STONE IDOL THIRTEEN FEET HIGH, AT COPAN.

Incidents of Travel in
CENTRAL AMERICA
CHIAPAS AND
YUCATAN

By JOHN L. STEPHENS

WITH ILLUSTRATIONS BY
FREDERICK CATHERWOOD

IN TWO VOLUMES
Volume I

DOVER PUBLICATIONS, INC.

NEW YORK

Published in Canada by General Publishing Company, Ltd.,
30 Lesmill Road, Don Mills, Toronto, Ontario.
Published in the United Kingdom by Constable and Company,
Ltd., 10 Orange Street, London WC 2.

This Dover edition, first published in 1969, is an
unabridged republication of the work originally published in 1841 by Harper & Brothers, New York, to
which has been added certain material (as specified
in the Publisher's Note) from the edition published
by Arthur Hall, Virtue & Co., London, in 1854.

Standard Book Number: 486-22404-X
Library of Congress Catalog Card Number: 74-95745

Manufactured in the United States of America
Dover Publications, Inc.
180 Varick Street
New York, N.Y. 10014

PUBLISHER'S NOTE

THIS edition is an unabridged republication of the first edition as published by Harper & Brothers, New York, in 1841. Captions have been supplied for those illustrations formerly lacking them. The following material, first published in a revised and abridged edition of the work prepared by Frederick Catherwood and published in 1854 by Arthur Hall, Virtue & Co, London, has been introduced into the present edition: (1) the Biographical Notice following this Note; (2) the illustrations in Volume One on pages 50 and 85 and facing pages 166, 267 and 290, and in Volume Two on page 419 and facing pages 274 and 336. The Lists of Illustrations to both volumes have been altered accordingly.

The large foldout map of the 1841 edition has been replaced by the more compact version (Volume One, facing page 10) from the edition of 1854. The portrait overleaf is also new to this edition.

JOHN LLOYD STEPHENS (1805–1852)

BIOGRAPHICAL NOTICE.

A SHORT biographical notice of my late fellow-traveller may not be uninteresting to the readers of the present volume. Mr. John Lloyd Stephens, the second son of Mr. Benjamin Stephens, was born at Shrewsbury in the State of New Jersey, in the United States of America, in the year 1805. Until the age of thirteen, Mr. Stephens studied at the school of Mr. Nelson, who, although blind, is described as an admirable teacher of the classics. For four years Mr. Stephens pursued his studies at Columbia College, New York, afterwards entered a law school, and when of age was admitted to the practice of the legal profession.

In the year 1834, the state of Mr. Stephens's health rendering it necessary for him to travel abroad, he visited many of the countries of Europe, extending his tour to Egypt and Syria. On his return to New York, he published "Incidents of Travel in Egypt, Arabia, Petræa, and the Holy Land," followed very shortly by "Incidents of Travel in Greece, Turkey, Russia, and Poland."

These works were received with great favour, and were very extensively read in the United States; and in this country have been several times reprinted, establishing Mr. Stephens's reputation as an excellent and agreeable writer of Travel and Narrative.

In 1839 Mr. Stephens and myself made arrangements for a tour in Central America, with a view to the examination of the remains of ancient art said to exist in the dense forests of those tropical regions.

Our preparations were scarcely completed, when Mr. Leggett, who was on the point of setting out as United States Minister for that country, died very suddenly, and upon application for it, Mr. Stephens immediately received the appointment. We had some misgivings lest it should interfere with our antiquarian pursuits, but Mr. Stephens contrived, as the reader will find, to combine the chase after a Government with a successful hunt for ruined cities. Our journey occupied about seven or eight months of the years 1839 and 1840.

The results of our researches were published in 1841. In the autumn of that year, we resumed our travels, and explored the Peninsula of Yucatan, and in 1843 a second work was brought out. After our last visit to Yucatan, we were urged to pursue the researches so successfully carried on in Central America by a journey to Peru, and Mr. Prescott, the admirable historian of that country, was of opinion that much useful information would thereby have been elicited. Mr. Stephens was, however, disinclined to undertake so distant an expedition, and was confirmed in this resolve by my being obliged to absent myself for several years on a professional engagement in the West Indies; he therefore remained in New York, and undertook the formation of the first American Ocean Steam Navigation Company, which in the end has proved highly successful. He next visited the Isthmus of Panama, with the view of forming a Railway across the narrow but difficult neck of land that separates the Atlantic and Pacific Oceans.

A Company was formed, of which he subsequently became the President, and a concession for the line was obtained from the Government of New Grenada. The necessary surveys were made, and the works began in 1850.* Having completed my engagement in the West Indies, I rejoined Mr. Stephens to assist in his great enterprise of spanning the Isthmus with a road of iron, and took charge of the works while he made a second journey to Santa Fé de Bogotá, the capital of New Grenada. We expected to meet in a few months, but Mr. Stephens's health, already much shattered by exposure in tropical regions, and mine still more so by a seven months' residence in one of the most unhealthy climates in the world, separated us for nearly two years; Mr. Stephens going to New York to recruit his strength, and I to California for the same object. Subsequently Mr. Stephens returned to the Isthmus, and by long and incautious exposure in that deadly climate in forwarding the interests of the Railway Company, brought on a disease which terminated fatally in the autumn of 1852.

As his fellow-traveller and intimate friend, I may be permitted to bear testimony to his kindly disposition, and the many excellent qualities of head and heart which endeared him to a large circle of friends and connexions.

F. CATHERWOOD.

* It is confidently expected that the Panama railway will be completed by the end of 1855, and will become the favourite route to Australia, as well as to California.

PREFACE.

THE author is indebted to Mr. Van Buren, late President of the United States, for the opportunity of presenting to the public the following pages. He considers it proper to say, that his diplomatic appointment was for a specific purpose, not requiring a residence at the capital, and the object of his mission being fulfilled or failing, he was at liberty to travel. At the time of his arrival in Central America, that country was distracted by a sanguinary civil war, which resulted, during his sojourn there, in the entire prostration of the Federal Government. By the protection and facilities afforded by his official character, he was enabled to accomplish what otherwise would have been impossible. His work embraces a journey of nearly three thousand miles in the interior of Central America, Chiapas, and Yucatan, including visits to eight ruined cities, with full illustrations from drawings taken on the spot by Mr. Catherwood. Its publication has been delayed on account of the engravings; but on one consideration the author does not regret the delay. Late intelligence from Central America enables him to express the belief that the state of anarchy in which he has represented that beautiful

1

country no longer exists; the dark clouds which hung over it have passed away, civil war has ceased, and Central America may be welcomed back among republics.

New-York, May, 1841.

CONTENTS

OF

THE FIRST VOLUME.

3

CHAPTER VI.

CHAPTER VII.

CHAPTER VIII.

CHAPTER IX.

CHAPTER X.

CHAPTER XI.

CHAPTER XII.

CHAPTER XIII.

CHAPTER XIV.

CHAPTER XV.

CHAPTER XVI.

CHAPTER XVII.

ILLUSTRATIONS

IN

VOLUME ONE

7

INCIDENTS OF TRAVEL

IN

CENTRAL AMERICA, CHIAPAS, AND YUCATAN.

CHAPTER I.

Departure.—The Voyage.—Arrival at Balize.—Mixing of Colours.—Government House.—Colonel M'Donald.—Origin of Balize.—Negro Schools.—Scene in a Court-room.—Law without Lawyers.—The Barracks.—Excursion in a Pitpan.—A Beginning of Honours.—Honours accumulating.— Departure from Balize.—Sweets of Office.

BEING intrusted by the President with a Special Confidential Mission to Central America, on Wednesday, the third of October, 1839, I embarked on board the British brig Mary Ann, Hampton, master, for the Bay of Honduras. The brig was lying in the North River, with her anchor apeak and sails loose, and in a few minutes, in company with a large whaling-ship bound for the Pacific, we were under way. It was before seven o'clock in the morning : the streets and wharves were still ; the Battery was desolate ; and, at the moment of leaving it on a voyage of uncertain duration, seemed more beautiful than I had ever known it before.

Opposite the Quarantine Ground, a few friends who had accompanied me on board left me ; in an hour the pilot followed ; at dusk the dark outline of the highlands of Neversink was barely visible, and the next morning we were fairly at sea.

My only fellow-passenger was Mr. Catherwood, an

9

experienced traveller and personal friend, who had passed more than ten years of his life in diligently studying the antiquities of the Old World ; and whom, as one familiar with the remains of ancient architectural greatness, I engaged, immediately on receiving my appointment, to accompany me in exploring the ruins of Central America.

Hurried on by a strong northeaster, on the ninth we were within the region of the trade-winds, on the tenth within the tropics, and on the eleventh, with the thermometer at 80°, but a refreshing breeze, we were moving gently between Cuba and St. Domingo, with both in full sight. For the rest, after eighteen days of boisterous weather, drenched with tropical rains, on the twenty-ninth we were driven inside the Lighthouse reef, and, avoiding altogether the regular pilot-ground, at midnight reached St. George's Bay, about twenty miles from Balize. A large brig, loaded with mahogany, was lying at anchor, with a pilot on board, waiting for favourable weather to put to sea. The pilot had with him his son, a lad about sixteen, cradled on the water, whom Captain Hampton knew, and determined to take on board.

It was full moonlight when the boy mounted the deck and gave us the pilot's welcome. I could not distinguish his features, but I could see that he was not white ; and his voice was as soft as a woman's. He took his place at the wheel, and, loading the brig with canvass, told us of the severe gales on the coast, of the fears entertained for our safety, of disasters and shipwrecks, and of a pilot who, on a night which we well remembered, had driven his vessel over a sunken reef.

At seven o'clock the next morning we saw Balize,

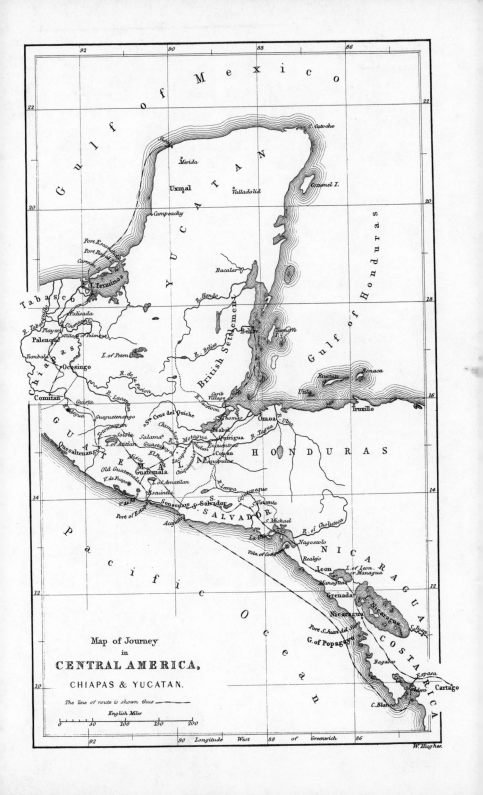

Map of Journey
in
CENTRAL AMERICA,
CHIAPAS & YUCATAN.

The line of route is shown thus ———

English Miles

0   50   100   150   200

W. Hughes.

appearing, if there be no sin in comparing it with cities consecrated by time and venerable associations, like Venice and Alexandrea, to rise out of the water. A range of white houses extended a mile along the shore, terminated at one end by the Government House, and at the other by the barracks, and intersected by the river Balize, the bridge across which formed a picturesque object; while the fort on a little island at the mouth of the river, the spire of a Gothic church behind the Government House, and groves of cocoanut-trees, which at that distance reminded us of the palm-trees of Egypt, gave it an appearance of actual beauty. Four ships, three brigs, sundry schooners, bungoes, canoes, and a steamboat, were riding at anchor in the harbour; alongside the vessels were rafts of mahogany; far out, a negro was paddling a log of the same costly timber; and the government dory which boarded us when we came to anchor was made of the trunk of a mahogany-tree.

We landed in front of the warehouse of Mr. Coffin, the consignee of the vessel. There was no hotel in the place, but Mr. Coffin undertook to conduct us to a lady who, he thought, could accommodate us with lodgings. The heavy rain from which we had suffered at sea had reached Balize. The streets were flooded, and in places there were large puddles, which it was difficult to cross. At the extreme end of the principal street we met the "lady," Miss ——, a mulatto woman, who could only give us board. Mr. Coffin kindly offered the use of an unoccupied house on the other side of the river to sleep in, and we returned.

By this time I had twice passed the whole length of the principal street, and the town seemed in the entire possession of blacks. The bridge, the market-place, the streets and stores were thronged with them, and I might have fancied myself in the capital of a negro republic. They were a fine-looking race, tall, straight, and athletic, with skins black, smooth, and glossy as velvet, and well dressed, the men in white cotton shirts and trousers, with straw hats, and the women in white frocks with short sleeves and broad red borders, and adorned with large red earrings and necklaces; and I could not help remarking that the frock was their only article of dress, and that it was the fashion of these sable ladies to drop this considerably from off the right shoulder, and to carry the skirt in the left hand, and raise it to any height necessary for crossing puddles.

On my way back I stopped at the house of a merchant, whom I found at what is called a second breakfast. The gentleman sat on one side of the table and his lady on the other. At the head was a British officer, and opposite him a mulatto; on his left was another officer, and opposite him also a mulatto. By chance a place was made for me between the two coloured gentlemen. Some of my countrymen, perhaps, would have hesitated about taking it, but I did not; both were well dressed, well educated, and polite. They talked of their mahogany works, of England, hunting, horses, ladies, and wine; and before I had been an hour in Balize I learned that the great work of practical amalgamation, the subject of so much angry controversy at home, had been going on quietly for generations; that colour was considered mere matter of taste; and that some of the most respectable inhabitants had black wives and mongrel children, whom they educated with as much care, and made money for with as much zeal, as if their skins were perfectly white.

I hardly knew whether to be shocked or amused at this condition of society ; and, in the mean time, joined Mr. Catherwood, to visit the house offered by Mr. Coffin. It was situated on the opposite side of the river, and the road to it was ankle deep in mud. At the gate was a large puddle, which we cleared by a jump ; the house was built on piles about two feet high, and underneath was water nearly a foot deep. We ascended on a plank to the sill of the door, and entered a large room occupying the whole of the first floor, and perfectly empty. The upper story was tenanted by a family of negroes ; in the yard was a house swarming with negroes ; and all over, in the yard and in front, were picturesque groups of little negroes of both sexes, and naked as they were born. We directed the room to be swept and our luggage brought there ; and, as we left the house, we remembered Captain Hampton's description before our arrival, and felt the point of his concluding remark, that Balize was the last place made.

We returned ; and, while longing for the comfort of a good hotel, received through Mr. Goff, the consul of the United States, an invitation from his excellency, Colonel M'Donald, to the Government House, and information that he would send the government dory to the brig for our luggage. As this was the first appointment I had ever held from government, and I was not sure of ever holding another, I determined to make the most of it, and accepted at once his excellency's invitation.

There was a steamboat for Yzabal, the port of Guatimala, lying at Balize ; and, on my way to the Government House, I called upon Señor Comyano, the agent, who told me that she was to go up the next day ;

but added, with great courtesy, that, if I wished it, he would detain her a few days for my convenience. Used to submitting to the despotic regulations of steamboat agents at home, this seemed a higher honour than the invitation of his excellency; but, not wishing to push my fortune too far, I asked a delay of one day only.

The Government House stands in a handsome situation at the extreme end of the town, with a lawn extending to the water, and ornamented with cocoanut-trees. Colonel M'Donald, a veteran six feet high, and one of the most military-looking men I ever saw, received me at the gate. In an hour the dory arrived with our luggage, and at five o'clock we sat down to dinner. We had at table Mr. Newport, chaplain, and for fifteen years parish clergyman at Balize; Mr. Walker, secretary of the government, and holding, besides, such a list of offices as would make the greatest pluralist among us feel insignificant; and several other gentlemen of Balize, office-holders, civil and military, in whose agreeable society we sat till eleven o'clock.

The next day we had to make preparations for our journey into the interior, besides which we had an opportunity of seeing a little of Balize. The Honduras Almanac, which assumes to be the chronicler of this settlement, throws a romance around its early history by ascribing its origin to a Scotch bucanier named Wallace. The fame of the wealth of the New World, and the return of the Spanish galleons laden with the riches of Mexico and Peru, brought upon the coast of America hordes of adventurers—to call them by no harsher name—from England and France, of whom Wallace, one of the most noted and daring, found refuge and security behind the keys and reefs which protect the harbour of Balize. The place where he built his log huts and fortalice is still pointed out; but their site is now occupied by warehouses. Strengthened by a close alliance with the Indians of the Moscheto shore, and by the adhesion of numerous British adventurers, who descended upon the coast of Honduras for the purpose of cutting mahogany, he set the Spaniards at defiance. Ever since, the territory of Balize has been the subject of negotiation and contest, and to this day the people of Central America claim it as their own. It has grown by the exportation of mahogany; but, as the trees in the neighbourhood have been almost all cut down, and Central America is so impoverished by wars that it offers but a poor market for British goods, the place is languishing, and will probably continue to dwindle away until the enterprise of her merchants discovers other channels of trade.

At this day it contains a population of six thousand, of which four thousand are blacks, who are employed by the merchants in gangs as mahogany cutters. Their condition was always better than that of plantation slaves; even before the act for the general abolition of slavery throughout the British dominions, they were actually free; and, on the thirty-first of August, 1839, a year before the time appointed by the act, by a general meeting and agreement of proprietors, even the nominal yoke of bondage was removed.

The event was celebrated, says the Honduras Almanac, by religious ceremonies, processions, bands of music, and banners with devices : " The sons of Ham respect the memory of Wilberforce ;" " The Queen, God bless her ;" " M'Donald forever ;" " Civil and religious liberty all over the world." Nelson Schaw, " a snowdrop of the first water," continues the Almanac, " advanced to his excellency, Colonel M'Donald, and spoke as follows : ' On the part of my emancipated brothers and sisters, I venture to approach your excellency, to entreat you to thank our most gracious Queen for all that she has done for us. We will pray for her ; we will fight for her ; and, if it is necessary, we will die for her. We thank your excellency for all you have done for us. God bless your excellency! God bless her excellency, Mrs. M'Donald, and all the royal family ! Come, my countymen, hurrah ! Dance, ye black rascals ; the flag of England flies over your heads, and every rustle of its folds knocks the fetters off the limbs of the poor slave. Hubbabboo Cochalorum Gee !' "

The negro schools stand in the rear of the Government House, and the boys' department consisted of about two hundred, from three to fifteen years of age, and of every degree of tinge, from nearly white down to two little native Africans bearing on their cheeks the scars of cuts made by their parents at home. These last were taken from on board a slave-ship captured by an English cruiser, brought into Balize, and, as provided for by the laws, on a drawing by lot, fell to the share of a citizen, who, entering into certain covenants for good treatment, is entitled to their services until they are twenty-one years old. Unfortunately, the master was not present, and I had no opportunity of learning the result of his experience in teaching ; but in this school, I was told, the brightest boys, and those who had improved most, were those who had in them the most white blood.

The mistress of the female department had had great experience in teaching ; and she told us that, though she had had many clever black girls under her charge, her white scholars were always the most quick and capable.

From the negro school we went to the Grand Court. It had been open about half an hour when I entered. On the back wall, in a massive mahogany tablet, were the arms of England; on a high platform beneath was a large circular table, around which were heavy mahogany chairs with high backs and cushions. The court consists of seven judges, five of whom were in their places. One of them, Mr. Walker, invited me to one of the vacant seats. I objected, on the ground that my costume was not becoming so dignified a position; he insisted, and I took my seat, in a roundabout jacket, upon a chair exceedingly comfortable for the administration of justice.

As before remarked, five of the judges were in their places; one of them was a mulatto. The jury was empannelled, and two of the jurors were mulattoes; one of them, as the judge who sat next me said, was a Sambo, or of the descending line, being the son of a mulatto woman and a black man. I was at a loss to determine the caste of a third, and inquired of the judge, who answered that he was his, the judge's, brother, and that his mother was a mulatto woman. The judge was aware of the feeling existing in the United States with regard to colour, and said that in Balize there was, in political life, no distinction whatever, except on the ground of qualifications and character; and hardly any in social life, even in contracting marriages.

I had noticed the judges and jurors, but I missed an important part of an English court. Where were the gentlemen of the bar ? Some of my readers will perhaps concur with Captain Hampton, that Balize was the last place made, when I tell them that there was not a single lawyer in the place, and never had been; but, lest some of my enterprising professional brethren should forthwith be tempted to pack their trunks for a descent upon the exempt city, I consider it my duty to add that I do not believe there is the least chance for one.

As there is no bar to prepare men for the bench, the judges, of course, are not lawyers. Of the five then sitting, two were merchants, one a mahogany cutter, and the mulatto, second to none of the others in character or qualifications, a doctor. This court is the highest tribunal for the trial of civil causes, and has jurisdiction of all amounts above £15. Balize is a place of large commercial transactions; contracts are daily made and broken, or misunderstood, which require the intervention of some proper tribunal to interpret and compel their fulfilment. And there was no absence of litigation; the calendar was large, and the courtroom crowded. The first cause called was upon an account, when the defendant did not appear, and a verdict was taken by default. In the next, the plaintiff stated his case, and swore to it; the defendant answered, called witnesses, and the cause was submitted to the jury. There was no case of particular interest. In one the parties became excited, and the defendant interrupted the plaintiff repeatedly, on which the latter, putting his hand upon the shoulder of his antagonist, said, in a coaxing way, " Now don't, George; wait a little, you shall have your turn. Don't interrupt me, and I won't you." All was done in a familiar and colloquial way; the parties were more or less known to each other, and judges and jurors were greatly influenced by knowledge of general character. I remarked that regularly the merits of the case were so clearly brought out, that, when it was committed to the jury, there was no question about the verdict; and so satisfactory has this system proved, that, though an appeal lies to the Queen in Council, as Mr. Evans, the foreman, told me, but one cause has been carried up in twenty-two years. Still it stands as an anomaly in the history of English jurisprudence; for, I believe, in every other place where the principles of the common law govern, the learning of the bench and the ingenuity of the bar are considered necessary to elicit the truth.

At daylight the next morning I was roused by Mr. Walker for a ride to the barracks. Immediately beyond the suburbs we entered upon an uncultivated country, low and flat, but very rich. We passed a racecourse, now disused and grown over. This is the only road opened, and there are no wheel-carriages in Balize. Between it and the inhabited part of Central America is a wilderness, unbroken even by an Indian path. There is no communication with the interior except by the Golfo Dolce or the Balize River; and, from the want of roads, a residence there is more confining than living on an island.

In half an hour we reached the barracks, situated on the opposite side of a small bay. The soldiers are all black, and are part of an old Jamaica regiment, most of them having been enlisted at the English recruiting stations in Africa. Tall and athletic, with red coats, and, on a line, bristling with steel, their ebony faces gave them a peculiarly warlike appearance. They carry themselves proudly, call themselves the " Queen's Gentlemen," and look down with contempt upon the " niggers."

We returned to breakfast, and immediately after

made an excursion in the government pit-pan. This is the same fashion of boat in which the Indians navigated the rivers of America before the Spaniards discovered it. European ingenuity has not contrived a better, though it has, perhaps, beautified the Indian model. Ours was about forty feet long, and six wide in the centre, running to a point at both ends, and made of the trunk of a mahogany-tree. Ten feet from the stern, and running forward, was a light wooden top, supported by fanciful stancheons, with curtains for protection against sun and rain; it had large cushioned seats, and was fitted up almost as neatly as the gondolas of Venice. It was manned by eight negro soldiers, who sat two on a seat, with paddles six feet long, and two stood up behind with paddles as steersmen. A few touches of the paddles gave brisk way to the pit-pan, and we passed rapidly the whole length of the town. It was an unusual thing for his excellency's pit-pan to be upon the water; citizens stopped to gaze at us, and all the idle negroes hurried to the bridge to cheer us. This excited our African boatmen, who, with a wild chant that reminded us of the songs of the Nubian boatmen on the Nile, swept under the bridge, and hurried us into the still expanse of a majestic river. Before the cheering of the negroes died away we were in as perfect a solitude as if removed thousands of miles from human habitations. The Balize River, coming from sources even yet but little known to civilized man, was then in its fulness. On each side was a dense, unbroken forest; the banks were overflowed; the trees seemed to grow out of the water, their branches spreading across so as almost to shut out the light of the sun, and reflected in the water as in a mirror. The sources of the river were occupied by the aboriginal owners, wild and free as Cortes found them. We had an eager desire to penetrate by it to the famous Lake of Peten, where the skeleton of the conquering Spaniard's horse was erected into a god by the astonished Indians; but the toil of our boatmen reminded us that they were paddling against a rapid current. We turned the pit-pan, and with the full power of the stream, a pull stronger, and a chant louder than before, amid the increased cheering of the negroes, swept under the bridge, and in a few minutes were landed at the Government House.

In order that we might embark at the hour appointed, Colonel M'Donald had ordered dinner at two o'clock, and, as on the two preceding days, had invited a small party to meet us. Perhaps I am wrong, but I should do violence to my feelings did I fail to express here my sense of the colonel's kindness. My invitation to the Government House was the fruit of my official character; but I cannot help flattering myself that some portion of the kindness shown me was the result of personal acquaintance. Colonel M'Donald is a soldier of the " twenty years' war," the brother of Sir John M'Donald, adjutant-general of England, and cousin of Marshal Macdonald of France. All his connexions and associations are military. At eighteen he entered Spain as an ensign, one of an army of ten thousand men, of whom, in less than six months, but four thousand were left. After being actively engaged in all the trying service of the Peninsular War, at Waterloo he commanded a regiment, and on the field of battle received the order of Companion of the Military Order of the Bath from the King of England, and that of Knight of the Order of St. Anne from the Emperor of Russia. Rich in recollections of a long

military life, personally acquainted with the public and
private characters of the most distinguished military
men of the age, his conversation was like reading a
page of history. He is one of a race that is fast passing away, and with whom an American seldom meets.

But to return. The large window of the dining-
room opened upon the harbour ; the steamboat lay in
front of the Government House, and the black smoke,
rising in columns from her pipe, gave notice that it was
time to embark. Before rising, Colonel M'Donald,
like a loyal subject, proposed the health of the Queen ;
after which he ordered the glasses to be filled to the
brim, and, standing up, he gave, " The health of Mr.
Van Buren, President of the United States," accompanying it with a warm and generous sentiment, and
the earnest hope of strong and perpetual friendship between England and America. I felt at the moment,
" Cursed be the hand that attempts to break it ;" and
albeit unused to taking the President and the people
upon my shoulders, I answered as well as I could.
Another toast followed to the health and successful
journey of Mr. Catherwood and myself, and we rose
from table. The government dory lay at the foot of
the lawn. Colonel M'Donald put his arm through
mine, and, walking away, told me that I was going
into a distracted country ; that Mr. Savage, the American consul in Guatimala, had, on a previous occasion,
protected the property and lives of British subjects ;
and, if danger threatened me, I must assemble the Europeans, hang out my flag, and send word to him. I
knew that these were not mere words of courtesy, and,
in the state of the country to which I was going, felt
the value of such a friend at hand. With the warmest
feelings of gratitude I bade him farewell, and stepped

into the dory. At the moment flags were run up at the government staff, the fort, the courthouse, and the government schooner, and a gun was fired from the fort. As I crossed the bay, a salute of thirteen guns was fired ; passing the fort, the soldiers presented arms, the government schooner lowered and raised her ensign, and when I mounted the deck of the steamboat, the captain, with hat in hand, told me that he had instructions to place her under my orders, and to stop wherever I pleased.

The reader will perhaps ask how I bore all these honours. I had visited many cities, but it was the first time that flags and cannon announced to the world that I was going away. I was a novice, but I endeavoured to behave as if I had been brought up to it ; and, to tell the truth, my heart beat, and I felt proud ; for these were honours paid to my country, and not to me.

To crown the glory of the parting scene, my good friend Captain Hampton had charged his two four-pounders, and when the steamboat got under way he fired one, but the other would not go off. The captain of the steamboat had on board one puny gun, with which he would have returned all their civilities ; but, as he told me, to his great mortification, he had no powder.

The steamboat in which we embarked was the last remnant of the stock in trade of a great Central American agricultural association, formed for building cities, raising the price of land, accommodating emigrants, and improvement generally. On the rich plains of the province of Vera Paz they had established the site of New Liverpool, which only wanted houses and a population to become a city. On the wheel of the boat was a brass circular plate, on which, in strange juxta-position, were the words " Vera Paz," " London." The captain was a small, weather-beaten, dried-up old Spaniard, with courtesy enough for a Don of old. The engineer was an Englishman, and the crew were Spaniards, Mestitzoes, and mulattoes, not particularly at home in the management of a steamboat.

Our only fellow-passenger was a Roman Catholic priest, a young Irishman, who had been eight months at Balize, and was now on his way to Guatimala by in-vitation of the provesor, by the exile of the archbishop the head of the church. The cabin was very com-fortable, but the evening was so mild that we took our tea on deck. At ten o'clock the captain came to me for orders. I have had my aspirations, but never ex-pected to be able to dictate to the captain of a steam-boat. Nevertheless, again as coolly as if I had been brought up to it, I designated the places I wished to visit, and retired. Verily, thought I, if these are the fruits of official appointments, it is not strange that men are found willing to accept them.

CHAPTER II.

Every one for himself.—Travellers' Tricks.—Puenta Gorda.—A Visit to the Carib Indians.—A Carib Crone.—A Baptism.—Rio Dolce.—Beautiful Scenery.—Yzabal.—Reception of the Padre.—A Barber in Office.—A Band of "Invincibles."—Parties in Central America.—A Compatriot.—A Grave in a Foreign Land.—Preparations for the Passage of "the Mountain."—A Road not Macadamized.—Perils by the Way.—A well-spiced Lunch.—The Mountain passed.

WE had engaged a servant, a French Spaniard, St. Domingo born and Omoa bred, bearing the name of Augustin; young, and, as we at first thought, not very sharp. Early in the morning he asked us what we would have for breakfast, naming eggs, chickens, &c. We gave him directions, and in due time sat down to breakfast. During the meal something occurred to put us on inquiry, and we learned that everything on the table, excepting the tea and coffee, belonged to the padre. Without asking any questions, or thinking of the subject at all, we had taken for granted that the steamboat made all necessary provisions for passengers; but, to our surprise, learned that the boat furnished nothing, and that passengers were expected to take care of themselves. The padre had been as ignorant and as improvident as we; but some good Catholic friends, whom he had married or whose children he had baptized, had sent on board contributions of various kinds, and, among other things—odd luggage for a traveller—a coop full of chickens. We congratulated the padre upon his good fortune in having us with him, and ourselves upon such a treasure as Augustin. I may mention, by-the-way, that, in the midst of Colonel M'Donald's hospitalities, Mr. Catherwood and I exhibited rather too much of the old traveller. When at dinner the last day, Mr. C. was called from table to superintend the removal of some luggage, and shortly after I was called out; and, fortunately for Colonel M'Donald and the credit of my country, I found Mr. C. quietly rolling up, to send back to New-York, a large blue cloak belonging to the colonel, supposing it to be mine. I returned to the table and mentioned to our host his narrow escape, adding that I had some doubt about a large canvass sack for bedding which I had found in my room, and, presuming it was one that had been promised me by Captain Hampton, had put on board the steamboat; but this too, it appeared, belonged to Colonel M'Donald, and for many years had carried his camp bed. The result was, that the colonel insisted upon our taking it, and I am afraid it was pretty well worn out before he received it again. The reader will infer from all this that Mr. C. and I, with the help of Augustin, were fit to travel in any country.

But to return. It was a beautiful day. Our course lay nearly south, directly along the coast of Honduras. In his last voyage Columbus discovered this part of the Continent of America, but its verdant beauties could not win him to the shore. Without landing, he continued on to the Isthmus of Darien, in search of that passage to India which was the aim of all his hopes, but which it was destined he should never see.

Steamboats have destroyed some of the most pleasing illusions of my life. I was hurried up the Hellespont, past Sestos and Abydos, and the Plain of Troy, under the clatter of a steam-engine; and it struck at the root of all the romance connected with the adventures of Columbus to follow in his track, accompanied by the clamour of the same panting monster. Nevertheless, it was very pleasant. We sat down under an awning; the sun was intensely hot, but we were sheltered, and had a refreshing breeze. The coast assumed an appearance of grandeur and beauty that realized my ideas of tropical regions. There was a dense forest to the water's edge. Beyond were lofty mountains, covered to their tops with perpetual green, some isolated, and others running off in ranges, higher and higher, till they were lost in the clouds.

At eleven o'clock we came in sight of Puenta Gorda, a settlement of Carib Indians, about a hundred and fifty miles down the coast, and the first place at which I had directed the captain to stop. As we approached we saw an opening on the water's edge, with a range of low houses, reminding me of a clearing in our forests at home. It was but a speck on the great line of coast; on both sides were primeval trees. Behind towered an extraordinary mountain, apparently broken into two, like the back of a two-humped camel. As the steamboat turned in, where steamboat had never been before, the whole village was in commotion: women and children were running on the bank, and four men descended to the water and came off in a canoe to meet us.

Our fellow-passenger, the padre, during his residence at Balize, had become acquainted with many of the Caribs, and, upon one occasion, by invitation from its chief, had visited a settlement for the purpose of marrying and baptizing the inhabitants. He asked whether we had any objection to his taking advantage of the opportunity to do the same here ; and, as we had none, at the moment of disembarking he appeared on deck with a large wash-hand basin in one hand, and a well-filled pocket-handkerchief in the other, containing his priestly vestments.

We anchored a short distance from the beach, and went ashore in the small boat. We landed at the foot of a bank about twenty feet high, and, ascending to the top, came at once, under a burning sun, into all the richness of tropical vegetation. Besides cotton and rice, the cahoon, banana, cocoanut, pineapple, orange, lemon, and plantain, with many other fruits which we did not know even by name, were growing with such luxuriance that at first their very fragrance was oppressive. Under the shade of these trees most of the inhabitants were gathered, and the padre immediately gave notice, in a wholesale way, that he had come to marry and baptize them. After a short consultation, a house was selected for the performance of the ceremonies, and Mr. Catherwood and I, under the guidance of a Carib, who had picked up a little English in his canoe expeditions to Balize, walked through the settlement.

It consisted of about five hundred inhabitants. Their native place was on the seacoast, below Truxillo, within the government of Central America; and having taken an active part against Morazan, when his party became dominant they fled to this place, being within the limits of the British authority. Though living apart, as a tribe of Caribs, not mingling their blood with that of their conquerors, they were completely civilized; retaining, however, the Indian passion for beads and ornaments. The houses or huts were built of poles about an inch thick, set upright in the ground, tied together with bark strings, and thatched with coroon leaves. Some had partitions and bedsteads made of the same materials; in every house were a grass hammock and a figure of the Virgin or of some tutelary saint; and we were exceedingly struck with the great progress made in civilization by these descendants of cannibals, the fiercest of all the Indian tribes whom the Spaniards encountered.

The houses extended along the bank, at some distance apart ; and the heat was so oppressive that, before reaching the last, we were about to turn back ; but our guide urged us to go on and see " one old woman," his grandmother. We followed and saw her. She was very old ; no one knew her age, but it was considerably over a hundred ; and, what gave her more interest in our eyes than the circumstance of her being the grandmother of our guide, she came from the island of St. Vincent, the residence of the most indomitable portion of her race ; and she had never been baptized. She received us with an idiotic laugh ; her figure was shrunken ; her face shrivelled, weazened, and wicked ; and she looked as though, in her youth, she had gloried in dancing at a feast of human flesh.

We returned, and found our friend, the padre, dressed in the contents of his pocket-handkerchief, quite a respectable-looking priest. By his side was our steamboat washbowl, filled with holy water, and in his hand a prayer-book. Augustin stood up, holding the stump of a tallow candle.

The Caribs, like most of the other Indians of Central America, have received the doctrines of Christianity as presented to them by the priests and monks of Spain, and are, in all things, strict observers of the forms prescribed. In this settlement, the visit of a padre was a rare but welcome occurrence. At first they seemed to have a suspicion that our friend was not orthodox, because he did not speak Spanish ; but when they saw him in his gown and surplice, with the burning incense, all distrust vanished.

There was little to be done in the way of marrying, there being a scarcity of men for that purpose, as most of them were away fishing or at work ; but a long file of women presented themselves, each with a child in her arms, for baptism. They were arranged around the wall in a circle, and the padre began. Of the first he asked a question which I believe is not to be found in the book, and which, in some places, it would be considered impertinent to put to a mother who offered her child for initiation into the Church, viz., whether she was married. She hesitated, smiled, laughed, and answered *no*. The padre told her that this was very wrong and unbecoming a good Christian woman, and advised her to take advantage of the present opportunity to marry the child's father. She answered that she would like to do so, but that he was away cutting mahogany ; and here, as his questions and her answers had to pass through an interpreter, the affair began to be complicated ; indeed, so many of the women interposed, all speaking at once, that the padre became aware he had touched upon delicate ground, and so passed on to the next.

In fact, even with the regular business our friend had enough to do. He understood but little Spanish ; his book was in Latin ; and not being able to translate as readily as the occasion required, he had employed the interval of our absence in copying on a slip of paper, from a Spanish Protestant prayer-book, the formal part of the baptismal service. In the confusion this was lost, and the padre was thrown back upon his Latin, to be translated into Spanish as required. After labouring a while, he turned to Augustin, and gave him in English the questions to put to the women. Augustin was a good Catholic, and listened to him with as much respect as if he had been the pope, but did not understand a word he said. I explained to Augustin in French, who explained to one of the men in Spanish, who explained to the women. This, of course, led to confusion ; but all were so devout and respectful, that, in spite of these tribulations, the ceremony was solemn. When he came to the Latin parts, our friend rattled it off as fast as if fresh from the Propaganda at Rome, and the Caribs were not much behindhand.

The padre had told us of the passion of the Caribs for a multiplicity of names ; and one of the women, after giving her child three or four, pointed to me, and told him to add mine. I am not very strict, but I did not care to assume wantonly the obligations of a godfather ; and, stopping the ceremony, begged the padre to get me released with the best grace he could. He promised to do so ; but it was an excessively hot day ; the room was crowded, the doors choked up, and by this time the padre, with his Latin, and English, and French, and Spanish, was in a profuse perspiration, and somewhat confused. I thought myself clear, till, a few moments afterward, a child was passed along for me to take in my arms ; but I was relieved on one point : I thought that it was the lady who had become a mother without being a wife, that wished her child to bear my name, but it was another ; still I most ungallantly avoided receiving the baby. On going away, however, the woman intercepted me, and, thrusting forward the child, called me compadre ; so that, without knowing it, I became godfather to a Carib child ; fortunately, its mother was an honest woman, and the father stood by at the time. In all probability I shall never have much to do with its training ; and I can only hope that in due season it will multiply the name and make it respectable among the Caribs.

We returned to the steamboat, and in a few minutes were again under way, steering for the Rio Dolce. An amphitheatre of lofty mountains stretches for many miles along the coast, and back till they are lost to the sight. In one small place this lofty range opens for the passage of a gentle river. On the right bank of the coast was one of the places I intended to visit. It was called by the familiar name of Livingston, in honour of the distinguished citizen of Louisiana whose criminal code was at that time introduced into Guatimala; and it was supposed, so advantageous was its position, that it would become the port of entry of Central America; but these expectations were not realized.

It was four o'clock in the afternoon, and, in steering toward it, the captain told me that, if we cast anchor, it would be necessary to lie there till morning. I was loth to lose the only opportunity I shall probably ever have of stopping a steamboat; but I had an eager, almost a burning curiosity to see the Golfo Dolce, and we all agreed that it would be wanton to lose such an opportunity of seeing it to advantage. I therefore directed the captain to move close to the bank and pass on.

The bank was elevated about thirty feet above the water, and rich and luxuriant as at Puenta Gorda. The site of the intended city was occupied by another tribe of Caribs, who, like the first, driven from their home by war, had followed up the coast, and, with that eye for the picturesque and beautiful in natural scenery which distinguishes the Indians everywhere, had fixed themselves upon this spot. Their leaf-thatched huts were ranged along the bank, shaded by

groves of plantain and cocoanut trees; canoes with
sails set were lying on the water, and men and women
were sitting under the trees gazing at us. It was a
soft and sunny scene, speaking peace and freedom
from the tumults of a busy world.

But, beautiful as it was, we soon forgot it; for a
narrow opening in a rampart of mountains wooed us
on, and in a few moments we entered the Rio Dolce.
On each side, rising perpendicularly from three to four
hundred feet, was a wall of living green. Trees grew
from the water's edge, with dense, unbroken foliage,
to the top; not a spot of barrenness was to be seen;
and on both sides, from the tops of the highest trees,
long tendrils descended to the water, as if to drink and
carry life to the trunks that bore them. It was, as its
name imports, a Rio Dolce, a fairy scene of Titan
land, combining exquisite beauty with colossal grandeur. As we advanced the passage turned, and in a
few minutes we lost sight of the sea, and were enclosed
on all sides by a forest wall; but the river, although
showing us no passage, still invited us onward. Could
this be the portal to a land of volcanoes and earthquakes, torn and distracted by civil war? For some
time we looked in vain for a single barren spot; at
length we saw a naked wall of perpendicular rock, but
out of the crevices, and apparently out of the rock itself, grew shrubs and trees. Sometimes we were so
enclosed that it seemed as if the boat must drive in
among the trees. Occasionally, in an angle of the
turns, the wall sunk, and the sun struck in with scorching force, but in a moment we were again in the deep-
est shade. From the fanciful accounts we had heard,
we expected to see monkeys gambolling among the
trees, and parrots flying over our heads; but all was as

quiet as if man had never been there before. The pelican, the stillest of birds, was the only living thing we saw, and the only sound was the unnatural bluster of our steam-engine. The wild defile that leads to the excavated city of Petra is not more noiseless or more extraordinary, but strangely contrasting in its steril desolation, while here all is luxuriant, romantic, and beautiful.

For nine miles the passage continued thus one scene of unvarying beauty, when suddenly the narrow river expanded into a large lake, encompassed by mountains and studded with islands, which the setting sun illuminated with gorgeous splendour. We remained on deck till a late hour, and awoke the next morning in the harbour of Yzabal. A single schooner of about forty tons showed the low state of her commerce. We landed before seven o'clock in the morning, and even then it was hot. There were no idlers on the bank, and the custom-house officer was the only person to receive us.

The town stands on a gentle elevation on the banks of the Golfo Dolce, with mountains piled upon mountains behind. We walked up the street to the square, on one side of which was the house of Messrs. Ampudia and Purroy, the largest and, except one they were then engaged in building, the only frame house in the place. The rest were all huts, built of poles and reeds, and thatched with leaves of the cahoon-tree. Opposite their door was a large shed, under which were bales of merchandise, and mules, muleteers, and Indians, for transporting goods across the Mico Mountain.

The arrival of the padre created a great sensation. It was announced by a joyful ringing of the church bells, and in an hour after he was dressed in his surplice and saying mass. The church stood at the head of the square, and, like the houses, was built of poles and thatched with leaves. In front, at a distance of ten or fifteen feet, was a large wooden cross. The floor was of bare earth, but swept clean and strewed with pine-leaves ; the sides were trimmed with branches and festoons of flowers, and the altar was ornamented with figures of the Virgin and saints, and wreaths of flowers. It was a long time since the people had had the privilege of hearing mass, and the whole population, Spaniards, Mestitzoes, and Indians, answered the unexpected but welcome call of the matin bell. The floor was covered with kneeling women having white shawls over their heads, and behind, leaning against the rude pillars, were the men ; and their earnestness and humility, the earthen floor and the thatched roof, were more imposing than the pomp of worship in the rich cathedrals of Europe or under the dome of St. Peter's.

After breakfast we inquired for a barber, and were referred to the collector of the port, who, we were told, was the best hair-cutter in the place. His house was no bigger than his neighbours', but inside hung a military saddle, with holsters and pistols, and a huge sword, the accoutrements of the collector when he sallied out at the head of his deputy to strike terror into the heart of a smuggler. Unfortunately, the honest Democrat was not at home ; but the deputy offered his own services. Mr. C. and I submitted ; but the padre, who wanted his crown shaved, according to the rules of his order, determined to wait the return of the collector.

I next called upon the commandant with my passport. His house was on the opposite side of the square. A soldier about fourteen years old, with a bell-crowned straw hat falling over his eyes like an extinguisher upon a candle, was standing at the door as sentinel. The troops, consisting of about thirty men and boys, were drawn up in front, and a sergeant was smoking a cigar and drilling them. The uniform purported to be a white straw hat, cotton trousers and shirt outside, musket, and cartridge-box. In one particular uniformity was strictly observed, viz., all were barefooted. The first process of calling off rank and file was omitted ; and, as it happened, a long-legged fellow, six feet high, stood next to a boy twelve or thirteen years old. The custom-house officer was with the sergeant, advising him ; and, after a manœuvre and a consultation, the sergeant walked up to the line, and with the palm of his hand struck a soldier on that part of the body which, in my younger days, was considered by the schoolmaster the channel of knowledge into a boy's brain.

The commandant of this hopeful band was Don Juan Peñol, a gentleman by birth and education, who, with others of his family, had been banished by General Morazan, and sought refuge in the United States. His predecessor, who was an officer of Morazan, had been just driven out by the Carrera party, and he was but twenty days in his place.

Three great parties at that time distracted Central America : that of Morazan, the former president of the Republic, in San Salvador, of Ferrera in Honduras, and of Carrera in Guatimala. Ferrera was a mulatto, and Carrera an Indian ; and, though not fighting for any common purpose, they sympathized in opposition to Morazan. When Mr. Montgomery visited Guatimala, it was just thrown into a ferment by the rising of Carrera, who was then regarded as the head of a

troop of banditti, a robber and assassin; his followers were called Cachurecos (meaning false coin), and
Mr. Montgomery told me that against him an official
passport would be no protection whatever. Now he
was the head of the party that ruled Guatimala. Señor Peñol gave us a melancholy picture of the state of
the country. A battle had just been fought near San
Salvador, between General Morazan and Ferrera, in
which the former was wounded, but Ferrera was routed, and his troops were cut to pieces, and he feared
Morazan was about to march upon Guatimala. He
could only give us a passport to Guatimala, which he
said would not be respected by General Morazan.

We felt interested in the position of Señor Peñol;
young, but with a face bearing the marks of care and
anxiety, a consciousness of the miserable condition of
the present, and fearful forebodings for the future.
To our great regret, the intelligence we received induced our friend the padre to abandon, for the present,
his intention of going to Guatimala. He had heard
all the terrible stories of Morazan's persecution and
proscription of the priests, and thought it dangerous to
fall into his hands; and I have reason to believe it
was the apprehension of this which ultimately drove
him from the country.

Toward evening I strolled through the town. The
population consists of about fifteen hundred Indians,
negroes, mulattoes, Mestitzoes, and mixed blood of
every degree, with a few Spaniards. Very soon I was
accosted by a man who called himself my countryman,
a mulatto from Baltimore, and his name was Philip.
He had been eight years in the country, and said that
he had once thought of returning home as a servant by
way of New-Orleans, but he had left home in such a

hurry that he forgot to bring with him his "Christian papers;" from which I inferred that he was what would be called in Maryland a runaway slave. He was a man of considerable standing, being fireman on board the steamboat at $23 a month; besides which, he did odd jobs at carpentering, and was, in fact, the principal architect in Yzabal, having then on his hands a contract for $3500 for building the new house of Messrs. Ampudia and Purroy. In other things, I am sorry to say, Philip was not quite so respectable; and I can only hope that it was not his American education that led him into some irregularities in which he seemed to think there was no harm. He asked me to go to his house and see his wife, but on the way I learned from him that he was not married; and he said, what I hope is a slander upon the good people of Yzabal, that he only did as all the rest did. He owned the house in which he lived, and for which, with the ground, he had paid twelve dollars; and being a householder and an American, I tried to induce him to take advantage of the opportunity of the padre's visit, and set a good example by getting married; but he was obstinate, and said that he did not like to be trammelled, and that he might go elsewhere and see another girl whom he liked better.

While standing at his door, Mr. Catherwood passed on his way to visit Mr. Rush, the engineer of the steamboat, who had been ill on board. We found him in one of the huts of the town, in a hammock, with all his clothes on. He was a man of Herculean frame, six feet three or four inches high, and stout in proportion; but he lay helpless as a child. A single candle stuck upon the dirt floor gave a miserable light, and a group of men of different races and colour, from the white-faced Saxon to the Indian and African, stood round him : rude nurses for one used to the comforts of an English home. I recollected that Yzabal was noted as a sickly place ; Mr. Montgomery, who published an interesting account of his visit to Guatimala in 1838, had told me that it was running the gauntlet for life even to pass through it, and I trembled for the poor Englishman. I remembered, too, what it is strange that I had before forgotten, that here Mr. Shannon, our chargé to Central America, died. Philip was with me, and knew where Mr. Shannon was buried, but in the dark he could not point out the spot. I intended to set out early in the morning ; and afraid that, in the hurry of departure, I might neglect altogether the sacred duty of visiting, in this distant place, the grave of an American, I returned to the house and requested Señor Ampudia to accompany me. We crossed the square, passed through the suburbs, and in a few minutes were outside of the town. It was so dark that I could scarcely see my way. Crossing a deep gulley on a plank, we reached a rising ground, open on the right, stretching away to the Golfo Dolce, and in front bounded by a gloomy forest. On the top was a rude fence of rough upright poles, enclosing the grave of some relative of Señor Ampudia ; and by the side of this was the grave of Mr. Shannon. There was no stone or fence, or hardly any elevation, to distinguish it from the soil around. It was a gloomy burial-place for a countryman, and I felt an involuntary depression of spirit. A fatality had hung over our diplomatic appointment to Central America : Mr. Williams, Mr. Shannon, Mr. Dewitt, Mr. Leggett, all who had ever held it, were dead. I recollected an expression in a letter from a near relative of Mr. Dewitt :

"May you be more fortunate than either of your predecessors has been." It was melancholy, that one who had died abroad in the service of his country was thus left on a wild mountain, without any stone to mark his grave. I returned to the house, directed a fence to be built around the grave of Mr. Shannon, and my friend the padre promised to plant at its head a cocoanut-tree.

At daylight the muleteers commenced loading for the passage of "the Mountain." At seven o'clock the whole caravan, consisting of nearly a hundred mules and twenty or thirty muleteers, was fairly under way. Our immediate party consisted of five mules; two for Mr. Catherwood and myself, one for Augustin, and two for luggage; besides which, we had four Indian carriers. If we had been consulted, perhaps at that time we should have scrupled to use men as beasts of burden; but Señor Ampudia had made all the arrangements for us. The Indians were naked, except a small piece of cotton cloth around the loins, and crossing in front between the legs. The loads were arranged so as to have on one side a flat surface. The Indians sat on the ground with their backs against the surface; passed a strap across the forehead, which supported the load; and, adjusting it on their shoulders, with the aid of a staff or the hand of a by-stander rose upon their feet. It seemed cruel; but, before much sympathy could be expended upon them, they were out of sight.

At eight o'clock Mr. C. and I mounted, each armed with a brace of pistols and a large hunting-knife, which we carried in a belt around the body; besides which, afraid to trust it in other hands, I had a mountain barometer slung over my shoulder. Augustin carried pistols and sword; our principal muleteer, who was mounted, carried a machete and a pair of murderous spurs, with rowels two inches long, on his naked heels; and two other muleteers accompanied us on foot, each carrying a gun.

A group of friendly by-standers gave us their adieus and good wishes; and, passing a few straggling houses which constituted the suburbs, we entered upon a marshy plain sprinkled with shrubs and small trees, and in a few minutes were in an unbroken forest. At every step the mules sank to their fetlocks in mud, and very soon we came to great puddles and mudholes, which reminded me of the breaking up of winter and the solitary horsepath in one of our primeval forests at home. As we advanced, the shade of the trees became thicker, the holes larger and deeper, and roots, rising two or three feet above the ground, crossed the path in every direction. I gave the barometer to the muleteer, and had as much as I could do to keep myself in the saddle. All conversation was at an end, and we kept as close as we could to the track of the muleteer; when he descended into a mudhole, and crawled out, the entire legs of his mule blue with mud, we followed, and came out as blue as he.

The caravan of mules, which had started before us, was but a short distance ahead, and in a little while we heard ringing through the woods the loud shout of the muleteers and the sharp crack of the whip. We overtook them at the bank of a stream which broke rapidly over a stony bed. The whole caravan was moving up the bed of the stream; the water was darkened by the shade of the overhanging trees; the muleteers, without shirts, and with their large trousers rolled up to the thighs and down from the waistband, were scattered among the mules : one was chasing a stray beast ; a second darting at one whose load was slipping off ; a third lifting up one that had fallen ; another, with his foot braced against a mule's side, straining at the girth ; all shouting, cursing, and lashing : the whole a mass of inextricable confusion, and presenting a scene almost terrific.

We held up to let them pass ; and, crossing the stream, rode a short distance on a level road, but over fetlock deep in mud ; and, cutting off a bend, fell into the stream ourselves in the middle of the caravan. The branches of the trees met over our heads, and the bed of the stream was so broken and stony that the mules constantly stumbled and fell. Leaving this, and continuing on a road the same as before, in an hour we reached the foot of the mountain. The ascent began precipitously, and by an extraordinary passage. It was a narrow gulley, worn by the tracks of mules and the washing of mountain torrents so deep that the sides were higher than our heads, and so narrow that we could barely pass through without touching. Our whole caravan moved singly through these muddy defiles, the muleteers scattered among them and on the bank above, extricating the mules as they stuck fast, raising them as they fell, arranging their cargoes, cursing, shouting, and lashing them on. If one stopped, all behind were blocked up, unable to turn. Any sudden start pressed us against the sides of the gulley, and there was no small danger of getting a leg crushed. Emerging from this defile, we came again among deep mudholes and projecting roots of trees, with the additional difficulty of a steep ascent. The trees, too, were larger, and their roots higher and extending farther ; and, above all, the mahogany-tree threw out its giant roots, high at the trunk and tapering, not round, like the roots of other trees, but straight, with sharp edges, traversing rocks and the roots of other trees. It was the last of the rainy season; the heavy rains from which we had suffered at sea had deluged the mountain, and it was in the worst state, to be passable; for sometimes it is not passable at all. For the last few days there had been no rain; but we had hardly congratulated ourselves upon our good fortune in having a clear day, when the forest became darker and the rain poured. The woods were of impenetrable thickness; and there was no view except that of the detestable path before us. For five long hours we were dragged through mudholes, squeezed in gulleys, knocked against trees, and tumbled over roots; every step required care and great physical exertion; and, withal, I felt that our inglorious epitaph might be, " tossed over the head of a mule, brained by the trunk of a mahogany-tree, and buried in the mud of the Mico Mountain." We attempted to walk, but the rocks and roots were so slippery, the mudholes so deep, and the ascents and descents so steep, that it was impossible to continue.

The mules were only half loaded, and even then several broke down; the lash could not move them; and scarcely one passed over without a fall. Of our immediate party, mine fell first. Finding that I could not save her with the rein, by an exertion that strained every nerve I lifted myself from off her back, and flung clear of roots and trees, but not of mud; and I had an escape from a worse danger: my dagger fell from its sheath and stood upright, with the handle in the mud, a foot of naked blade. Mr. Catherwood was thrown with such violence, that for a few moments, feeling the helplessness of our condition, I was horror-struck. Long before this he had broken silence to utter an exclamation which seemed to come from the bottom of his heart, that, if he had known of this "mountain," I might have come to Central America alone ; if I had had any tendency to be a little uplifted by the honours I received at Balize, I was brought down by this high way to my capital. Shortly after Augustin's mule fell backward ; he kicked his feet out of the stirrups, and attempted to slide off behind ; but the mule rolled, and caught him with his left leg under, and, but for his kicking, I should have thought that every bone in his body was broken. The mule kicked worse than he ; but they rose together, and without any damage except that the mud, which before lay upon them in spots, was now formed into a regular plaster.

We were toiling on toward the top of the mountain, when, at a sudden turn, we met a solitary traveller. He was a tall, dark-complexioned man, with a broad-brimmed Panama hat, rolled up at the sides ; a striped woollen Guatimala jacket, with fringe at the bottom ; plaid pantaloons, leather spatterdashes, spurs, and sword ; he was mounted on a noble mule with a high-peaked saddle, and the butts of a pair of horseman's pistols peeped out of the holsters. His face was covered with sweat and mud ; his breast and legs were spattered, and his right side was a complete incrustation ; altogether, his appearance was fearful. It seemed strange to meet any one on such a road ; and, to our surprise, he accosted us in English. He had set out with muleteers and Indians, but had lost them in some of the windings of the woods, and was seeking his way alone. He had crossed the mountain twice before, but had never known it so bad ; he had been thrown twice; once his mule rolled over him, and nearly crushed him; and now she was so frightened that he could hardly urge her along. He dismounted, and the trembling beast and his own exhausted state confirmed all that he had said. He asked us for brandy, wine, or water, anything to revive him; but, unfortunately, our stores were ahead, and for him to go back one step was out of the question. Imagine our surprise, when, with his feet buried in the mud, he told us that he had been two years in Guatimala "negotiating" for a bank charter. Fresh as I was from the land of banks, I almost thought he intended a fling at me; but he did not look like one in a humour for jesting; and, for the benefit of those who will regard it as an evidence of incipient improvement, I am able to state that he had the charter secured when he rolled over in the mud, and was then on his way to England to sell the stock. He told us, too, what seemed in better keeping with the scene, that Carrera had marched toward St. Salvador, and a battle was daily expected between him and Morazan.

But neither of us had time to lose; and parting, though with some reluctance, almost as abruptly as we had met, we continued our ascent. At one o'clock, to our inexpressible satisfaction, we reached the top of the mountain. Here we found a clearing of about two hundred feet in diameter, made for the benefit of benighted muleteers; in different places were heaps of ashes and burned stumps of wood, the remains of their fires. It was the only place on the mountain which the sun could reach, and here the ground was dry; but the view was bounded by the clearing.

We dismounted, and would have lunched, but had no water to drink; and, after a few minutes' rest, resumed our journey. The descent was as bad as the ascent; and, instead of stopping to let the mules breathe, as they had done in ascending, the muleteers seemed anxious to determine in how short a time they could tumble them down the mountain. In one of the muddiest defiles we were shut up by the falling of a mule before, and the crowding upon us of all behind; and, at the first convenient place, we stopped until the whole caravan had passed. The carefulness of the mules was extraordinary. For an hour I watched the movements of the one before me. At times he put one of his fore feet on a root or stone, and tried it as a man would; sometimes he drew his fore legs out of a bed of mud from the shoulders, and sometimes it was one continued alternation of sinking and pulling out.

This is the great high road to the city of Guatimala, which has always been a place of distinction in Spanish America. Almost all the travel and merchandise from Europe passes over it; and our guide said that the reason it was so bad was because it was traversed by so many mules. In some countries this would be a reason for making it better; but it was pleasant to find that the people to whom I was accredited were relieved from one of the sources of contention at home, and did not trouble themselves with the complicated questions attendant upon internal improvements.*

In two hours we reached a wild river or mountain torrent, foaming and breaking over its rocky bed, and shaded by large trees. It was called El Arroyo del Muerto, or Stream of the Dead. The muleteers were already distributed on the rocks or under the shade of

---

* Since that time the Constituent Assembly of Guatimala has imposed a tax of one dollar upon every bale of merchandise that passes over the mountain, for the improvement of the road.

the trees, eating their frugal meal of corn-cakes; the mules were in the river, or scattered along the bank; and we selected a large tree, which spread its branches over us like a roof, and so near the stream that we could dip our drinking-cups into the water.

All the anxiety which I had been able to spare during the day from myself I had bestowed upon the barometer on the back of the guide. He carried, besides, a small white pitcher, with a red rim, on the belt of his machete, of which he was very proud and very careful; and several times, after a stumble and a narrow escape, he turned round and held up the pitcher with a smile, which gave me hopes of the barometer; and, in fact, he had carried it through without its being broken; but, unfortunately, the quicksilver was not well secured, and the whole had escaped. It was impossible to repair it in Guatimala, and the loss of this barometer was a source of regret during our whole journey; for we ascended many mountains, the heights of which have never been ascertained.

But we had another misadventure, which, at the moment, touched us more nearly. We sat on the ground, Turkish fashion, with a vacant space between us. Augustin placed before us a well-filled napkin; and, as we dipped water from the clear stream by our side, a spirit of other days came over us, and we spoke in contempt of railroads, cities, and hotels; but oh, publicans, you were avenged. We unrolled the napkin, and the scene that presented itself was too shocking, even for the strongest nerves. We had provided bread for three days, eggs boiled hard, and two roasted fowls for as long as they might last. Augustin had forgotten salt, but he had placed in the napkin a large paper of gunpowder as an adventure of his own. The paper was broken, and the bread, fowls, and eggs were thoroughly seasoned with this new condiment. All the beauty of the scene, all our equanimity, everything except our tremendous appetites, left us in a moment. Country taverns rose up before us ; and we, who had been so amiable, abused Augustin, and wished him the whole murderous seasoning in his own body. We could not pick out enough to satisfy hunger. It was perhaps the most innocent way of tasting gunpowder, but even so it was a bitter pill. We picked and made excavations for immediate use, but the rest of our stores was lost.

This over, we mounted, and, fording the stream, continued our descent. Passing off by a spur of the mountain, we came out upon an open ridge, commanding a view of an extensive savannah. Very soon we reached a fine table of land, where a large party of muleteers on their way to Yzabal were encamped for the night. Bales of indigo, which formed their cargoes, were piled up like a wall ; their mules were pasturing quietly near them, and fires were burning to cook their suppers. It was a great satisfaction to be once more in an open country, and to see the mountain, with its dense forest, lighted up by the setting sun, grand and gloomy, and ourselves fairly out of it. With ten hours of the hardest riding I ever went through, we had made only twelve miles.

Descending from this table, we entered a plain thickly wooded, and in a few minutes reached a grove of wild palm-trees of singular beauty. From the top of a tall naked stem grew branches twenty or thirty feet long, spreading from the trunk, and falling outward with a graceful bend, like enormous plumes of feathers ; the trees stood so close that the bending branches

met, and formed arches, in some places as regular as
if constructed by art ; and as we rode among them, there
was a solemn stillness, an air of desolation, that reminded us of the columns of an Egyptian temple.

Toward dark we reached the rancho of Mico. It
was a small house, built of poles and plastered with
mud. Near it, and connected by a shed thatched with
branches, was a larger house, built of the same material, expressly for the use of travellers. This was already occupied by two parties from Guatimala, one of
which consisted of the Canonigo Castillo, his clerical
companion or secretary, and two young Pavons. The
other was a French merchant on his way to Paris.
Mr. C. and I were picturesque-looking objects, not
spattered, but plastered with mud from head to foot ;
but we were soon known, and received from the whole
company a cordial welcome to Central America.

Their appearance was such as gave me a highly
favourable opinion of the description of persons I
should meet at Guatimala. The canonigo was one of
the first men in the country in position and character,
and was then on his way to Havana on a delicate political mission, being sent by the Constituent Assembly to invite back the archbishop, who had been banished by General Morazan ten years before. He undertook to do the honours, and set before us chocolate and what he called the " national dish," fregoles,
or black beans fried, which, fortunately for our subse-
quent travels, we " cottoned" to at once. We were
very tired, but agreeable company was better than
sleep. The canonigo had been educated at Rome,
and passed the early part of his life in Europe ; the
Frenchman was from Paris ; the young Pavons were
educated in New-York ; and we sat till a late hour,

our clothes stiff with mud, talking of France, Italy,
and home. At length we hung up our hammocks.
We had been so much occupied that we had paid no
attention to our luggage ; and, when we wanted to procure a change of raiment, could not find our men, and
were obliged to turn in as we were ; but, with the satisfactory feeling that we had passed " the mountain,"
we soon fell asleep.

ENTERING THE RIO DOLCE.

CHAPTER III.

BEFORE daylight I was out of doors. Twenty or thirty men, muleteers and servants, were asleep on the ground, each lying on his back, with his black *chamar* wound round him, covering his head and feet. As the day broke they arose. Very soon the Frenchman got up, took chocolate, and, after an hour's preparation, started. The canonigo set off next. He had crossed the mountain twenty years before, on his first arrival in the country, and still retained a full recollection of its horrors. He set off on the back of an Indian, in a *silla*, or chair with a high back and top to protect him from the sun. Three other Indians followed as relay carriers, and a noble mule for his relief if he should become tired of the chair. The Indian was bent almost double, but the canonigo was in high spirits, smoking his cigar, and waving his hand till he was out of sight. The Pavons started last, and we were left alone.

Still none of our men came. At about eight o'clock two made their appearance ; they had slept at a rancho near by, and the others had gone on with the luggage. We were excessively provoked ; but, enduring as we might the discomfort of our clothes stiff with mud, saddled and set off.

We saw no more of our caravan of mules, and our muleteer of the barometer had disappeared without

notice, and left us in the hands of two understrap-
pers.

Our road lay over a mountainous country, but generally clear of wood ; and in about two hours we reached a collection of ranchos, called El Posos. One of
our men rode up to a hut and dismounted, as if he
were at home. The woman of the house chided him
for not having come the night before, which he gruffly
ascribed to us ; and it was evident that we stood a
chance of losing him too. But we had a subject of
more immediate interest in the want of a breakfast.
Our tea and coffee, all that we had left after the destruction of our stores by gunpowder, were gone forward, and for some time we could get nothing. And
here, in the beginning of our journey, we found a scarcity of provant greater than we had ever met with before in any inhabited country. The people lived exclusively upon tortillas—flat cakes made of crushed
Indian corn, and baked on a clay griddle—and black
beans. Augustin bought some of these last, but they
required several hours' soaking before they could be
eaten. At length he succeeded in buying a fowl,
through which he ran a stick, and smoked it over a
fire, without dressing of any kind, and which, with tortillas, made a good meal for a penitentiary system of
diet. As we had expected, our principal muleteer was
unable to tear himself away ; but, like a dutiful husband, he sent, by the only one that was now left, a
loving message to his wife at Gualan.

At the moment of starting, our remaining attendant
said he could not go until he had made a pair of shoes,
and we were obliged to wait; but it did not take long.
Standing on an untanned cowhide, he marked the size
of his feet with a piece of coal, cut them out with his

machete, made proper holes, and, passing a leather
string under the instep, around the heel, and between
the great *doigt du pied* and the one next to it, was
shod.

Again our road lay on the ridge of a high mountain,
with a valley on each side. At a distance were beautiful hillsides, green, and ornamented with pine-trees
and cattle grazing upon them, that reminded us of park
scenery in England. Often points presented themselves, which at home would have been selected as
sites for dwellings, and embellished by art and taste.
And it was a land of perpetual summer; the blasts
of winter never reach it; but, with all its softness and
beauty, it was dreary and desolate.

At two o'clock it began to rain; in an hour it cleared off, and from the high mountain ridge we saw the
Motagua River, one of the noblest in Central America,
rolling majestically through the valley on our left.
Descending by a wild, precipitous path, at four o'clock
we reached the bank directly opposite Encuentros. It
was one of the most beautiful scenes I ever beheld:
all around were giant mountains, and the river, broad
and deep, rolled through them with the force of a
mighty torrent.

On the opposite bank were a few houses, and two
or three canoes lay in the water, but not a person was
in sight. By loud shouting we brought a man to the
bank, who entered one of the canoes and set her adrift;
he was immediately carried far down the stream; but,
taking advantage of an eddy, he brought her across to
the place where we stood. Our luggage, the saddles,
bridles, and other trappings of the mules, were put on
board, and we embarked. Augustin sat in the stern,
holding the halter of one of the mules, and leading her

like a decoy duck; but the rest had no disposition to
follow. The muleteer drove them in up to their necks,
but they ran back to the shore. Several times, by pelt-
ing them with sticks and stones, he drove them in as
before. At length he stripped himself; and, wading
to the depth of his breast, with a stick ten or twelve
feet long, succeeded in getting them all afloat, and on a
line within the reach of his stick. Any one that turned toward the shore received a blow on his nose, and
at length they all set their faces for the opposite bank;
their little heads were all that we could see, aimed directly across, but carried down by the current. One
was carried below the rest; and, when she saw her
companions landing, she raised a frightened cry, and
almost drowned herself in struggling to reach them.

During all this time we sat in the canoe, with the
hot sun beating upon our heads. For the last two
hours we had suffered excessively from heat; our
clothes were saturated with perspiration and stiff with
mud, and we looked forward almost with rapture to a
bath in the Motagua and a change of linen. We landed, and walked up to the house in which we were to
pass the night. It was plastered and whitewashed,
and adorned with streaks of red in the shape of festoons; and in front was a fence made of long reeds,
six inches in diameter, split into two; altogether the
appearance was favourable. To our great vexation,
our luggage had gone on to a rancho three leagues beyond. Our muleteers refused to go any farther. We
were unpleasantly situated, but we did not care to leave
so soon the Motagua river. Our host told us that his
house and all that he had were at our disposal; but he
could give us nothing to eat; and, telling Augustin to
ransack the village, we returned to the river. Every-

where the current was too rapid for a quiet bath.   Calling our canoe man, we returned to the opposite side,
and in a few minutes were enjoying an ablution, the
luxury of which can only be appreciated by those who,
like us, had crossed the Mico Mountain without throwing away their clothes.

There was an enjoyment in this bath greater even
than that of cooling our heated bodies. It was the
moment of a golden sunset. We stood up to our necks
in water clear as crystal, and calm as that of some
diminutive lake, at the margin of a channel along
which the stream was rushing with arrowy speed. On
each side were mountains several thousand feet high,
with their tops illuminated by the setting sun ; on a
point above us was a palm-leafed hut, and before it a
naked Indian sat looking at us ; while flocks of parrots,
with brilliant plumage, almost in thousands, were flying
over our heads, catching up our words, and filling the
air with their noisy mockings. It was one of those
beautiful scenes that so rarely occur in human life, almost realizing dreams. Old as we were, we might
have become poetic, but that Augustin came down to
the opposite bank, and, with a cry that rose above the
chattering of parrots and the loud murmur of the river,
called us to supper.

We had one moment of agony when we returned to
our clothes. They lay extended upon the bank, emblems of men who had seen better days. The setting
sun, which shed over all a soft and mellow lustre, laid
bare the seams of mud and dirt, and made them hideous. We had but one alternative, and that was to go
without them. But, as this seemed to be trenching
upon the proprieties of life, we picked them up and
put them on reluctant. I am not sure, however, but

that we made an unnecessary sacrifice of personal comfort.   The proprieties of life are matters of convention-
al usage.   Our host was a don ; and when we presented our letter he received us with great dignity in a single garment, loose, white, and very laconic, not quite
reaching his knees.   The dress of his wife was no less
easy ; somewhat in the style of the oldfashioned shortgown and petticoat, only the shortgown and whatever
else is usually worn under it were wanting, and their
place supplied by a string of beads, with a large cross
at the end.   A dozen men and half-grown boys, naked
except the small covering formed by rolling the trousers
up and down in the manner I have mentioned, were
lounging about the house ; and women and girls in
such extremes of undress, that a string of beads seemed quite a covering for modesty.

Mr. C. and I were in a rather awkward predicament
for the night.   The general reception-room contained
three beds, made of strips of cowhide interlaced.   The
don occupied one ; he had not much undressing to do,
but what little he had, he did by pulling off his shirt.
Another bed was at the foot of my hammock.   I was
dozing, when I opened my eyes, and saw a girl about
seventeen sitting sideway upon it, smoking a cigar.
She had a piece of striped cotton cloth tied around her
waist, and falling below her knees ; the rest of her
dress was the same which Nature bestows alike upon
the belle of fashionable life and the poorest girl; in
other words, it was the same as that of the don's wife,
with the exception of the string of beads.   At first I
thought it was something I had conjured up in a dream;
and as I waked up perhaps I raised my head, for she
gave a few quick puffs of her cigar, drew a cotton
sheet over her head and shoulders, and lay down to

sleep. I endeavoured to do the same. I called to
mind the proverb, that " travelling makes strange bed-
fellows." I had slept pellmell with Greeks, Turks,
and Arabs. I was beginning a journey in a new country; it was my duty to conform to the customs of the
people; to be prepared for the worst, and submit with
resignation to whatever might befall me.

As guests, it was pleasant to feel that the family made
no strangers of us. The wife of the don retired with the
same ceremonies. Several times during the night we
were waked by the clicking of flint and steel, and saw
one of our neighbours lighting a cigar. At daylight
the wife of the don was enjoying her morning slumber.
While I was dressing she bade me good-morning, removed the cotton covering from her shoulders, and
arose dressed for the day.

We started early, and for some distance our road
lay along the banks of the Motagua, almost as beautiful by morning as by evening light. In an hour we
commenced ascending the spur of a mountain; and,
reaching the top, followed the ridge. It was high and
narrow, commanding on both sides an almost boundless view, and seemed selected for picturesque effect.
The scenery was grand, but the land wild and uncultivated, without fences, enclosures, or habitations. A
few cattle were wandering wild over the great expanse,
but without imparting that domestic aspect which in
other countries attends the presence of cattle. We met
a few Indians, with their machetes, going to their morning's work, and a man riding a mule, with a woman
before him, his arm encircling her waist.

I was riding ahead of my companions, and on the
summit of the ridge, a little aside from the road, saw
a little white girl, perfectly naked, playing before a

rancho.   As most of the people we met were Indians
or Ladinos, I was attracted by her appearance, and
rode up to the rancho.   The proprietor, in the easy
costume of our host of Encuentros, was swinging in a
hammock under the portico, and smoking a cigar.   At
a little distance was a shed thatched with stalks and
leaves of Indian corn, and called the *cucinera*, or kitch-
en.   As usual, while the don was lolling in his hammock, the women were at work.

I rode on to the *cucinera*, and dismounted.   The
party consisted of the mother and a pretty daughter-
in-law of about nineteen, and two daughters of about
fifteen and seventeen.   The reader is perhaps curious
about costumes; but having given him an insight into
those of this country, he will not require any farther descriptions.   In honour of my visit, the mother
snatched up the little girl who had attracted me to the
rancho, carried her inside, and slipped over her head
a garment which, I believe, is generally worn by little
girls; but in a few minutes my young friend disen-
cumbered herself of her finery, and was toddling about
with it under her arm.

The whole family was engaged in making tortillas.
This is the bread of Central and of all Spanish America, and the only species to be found except in the principal towns.   At one end of the *cucinera* was an elevation, on which stood a comal or griddle, resting on
three stones, with a fire blazing under it.   The daugh-
ter-in-law had before her an earthen vessel containing
Indian corn soaked in lime-water to remove the husk;
and, placing a handful on an oblong stone curving inward, mashed it with a stone roller into a thick paste.
The girls took it as it was mashed, and patting it with
their hands into flat cakes, laid them on the griddle to

bake. This is repeated for every meal, and a great part of the business of the women consists in making tortillas.

When Mr. Catherwood arrived the tortillas were smoking, and we stopped to breakfast. They gave us the only luxury they had, coffee made of parched corn, which, in compliment to their kindness, we drank. Like me, Mr. C. was struck with the personal beauty of this family group. With the advantages of dress and education, they might be ornaments in cultivated society; but it is decreed otherwise, and these young girls will go through life making tortillas.

For an hour longer we continued on the ridge of the mountain, then entered a more woody country, and in half an hour came to a large gate, which stood directly across the road like a tollbar. It was the first token we had seen of individual or territorial boundary, and in other countries would have formed a fitting entrance to a princely estate; for the massive frame, with all its posts and supporters, was of solid mahogany. The heat was now intense. We entered a thick wood and forded a wild stream, across which pigs were swimming. Soon after we came to a cochineal plantation, and passed through a long lane thickly bordered and overshaded with shrubs and trees, close to suffocation. We emerged into an open plain, on which the sun beat with almost intolerable power; and, crossing the plain, at about three o'clock entered Gualan. There was not a breath of air; the houses and the earth seemed to throw out heat. I was confused, my head swam, and I felt in danger of a stroke of the sun. At that moment there was a slight shock of earthquake. I was unconscious of it, but was almost overpowered by the excessive heat and closeness of atmosphere which accompanied it.

We rode up to the house of Donna Bartola, to whom we had a letter of recommendation, and I cannot describe the satisfaction with which I threw myself into a hammock. Shade and quiet restored me. For the first time since we left Yzabal we changed our clothes; for the first time, too, we dined.

Toward evening we strolled through the town. It stands on a table of breccia rock, at the junction of two noble rivers, and is encircled by a belt of mountains. One principal street, the houses of one story, with piazzas in front, terminates in a plaza or public square, at the head of which stands a large church with a Gothic door; and before it, at a distance of ten or twelve yards, was a cross about twenty feet high. The population is about ten thousand, chiefly Mestitzoes. Leaving the plaza, we walked down to the Motagua. On the bank a boat was in process of construction, about fifty feet long and ten wide, entirely of mahogany. Near it a party of men and women were fording the stream, carrying their clothes above their heads; and around a point three women were bathing. There are no ancient associations connected with this place; but the wildness of the scene, the clouds, the tints of the sky, and the setting sun reflected upon the mountains, were beautiful. At dark we returned to the house. Except for the companionship of some thousands of ants, which blackened the candles and covered everything perishable, we had a room to ourselves.

Early in the morning we were served with chocolate and a small roll of sweet bread. While at breakfast our muleteer came, reiterating a demand for settlement, and claiming three dollars more than was due.

We refused to pay him, and he went away furious. In half an hour an alguazil came to me with a summons to the alcalde. Mr. Catherwood, who was, at the moment, cleaning his pistols, cheered me by threatening, if they put me in prison, to bombard the town. The cabildo, or house of the municipality, was at one side of the plaza. We entered a large room, one end of which was partitioned off by a wooden railing. Inside sat the alcalde and his clerk, and outside was the muleteer, with a group of half-naked fellows as his backers. He had reduced his claim to one dollar, doubtless supposing that I would pay that rather than have any trouble. It was not very respectable to be sued for a dollar; but I looked in his face on entering, and resolved not to pay a cent. I did not, however, claim my privilege under the law of nations, but defended the action on the merits, and the alcalde decided in my favour; after which I showed him my passport, and he asked me inside the bar and offered me a cigar.

This over, I had more important business. The first was to hire mules, which could not be procured till the day but one after. Next I negotiated for washing clothes, which was a complicated business, for it was necessary to specify which articles were to be washed, which ironed, and which starched, and to pay separately for washing, ironing, soap, and starch; and, lastly, I negotiated with a tailor for a pair of pantaloons, purchasing separately stuff, lining, buttons, and thread, the tailor finding needles and thimble himself.

Toward evening we again walked to the river, returned, and taught Donna Bartola how to make tea. By this time the whole town was in commotion preparatory to the great ceremony of praying to the Santa

Lucia. Early in the morning, the firing of muskets, petards, and rockets had announced the arrival of this unexpected but welcome visiter, one of the holiest saints of the calendar, and, next to San Antonio, the most celebrated for the power of working miracles. Morazan's rise into power was signalized by a persecution of the clergy : his friends say that it was the purification of a corrupt body ; his enemies, that it was a war against morality and religion. The country was at that time overrun with priests, friars, and monks of different orders. Everywhere the largest buildings, the best cultivated lands, and a great portion of the wealth of the country were in their hands. Many, no doubt, were good men ; but some used their sacred robes as a cloak for rascality and vice, and most were drones, reaping where they did not sow, and living luxuriously by the sweat of other men's brows. At all events, and whatever was the cause, the early part of Morazan's administration was signalized by hostility to them as a class ; and, from the Archbishop of Guatimala down to the poorest friar, they were in danger ; some fled, others were banished, and many were torn by rude soldiers from their convents and churches, hurried to the seaports, and shipped for Cuba and old Spain, under sentence of death if they returned. The country was left comparatively destitute ; many of the churches fell to ruins ; others stood, but their doors were seldom opened ; and the practice and memory of their religious rites were fading away. Carrera and his Indians, with the mystic rites of Catholicism ingrafted upon the superstitions of their fathers, had acquired a strong hold upon the feelings of the people by endeavouring to bring back the exiled clergy and to restore the influence of the church. The tour of the Santa Lucia was regarded as an indication of a change of feeling and government; as a prelude to the restoration of the influence of the church and the revival of ceremonies dear to the heart of the Indian. As such, it was hailed by all the villages through which she had passed; and that night she would receive the prayers of the Christians of Gualan.

The Santa Lucia enjoyed a peculiar popularity from her miraculous power over the affections of the young; for any young man who prayed to her for a wife, or any young woman who prayed for a husband, was sure to receive the object of such prayer; and if the person praying indicated to the saint the individual wished for, the prayer would be granted, provided such individual was not already married. It was not surprising that a saint with such extraordinary powers, touching so directly the tenderest sensibilities, created a sensation in a place where the feelings, or, rather, the passions, are particularly turned to love.

Donna Bartola invited us to accompany her, and, setting out, we called upon a friend of hers; during the whole visit, a servant girl sat with her lap full of tobacco, making straw cigars for immediate use. It was the first time we had smoked with ladies, and, at first, it was rather awkward to ask one for a light; but we were so thoroughly broken in that night that we never had any delicacy afterward. The conversation turned upon the saint and her miraculous powers; and when we avowed ourselves somewhat skeptical, the servant girl, with that familiarity, though not want of respect, which exists throughout Central America, said that it was wicked to doubt; that she had prayed to the saint herself, and two months afterward she was married, and to the very man she prayed for, though at the time he had no idea of her, and, in fact, wanted another girl.

With this encouragement, locking the house, and accompanied by children and servants, we set out to pay our homage to the saint. The sound of a violin and the firing of rockets indicated the direction of her temporary domicil. She had taken up her residence in the hut of a poor Indian in the suburbs; and, for some time before reaching it, we encountered crowds of both sexes, and all ages and colours, and in every degree of dress and undress, smoking and talking, and sitting or lying on the ground in every variety of attitude. Room was made for our party, and we entered the hut.

It was about twenty feet square, thatched on the top and sides with leaves of Indian corn, and filled with a dense mass of kneeling men and women. On one side was an altar, about four feet high, covered with a clean white cotton cloth. On the top of the altar was a frame, with three elevations, like a flower-stand, and on the top of that a case, containing a large wax doll, dressed in blue silk, and ornamented with gold leaf, spangles, and artificial flowers. This was the Santa Lucia. Over her head was a canopy of red cotton cloth, on which was emblazoned a cross in gold. On the right was a sedan chair, trimmed with red cotton and gold leaf, being the travelling equipage of the saint; and near it were Indians in half-sacerdotal dress, on whose shoulders she travelled; festoons of oranges hung from the roof, and the rough posts were inwrapped with leaves of the sugar-cane. At the foot of the altar was a mat, on which girls and boys were playing; and a little fellow about six years old, habited in the picturesque costume of a straw hat, and that only, was coolly surveying the crowd.

The ceremony of praying had already begun, and the music of a drum, a violin, and a flageolet, under the di-

rection of the Indian master of ceremonies, drowned
the noise of voices. Donna Bartola, who was a widow,
and the other ladies of our party, fell on their knees; and,
recommending myself to their prayers, I looked on without doing anything for myself, but I studied attentively the faces of those around me. There were some of
both sexes who could not strictly be called young; but
they did not, on that account, pray less earnestly. In
some places people would repel the imputation of being
desirous to procure husband or wife; not so in Gualan:
they prayed publicly for what they considered a bless-
ing. Some of the men were so much in earnest that
perspiration stood in large drops upon their faces; and
none thought that praying for a husband need tinge the
cheek of a modest maiden. I watched the countenance
of a young Indian girl, beaming with enthusiasm and
hope; and, while her eyes rested upon the image of the
saint and her lips moved in prayer, I could not but imagine that her heart was full of some truant, and perhaps unworthy lover.

Outside the hut was an entirely different scene. Near
by were rows of kneeling men and women, but beyond
were wild groups of half-naked men and boys, setting
off rockets and fireworks. As I moved through, a
flash rose from under my feet, and a petard exploded
so near that the powder singed me; and, turning round,
I saw hurrying away my rascally muleteer. Beyond
were parties of young men and women dancing by the
light of blazing pine sticks. In a hut at some little distance were two haggard old women, with large caldrons
over blazing fires, stirring up and serving out the contents with long wooden ladles, and looking like witches
dealing out poison instead of love-potions.

At ten o'clock the prayers to the saint died away, and

the crowd separated into groups and couples, and many fell into what in English would be called flirtations. A mat was spread for our party against the side of the hut, and we all lighted cigars and sat down upon it. Cups made of small gourds, and filled from the caldrons with a preparation of boiled Indian corn sweetened with various *dolces*, were passed from mouth to mouth, each one sipping and passing it on to the next; and this continued, without any interruption, for more than an hour. We remained on the ground till after midnight, and then were among the first to leave. On the whole, we concluded that praying to the Santa Lucia must lead to matrimony; and I could not but remark that, in the way of getting husbands and wives, most seemed disposed to do something for themselves, and not leave all to the grace of the saint.

The next day it was excessively hot, and we remained within doors. In the evening we visited the padre, who had just returned from a neighbouring village. He was a short, fat man, and had on a white nightcap, a blue striped jacket, and white pantaloons, and we found him swinging in a hammock and smoking a cigar. He had a large household of women and children; but as to the relation in which they stood to him, people differed. He gave us more information in regard to the country than we had yet been able to obtain, and particularly in regard to Copan, a ruined city which we wished to visit. He was familiar with the history of the Indians, and understood thoroughly the character of the present race; and, in answer to our question if they were all Christians, said that they were devout and religious, and had a great respect for the priests and saints. With this he hitched up his bursting pantaloons, and lighted another cigar. We might have smiled at the idea of his confounding his comfortable figure with the saints; but he had so much good sense and good feeling that we were not disposed to be captious.

The next morning our muleteer came, but, through some misunderstanding, he had not mules enough to carry all our luggage. Rather than wait, we started without him, and left part of the baggage for him to bring on to Zacapa the next day.

Leaving Gualan, we had on our right the Motagua River, which had now become to us a friend, and beyond it the great range of the mountains of Vera Paz, six or eight thousand feet high. In an hour we commenced ascending. Soon we were in a wilderness of flowers; shrubs and bushes were clothed in purple and red; and on the sides of the mountain, and in the ravines leading down to the river, in the wildest positions, were large trees so covered with red that they seemed a single flower. In three hours we descended from our mountain height, and came once more to the river side, where it was rolling swiftly, and in some places breaking into rapids. We followed for about an hour, and rose again several thousand feet. At two o'clock we reached the village of San Pablo, situated on a lofty table of land, looking down upon the river, and having its view bounded by the mountains of Vera Paz. The church stood at the entrance of the village. We turned our mules loose to graze, and took our meal in the porch. It was a beautiful position, and two waterfalls, shining like streaks of silver on the distant mountain side, reminded us of cascades in Switzerland.

We procured a guide from the alcalde to conduct us to Zacapa; and, resuming our journey, for two hours more had the same great range upon our right. The sun was obscured, but occasionally it broke through and lighted up the sides of the mountains, while the tops were covered with clouds. At four o'clock we had a distant view of the great plain of Zacapa, bounded on the opposite side by a triangular belt of mountains, at the foot of which stood the town. We descended and crossed the plain, which was green and well cultivated ; and, fording a stream, ascended a rugged bank and entered the town.

It was by far the finest we had seen. The streets were regular, and the houses plastered and whitewashed, with large balconied windows and piazzas. The church was two hundred and fifty feet long, with walls ten feet thick, and a façade rich with Moorish devices. It was built in the form of a Latin cross. In one end of the cross was a tailor's shop, and the other was roofless. At one corner was a belfry, consisting of four rough trunks of trees supporting a peaked roof covered with tiles. Two bells were suspended from a rude beam ; and, as we passed, a half-naked Indian was standing on a platform underneath, ringing for vespers.

We rode up to the house of Don Mariano Durante, one of the largest and best in the place, being about a hundred feet front, and having a corridor extending the whole length, paved with square stones. The door was opened by a respectable-looking St. Domingo negro, who told us, in French, that Señor Durante was not at home, but that the house was at our service ; and, going round to a *porte cochère* alongside, admitted us into a large courtyard ornamented with trees and flowers, at one side of which was a *cabelleria* or stable. We left our mules in the hands of the servants, and entered a sala or reception-room covering nearly the whole front, with large windows reaching down to the floor and iron balconies, and furnished with tables, a European bureau, and chairs. In the centre of the room and in the windows hung cages, handsomely made and gilded, containing beautiful singing-birds of the country, and two fine canary birds from Havana. This was the residence of two bachelor brothers, who, feeling for the wants of travellers in a country entirely destitute of hotels, kept a door always open for their accommodation. We had candles lighted, and made ourselves at home. I was sitting at a table writing, when we heard the tramp of mules outside, and a gentleman entered, took off his sword and spurs, and laid his pistols upon the table. Supposing him to be a traveller like ourselves, we asked him to take a seat; and, when supper was served, invited him to join us. It was not till bedtime that we found we were doing the honours to one of the masters of the house. He must have thought us cool, but I flatter myself he had no reason to complain of any want of attention.

CHAPTER IV.

Purchasing a Bridle.—A School and its Regulations.—Conversation with an In-
dian.— Spanish Translation of the " Spy."—Chiquimula.—A Church in Ruins.
—A Veteran of the French Empire.—St. Stephanos.—A Land of Mountains.—
An Affair with a Muleteer.—A deserted Village.—A rude Assault.—Arrest.—
Imprisonment.—Release.

THE next day we were obliged to wait for our muleteer. Our guide of the night before had stolen one of
our bridles ; and here we found the beginning of an
annoyance which attended us throughout Central America, in the difficulty of buying anything ready made.
There was a blacksmith who had a bit partly made, but
had not charcoal enough to finish it. Fortunately, during the day an Indian arrived with a backload, and the
bridle was completed. The headstall we bought of a
saddler, and the reins, which were of platted leather like
the lash of a whip, we were lucky enough to obtain
ready made. The arrival of the charcoal enabled the
blacksmith to fit us out with one pair of spurs.

At Zacapa, for the first time, we saw a schoolhouse.
It was a respectable-looking building, with columns in
front, and against the wall hung a large card, headed,

" 1st Decurion (a student who has the care of ten other students).   2d Decurion.
MONITOR, &c.

" Interior regulation for the good government of the school of first letters of this
town, which ought to be observed strictly by all the boys composing it," &c.,

with a long list of complicated articles, declaring the
rewards and punishments. The school, for the government of which these regulations were intended, consisted of five boys, two besides the decurions and monitor.
It was nearly noon, and the master, who was the clerk
of the alcalde, had not yet made his appearance. The

only books I saw were a Catholic prayer-book and a translation of Montesquieu's Spirit of the Laws. The boys were fine little fellows, half white; and with one of them I had a trial of sums in addition, and then of exercises in handwriting, in which he showed himself very proficient, writing in Spanish, in a hand which I could not mistake, " Give me sixpence."

We were rather at a loss what to do with ourselves, but in the afternoon our host called in an Indian for the purpose of enabling us to make a vocabulary of Indian words. The first question I asked him was the name of God, to which he answered, Santissima Trinidad. Through our host I explained to him that I did not wish the Spanish, but the Indian name, and he answered as before, Santissima Trinidad, or Dios. I shaped my question in a variety of ways, but could get no other answer. He was of a tribe called Chinaute, and the inference was, either that they had never known any Great Spirit who governed and directed the universe, or that they had undergone such an entire change in matters of religion that they had lost their own appellation for the Deity.

In the evening the town was thrown into excitement by the entry of a detachment of Carrera's soldiers, on their way to Yzabal to receive and escort a purchase of muskets. The house of our friend was a gathering-place of residents, and, as usual, the conversation turned upon the revolutionary state of the country. Some of them, as soon as they knew my official character, were anxious for me to go directly to San Salvador, the head-quarters of the Morazan or Federal party, and assured me that the road to Guatimala was occupied by the troops of Carrera, and dangerous to travel over. I knew too much of the effect of party spirit to put implicit faith in what partisans told me, and endeavoured to change the subject. Our host asked me whether we had any wars in my country, and said he knew that we had had one revolution, for he had read La Historia de la Revolution de los Estados Unidos del Norte, in four volumes, in which General Washington appeared under the name of Harper, and Jack Lawton and Dr. Sitgreaves were two of the principal characters; from which I learned, what will perhaps be new to some of my readers, that in the Spanish translation the tale of the "Spy" is called a History of the American Revolution.

Our muleteer did not make his appearance till late the next day. In the mean time, I had had an opportunity of acquiring much information about the roads and the state of the country; and, being satisfied that, so far as regarded the purpose of my mission, it was not necessary to proceed immediately to Guatimala, and, in fact, that it was better to wait a little while and see the result of the convulsions that then distracted the country, we determined to visit Copan. It was completely out of the line of travel, and, though distant only a few days' journey, in a region of country but little known, even at Zacapa; but our muleteer said that he knew the road, and made a contract to conduct us thither in three days, arranging the different stages beforehand, and from thence direct to Guatimala.

At seven o'clock the next morning we started. Although both my companion and myself were old travellers, our luggage was in bad packages for travelling with mules over a mountainous country—hard to put on and easy to fall off; and, in keeping with this, we had but one pair of spurs between us. In an hour we forded the Motagua, still a broad stream, deep, and with a rapid current; and coming out with our feet and legs wet diminished somewhat the regret with which we bade farewell for a while to the beautiful river. For an hour longer we continued on the plain of Zacapa, cultivated for corn and cochineal, and divided by fences of brush and cactus. Beyond this the country became broken, arid, and barren, and very soon we commenced ascending a steep mountain. In two hours we reached the top, three or four thousand feet high, and, looking back, had a fine view of the plain and town of Zacapa. Crossing the ridge, we reached a bold precipitous spur, and very soon saw before us another extensive plain, and, afar off, the town of Chiquimula, with its giant church. On each side were immense ravines, and the opposite heights were covered with pale and rose-coloured mimosa. We descended by a long and zigzag path, and reached the plain, on which were growing corn, cochineal, and plantain. Once more fording a stream, we ascended a bank, and at two o'clock entered Chiquimula, the head of the department of that name. In the centre of the plaza was a fine fountain, shaded by palm-trees, at which women were filling their water-jars, and on the sides were the church and cabildo. On one corner was a house, to which we were attracted by the appearance of a woman at the door. I may call her a lady, for she wore a frock not open behind, and shoes and stockings, and had a face of uncommon interest, dark, and with finely-pencilled eyebrows. To heighten the effect of her appearance, she gave us a gracious welcome to her house, and in a few minutes the shed was lumbered with our multifarious luggage.

After a slight lunch we took our guns, and, walking down to the edge of the table of land, saw, what had attracted our attention at a great distance, a gigantic church in ruins. It was seventy-five feet front and two hundred and fifty feet deep, and the walls were ten feet thick. The façade was adorned with ornaments and figures of the saints, larger than life. The roof had fallen, and inside were huge masses of stone and mortar, and a thick growth of trees. It was built by the Spaniards on the site of the old Indian village; but, having been twice shattered by earthquakes, the inhabitants had deserted it, and built the town where it now stands. The ruined village was now occupied as a campo santo, or burial-place; inside the church were the graves of the principal inhabitants, and in the niches of the wall were the bones of priests and monks, with their names written under them. Outside were the graves of the common people, untended and uncared for, with the barrow of laced sticks which had carried the body to the grave laid upon the top, and slightly covered with earth. The bodies had decayed, the dirt fallen in, and the graves were yawning. Around this scene of desolation and death nature was rioting in beauty; the ground was covered with flowers, and parrots on every bush and tree, and flying in flocks over our heads, wanton in gayety of colours, with senseless chattering disturbed the stillness of the grave.

We returned to the town, and found about twelve hundred soldiers drawn up in the plaza for evening parade. Their aspect was ferocious and banditti-like, and it was refreshing to see convicts peeping through the gratings of the prison, and walking in chains on the plaza, as it gave an idea that sometimes crimes were punished. With all their ferocity of appearance, the officers, mounted on prancing mules or very small horses, almost hidden in saddle-cloth and armour, wore an air bordering upon the mock heroic. While we were looking at them, General Cascara, the commandant of the department, attended by a servant, rode up to the line. He was an Italian, upward of sixty, who had served under Napoleon in Italy, and on the downfall of the emperor had fled to Central America. Banished by Morazan, and eight years in exile, he had just returned to the country, and six months before had been appointed to this command. He was ghastly pale, and evidently in feeble health; and I could not but think that, if recollections of the pomp of war under the emperor ever crossed his mind, he must needs blush at his barefooted detachment.

He returned to his house, whither we followed and presented our passport. Like the commandant at Yzabal, he seemed ill at ease, and spoke much of the distracted state of the country. He was dissatisfied, too, with the route I proposed taking; and though I told him it was merely to visit the ruins of Copan, he was evidently apprehensive that I intended going to San Salvador to present my credentials to the Federal government. He *viséd* the passport, however, as I required; though, after we left, he called Augustin back, and questioned him very closely as to our purposes. I was indignant, but smothered my feelings in consideration of the distracted state of the country, and the game of life and death that was then playing throughout the land.

We returned to the house and the interesting lady who had welcomed us to it. As yet we did not know whether she was *señora* or *señorita;* but, unhappily, we found that a man whom we supposed her father was her husband. When we inquired of her about a fine boy ten years old, whom we supposed to be her brother, she answered, " es mio," he is mine ; and, as if it was fated that the charm of her appearance should be broken, when, according to the rules of courtesy, I offered for her choice a cigar and a puro, she took the latter. But it was so long since I had seen a woman who was at all attractive, and her face was so interesting, her manners were so good, her voice so sweet, the Spanish words rolled so beautifully from her lips, and her frock was tied so close behind, that, in spite of ten-year-old boy and puro, I clung to my first impressions.

The next morning we rose early. Our interesting hostess and her fatherly husband were up betimes to assist us. It would have been an offence to the laws of hospitality to offer them money; but Mr. C. gave the boy a penknife, and I put on the finger of the señora a gold ring, with the motto, "Souvenir d'amitié." It was in French, and her husband could not understand it, nor, unfortunately, could she.

At seven o'clock we started. Passing the ruined church and the old village, we rode over a rich valley, so well cultivated with Indian corn that it gave a key to the boy's question, Whether we had come to Chiquimula to buy maize ? At a league's distance we came to the village of St. Stephanos, where, amid a miserable collection of thatched huts, stood a gigantic church, like that at Chiquimula, roofless, and falling to ruins. We were now in a region which had been scourged by civil war. A year before the village had been laid waste by the troops of Morazan.

Passing the village, we came upon the bank of a stream, in some places diverted into water-courses for irrigating the land; and on the other side of the stream was a range of high mountains. Continuing along it, we met an Indian, who advised our muleteer that the camino real for Copan was on the opposite side of the river, and across the range of mountains. We returned and forded the river ; a great part of the bed was dry, and we rode along it for some distance, but could find no path that led up the mountain. At length we struck one, but it proved to be a cattle-path, and we wandered for more than an hour before we found the camino real ; and this royal road was barely a track by which a single mule could climb. It was evident that our muleteer did not know the road, and the region we were entering was so wild that we had some doubts about following him. At eleven we reached the top of the mountain, and, looking back, saw at a great distance, and far below us, the town of Chiquimula ; on the right, up the valley, the village of St. Helena ; and, rising above a few thatched huts, another gigantic and roofless church. On each side were mountains still higher than ours, some grand and gloomy, with their summits buried in the clouds ; others in the form of cones and pyramids, so wild and fantastic that they seemed sporting with the heavens, and I almost wished for wings to fly and light upon their tops. Here, on heights apparently inaccessible, we saw the wild hut of an Indian, with his milpa or patch of Indian corn. Clouds gathered around the mountains, and for an hour we rode in the rain ; when the sun broke through we saw the mountain tops still towering above us, and on our right, far below us, a deep valley. We descended, and found it narrower and more beautiful than any we had yet seen, bounded by ranges of mountains several thousand feet high, and having on its left a range of extraordinary beauty, with a red soil of sandstone, without any brush or underwood, and covered with gigantic pines. In front, rising above the miserable huts of the village, and seeming to bestride the valley, was the gigantic church of St. John the Hermit, reminding me of the

Church of St. John in the wilderness of Judea, but the situation was even more beautiful. At two o'clock we crossed the stream and entered the village. Opposite the church the muleteer told us that the day's work was over, but, with all our toils, we had made only fifteen miles, and were unwilling to stop so soon. The exceeding beauty of the place might have tempted us, but the only good plastered hut was occupied by a band of ruffianly soldiers, and we rode on. The muleteer followed with curses, and vented his spite in lashing the mules. Again we crossed the stream, and, continuing up the valley along the dry bed, which bore marks of the flood that washed it in the rainy season, in an hour we crossed it half a dozen times. Heavy clouds rested on the mountains, and again we had rain. At four o'clock we saw on a high table on the left the village of Hocotan, with another gigantic church. According to the route agreed upon with the muleteer, this should have been the end of our first day's journey. We had been advised that the cura could give us much information about the ruins of Copan, and told him to cross over and stop there; but he refused, and, hurrying on the mules, added that we had refused to stop when he wished, and now he would not stop for us. I could not spur my mule beyond her own gait, and, unable to overtake him, jumped off and ran after him on foot. Accidentally I put my hand on my pistols, to steady them in my belt, and he fell back and drew his machete. We came to a parley. He said that if we went there we could not reach Copan the next day; whereupon, willing to make a retreat, and wishing to leave him no excuse for failing, we continued.

At six o'clock we rose upon a beautiful table of land, on which stood another gigantic church. It was the

seventh we had seen that day, and, coming upon them
in a region of desolation, and by mountain paths which
human hands had never attempted to improve, their colossal grandeur and costliness were startling, and gave
evidence of a retrograding and expiring people. This
stood in a more desolate place than any we had yet
seen. The grass was green, the sod unbroken even by
a mule path, not a human being was in sight, and even
the gratings of the prison had no one looking through
them. It was, in fact, a picture of a deserted village.
We rode up to the cabildo, the door of which was fastened and the shed barricaded, probably to prevent the
entrance of straggling cattle. We tore away the fast-
enings, broke open the door, and, unloading the mules,
sent Augustin on a foraging expedition. In half an
hour he returned with *one* egg, being all that he was
able to procure ; but he had waked up the village, and
the alcalde, an Indian with a silver-headed cane, and
several alguazils with long thin rods or wands of office,
came down to examine us. We showed them our passport, and told them where we were going, at which,
with their characteristic indifference of manner, they
expressed no surprise. They could not read the passport, but they examined the seal and returned it. We
asked them for eggs, fowls, milk, &c., to all of which
they answered, what afterward became but too familiar,
" no hay," " there is none," and in a few minutes they
retired and left us to ourselves.

The cabildo was about forty feet long and twenty
broad, with plastered walls ; its furniture consisted of
a large table and two benches with high backs, and the
alcalde sent us a jar of water. We abused the muleteer for stopping at a place where we could get nothing
to eat, and made our dinner and supper upon bread and

chocolate, taking care not to give him any.   There were
pins in the walls for swinging hammocks, and in the
evening we prepared for sleep.   Mr. C. was in his hammock, and I was half undressed, when the door was
suddenly burst open, and twenty-five or thirty men
rushed in, the alcalde, alguazils, soldiers, Indians, and
Mestitzoes, ragged and ferocious-looking fellows, and
armed with staves of office, swords, clubs, muskets, and
machetes, and carrying blazing pine sticks.   At the
head of them was a young officer of about twenty-eight
or thirty, with a glazed hat and sword, and a knowing
and wicked expression, whom we afterward understood
to be a captain of one of Carrera's companies.   The
alcalde was evidently intoxicated, and said that he
wished to see my passport again.   I delivered it to him,
and he handed it over to the young officer, who examined it, and said that it was not valid.   In the mean
time, Mr. Catherwood and I dressed ourselves.   I was
not very familiar with the Spanish language, and,
through Augustin, explained my official character, and
directed him particularly to the endorsements of Commandant Peñol and General Cascara.   He paid no regard to my explanations; the alcalde said that he had
seen a passport once before, and that it was printed,
and on a small piece of paper not bigger than his hand;
whereas mine was the one given by government on a
quarto sheet.   Besides this, they said that the seal of
General Cascara was only that of the department of
Chiquimula, and it ought to be that of the state of Guatimala.   I did all in my power to show the insufficiency
of these objections; but, after a warm altercation, the
young man said that we should not proceed on our journey, but must remain at Comotan until information
could be sent to Chiquimula, and orders received from

that place. We had no disposition to remain in such hands; threatened them with the consequences of throwing any obstructions in our way; and I at length said that, rather than be detained there and lose time, I would abandon my journey to Copan altogether, and return by the road on which I came; but both the officer and the alcalde said peremptorily that we should not leave Comotan.

The young man then told me to give up my passport. I answered that the passport was given me by my own government; that it was the evidence of my official character, necessary for my personal security, and I would not give it up. Mr. Catherwood made a learned exposition of the law of nations, the right of an ambassador, and the danger of bringing down upon them the vengeance of the government del Norte, which I sustained with some warmth, but it was of no use. At length I told him again that I would not give up the passport, but offered to go with it myself, under a guard of soldiers, to Chiquimula, or wherever else they chose to send it; he answered insultingly that we should not go to Chiquimula or anywhere else; neither forward nor backward; that we must stay where we were, and must give up the passport. Finding arguments and remonstrances of no use, I placed the paper inside my vest, buttoned my coat tight across my breast, and told him he must get it by force; and the officer, with a gleam of satisfaction crossing his villanous face, responded that he would. I added that, whatever might be the immediate result, it would ultimately be fatal to them; to which he answered, with a sneer, that they would run the risk. During the whole time, the band of cowardly ruffians stood with their hands on their swords and machetes, and two assassin-looking scoundrels sat on a bench with muskets against their shoulders, and the muzzles pointed within three feet of my breast. If we had been longer in the country we should have been more alarmed; but as yet we did not know the sanguinary character of the people, and the whole proceeding was so outrageous and insulting that it roused our indignation more than our fears. Augustin, who, from having had a cut across the head with a machete, which did not kill him, was always bellicose, begged me in French to give the order to fire, and said that one round would scatter them all. We had eleven charges, all sure; we were excited, and, if the young man himself had laid his hands upon me, I think I should have knocked him down at least; but, most fortunately, before he had time to give his order to fall upon us, a man, who entered after the rest, of a better class, wearing a glazed hat and round-about jacket, stepped forward and asked to see the passport. I was determined not to trust it out of my hands, and held it up before a blazing pine stick while he read it, and, at Mr. Catherwood's request, aloud.

I have since doubted whether even the officer had read it, or, if so, whether he had communicated its contents, for it produced an effect upon the alcalde and his alguazils; and, after some moments of anxious suspense to us, they forbore to execute their threat, but said that we must remain in custody. I demanded a courier, to carry a letter immediately to General Cascara, which they refused; but, on my offering to pay the expense of the courier, the alcalde promised to send it. Knowing General Cascara to be an Italian, and afraid to trust my Spanish, I wrote a note, which Mr. C. translated into Italian, informing him of our arrest and imprisonment; that we had exhibited to the alcalde and soldiers who arrested us my special passport from my own government, with the endorsements of Commandant Peñol and himself, certifying my official character, which were not deemed sufficient ; demanding to be set at liberty immediately, and allowed to proceed on our journey without farther molestation ; and adding that we should, of course, represent to the government at Guatimala, and also to my own, the manner in which we had been treated. Not to mince matters, Mr. Catherwood signed the note as Secretary ; and, having no official seal with me, we sealed it, unobserved by anybody, with a new American half dollar, and gave it to the alcalde. The eagle spread his wings, and the stars glittered in the torchlight. All gathered round to examine it, and retired, locking us up in the cabildo, stationing twelve men at the door with swords, muskets, and machetes ; and, at parting, the officer told the alcalde that, if we escaped during the night, his head should answer for it.

The excitement over, Mr. C. and I were exhausted. We had made a beautiful beginning of our travels ; but a month from home, and in the hands of men who would have been turned out of any decent state prison lest they should contaminate the boarders. A peep at our beautiful keepers did not reassure us. They were sitting under the shed, directly before the door, around a fire, their arms in reach, and smoking cigars. Their whole stock of wearing apparel was not worth a pair of old boots ; and with their rags, their arms, their dark faces reddened by the firelight, their appearance was ferocious ; and, doubtless, if we had attempted to escape, they would have been glad of the excuse for murder. We opened a basket of wine with which Col. M'Donald had provided us, and drank his health. We were

relieved from immediate apprehensions, but our prospects were not pleasant; and, fastening the door as well
as we could inside, we again betook ourselves to our
hammocks.

During the night the door was again burst open, and
the whole ruffianly band entered, as before, with swords,
muskets, machetes, and blazing pine sticks. In an instant we were on our feet, and my hurried impression
was, that they had come to take the passport; but, to
our surprise, the alcalde handed me back the letter with
the big seal, said there was no use in sending it, and
that we were at liberty to proceed on our journey when
we chose.

We were too well pleased to ask any questions, and
to this day do not know why we were arrested. My
belief is, that if we had quailed at all, and had not kept
up a high, threatening tone to the last, we should not have
been set free; and I have no doubt that the big seal did
much in our behalf. Our indignation, however, was not
the less strong that we considered ourselves safe in
pouring it out. We insisted that the matter should not
end here, and that the letter should go to General Cascara. The alcalde objected; but we told him that, if not
sent, it would be the worse for him; and, after some delay, he thrust it into the hands of an Indian, and beat
him out of doors with his staff; and in a few minutes
the guard was withdrawn, and they all left us.

It was now nearly daylight, and we did not know
what to do; to continue was to expose ourselves to a
repetition of the same treatment, and perhaps, as we
advanced farther into the interior, with a worse result.
Undetermined, for the third time we turned into our
hammocks. At broad daylight we were again roused
by the alcalde and his alguazils, but this time they came

to pay us a visit of ceremony. The soldiers, who had accidentally passed through the village, and had made all the disturbance, had left. After some deliberation we determined to continue ; and, charging the alcalde again about the letter to General Cascara, turned our backs upon him and his alguazils. In a few minutes they all withdrew. We took a cup of chocolate, loaded our mules, and, when we left, the place was as desolate as when we entered. Not a person had been there to welcome us, and there was not one to bid us farewell.

"WE SAW A GIGANTIC CHURCH IN RUINS" (see p. 73).

CHAPTER V.

TURNING away from the church, we passed the brow
of a hill, behind which was a collection of huts almost
concealed from sight, and occupied by our friends of the
night before. Very soon we commenced ascending a
mountain. At a short distance we met a corpse borne
on a rude bier of sticks, upon the shoulders of Indians,
naked except a piece of cotton cloth over the loins, and
shaking awfully under the movements of its carriers.
Soon after we met another, borne in the same way, but
wrapped in matting, and accompanied by three or four
men and a young woman. Both were on their way to
the graveyard of the village church. Ascending, we
reached the top of a mountain, and saw behind us a
beautiful valley extending toward Hocotan, but all
waste, and suggesting a feeling of regret that so beautiful a country should be in such miserable hands.

At half past twelve we descended to the banks of the
Copan River. It was broad and rapid, and in the middle was a large sandbar. We had difficulty in fording
it; and some of the baggage, particularly the beds and
bedding, got wet. From the opposite side we again
commenced ascending another ridge, and from the top
saw the river winding through the valley. As we crossed, by a sudden turn it flowed along the base, and we
looked directly down upon it. Descending this mount-

ain, we came to a beautiful stream, where a gray-haired Indian woman and a pretty little girl, pictures of youth and old age, were washing clothes. We dismounted, and sat down on the bank to wait for the muleteer. I forgot to mention that he had with him a boy about thirteen or fourteen years old, a fine little fellow, upon whom he imposed the worst part of the burden, that of chasing the mules, and who really seemed, like Baron Munchausen's dog, in danger of running his legs off.

Our breach with the muleteer had not been healed, and at first we ascribed to him some agency in our troubles at Comotan. At all events, if it had not been for him, we should not have stopped there. All day he had been particularly furious with the mules, and they had been particularly perverse, and now they had gone astray ; and it was an hour before we heard his spiteful voice, loading them with curses. We mounted again, and at four o'clock saw at a distance a hacienda, on the opposite side of a valley. It stood alone, and promised a quiet resting-place for the night. We turned off from the *camino real* into a wild path, stony, and overgrown with bushes, and so steep that we were obliged to dismount, let the mules go ahead, and hold on ourselves by the bushes to descend. At the foot of the hill we mounted and crossed a stream, where a little boy, playing in the water, saluted me by crossing his arms upon his breast, and then passed on to Mr. Catherwood. This was a favourable omen ; and, as we climbed up a steep hill, I felt that here, in this lonely spot, away from the gathering-places of men, we must meet kindness. On the top of the hill a woman, with a naked child in her arms and a smile on her face, stood watching our toilsome ascent ; and when we asked her if we could make posada there, she answered, in the kindest phrase of the country, with a face that spoke even a warmer welcome than her words, " como non ?" " why not ?" and when she saw that our servant had pineapples in his alforgas, she asked why he brought them, and if he did not know that she had plenty.

The situation of the hacienda of San Antonio was wildly beautiful. It had a clearing for a cowyard, a plantation of corn, tobacco, and plantains, and the opening gave a view of the high mountains by which it was surrounded. The house was built of poles plastered with mud, and against the wall in front of the door was a figure of the Saviour on the cross, on a white cotton cloth hung round with votive offerings. The naked child which the mother carried in her arms was called Maria de los Angelos. While supper was in preparation the master of the house arrived, a swarthy, grim-looking fellow, with a broad-brimmed sombrero and huge whiskers, and mounted on a powerful young horse, which he was just breaking to the mountain-roads ; when he knew that we were strangers asking hospitality, his harsh features relaxed, and he repeated the welcome the woman had given us.

Unfortunately, the boy of the muleteer was taken very ill ; his master paid no attention to him, and, while the poor little fellow was groaning under a violent fever, ate on with perfect indifference. We made him a comfortable bed on the piazza, and Mr. Catherwood gave him a dose of medicine. Our evening passed very differently from the last. Our host and hostess were a kind-hearted and simple couple. It was the first time they had ever met with men from another country, and they asked many questions, and examined our little travelling apparatus, particularly our plated cups, knives, forks, and spoons ; we showed them our watches, compass, sextant, chronometer, thermometer, telescope, &c., and the woman, with great discernment, said that we must be very rich, and had "muchos idées," "many ideas." They asked us about our wives, and we learned that our simple-minded host had two, one of whom lived at Hocotan, and that he passed a week alternately with each. We told him that in England he would be transported, and in the North imprisoned for life for such indulgences, to which he responded that they were barbarous countries; and the woman, although she thought a man ought to be content with one, said that it was no *peccato* or crime to have two; but I heard them say, *sotto voce*, that we were "mas Christianos," or better Christians than they. He assisted us in swinging our hammocks, and about nine o'clock we drove out the dogs and pigs, lighted cigars, and went to bed. Including servants, women, and children, we numbered eleven in the room. All around were little balls of fire, shining and disappearing with the puffs of the cigars. One by one these went out, and we fell asleep.

In the morning we all rose together. The boy was much better, but we did not think him in a condition to travel. His brutal master, however, insisted upon his going. For all that our kind friends had done for us, they would have charged us nothing; but, besides compensating them in money, we distributed among them various trifles, and, when bidding them farewell, I saw with regret a ring which I had given her sparkling on his finger. After we had mounted, the little boy whom we had met at the stream came staggering under a load of six freshly-cut pineapples; and even when we had started, the woman ran after me with a piece of fresh sugarcane.

All parted at the hacienda of San Antonio with kind feelings except our surly muleteer, who was indignant, as he said, that we made presents to everybody except to him. The poor boy was most grateful, and, unfortunately for him, we had given him a knife, which made the muleteer jealous.

Almost immediately from the hacienda we entered a thick wood, dense as that of the Mico Mountain, and almost as muddy. The ascent was toilsome, but the top was open, and so covered with that beautiful plant that we called it the Mountain of Aloes. Some were just peeping out of the ground, others were twenty or thirty feet high, and some gigantic stalks were dead ; flowers which would have kindled rapture in the breast of beauty had bloomed and died on this desolate mountain, unseen except by a passing Indian.

In descending we lost the path, and wandered for some time before we recovered it. Almost immediately we commenced ascending another mountain, and from its top looked completely over a third, and, at a great distance, saw a large hacienda. Our road lay directly along the edge of a precipice, from which we looked down upon the tops of gigantic pines at a great distance beneath us. Very soon the path became so broken, and ran so near the edge of a precipice, that I called to Mr. Catherwood to dismount. The precipice was on the left side, and I had advanced so far that, on the back of a perverse mule, I did not venture to make any irregular movement, and rode for some moments in great anxiety. Somewhere on this road, but unmarked by any visible sign, we crossed the boundary-line of the state of Guatimala and entered Honduras.

At two o'clock we reached the village of Copan,

which consisted of half a dozen miserable huts thatched with corn. Our appearance created a great sensation. All the men and women gathered around us to
gaze. We inquired immediately for the ruins, but none
of the villagers could direct us to them, and all advised
us to go to the hacienda of Don Gregorio. We had no
wish to stop at a village, and told the muleteer to go on,
but he refused, and said that his engagement was to
conduct us to Copan. After a long wrangle we prevailed, and, riding through a piece of woods, forded
once more the Copan River, and came out upon a clearing, on one side of which was a hacienda, with a tile
roof, and having cucinera and other outbuildings, evidently the residence of a rich proprietor. We were
greeted by a pack of barking dogs, and all the door-
ways were filled with women and children, who seemed in no small degree surprised at our appearance.
There was not a man in sight; but the women received us kindly, and told us that Don Gregorio would
return soon, and would conduct us to the ruins. Immediately the fire was rekindled in the cucinera, the
sound of the patting of hands gave notice of the making of tortillas, and in half an hour dinner was ready.
It was served up on a massive silver plate, with water
in a silver tankard, but without knife, fork, or spoon;
soup or caldo was served in cups to be drunk. Nevertheless, we congratulated ourselves upon having fallen
into such good quarters.

In a short time a young man arrived on horseback,
gayly dressed, with an embroidered shirt, and accompanied by several men driving a herd of cattle. An ox
was selected, a rope thrown around its horns, and the
animal was drawn up to the side of the house, and,
by another rope around its legs, thrown down. Its feet

were tied together, its head drawn back by a rope tied from its horns to its tail, and with one thrust of the machete the artery of life was severed. The pack of hungry dogs stood ready, and, with a horrible clicking, lapped up the blood with their tongues. All the women were looking on, and a young girl took a puppy dog and rubbed its nose in the crimson stream, to give it early a taste for blood. The ox was skinned, the meat separated from the bones, and, to the entire destruction of steaks, sirloins, and roasting-pieces, in an hour the whole animal was hanging in long strings on a line before the door.

During this operation Don Gregorio arrived. He was about fifty, had large black whiskers, and a beard of several days' growth; and, from the behaviour of all around, it was easy to see that he was a domestic tyrant. The glance which he threw at us before dismounting seemed to say, " Who are *you?*" but, without a word, he entered the house. We waited until he had finished his dinner, when, supposing that to be the favourable moment, I entered the house. In my intercourse with the world I have more than once found my overtures to an acquaintance received coldly, but I never experienced anything quite so cool as the don's reception of me. I told him that we had come into that neighbourhood to visit the ruins of Copan, and his manner said, What's that to me? but he answered that they were on the other side of the river. I asked him whether we could procure a guide, and again he said that the only man who knew anything about them lived on the other side of the river. As yet we did not make sufficient allowance for the distracted state of the country, nor the circumstance that a man might incur danger to himself by giving shelter to suspected persons; but, relying on the reputation of the country for hospitality, and the proof of it which we had already met with, I was rather slow in coming to the disagreeable conclusion that we were not welcome. This conclusion, however, was irresistible. The don was not pleased with our looks. I ordered the muleteer to saddle the mules; but the rascal enjoyed our confusion, and positively refused to saddle his beasts again that day. We applied to Don Gregorio himself, offering to pay him; and, as Augustin said, in the hope of getting rid of us, he lent us two, on which to ride back to the village. Unfortunately, the guide we sought was away; a brisk cock-fight was then pending, and we received no encouragement, either from the appearance of the people or from invitation, to bring back our luggage to that place. And we learned, what was very provoking, that Don Gregorio was the great man of Copan; the richest man, and the petty tyrant; and that it would be most unfortunate to have a rupture with him, or even to let it be known at the village that we were not well received at his house. Reluctantly, but in the hope of making a more favourable impression, we returned to the hacienda. Mr. C. dismounted on the steps, and took a seat on the piazza. I happened to dismount outside; and, before moving, took a survey of the party. The don sat on a chair, with our detestable muleteer by his side, and a half-concealed smile of derision on his face, talking of " idols," and looking at me. By this time eight or ten men, sons, servants, and labourers, had come in from their day's work, but not one offered to take my mule, or made any of those demonstrations of civility which are always shown to a welcome guest. The women turned away their heads, as if they had been reproved for receiving us; and all the men, taking their cue from

the don, looked so insulting, that I told Mr. Catherwood
we would tumble our luggage into the road, and curse
him for an inhospitable churl; but Mr. Catherwood
warned me against it, urging that, if we had an open
quarrel with him, after all our trouble we would be prevented seeing the ruins.   The don probably suspected
something of what passed; and, fearing that he might
push things too far, and bring a stain upon his name,
pointed to a chair, and asked me to take a seat.   With
a great effort, I resolved to smother my indignation until I could pour it out with safety.   Augustin was very
indignant at the treatment we received; on the road he
had sometimes swelled his own importance by telling
of the flags hoisted and cannon fired when we left Balize; and here he hoisted more flags and fired more
guns than usual, beginning with forty guns, and afterward going on to a cannonade; but it would not do.
The don did not like us, and probably was willing to
hoist flags, and fire cannons too, as at Balize, when we
should go away.

Toward evening the skin of an ox was spread upon
the piazza, corn in ears thrown upon it, and all the men,
with the don at their head, sat down to shell it.   The
cobs were carried to the kitchen to burn, the corn taken
up in baskets, and three pet hogs, which had been grunt-
ing outside in expectation of the feast, were let in to
pick up the scattered grains.   During the evening no
notice was taken of us, except that the wife of the don
sent a message by Augustin that supper was preparing;
and our wounded pride was relieved, and our discontent
somewhat removed, by an additional message that they
had an oven and flour, and would bake us some bread
if we wished to buy it.

After supper all prepared for sleep.   The don's house

had two sides, an inside and an out. The don and his family occupied the former, and we the latter; but we had not even this to ourselves. All along the wall were frames made of sticks about an inch thick, tied together with bark strings, over which the workmen spread an untanned oxhide for a bed. There were three hammocks besides ours, and I had so little room for mine that my body described an inverted parabola, with my heels as high as my head. It was vexatious and ridiculous; or, in the words of the English tourist in Fra Diavolo, it was "shocking! positively shocking!"

In the morning Don Gregorio was in the same humour. We took no notice of him, but made our toilet under the shed with as much respect as possible to the presence of the female members of the family, who were constantly passing and repassing. We had made up our minds to hold on and see the ruins; and, fortunately, early in the morning, one of the crusty don's sons, a civil young man, brought over from the village Jose, the guide of whom we stood in need.

By reason of many vexatious delays, growing out of difficulties between Jose and the muleteer, we did not get away until nine o'clock. Very soon we left the path or road, and entered a large field, partially cultivated with corn, belonging to Don Gregorio. Riding some distance through this, we reached a hut, thatched with corn-leaves, on the edge of the woods, at which some workmen were preparing their breakfast. Here we dismounted, and, tying our mules to trees near by, entered the woods, Jose clearing a path before us with a machete; soon we came to the bank of a river, and saw directly opposite a stone wall, perhaps a hundred feet high, with furze growing out of the top, running north and south along the river, in some places fallen, but in

others entire. It had more the character of a structure than any we had ever seen, ascribed to the aborigines of America, and formed part of the wall of Copan, an ancient city, on whose history books throw but little light.

I am entering abruptly upon new ground. Volumes without number have been written to account for the first peopling of America. By some the inhabitants of this continent have been regarded as a separate race, not descended from the same common father with the rest of mankind; others have ascribed their origin to some remnant of the antediluvian inhabitants of the earth, who survived the deluge which swept away the greatest part of the human species in the days of Noah, and hence have considered them the most ancient race of people on the earth. Under the broad range allowed by a descent from the sons of Noah, the Jews, the Canaanites, the Phœnicians, the Carthaginians, the Greeks, the Scythians in ancient times; the Chinese, the Swedes, the Norwegians, the Welsh, and the Spaniards in modern, have had ascribed to them the honour

of peopling America. The two continents have been
joined together and rent asunder by the shock of an
earthquake ; the fabled island of Atlantis has been lifted out of the ocean ; and, not to be behindhand, an
enterprising American has turned the tables on the Old
World, and planted the ark itself within the State of
New-York.

The monuments and architectural remains of the
aborigines have heretofore formed but little part of the
groundwork for these speculations. Dr. Robertson, in
his History of America, lays it down as " a certain principle, that America was not peopled by any nation of
the ancient continent which had made considerable
progress in civilization."   "The inhabitants of the
New World," he says, " were in a state of society so
extremely rude as to be unacquainted with those arts
which are the first essays of human ingenuity in its advance toward improvement."   Discrediting the glow-
ing accounts of Cortez and his companions, of soldiers,
priests, and civilians, all concurring in representations
of the splendour exhibited in the buildings of Mexico,
he says that the " houses of the people were mere huts,
built with turf, or mud, or the branches of trees, like
those of the rudest Indians."   The temple of Cholula
was nothing more than " a mound of earth, without any
steps or any facing of stone, covered with grass and
shrubs ;" and, on the authority of persons long resident
in New Spain, and who professed to have visited every
part of it, he says that " there is not, in all the extent of
that vast empire, a single monument or vestige of any
building more ancient than the conquest."   At that
time, distrust was perhaps the safer side for the historian ; but since Dr. Robertson wrote a new flood of light

has poured upon the world, and the field of American antiquities has been opened.

The ignorance, carelessness, and indifference of the inhabitants of Spanish America on this subject are matter of wonder. In our own country, the opening of forests and the discovery of tumuli or mounds and fortifications, extending in ranges from the lakes through the valleys of the Ohio and Mississippi, mummies in a cave in Kentucky, the inscription on the rock at Dighton, supposed to be in Phœnician characters, and the ruins of walls and a great city in Arkansas and Wisconsin Territory, had suggested wild and wandering ideas in regard to the first peopling of this country, and the strong belief that powerful and populous nations had occupied it and had passed away, whose histories are entirely unknown. The same evidences continue in Texas, and in Mexico they assume a still more definite form.

The first new light thrown upon this subject as regards Mexico was by the great Humboldt, who visited that country at a time when, by the jealous policy of the government, it was almost as much closed against strangers as China is now. No man could have better deserved such fortune. At that time the monuments of the country were not a leading object of research; but Humboldt collected from various sources information and drawings, particularly of Mitla, or the Vale of the Dead; Xoxichalco, a mountain hewed down and terraced, and called the Hill of Flowers; and the great pyramid or Temple of Cholula he visited himself, of all which his own eloquent account is within reach of the reader. Unfortunately, of the great cities beyond the Vale of Mexico, buried in forests, ruined, desolate, and without a name, Humboldt never heard, or, at least,

he never visited them.   It is but lately that accounts of
their existence reached Europe and our own country.
These accounts, however vague and unsatisfactory, had
roused our curiosity; though I ought perhaps to say
that both Mr. C. and I were somewhat skeptical, and
when we arrived at Copan, it was with the hope, rather
than the expectation, of finding wonders.

Since the discovery of these ruined cities the prevailing theory has been, that they belonged to a race long
anterior to that which inhabited the country at the time
of the Spanish conquest.   With regard to Copan, mention is made by the early Spanish historians of a place
of that name, situated in the same region of country in
which these ruins are found, which then existed as an
inhabited city, and offered a formidable resistance to the
Spanish arms, though there are circumstances which
seem to indicate that the city referred to was inferior in
strength and solidity of construction, and of more modern origin.

It stood in the old province of Chiquimula de Sierras,
which was conquered by the officers of Pedro de Alvarado, but not one of the Spanish historians has given any
particulars of this conquest.   In 1530 the Indians of the
province revolted, and attempted to throw off the yoke
of Spain.   Hernando de Chaves was sent to subdue
them, and, after many sanguinary battles, he encamped
before Esquipulas, a place of arms belonging to a powerful cacique, which, on the fourth day, to use the words
of the cacique himself, " more out of respect to the public tranquillity than from fear of the Spanish arms, determined to surrender," and, with the capital, the whole
province submitted again to the Spanish dominion.

The cacique of Copan, whose name was Copán Calel,
had been active in exciting the revolt and assisting the

insurgents. Hernando de Chaves determined to pun-
ish him, and marched against Copan, then one of the
largest, most opulent, and most populous places of the
kingdom. The camp of the cacique, with his auxiliaries, consisted of thirty thousand men, well disci-
plined, and veterans in war, armed with wooden swords
having stone edges, arrows, and slings. On one side,
says the historian, it was defended by the ranges of
mountains of Chiquimula and Gracios a Dios, and on
the opposite side by a deep fosse, and an intrenchment
formed of strong beams of timber, having the interstices
filled with earth, with embrasures, and loopholes for
the discharge of arrows. Chaves, accompanied by
some horsemen, well armed, rode to the fosse, and
made sign that he wished to hold conference. The
cacique answered with an arrow. A shower of arrows,
stones, and darts followed, which compelled the Spaniards to retreat. The next day Chaves made an attack
upon the intrenchment. The infantry wore loose coats
stuffed with cotton ; swords and shields ; the horsemen
wore breastplates and helmets, and their horses were
covered. The Copanes had each a shield covered with
the skin of the danta on his arm, and his head guarded
by bunches of feathers. The attack lasted the whole
day. The Indians, with their arrows, javelins, and
pikes, the heads of which were hardened by fire, main-
tained their ground. The Spaniards were obliged to
retreat. Chaves, who had fought in the thickest of the
battle, was alarmed at the difficulties of the enterprise
and the danger to the credit of the Spanish arms, but
received information that in one place the depth of the
ditch which defended Copan was but trifling, and the
next day he proceeded to the spot to make an attack
there. The Copanes had watched his movements, and

manned the intrenchment with their bravest soldiers.
The infantry were unable to make a lodgment. The
cavalry came to their assistance. The Indians brought
up their whole force, and the Spaniards stood like
rocks, impassable to pikes, arrows, and stones. Several times they attempted to scale the intrenchments,
and were driven back into the fosse. Many were killed
on both sides, but the battle continued without advantage to either until a brave horseman leaped the ditch,
and, his horse being carried violently with his breast
against the barrier, the earth and palisadoes gave way,
and the frightened horse plunged among the Indians.
Other horsemen followed, and spread such terror among
the Copanes, that their lines were broken and they fled.
Copán Calel rallied at a place where he had posted a
body of reserve; but, unable to resist long, retreated,
and left Copan to its fate.

   This is the account which the Spanish historians have
given of Copan; and, as applied to the city, the wall of
which we saw from the opposite side of the river, it appeared to us most meager and unsatisfactory; for the
massive stone structures before us had little the air of
belonging to a city, the intrenchment of which could be
broken down by the charge of a single horseman. At
this place the river was not fordable; we returned to
our mules, mounted, and rode to another part of the
bank, a short distance above. The stream was wide,
and in some places deep, rapid, and with a broken and
stony bottom. Fording it, we rode along the bank by
a footpath encumbered with undergrowth, which Jose
opened by cutting away the branches, until we came to
the foot of the wall, where we again dismounted and
tied our mules.

   The wall was of cut stone, well laid, and in a good

state of preservation. We ascended by large stone
steps, in some places perfect, and in others thrown down
by trees which had grown up between the crevices, and
reached a terrace, the form of which it was impossible
to make out, from the density of the forest in which it
was enveloped. Our guide cleared a way with his machete, and we passed, as it lay half buried in the earth,
a large fragment of stone elaborately sculptured, and
came to the angle of a structure with steps on the sides,
in form and appearance, so far as the trees would ena-
ble us to make it out, like the sides of a pyramid. Di-
verging from the base, and working our way through
the thick woods, we came upon a square stone column, about fourteen feet high and three feet on each
side, sculptured in very bold relief, and on all four of
the sides, from the base to the top. The front was the
figure of a man curiously and richly dressed, and the
face, evidently a portrait, solemn, stern, and well fitted
to excite terror. The back was of a different design,
unlike anything we had ever seen before, and the sides
were covered with hieroglyphics. This our guide called
an "Idol;" and before it, at a distance of three feet, was
a large block of stone, also sculptured with figures and
emblematical devices, which he called an altar. The
sight of this unexpected monument put at rest at once
and forever, in our minds, all uncertainty in regard to
the character of American antiquities, and gave us the
assurance that the objects we were in search of were interesting, not only as the remains of an unknown people, but as works of art, proving, like newly-discovered
historical records, that the people who once occupied
the Continent of America were not savages. With an
interest perhaps stronger than we had ever felt in wandering among the ruins of Egypt, we followed our

guide, who, sometimes missing his way, with a constant
and vigorous use of his machete, conducted us through
the thick forest, among half-buried fragments, to fourteen monuments of the same character and appearance,
some with more elegant designs, and some in workmanship equal to the finest monuments of the Egyptians ;
one displaced from its pedestal by enormous roots; another locked in the close embrace of branches of trees,
and almost lifted out of the earth; another hurled to
the ground, and bound down by huge vines and creepers; and one standing, with its altar before it, in a
grove of trees which grew around it, seemingly to
shade and shroud it as a sacred thing; in the solemn
stillness of the woods, it seemed a divinity mourning
over a fallen people. The only sounds that disturbed
the quiet of this buried city were the noise of monkeys
moving among the tops of the trees, and the cracking
of dry branches broken by their weight. They moved
over our heads in long and swift processions, forty or
fifty at a time, some with little ones wound in their
long arms, walking out to the end of boughs, and
holding on with their hind feet or a curl of the tail,
sprang to a branch of the next tree, and, with a noise
like a current of wind, passed on into the depths of the
forest. It was the first time we had seen these mock-
eries of humanity, and, with the strange monuments
around us, they seemed like wandering spirits of the
departed race guarding the ruins of their former habitations.

We returned to the base of the pyramidal structure,
and ascended by regular stone steps, in some places
forced apart by bushes and saplings, and in others
thrown down by the growth of large trees, while some
remained entire. In parts they were ornamented with

sculptured figures and rows of death's heads. Climbing
over the ruined top, we reached a terrace overgrown
with trees, and, crossing it, descended by stone steps
into an area so covered with trees that at first we could
not make out its form, but which, on clearing the way
with the machete, we ascertained to be a square, and
with steps on all the sides almost as perfect as those of
the Roman amphitheatre. The steps were ornamented
with sculpture, and on the south side, about half way
up, forced out of its place by roots, was a colossal
head, evidently a portrait. We ascended these steps,
and reached a broad terrace a hundred feet high, overlooking the river, and supported by the wall which we
had seen from the opposite bank. The whole terrace
was covered with trees, and even at this height from
the ground were two gigantic Ceibas, or wild cotton-
trees of India, above twenty feet in circumference, extending their half-naked roots fifty or a hundred feet
around, binding down the ruins, and shading them with
their wide-spreading branches. We sat down on the
very edge of the wall, and strove in vain to penetrate
the mystery by which we were surrounded. Who
were the people that built this city? In the ruined cities of Egypt, even in the long-lost Petra, the
stranger knows the story of the people whose vestiges are around him. America, say historians, was
peopled by savages; but savages never reared these
structures, savages never carved these stones. We
asked the Indians who made them, and their dull answer was " Quien sabe?" " who knows?"

There were no associations connected with the
place; none of those stirring recollections which hal-
low Rome, Athens, and

" The world's great mistress on the Egyptian plain;"

but architecture, sculpture, and painting, all the arts which embellish life, had flourished in this overgrown forest; orators, warriors, and statesmen, beauty, ambition, and glory, had lived and passed away, and none knew that such things had been, or could tell of their past existence. Books, the records of knowledge, are silent on this theme. The city was desolate. No remnant of this race hangs round the ruins, with traditions handed down from father to son, and from generation to generation. It lay before us like a shattered bark in the midst of the ocean, her masts gone, her name effaced, her crew perished, and none to tell whence she came, to whom she belonged, how long on her voyage, or what caused her destruction; her lost people to be traced only by some fancied resemblance in the construction of the vessel, and, perhaps, never to be known at all. The place where we sat, was it a citadel from which an unknown people had sounded the trumpet of war? or a temple for the worship of the God of peace? or did the inhabitants worship the idols made with their own hands, and offer sacrifices on the stones before them? All was mystery, dark, impenetrable mystery, and every circumstance increased it. In Egypt the colossal skeletons of gigantic temples stand in the unwatered sands in all the nakedness of desolation; here an immense forest shrouded the ruins, hiding them from sight, heightening the impression and moral effect, and giving an intensity and almost wildness to the interest.

Late in the afternoon we worked our way back to the mules, bathed in the clear river at the foot of the wall, and returned to the hacienda. Our grateful muleteer-boy had told of his dreadful illness, and the extraordinary cure effected by Mr. Catherwood; and we found

at the hacienda a ghastly-looking man, worn down by
fever and ague, who begged us for "remedios." An
old lady on a visit to the family, who had intended to
go home that day, was waiting to be cured of a malady
from which she had suffered twenty years. Our medi-
cine-chest was brought out, and this converted the wife
of the don into a patient also. Mr. C.'s reputation rose
with the medicines he distributed ; and in the course of
the evening he had under his hands four or five women
and as many men. We wanted very much to practice
on the don, but he was cautious. The percussion caps
of our pistols attracted the attention of the men; and
we showed them the compass and other things, which
made our friend at San Antonio suppose we were "very
rich," and "had many ideas." By degrees we became
on social terms with all the house except the master,
who found a congenial spirit in the muleteer. He had
taken his ground, and was too dignified and obstinate
to unbend. Our new friends made more room for our
hammocks, and we had a better swing for the night.

In the morning we continued to astonish the people
by our strange ways, particularly by brushing our teeth,
an operation which, probably, they saw then for the first
time. While engaged in this, the door of the house
opened, and Don Gregorio appeared, turning his head
away to avoid giving us a buenos dios. We resolved
not to sleep another night under his shed, but to take
our hammocks to the ruins, and, if there was no building to shelter us, to hang them up under a tree. My
contract with the muleteer was to stop three days at
Copan; but there was no bargain for the use of the mules
during that time, and he hoped that the vexations we
met with would make us go on immediately. When he
found us bent on remaining, he swore he would not

carry the hammocks, and would not remain one day over, but at length consented to hire the mules for that day.

Before we started a new party, who had been conversing some time with Don Gregorio, stepped forward, and said that he was the owner of " the idols ;" that no one could go on the land without his permission ; and handed me his title papers. This was a new difficulty. I was not disposed to dispute his title, but read his papers as attentively as if I meditated an action in ejectment ; and he seemed relieved when I told him his title was good, and that, if not disturbed, I would make him a compliment at parting. Fortunately, he had a favour to ask. Our fame as physicians had reached the village, and he wished remedios for a sick wife. It was important to make him our friend ; and, after some conversation, it was arranged that Mr. C., with several workmen whom we had hired, should go on to the ruins, as we intended, to make a lodgment there, while I would go to the village and visit his wife.

Our new acquaintance, Don Jose Maria Asebedo, was about fifty, tall, and well dressed ; that is, his cotton shirt and pantaloons were clean ; inoffensive, though ignorant ; and one of the most respectable inhabitants of Copan. He lived in one of the best huts of the village, made of poles thatched with corn-leaves, with a wooden frame on one side for a bed, and furnished with a few pieces of pottery for cooking. A heavy rain had fallen during the night, and the ground inside the hut was wet. His wife seemed as old as he, and, fortunately, was suffering from a rheumatism of several years' standing. I say fortunately, but I speak only in reference to ourselves as medical men, and the honour of the profession accidentally confided to our hands. I told her

that if it had been a recent affection, it would be more
within the reach of art; but, as it was a case of old
standing, it required time, skill, watching of symptoms,
and the effect of medicine from day to day; and, for
the present, I advised her to take her feet out of a puddle of water in which she was standing, and promised
to consult Mr. Catherwood, who was even a better
medico than I, and to send her a liniment with which
to bathe her neck.

This over, Don Jose Maria accompanied me to the
ruins, where I found Mr. Catherwood with the Indian
workmen. Again we wandered over the whole ground
in search of some ruined building in which we could
take up our abode, but there was none. To hang up
our hammocks under the trees was madness; the
branches were still wet, the ground muddy, and again
there was a prospect of early rain; but we were determined not to go back to Don Gregorio's. Don Mariano said that there was a hut near by, and conducted
me to it. As we approached, we heard the screams of a
woman inside, and, entering, saw her rolling and toss-
ing on a bull's-hide bed, wild with fever and pain; and,
starting to her knees at the sight of me, with her hands
pressed against her temples, and tears bursting from
her eyes, she begged me, for the love of God, to give
her some remedios. Her skin was hot, her pulse very
high; she had a violent intermitting fever. While inquiring into her symptoms, her husband entered the hut,
a white man, about forty, dressed in a pair of dirty cotton drawers, with a nether garment hanging outside, a
handkerchief tied around his head, and barefooted; and
his name was *Don* Miguel. I told him that we wished to
pass a few days among the ruins, and asked permission
to stop at his hut. The woman, most happy at having

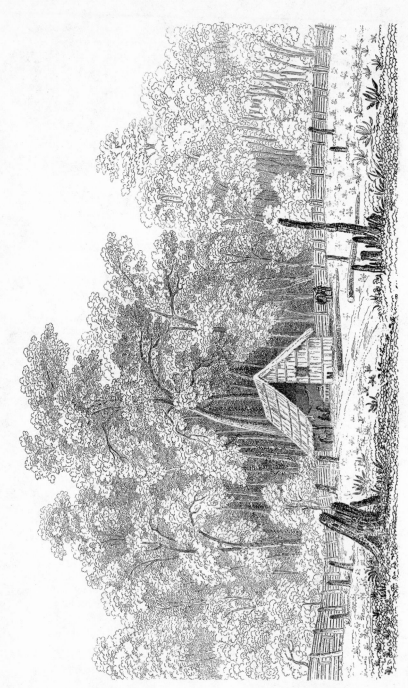

RANCHO AT COPAN.

a skilful physician near her, answered for him, and I returned to relieve Mr. Catherwood, and add another to his list of patients. The whole party escorted us to the hut, bringing along only the mule that carried the hammocks; and by the addition of Mr. C. to the medical corps, and a mysterious display of drawing materials and measuring rods, the poor woman's fever seemed frightened away.

The hut stood on the edge of a clearing, on the ground once covered by the city, with a stone fragment, hollowed out and used as a drinking-vessel for cattle, almost at the very door. The clearing was planted with corn and tobacco, and bounded on each side by the forest. The hut was about sixteen feet square, with a peaked roof, thatched with husks of Indian corn, made by setting in the ground two upright poles with crotches, in which another pole was laid to support the peak of the roof, and similar supports on each side, but only about four feet high. The gable end was the front, and one half of it was thatched with corn-leaves, while the other remained open. The back part was thatched, and piled up against it was Indian corn three ears deep. On one side the pile was unbroken, but on the other it was used down to within three or four feet of the ground. In the corner in front was the bed of Don Miguel and his wife, protected by a bull's hide fastened at the head and side. The furniture consisted of a stone roller for mashing corn, and a comal or earthen griddle for baking tortillas; and on a rude shelf over the bed were two boxes, which contained the wardrobe and all the property of Don Miguel and his wife, except Bartalo, their son and heir, an overgrown lad of twenty, whose naked body seemed to have burst up out of a pair of boy's trousers, disdaining a shirt, his stomach swollen by a distressing liver complaint, and that and his livid face clouded with dirt. There was only room enough for one hammock, and, in fact, the cross-sticks were not strong enough to support two men. The pile of corn which had been used down was just high and broad enough for a bed ; by consent, I took this for my sleeping-place, and Mr. Catherwood hung up his hammock ; we were so glad at being relieved from the churlish hospitality of Don Gregorio, and so near the ruins, that all seemed snug and comfortable.

After a noonday meal I mounted the luggage-mule, with only a halter to hold her, and, accompanied by Augustin on foot, set out for Don Gregorio's, for the purpose of bringing over the luggage. The heavy rains had swollen the river, and Augustin was obliged to strip himself in order to ford it. Don Gregorio was not at home ; and the muleteer, as usual, glad of a difficulty, said that it was impossible to cross the river with a cargo that day. Regularly, instead of helping us in our little difficulties, he did all that he could to increase them. He knew that, if we discharged him, we could get no mules in Copan except by sending off two days' journey ; that we had no one on whom we could rely to send ; and that the delay would be at least a week. Uncertain at what moment it might be advisable to leave, and not wishing to be left destitute, I was compelled to hire him to remain, at a price which was considered so exorbitant that it gave me a reputation for having "mucha plata," which, though it might be useful at home, I did not covet at Copan ; and, afraid to trust me, the rascal stipulated for daily payments. At that time I was not acquainted with the cash system of business prevailing in the country. The barbarians are not satisfied with your custom unless you pay them besides; and the whole, or a large portion, must be in advance. I was accidentally in arrears to the muleteer; and, while I was congratulating myself on this only security for his good behaviour, he was torturing himself with the apprehension that I did not mean to pay at all.

In the mean time it began to rain; and, settling my accounts with the señora, thanking her for her kindness, leaving an order to have some bread baked for the next day, and taking with me an umbrella and a blue bag, contents unknown, belonging to Mr. Catherwood, which he had particularly requested me to bring, I set out on my return. Augustin followed with a tin teapot, and some other articles for immediate use. Entering the woods, the umbrella struck against the branches of the trees, and frightened the mule; and, while I was endeavouring to close it, she fairly ran away with me. Having only a halter, I could not hold her; and, knocking me against the branches, she ran through the woods, splashed into the river, missing the fording-place, and never stopped till she was breast-deep. The river was swollen and angry, and the rain pouring down. Rapids were foaming a short distance below. In the effort to restrain her, I lost Mr. Catherwood's blue bag, caught at it with the handle of the umbrella, and would have saved it if the beast had stood still; but as it floated under her nose she snorted and started back. I broke the umbrella in driving her across; and, just as I touched the shore, saw the bag floating toward the rapids, and Augustin, with his clothes in one hand and the teapot in the other, both above his head, steering down the river after it. Supposing it to contain some indispensable drawing materials, I dashed among the thickets on the bank in the

hope of intercepting it, but became entangled among
branches and vines. I dismounted and tied my mule,
and was two or three minutes working my way to the
river, where I saw Augustin's clothes and the teapot,
but nothing of him, and, with the rapids roaring below,
had horrible apprehensions. It was impossible to continue along the bank ; so, with a violent effort, I jumped across a rapid channel to a ragged island of sand
covered with scrub bushes, and, running down to the
end of it, saw the whole face of the river and the rapids, but nothing of Augustin. I shouted with all my
strength, and, to my inexpressible relief, heard an answer, but, in the noise of the rapids, very faint ; presently he appeared in the water, working himself around
a point, and hauling upon the bushes. Relieved about
him, I now found myself in a quandary. The jump
back was to higher ground, the stream a torrent, and,
the excitement over, I was afraid to attempt it. It would
have been exceedingly inconvenient for me if Augustin
had been drowned. Making his way through the
bushes and down to the bank opposite with his dripping body, he stretched a pole across the stream, by
springing upon which I touched the edge of the bank,
slipped, but hauled myself up by the bushes with the
aid of a lift from Augustin. All this time it was rain-
ing very hard ; and now I had forgotten where I tied
my mule. We were several minutes looking for her ;
and wishing everything but good luck to the old bag,
I mounted. Augustin, principally because he could
carry them more conveniently on his back, put on his
clothes.

Reaching the village, I took shelter in the hut of Don
Jose Maria, while Augustin, being in that happy state
that cannot be made worse, continued through the rain.

There was no one in the hut but a little girl, and the moment the rain abated I followed. I had another stream to cross, which was also much swollen, and the road was flooded. The road lay through a thick forest; very soon the clouds became blacker than ever; on the left was a range of naked mountains, the old stone quarries of Copan, along which the thunder rolled fearfully, and the lightning wrote angry inscriptions on its sides. An English tourist in the United States admits the superiority of our thunder and lightning. I am pertinacious on all points of national honour, but concede this in favour of the tropics. The rain fell as if floodgates were opened from above; and while my mule was slipping and sliding through the mud I lost my road. I returned some distance, and was again retracing my steps, when I met a woman, barefooted, and holding her dress above her knees, who proved to be my rheumatic patient, the wife of Don Jose Maria. While inquiring the road, I told her that she was setting at naught the skill of the physician, and added, what I believed to be very true, that she need not expect to get well under our treatment. I rode on some distance, and again lost my way. It was necessary to enter the woods on the right. I had come out by a footpath which I had not noticed particularly. There were cattle-paths in every direction, and within the line of a mile I kept going in and out, without hitting the right one. Several times I saw the print of Augustin's feet, but soon lost them in puddles of water, and they only confused me more; at length I came to a complete stand-still. It was nearly dark; I did not know which way to turn; and as Mr. Henry Pelham did when in danger of drowning in one of the gutters of Paris, I stood still and hallooed. To my great joy,

I was answered by a roar from Augustin, who had been lost longer than I, and was in even greater tribulation. He had the teapot in his hand, the stump of an unlighted cigar in his mouth, was plastered with mud from his head to his heels, and altogether a most distressful object. We compared notes, and, selecting a path, shouting as we went, our united voices were answered by barking dogs and Mr. Catherwood, who, alarmed at our absence, and apprehending what had happened, was coming out with Don Miguel to look for us. I had no change of clothes, and therefore stripped and rolled myself up in a blanket in the style of a North American Indian. All the evening peals of thunder crashed over our heads, lightning illuminated the dark forest and flashed through the open hut, the rain fell in torrents, and Don Miguel said that there was a prospect of being cut off for several days from all communication with the opposite side of the river and from our luggage. Nevertheless, we passed the evening with great satisfaction, smoking cigars of Copan tobacco, the most famed in Central America, of Don Miguel's own growing and his wife's own making.

Don Miguel, like myself that evening, had but little wearing apparel; but he was an intelligent and educated man, could read and write, bleed, and draw teeth or a law paper; literary in his tastes, for he asked Augustin if we had any books: he said their being in English made no difference—books were good things; and it was delightful to hear him express his contempt for the understanding of Don Gregorio. He was a sub-tenant on the estate, at a rent of four dollars a year, and was generally behindhand in his payments: he said he had not much to offer us; but we felt, what was better than a canopied bed, that we were welcome guests. In fact, all were pleased. His wife expected us to drive away her fever and ague; Bartalo made sure that we would reduce the protuberance of his stomach; and Don Miguel liked our society. In these happy circumstances, the raging of the elements without did not disturb us.

All day I had been brooding over the title-deeds of Don Jose Maria, and, drawing my blanket around me, suggested to Mr. Catherwood " an operation." (Hide your heads, ye speculators in up-town lots!) To buy Copan! remove the monuments of a by-gone people from the desolate region in which they were buried, set them up in the " great commercial emporium," and found an institution to be the nucleus of a great national museum of American antiquities! But quere, Could the " idols" be removed? They were on the banks of a river that emptied into the same ocean by which the docks of New-York are washed, but there were rapids below; and, in answer to my inquiry, Don Miguel said these were impassable. Nevertheless, I should have been unworthy of having passed through the times " that tried men's souls" if I had not had an alternative; and this was to exhibit by sample: to cut one up and remove it in pieces, and make casts of the others. The casts of the Parthenon are regarded as precious memorials in the British Museum, and casts of Copan would be the same in New-York. Other ruins might be discovered even more interesting and more accessible. Very soon their existence would become known and their value appreciated, and the friends of science and the arts in Europe would get possession of them. They belonged of right to us, and, though we did not know how soon we might be kicked out our-

selves, I resolved that ours they should be ; with visions
of glory and indistinct fancies of receiving the thanks
of the corporation flitting before my eyes, I drew my
blanket around me, and fell asleep.

CHAPTER VI.

How to begin.— Commencement of Explorations.— Interest created by these Ruins.—Visit from the Alcalde.—Vexatious Suspicions.—A welcome Visiter. —Letter from General Cascara.—Buying a City.—Visit from Don Gregorio's Family.—Distribution of Medicines.

AT daylight the clouds still hung over the forest; as the sun rose they cleared away; our workmen made their appearance, and at nine o'clock we left the hut. The branches of the trees were dripping wet, and the ground very muddy. Trudging once more over the district which contained the principal monuments, we were startled by the immensity of the work before us, and very soon we concluded that to explore the whole extent would be impossible. Our guides knew only of this district; but having seen columns beyond the village, a league distant, we had reason to believe that others were strewed in different directions, completely buried in the woods, and entirely unknown. The woods were so dense that it was almost hopeless to think of penetrating them. The only way to make a thorough exploration would be to cut down the whole forest and burn the trees. This was incompatible with our immediate purposes, might be considered taking liberties, and could only be done in the dry season. After deliberation, we resolved first to obtain drawings of the sculptured columns. Even in this there was great difficulty. The designs were very complicated, and so different from anything Mr. Catherwood had ever seen before as to be perfectly unintelligible. The cutting was in very high relief, and required a strong body of light to bring up the figures ; and the foliage was so thick, and the shade so deep, that drawing was impossible.

After much consultation, we selected one of the "idols," and determined to cut down the trees around it, and thus lay it open to the rays of the sun. Here again was difficulty. There was no axe ; and the only instrument which the Indians possessed was the ma- chete, or chopping-knife, which varies in form in differ- ent sections of the country ; wielded with one hand, it was useful in clearing away shrubs and branches, but almost harmless upon large trees ; and the Indians, as in the days when the Spaniards discovered them, ap- plied to work without ardour, carried it on with little activity, and, like children, were easily diverted from it. One hacked into a tree, and, when tired, which happened very soon, sat down to rest, and another re- lieved him. While one worked there were always several looking on. I remembered the ring of the woodman's axe in the forests at home, and wished for a few long-sided Green Mountain boys. But we had been buffeted into patience, and watched the Indians while they hacked with their machetes, and even won- dered that they succeeded so well. At length the trees were felled and dragged aside, a space cleared around the base, Mr. C.'s frame set up, and he set to work. I took two Mestitzoes, Bruno and Francisco, and, offer- ing them a reward for every new discovery, with a compass in my hand set out on a tour of exploration. Neither had seen "the idols" until the morning of our first visit, when they followed in our train to laugh at los Ingleses ; but very soon they exhibited such an interest that I hired them. Bruno attracted my attention by his admiration, as I supposed, of my person ; but I found it

was of my coat, which was a long shooting-frock, with
many pockets; and he said that he could make one
just like it except the skirts. He was a tailor by profession, and in the intervals of a great job upon a
roundabout jacket, worked with his machete. But he
had an inborn taste for the arts. As we passed through
the woods, nothing escaped his eye, and he was profes-
sionally curious touching the costumes of the sculptured
figures. I was struck with the first development of
their antiquarian taste. Francisco found the feet and
legs of a statue, and Bruno a part of the body to match,
and the effect was electric upon both. They searched
and raked up the ground with their machetes till they
found the shoulders, and set it up entire except the
head; and they were both eager for the possession of
instruments with which to dig and find this remaining
fragment.

It is impossible to describe the interest with which I
explored these ruins. The ground was entirely new;
there were no guide-books or guides; the whole was
a virgin soil. We could not see ten yards before us,
and never knew what we should stumble upon next.
At one time we stopped to cut away branches and vines
which concealed the face of a monument, and then to
dig around and bring to light a fragment, a sculptured
corner of which protruded from the earth. I leaned
over with breathless anxiety while the Indians worked,
and an eye, an ear, a foot, or a hand was disentombed;
and when the machete rang against the chiselled stone,
I pushed the Indians away, and cleared out the loose
earth with my hands. The beauty of the sculpture, the
solemn stillness of the woods, disturbed only by the
scrambling of monkeys and the chattering of parrots,
the desolation of the city, and the mystery that hung

over it, all created an interest higher, if possible, than I had ever felt among the ruins of the Old World. After several hours' absence I returned to Mr. Catherwood, and reported upward of fifty objects to be copied.

I found him not so well pleased as I expected with my report. He was standing with his feet in the mud, and was drawing with his gloves on, to protect his hands from the moschetoes. As we feared, the designs were so intricate and complicated, the subjects so entirely new and unintelligible, that he had great difficulty in drawing. He had made several attempts, both with the camera lucida and without, but failed to satisfy himself or even me, who was less severe in criticism. The " idol" seemed to defy his art; two monkeys on a tree on one side appeared to be laughing at him, and I felt discouraged and despondent. In fact, I made up my mind, with a pang of regret, that we must abandon the idea of carrying away any materials for antiquarian speculation, and must be content with having seen them ourselves. Of that satisfaction nothing could deprive us. We returned to the hut with our interest undiminished, but sadly out of heart as to the result of our labours.

Our luggage had not been able to cross the river, but the blue bag which had caused me so many troubles was recovered. I had offered a dollar reward, and Bartalo, the heir-apparent of the lesseeship of our hut, had passed the day in the river, and found it entangled in a bush upon the bank. His naked body seemed glad of its accidental washing, and the bag, which we supposed to contain some of Mr. C.'s drawing materials, being shaken, gave out a pair of old boots, which, however, were at that time worth their weight in gold, being water-proof, and cheered Mr. Catherwood's droop-

ing spirits, who was ill with a prospective attack of fever and ague or rheumatism, from standing all day in
the mud. Our men went home, and Frederico had orders, before coming to work in the morning, to go to
Don Gregorio's and buy bread, milk, candles, lard, and
a few yards of beef. The door of the hut looked toward the west, and the sun set over the dark forest in
front with a gorgeousness I have never seen surpassed.
Again, during the night, we had rain, with thunder and
lightning, but not so violent as the night before, and in
the morning it was again clear.

That day Mr. Catherwood was much more successful in his drawings; indeed, at the beginning the light
fell exactly as he wished, and he mastered the difficulty.
His preparations, too, were much more comfortable, as
he had his water-proofs, and stood on a piece of oiled
canvass, used for covering luggage on the road. I
passed the morning in selecting another monument,
clearing away the trees, and preparing it for him to
copy. At one o'clock Augustin came to call us to dinner. Don Miguel had a patch of beans, from which
Augustin gathered as many as he pleased, and, with the
fruits of a standing order for all the eggs in the village,
being three or four a day, strings of beef, and bread and
milk from the hacienda, we did very well. In the afternoon we were again called off by Augustin, with a
message that the alcalde had come to pay us a visit.
As it was growing late, we broke up for the day, and
went back to the hut. We shook hands with the alcalde, and gave him and his attendants cigars, and were
disposed to be sociable; but the dignitary was so tipsy
he could hardly speak. His attendants sat crouching
on the ground, swinging themselves on their knee-
joints, and, though the positions were different, re-

minding us of the Arabs. In a few minutes the alcalde started up suddenly, made a staggering bow, and left us, and they all followed, Don Miguel with them. While we were at supper he returned, and it was easy to see that he, and his wife, and Bartalo were in trouble, and, as we feared, the matter concerned us.

While we were busy with our own affairs, we had but little idea what a sensation we were creating in the village. Not satisfied with getting us out of his house, Don Gregorio wanted to get us out of the neighbourhood. Unluckily, besides his instinctive dislike, we had offended him in drawing off some of his workmen by the high prices which, as strangers, we were obliged to pay, and he began to look upon us as rivals, and said everywhere that we were suspicious characters; that we should be the cause of disturbing the peace of Copan, and introducing soldiers and war into the neighbourhood. In confirmation of this, two Indians passed through the village, who reported that we had escaped from imprisonment, had been chased to the borders of Honduras by a detachment of twenty-five soldiers under Landaveri, the officer who arrested us, and that, if we had been taken, we would have been shot. The alcalde, who had been drunk ever since our arrival, resolved to visit us, to solve the doubts of the village, and take those measures which the presence of such dangerous persons and the safety of the country might require. But this doughty purpose was frustrated by a ludicrous circumstance. We made it a rule to carry our arms with us to the ruins, and when we returned to the hut to receive his visit, as usual, each of us had a brace of pistols in his belt and a gun in hand; and our appearance was so formidable that the alcalde was frightened at his own audacity in having thought of catechising us, and fairly sneaked off. As soon as he reached the woods, his attendants reproached him for not executing his purpose, and he said, doggedly, that he was not going to have anything to say to men armed as we were. Roused at the idea of our terrible appearance, we told Don Miguel to advise the alcalde and the people of the village that they had better keep out of our way and let us alone. Don Miguel gave a ghastly smile; but all was not finished. He said that he had no doubt himself of our being good men, but we were suspected; the country was in a state of excitement; and he was warned that he ought not to harbour us, and would get into difficulty by doing so. The poor woman could not conceal her distress. Her head was full of assassinations and murders, and though alarmed for their safety, she was not unmindful of ours; she said that, if any soldiers came into the village, we would be murdered, and begged us to go away.

We were exceedingly vexed and disturbed by these communications, but we had too much at stake to consent to be driven away by apprehensions. We assured Don Miguel that no harm could happen to him; that it was all false and a mistake, and that we were above suspicion. At the same time, in order to convince him, I opened my trunk, and showed him a large bundle of papers, sealed credentials to the government and private letters of introduction in Spanish to prominent men in Guatimala, describing me as "Encargado de los Negocios de los Estados Unidos del Norte," and one very special from Don Antonio Aycinena, now in this city, formerly colonel in the Central army, and banished by Morazan, to his brother the Marquis Aycinena, the leader of the Central party, which was dominant in that district in the civil war then raging, recommending me very highly, and stating my purpose of travelling through the country.   This last letter was more important than anything else ; and if it had been directed to one of the opposite party in politics, it would have been against us, as confirming the suspicion of our being " ennemigos." Never was greatness so much under a shade.   Though vexatious, it was almost amusing to be obliged to clear up our character to such a miserable party as Don Miguel, his wife, and Barta- lo ; but it was indispensable to relieve them from doubts and anxieties, enabling us to remain quietly in their wretched hut ; and the relief they experienced, and the joy of the woman in learning that we were tolerably respectable people, not enemies, and not in danger of being put up and shot at, were most grateful to us.

Nevertheless, Don Miguel advised us to go to Guati- mala or to General Cascara, procure an order to visit the ruins, and then return.   We had made a false step in one particular ; we should have gone direct to Guati- mala, and returned with a passport and letters from the government ; but, as we had no time to spare, and did not know what there was at Copan, probably if we had not taken it on the way we should have missed it alto- gether.   And we did not know that the country was so completely secluded ; the people are less accustomed to the sight of strangers than the Arabs about Mount Sinai, and they are much more suspicious.   Colonel Galindo was the only stranger who had been there before us, and he could hardly be called a stranger, for he was a colonel in the Central American service, and visited the ruins under a commission from the government.   Our visit has perhaps had some influence upon the feelings of the people ; it has, at all events, taught Don Gre- gorio that strangers are not easily got rid of ; but I advise any one who wishes to visit these ruins in peace, to go to Guatimala first, and apply to the government for all the protection it can give. As to us, it was too late to think of this, and all we had to do was to maintain our ground as quietly as we could. We had no apprehension of soldiers coming from any other place merely to molest us. Don Miguel told us, what we had before observed, that there was not a musket in the village; the quality and excellence of our arms were well known; the muleteer had reported that we were outrageous fellows, and had threatened to shoot him; and the alcalde was an excessive coward. We formed an alliance, offensive and defensive, with Don Miguel, his wife, and Bartalo, and went to sleep. Don Miguel and his wife, by-the-way, were curious people; they slept with their heads at different ends of the bed, so that, in the unavoidable accompaniment of smoking, they could clear each other.

In the morning we were relieved from our difficulty, and put in a position to hurl defiance at the traducers of our character. While the workmen were gathering outside the hut, an Indian courier came trotting through the cornfield up to the door, who inquired for Señor Ministro; and pulling off his petate, took out of the crown a letter, which he said he was ordered by General Cascara to deliver into the right hands. It was directed to "Señor Catherwood, à Comotan ó donde se halle," conveying the expression of General Cascara's regret for the arrest at Comotan, ascribing it to the ignorance or mistake of the alcalde and soldiers, and enclosing, besides, a separate passport for Mr. Catherwood. I have great satisfaction in acknowledging the receipt of this letter; and the promptness with which General Cascara despatched it to "Comotan, or wherever he may be found," was no less than I expected from his character and station. I requested Don Miguel to read it aloud, told the Indian to deliver our compliments to General Cascara, and sent him to the village to breakfast, with a donation which I knew would make him publish the story with right emphasis and discretion. Don Miguel smiled, his wife laughed, and a few spots of white flashed along Bartalo's dirty skin. Stocks rose, and I resolved to ride to the village, strengthen the cords of friendship with Don Jose Maria, visit our patients, defy Don Gregorio, and get up a party in Copan.

Mr. Catherwood went to the ruins to continue his drawings, and I to the village, taking Augustin with me to fire the Balize guns, and buy up eatables for a little more than they were worth. My first visit was to Don Jose Maria. After clearing up our character, I broached the subject of a purchase of the ruins; told him that, on account of my public business, I could not remain as long as I desired, but wished to return with spades, pickaxes, ladders, crowbars, and men, build a hut to live in, and make a thorough exploration; that I could not incur the expense at the risk of being refused permission to do so; and, in short, in plain English, asked him, What will you take for the ruins? I think he was not more surprised than if I had asked to buy his poor old wife, our rheumatic patient, to practice medicine upon. He seemed to doubt which of us was out of his senses. The property was so utterly worthless that my wanting to buy it seemed very suspicious. On examining the paper, I found that he did not own the fee, but held under a lease from Don Bernardo de Aguila, of which three years were unexpired. The tract consisted of about six thousand acres, for which he paid eighty dollars a year; he was at a loss what to do, but told me that he would reflect upon it, consult his wife, and give me an answer at the hut the next day.   I then visited the alcalde, but he was too tipsy to be susceptible of any impression; prescribed for several patients; and instead of going to Don Gregorio's, sent him a polite request by Don Jose Maria to mind his own business and let us alone; returned, and passed the rest of the day among the ruins.   It rained during the night, but again cleared off in the morning, and we were on the ground early.   My business was to go around with workmen to clear away trees and bushes, dig, and excavate, and prepare monuments for Mr. Catherwood to copy.   While so engaged, I was called off by a visit from Don Jose Maria, who was still undecided what to do; and not wishing to appear too anxious, told him to take more time, and come again the next morning.

The next morning he came, and his condition was truly pitiable.   He was anxious to convert unproductive property into money, but afraid, and said that I was a stranger, and it might bring him into difficulty with the government.   I again went into proof of character, and engaged to save him harmless with the government or release him.   Don Miguel read my letters of recommendation, and re-read the letter of General Cascara.   He was convinced, but these papers did not give him a right to sell me his land; the shade of suspicion still lingered; for a finale, I opened my trunk, and put on a diplomatic coat, with a profusion of large eagle buttons.   I had on a Panama hat, soaked with rain and spotted with mud, a check shirt, white pantaloons, yellow up to the knees with mud, and was about as outré as the negro king who received a company of British officers on the coast of Africa in a cocked hat

and military coat, without any inexpressibles ; but Don
Jose Maria could not withstand the buttons on my coat ;
the cloth was the finest he had ever seen ; and Don
Miguel, and his wife, and Bartalo realized fully that
they had in their hut an illustrious incognito. The only
question was who should find paper on which to draw
the contract. I did not stand upon trifles, and gave
Don Miguel some paper, who took our mutual instructions, and appointed the next day for the execution of
the deed.

The reader is perhaps curious to know how old
cities sell in Central America. Like other articles of
trade, they are regulated by the quantity in market,
and the demand ; but, not being staple articles, like
cotton and indigo, they were held at fancy prices, and
at that time were dull of sale. I paid fifty dollars for
Copan. There was never any difficulty about price.
I offered that sum, for which Don Jose Maria thought
me only a fool ; if I had offered more, he would probably have considered me something worse.

We had regular communications with the hacienda
by means of Francisco, who brought thence every morning a large waccal of milk, carrying it a distance of
three miles, and fording the river twice. The ladies
of the hacienda had sent us word that they intended
paying us a visit, and this morning Don Gregorio's
wife appeared, leading a procession of all the women
of the house, servants, and children, with two of her
sons. We received them among the ruins, seated them
as well as we could, and, as the first act of civility, gave
them cigars all around. It can hardly be believed, but
not one of them, not even Don Gregorio's sons, had
ever seen the " idols" before, and now they were much
more curious to see Mr. C.'s drawings. In fact, I be-

lieve it was the fame of these drawings that procured us the honour of their visit. In his heart Mr. C. was not much happier to see them than the old don was to see us, as his work was stopped, and every day was precious. As I considered myself in a manner the proprietor of the city, I was bound to do the honours; and, having cleared paths, led them around, showing off all the lions as the cicerone does in the Vatican or the Pitti Palace; but I could not keep them away, and, to the distress of Mr. C., brought them all back upon him.

Obliged to give up work, we invited them down to the hut to see our accommodations. Some of them were our patients, and reminded us that we had not sent the medicines we promised. The fact is, we avoided giving medicines when we could, among other reasons, from an apprehension that if any one happened to die on our hands we should be held responsible; but our reputation was established; honours were buckled on our backs, and we were obliged to wear them. These ladies, in spite of Don Gregorio's crustiness, had always treated us kindly, and we would fain have shown our sense of it in some other mode than by giving them physic; but, to gratify them in their own way, we distributed among them powders and pills, with written directions for use; and when they went away escorted them some distance, and had the satisfaction of hearing that they avenged us on Don Gregorio by praises of our gallantry and attentions.

CHAPTER VII.

Survey of the Ruins.—Account of them by Huarros and by Colonel Galindo. —Their Situation.—Their Extent.—Plan of Survey.—Pyramidal Structures.— Rows of Death's Heads.—Remarkable Portrait.—"Idols."—Character of the Engravings.—Ranges of Terraces.—A Portrait.—Courtyards.—Curious Altar. —Tablets of Hieroglyphics.—Gigantic Head.—Stone Quarries.—More Applicants for Medicine. —"Idols" and Altars.—Buried Image.—Material of the Statues.—Idols originally painted.—Circular Altar.—Antiquity of Copan.

THAT night there was no rain, and the next day, as the ground was somewhat dry, we commenced a regular survey of the ruins. It was my first essay in engineering. Our surveying apparatus was not very extensive. We had a good surveying compass, and the rest consisted of a reel of tape which Mr. C. had used in a survey of the ruins of Thebes and Jerusalem. My part of the business was very scientific. I had to direct the Indians in cutting straight lines through the woods, make Bruno and Frederico stick their hats on poles to mark the stations, and measure up to them. The second day we were thoroughly in the spirit of it.

That day Don Jose Maria refused to execute the contract. Don Gregorio was the cause. He had ceased to interfere with us, but at the idea of our actually taking root in the neighbourhood he could not contain himself, and persuaded Don Jose Maria that he would get into difficulty by having anything to do with us; he even told him that General Cascara's passport was worthless, and that General Cascara himself had gone over to Morazan. He carried his point for the moment, but in the end we beat him, and the contract was executed.

After three days of very hard but very interesting labour, we finished the survey, the particulars of which I intend to inflict upon the reader; but before doing so

I will mention the little that was previously known of these ruins.

Huarros, the historian of Guatimala, says, " Francisco de Fuentes, who wrote the Chronicles of the Kingdom of Guatimala, assures us that in his time, that is, in the year 1700, the great circus of Copan still remained entire. This was a circular space surrounded by stone pyramids about six yards high, and very well constructed. At the bases of these pyramids were figures, both male and female, of very excellent sculpture, which then retained the colours they had been enamelled with, and, what was not less remarkable, the whole of them were habited *in the Castilian costume.* In the middle of this area, elevated above a flight of steps, was the place of sacrifice. The same author affirms that at a short distance from the circus there was a portal constructed of stone, on the columns of which were the figures of men, likewise represented in *Spanish habits,* with hose, and ruff around the neck, sword, cap, and short cloak. On entering the gateway there are two fine stone pyramids, moderately large and lofty, from which is suspended a hammock that contains two human figures, one of each sex, clothed in the Indian style. Astonishment is forcibly excited on viewing this structure, because, large as it is, there is no appearance of the component parts being joined together ; and though entirely of one stone, and of an enormous weight, it may be put in motion by the slightest impulse of the hand."

From this time, that is, from the year 1700, there is no account of these ruins until the visit of Colonel Galindo in 1836, before referred to, who examined them under a commission from the Central American government, and whose communications on the subject were published in the proceedings of the Royal Geographical Society of Paris, and in the Literary Gazette of London. He is the only man in that country who has given any attention *at all* to the subject of antiquities, or who has ever presented Copan to the consideration of Europe and our own country. Not being an artist, his account is necessarily unsatisfactory and imperfect, but it is not exaggerated. Indeed, it falls short of the marvellous account given by Fuentes one hundred and thirty-five years before, and makes no mention of the moveable stone hammock, with the sitting figures, which were our great inducement to visit the ruins. No plans or drawings have ever been published, nor anything that can give even an idea of that valley of romance and wonder, where, as has been remarked, the genii who attended on King Solomon seem to have been the artists.

It lies in the district of country now known as the State of Honduras, one of the most fertile valleys in Central America, and to this day famed for the superiority of its tobacco. Mr. Catherwood made several attempts to determine the longitude, but the artificial horizon which we took with us expressly for such purposes had become bent, and, like the barometer, was useless. The ruins are on the left bank of the Copan River, which empties into the Motagua, and so passes into the Bay of Honduras near Omoa, distant perhaps three hundred miles from the sea. The Copan River is not navigable, even for canoes, except for a short time in the rainy season. Falls interrupt its course before it empties into the Motagua. Cortez, in his terrible journey from Mexico to Honduras, of the hardships of which, even now, when the country is comparatively open, and free from masses of enemies, it is difficult to

South

East

West

North

A   Square Altar sculptured on the four sides and top.
B   Statue erect.
C   Statue and Altar,
D   do.
E   do.   Fallen do. with many fragments on side of Pyramid.
F   Colossal Head.
G   Remains of sculptured figures.
H   Colossal Head,
I   Sepulchre and underground passage leading to the River.
J   Remains of 2 circular Towers with Stairs.
K   Statue and Altar, (Fallen.)
L   Statue and Altar, (Erect.)
M   do.   do.
N   do.   do.
O   do.   do.   (Fallen)
P   do.   do.   (Erect.)

Q   Statue and Altar, (Erect.)
R   do.   do.   (Fallen.)
S   Statue of Female with Altar, (Erect.)
T   Beautiful Fragment, partly buried.
U   Court Yard, with steps on three sides,
V   Entrance, with remains of Statue or Columns.
W   Pyramidal Building, Steps 10 ft. wide, and 6 ft. high
X   Area, overgrown with Trees.
Y YYYY   Remains of Walls.
Z ZZZZZZ   Remains of Pyramidal Buildings.

The dotted line shows the boundaries of the survey.

Indian Rubber, Mahogany, Cedar, and other large trees are
dispersed over the Ruins.

RIVER COPAN

Boundary of the survey

PLAN

OF

COPAN

Scale of English Feet.

100   50   0   100   200   300 F.ᵗ

F. Catherwood.

form a conception, must have passed within two days' march of this city.

The extent along the river, as ascertained by monuments still found, is more than two miles. There is one monument on the opposite side of the river, at the distance of a mile, on the top of a mountain two thousand feet high. Whether the city ever crossed the river, and extended to that monument, it is impossible to say. I believe not. At the rear is an unexplored forest, in which there may be ruins. There are no remains of palaces or private buildings, and the principal part is that which stands on the bank of the river, and may, perhaps, with propriety be called the Temple.

This temple is an oblong enclosure. The front or river wall extends on a right line north and south six hundred and twenty-four feet, and it is from sixty to ninety feet in height. It is made of cut stones, from three to six feet in length, and a foot and a half in breadth. In many places the stones have been thrown down by bushes growing out of the crevices, and in one place there is a small opening, from which the ruins are sometimes called by the Indians Las Ventanas, or the windows. The other three sides consist of ranges of steps and pyramidal structures, rising from thirty to one hundred and forty feet in height on the slope. The whole line of survey is two thousand, eight hundred and sixty-six feet, which, though gigantic and extraordinary for a ruined structure of the aborigines, that the reader's imagination may not mislead him, I consider it necessary to say, is not so large as the base of the great Pyramid of Ghizeh.

The engraving opposite gives the plan according to our survey, a reference to which will assist the reader to understand the description.

To begin on the right : Near the southwest corner of the river wall and the south wall is a recess, which was probably once occupied by a colossal monument fronting the water, no part of which is now visible ; probably it has fallen and been broken, and the fragments have been buried or washed away by the floods of the rainy season. Beyond are the remains of two small pyramidal structures, to the largest of which is attached a wall running along the west bank of the river ; this appears to have been one of the principal walls of the city ; and between the two pyramids there seems to have been a gateway or principal entrance from the water.

The south wall runs at right angles to the river, beginning with a range of steps about thirty feet high, and each step about eighteen inches square. At the southeast corner is a massive pyramidal structure one hundred and twenty feet high on the slope. On the right are other remains of terraces and pyramidal buildings; and here also was probably a gateway, by a passage about twenty feet wide, into a quadrangular area two hundred and fifty feet square, two sides of which are massive pyramids one hundred and twenty feet high on the slope.

At the foot of these structures, and in different parts of the quadrangular area, are numerous remains of sculpture. At the point marked E is a colossal monument richly sculptured, fallen, and ruined. Behind it fragments of sculpture, thrown from their places by trees, are strewed and lying loose on the side of the pyramid, from the base to the top ; and among them our attention was forcibly arrested by rows of death's heads of gigantic proportions, still standing in their places about half way up the side of the pyramid ; the effect was extraordinary. The engraving which follows represents one of them.

At the time of our visit, we had no doubt that these were death's heads; but it has been suggested to me that the drawing is more like the scull of a monkey than that of a man. And, in connexion with this remark, I add what attracted our attention, though not so forcibly at the time. Among the fragments on this side were the remains of a colossal ape or baboon, strongly resembling in outline and appearance the four monstrous animals which once stood in front attached to the base of the obelisk of Luxor, now in Paris,* and which, under the name of Cynocephali, were worshipped at Thebes. This fragment was about six feet high. The head was wanting; the trunk lay on the side of the pyramid, and we rolled it down several steps, when it fell among a mass of stones, from which we could not disengage it. We had no such idea at the time, but it is not absurd to suppose the sculptured sculls to be intended for the heads of monkeys, and that these ani-

* As it stands in Paris, these figures are wanting to make it complete as it stood at Thebes, the obelisk alone having been removed.

mals were worshipped as deities by the people who built Copan.

Among the fragments lying on the ground, near this place, is a remarkable portrait, of which the following engraving is a representation. It is probably the por-

trait of some king, chieftain, or sage. The mouth is injured, and part of the ornament over the wreath that crowns the head. The expression is noble and severe, and the whole character shows a close imitation of nature.

At the point marked D stands one of the columns or "idols" which give the peculiar character to the ruins of Copan, the front of which forms the frontispiece to this volume, and to which I particularly request the attention of the reader. It stands with its face to the east, about six feet from the base of the pyramidal wall. It is thirteen feet in height, four feet in front, and three deep, sculptured on all four of its sides from the base to the top, and one of the richest and most elaborate specimens in the whole extent of the ruins. Originally it was painted, the marks of red colour being still distinctly visible. Before it, at a distance of about eight feet, is a large block of sculptured stone, which the Indians call an altar. The subject of the front is a full-length figure, the face wanting beard, and of a feminine cast, though the dress seems that of a man. On the two sides are rows of hieroglyphics, which probably recite the history of this mysterious personage.

As the monuments speak for themselves, I shall abstain from any verbal description; and I have so many to present to the reader, all differing very greatly in detail, that it will be impossible, within reasonable limits, to present our own speculations as to their character. I will only remark that, from the beginning, our great object and effort was to procure true copies of the originals, adding nothing for effect as pictures. Mr. Catherwood made the outline of all the drawings with the camera lucida, and divided his paper into sections, so as to preserve the utmost accuracy of proportion. The engravings were made with the same regard to truth, from drawings reduced by Mr. Catherwood himself, the originals being also in the hands of the engraver; and I consider it proper to mention that a portion of them, of which the frontispiece was one, were sent to London, and executed by engravers on wood whose names stand among the very first in England; yet, though done with exquisite skill, and most effective as pictures, they failed in giving the true character and expression of the originals; and, at some considerable loss both of time and money, were all thrown aside, and re-engraved on steel. Proofs of every plate were given to Mr. Catherwood, who made such corrections as were necessary; and, in my opinion, they are as true copies as can be presented; and, except the stones themselves, the reader cannot have better materials for speculation and study.

Following the wall, at the place marked C is another monument or idol of the same size, and in many respects similar. The engraving opposite represents the back. The character of this image, as it stands at the foot of the pyramidal wall, with masses of fallen stone resting against its base, is grand, and it would be difficult to exceed the richness of the ornament and sharpness of the sculpture. This, too, was painted, and the red is still distinctly visible.

The whole quadrangle is overgrown with trees, and interspersed with fragments of fine sculpture, particularly on the east side, and at the northeast corner is a narrow passage, which was probably a third gateway.

On the right is a confused range of terraces running off into the forest, ornamented with death's heads, some of which are still in position, and others lying about as they have fallen or been thrown down. Turning northward, the range on the left hand continues a high, massive pyramidal structure, with trees growing out of it to the very top. At a short distance is a detached pyramid, tolerably perfect, marked on the plan Z, about fifty feet square and thirty feet high. The range continues for a distance of about four hundred feet, decreasing somewhat in height, and along this there are but few remains of sculpture.

The range of structures turns at right angles to the left, and runs to the river, joining the other extremity

F. Catherwood   H. Jordan

STONE STATUE (*front view*).

of the wall, at which we began our survey. The bank was elevated about thirty feet above the river, and had been protected by a wall of stone, most of which had fallen down. Among the fragments lying on the ground on this side is the portrait here given.

The plan was complicated, and, the whole ground being overgrown with trees, difficult to make out. There was no entire pyramid, but, at most, two or three pyramidal sides, and these joined on to terraces or other structures of the same kind. Beyond the wall of enclosure were walls, terraces, and pyramidal elevations running off into the forest, which sometimes confused us. Probably the whole was not erected at the same time, but additions were made and statues erected by different kings, or, perhaps, in commemoration of important events in the history of the city. Along the whole line were ranges of steps with pyramidal elevations, probably crowned on the top with buildings or altars now ruined. All these steps and the pyramidal sides were painted, and the reader may imagine the effect when the whole country was clear of forest, and priest and people were ascending from the outside to the terraces, and thence to the holy places within to pay their adoration in the temple.

Within this enclosure are two rectangular court-yards, having ranges of steps ascending to terraces. The area of each is about forty feet above the river. Of the larger and most distant from the river the steps have all fallen, and constitute mere mounds. On one side, at the foot of the pyramidal wall, is the monument or "idol" marked B, of which the engraving repre-sents the front. It is about the same height with the others, but differs in shape, being larger at the top than below. Its appearance and character are tasteful and pleasing, but the sculpture is in much lower relief; the expression of the hands is good, though somewhat formal. The figure of a man shows the relative height. The back and sides are covered with hieroglyphics.

Near this, at the point marked A, is a remarkable altar, which perhaps presents as curious a subject of speculation as any monument in Copan. The altars, like the idols, are all of a single block of stone. In general they are not so richly ornamented, and are more faded and worn, or covered with moss; some were completely buried, and of others it was difficult to make out more than the form. All differed in fashion, and doubtless had some distinct and peculiar reference to the idols before which they stood. This stands on four globes cut out of the same stone; the sculpture is in bas-relief, and it is the only specimen of that kind of sculpture found at Copan, all the rest being in bold alto-relievo. It is six feet square and four feet high, and the top is divided into thirty-six tablets of hiero-glyphics, which beyond doubt record some event in the history of the mysterious people who once inhabited the

FRONT OF STONE IDOL.

city.   The lines are still distinctly visible, and a faithful
copy appears in the following cut.

CATHERWOOD D.   ANDERSON S.

The next two engravings exhibit the four sides of this
altar.   Each side represents four individuals.   On the
west side are the two principal personages, chiefs or
warriors, with their faces opposite each other, and apparently engaged in argument or negotiation.   The
other fourteen are divided into two equal parties, and
seem to be following their leaders.   Each of the two
principal figures is seated cross-legged, in the Oriental
fashion, on a hieroglyphic which probably designates
his name and office, or character, and on three of which

the serpent forms part.   Between the two principal personages is a remarkable cartouche, containing two hieroglyphics well preserved, which reminded us strongly of the Egyptian method of giving the names of the
kings or heroes in whose honour monuments were erected.   The headdresses are remarkable for their curious
and complicated form ; the figures have all breastplates,
and one of the two principal characters holds in his
hand an instrument, which may, perhaps, be considered
a sceptre ; each of the others holds an object which can
be only a subject for speculation and conjecture.   It
may be a weapon of war, and, if so, it is the only thing
of the kind found represented at Copan.   In other
countries, battle-scenes, warriors, and weapons of war
are among the most prominent subjects of sculpture ;
and from the entire absence of them here there is reason to believe that the people were not warlike, but
peaceable, and easily subdued.

The other courtyard is near the river.   By cutting
down the trees, we discovered the entrance to be on
the north side, by a passage thirty feet wide and about
three hundred feet long.   On the right is a high range
of steps rising to the terrace of the river wall.   At the
foot of this are six circular stones, from eighteen inches
to three feet in diameter, perhaps once the pedestals of
columns or monuments now fallen and buried.   On the
left side of the passage is a high pyramidal structure,
with steps six feet high and nine feet broad, like the
side of one of the pyramids at Saccara, and one hundred and twenty-two feet high on the slope.   The top
is fallen, and has two immense Ceiba trees growing out
of it, the roots of which have thrown down the stones,
and now bind the top of the pyramid.   At the end of
the passage is the area or courtyard, probably the great

WEST SIDE.

NORTH SIDE.

ALTAR.

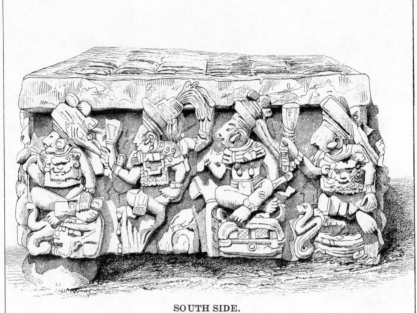

SOUTH SIDE.

EAST SIDE.

F. Catherwood.

A.L. Dick.

ALTAR.

GIGANTIC HEAD.

circus of Fuentes, but which, instead of being circular, is rectangular, one hundred and forty feet long and ninety broad, with steps on all the sides. This was probably the most holy place in the temple. Beyond doubt it had been the theatre of great events and of imposing religious ceremonies ; but what those ceremonies were, or who were the actors in them, or what had brought them to such a fearful close, were mysteries which it was impossible to fathom. There was no idol or altar, nor were there any vestiges of them. On the left, standing alone, two thirds of the way up the steps, is the gigantic head opposite. It is moved a little from its place, and a portion of the ornament on one side has been thrown down some distance by the expansion of the trunk of a large tree, as shown by the drawing. The head is about six feet high, and the style good. Like many of the others, with the great expansion of the eyes it seems intended to inspire awe. On either side of it, distant about thirty or forty feet, and rather lower down, are other fragments of sculpture of colossal dimensions and good design, and at the foot are two colossal heads turned over and partly buried, well worthy the attention of future travellers and artists. The whole area is overgrown with trees and encumbered with decayed vegetable matter, with fragments of curious sculpture protruding above the surface, which, probably with many others completely buried, would be brought to light by digging.

On the opposite side, parallel with the river, is a range of fifteen steps to a terrace twelve feet wide, and then fifteen steps more to another terrace twenty feet wide, extending to the river wall. On each side of the centre of the steps is a mound of ruins, apparently of a circular tower. About half way up the steps on this side is a pit five feet square and seventeen feet deep, cased with stone. At the bottom is an opening two feet four inches high, with a wall one foot nine inches thick, which leads into a chamber ten feet long, five feet eight inches wide, and four feet high. At each end is a niche one foot nine inches high, one foot eight inches deep, and two feet five inches long. Colonel Galindo first broke into this sepulchral vault, and found the niches and the ground full of red earthenware dishes and pots, more than fifty of which, he says, were full of human bones, packed in lime. Also several sharpedged and pointed knives of chaya, a small death's head carved in a fine green stone, its eyes nearly closed, the lower features distorted, and the back symmetrically perforated by holes, the whole of exquisite workmanship. Immediately above the pit which leads to this vault is a passage leading through the terrace to the river wall, from which, as before mentioned, the ruins are sometimes called Las Ventanas, or the windows. It is one foot eleven inches at the bottom, and one foot at the top, in ⌐⌐ this form, and barely large enough for a man to crawl through on his face.

There were no remains of buildings. In regard to the stone hammock mentioned by Fuentes, and which, in fact, was our great inducement to visit these ruins, we made special inquiry and search for it, but saw nothing of it. Colonel Galindo does not mention it. Still it may have existed, and may be there still, broken and buried. The padre of Gualan told us that he had seen it, and in our inquiries among the Indians we met with one who told us that he had heard his father say that *his* father, two generations back, had spoken of such a monument.

I have omitted the particulars of our survey; the difficulty and labour of opening lines through the trees; climbing up the sides of the ruined pyramids; measuring steps, and the aggravation of all these from our want of materials and help, and our imperfect knowledge of the language. The people of Copan could not comprehend what we were about, and thought we were practising some black art to discover hidden treasure. Bruno and Francisco, our principal coadjutors, were completely mystified, and even the monkeys seemed embarrassed and confused; these counterfeit presentments of ourselves aided not a little in keeping alive the strange interest that hung over the place. They had no "monkey tricks," but were grave and solemn as if officiating as the guardians of consecrated ground. In the morning they were quiet, but in the afternoon they came out for a promenade on the tops of the trees; and sometimes, as they looked steadfastly at us, they seemed on the point of asking us why we disturbed the repose of the ruins. I have omitted, too, what aggravated our hardships and disturbed our sentiment, apprehensions from scorpions, and bites of moschetoes and garrapatas or ticks, the latter of which, in spite of precautions (pantaloons tied tight over our boots and coats buttoned close in the throat), got under our clothes, and buried themselves in the flesh; at night, moreover, the hut of Don Miguel was alive with fleas, to protect ourselves against which, on the third night of our arrival we sewed up the sides and one end of our sheets, and thrust ourselves into them as we would into a sack. And while in the way of mentioning our troubles I may add, that during this time the flour of the hacienda gave out, we were cut off from bread, and brought down to tortillas.

The day after our survey was finished, as a relief we set out for a walk to the old stone quarries of Copan. Very soon we abandoned the path along the river, and turned off to the left. The ground was broken, the forest thick, and all the way we had an Indian before us with his machete, cutting down branches and saplings. The range lies about two miles north from the river, and runs east and west. At the foot of it we crossed a wild stream. The side of the mountain was overgrown with bushes and trees. The top was bare, and commanded a magnificent view of a dense forest, broken only by the winding of the Copan River, and the clearings for the haciendas of Don Gregorio and Don Miguel. The city was buried in forest and entirely hidden from sight. Imagination peopled the quarry with workmen, and laid bare the city to their view. Here, as the sculptor worked, he turned to the theatre of his glory, as the Greek did to the Acropolis of Athens, and dreamed of immortal fame. Little did he imagine that the time would come when his works would perish, his race be extinct, his city a desolation and abode for reptiles, for strangers to gaze at and wonder by what race it had once been inhabited.

The stone is of a soft grit. The range extended a long distance, seemingly unconscious that stone enough had been taken from its sides to build a city. How the huge masses were transported over the irregular and broken surface we had crossed, and particularly how one of them was set up on the top of a mountain two thousand feet high, it was impossible to conjecture. In many places were blocks which had been quarried out and rejected for some defect; and at one spot, midway in a ravine leading toward the river, was a gigantic block, much larger than any we saw in the city, which was probably on its way thither, to be carved and set up as an ornament, when the labours of the workmen were arrested. Like the unfinished blocks in the quarries at Assouan and on the Pentelican Mountain, it remains as a memorial of baffled human plans.

We remained all day on the top of the range. The close forest in which we had been labouring made us feel more sensibly the beauty of the extended view. On the top of the range was a quarried block. With the chay stone found among the ruins, and supposed to be the instrument of sculpture, we wrote our names upon it. They stand alone, and few will ever see them. Late in the afternoon we returned, and struck the river about a mile above the ruins, near a stone wall with a circular building and a pit, apparently for a reservoir.

As we approached our hut we saw two horses with side-saddles tied outside, and heard the cry of a child within. A party had arrived, consisting of an old woman and her daughter, son, and his wife and child, and their visit was to the medicos. We had had so many applications for remedios, our list of patients had increased so rapidly, and we had been so much annoyed every evening with weighing and measuring medicines, that, influenced also by the apprehensions before referred to, we had given out our intention to discontinue practice; but our fame had extended so far that these people had actually come from beyond San Antonio, more than thirty miles distant, to be cured, and it was hard to send them away without doing something for them. As Mr. C. was the medico in whom the public had most confidence, I scarcely paid any attention to them, unless to observe that they were much more respectable in dress and appearance than any patients we had had except the members of Don Grego-

rio's family; but during the evening I was attracted
by the tone in which the mother spoke of the daughter,
and for the first time noticed in the latter an extreme
delicacy of figure and a pretty foot, with a neat shoe
and clean stocking. She had a shawl drawn over her
head, and on speaking to her she removed the shawl,
and turned up a pair of the most soft and dovelike eyes
that mine ever met. She was the first of our patients
in whom I took any interest, and I could not deny myself the physician's privilege of taking her hand in
mine. While she thought we were consulting in regard to her malady, we were speaking of her interesting
face ; but the interest which we took in her was melancholy and painful, for we felt that she was a delicate
flower, born to bloom but for a season, and, even at the
moment of unfolding its beauties, doomed to die.

The reader is aware that our hut had no partition
walls. Don Miguel and his wife gave up their bed to
two of the women ; she herself slept on a mat on the
ground with the other. Mr. C. slept in his hammock,
I on my bed of Indian corn, and Don Miguel and the
young men under a shed out of doors.

I passed two or three days more in making the clearings and preparations, and then Mr. Catherwood had
occupation for at least a month. When we turned off
to visit these ruins, we did not expect to find employment for more than two or three days, and I did not
consider myself at liberty to remain longer. I apprehended a desperate chase after a government ; and fearing that among these ruins I might wreck my own political fortunes, and bring reproach upon my political
friends, I thought it safer to set out in pursuit. A
council was called at the base of an idol, at which Mr.
C. and I were both present. It was resumed in Don

Miguel's hut. The subject was discussed in all its bearings. All the excitement in the village had died away; we were alone and undisturbed; Mr. C. had under his dominion Bruno and Francisco, Don Miguel, his wife, and Bartalo. We were very reluctant to separate, but it was agreed, nem. con., for me to go on to Guatimala, and for Mr. Catherwood to remain and finish his drawings. Mr. Catherwood did remain, and, after many privations and difficulties, was compelled to leave on account of illness. He returned a second time and completed them, and I give the result of the whole.

At a short distance from the Temple, within terraced walls, probably once connected with the main building, are the "idols" which give the distinctive character to the ruins of Copan; and if the reader will look on the map, and follow the line marked "pathway to Don Miguel's house," toward the end on the right he will see the place where they stand. Near as they are, the forest was so dense that one could not be seen from the other. In order to ascertain their juxtaposition, we cut vistas through the trees, and took the bearings and distances; and I introduce them in the order in which they stand. The first is on the left of the pathway, at the point marked K. This statue is fallen and the face destroyed. It is twelve feet high, three feet three inches on one side, and four feet on the other. The altar is sunk in the earth, and we give no drawing of either.

At a distance of two hundred feet stands the one marked S. It is eleven feet eight inches high, three feet four inches on each side, and stands with its front to the east on a pedestal six feet square, the whole resting on a circular stone foundation sixteen feet in diameter. Before it, at a distance of eight feet ten inches, is an altar, partly buried, three feet three inches above the ground, seven feet square, and standing diagonally to the "idol." It is in high relief, boldly sculptured, and in a good state of preservation.

The engravings which follow represent the front and back view. The front, from the absence of a beard and from the dress, we supposed to be the figure of a woman, and the countenance presents traits of individuality, leading to the supposition that it is a portrait.

The back is a different subject. The head is in the centre, with complicated ornaments over it, the face broken, the border gracefully disposed, and at the foot are tablets of hieroglyphics. The altar is introduced on one side, and consists of four large heads strangely grouped together, so as not to be easily made out. It could not be introduced in its proper place without hiding the lower part of the "idol." In drawing the front, Mr. Catherwood always stood between the altar and the "idol."

F. Catherwood   J. Halpin

STONE IDOL (*front view*).

STONE IDOL (*back view*).

IDOL HALF BURIED.

A little behind this is the monument marked T. It is one of the most beautiful in Copan, and in workmanship is equal to the finest Egyptian sculpture. Indeed, it would be impossible, with the best instruments of modern times, to cut stones more perfectly. It stands at the foot of a wall of steps, with only the head and part of the breast rising above the earth. The rest is buried, and probably as perfect as the portion which is now visible. When we first discovered it, it was buried up to the eyes. Arrested by the beauty of the sculpture, and by its solemn and mournful position, we commenced excavating. As the ground was level up to that mark, the excavation was made by loosening the earth with the machete, and scooping it out with the hands. As we proceeded, the earth formed a wall around and increased the labour. The Indians struck so carelessly with their machetes, that, afraid to let them work near the stone, we cleared it with our own hands. It was impossible, however, to continue; the earth was matted together by roots which entwined and bound the monument. It required a complete throwing out of the earth for ten or twelve feet around ; and without any proper instruments, and afraid of injuring the sculpture, we preferred to let it remain, to be excavated by ourselves at some future time or by some future traveller. Whoever he may be, I almost envy him the satisfaction of doing it. The outline of the trees growing around it is given in the engraving.

Toward the south, at a distance of fifty feet, is a mass of fallen sculpture, with an altar, marked R on the map; and at ninety feet distance is the statue marked Q, standing with its front to the east, twelve feet high and three feet square, on an oblong pedestal seven feet in front and six feet two inches on the sides. Before it, at a distance of eight feet three inches, is an altar five feet eight inches long, three feet eight inches broad, and four feet high.

The face of this "idol" is decidedly that of a man. The beard is of a curious fashion, and joined to the mustache and hair. The ears are large, though not resembling nature; the expression is grand, the mouth partly open, and the eyeballs seem starting from the sockets; the intention of the sculptor seems to have been to excite terror. The feet are ornamented with sandals, probably of the skins of some wild animals, in the fashion of that day.

The back of this monument contrasts remarkably with the horrible portrait in front. It has nothing grotesque or pertaining to the rude conceits of Indians, but is noticeable for its extreme grace and beauty. In our daily walks we often stopped to gaze at it, and the more we gazed the more it grew upon us. Others seemed intended to inspire terror, and, with their altars before them, sometimes suggested the idea of a blind, bigoted, and superstitious people, and sacrifices of human victims. This always left a pleasing impression; and there was a higher interest, for we considered that in its medallion tablets the people who reared it had published a record of themselves, through which we might one day hold conference with a perished race, and unveil the mystery that hung over the city.

IDOL (*front view*).

F. Catherwood   J. Halpin

IDOL (*back view*).

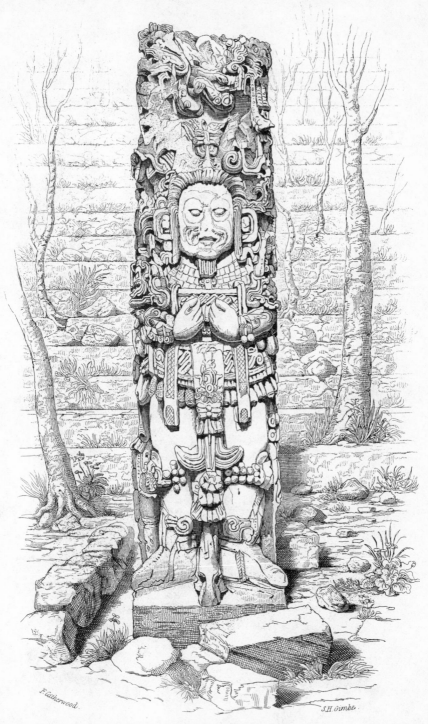

IDOL (*front view*).

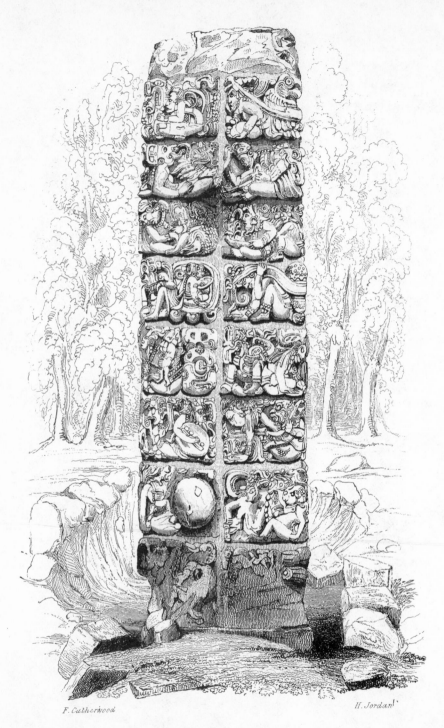

F. Catherwood

H. Jordan

IDOL (*back view*).

At a distance of one hundred and forty-two feet in a southeasterly direction is the idol marked P. It stands at the foot of a wall rising in steps to the height of thirty or forty feet; originally much higher, but the rest fallen and in ruins. Its face is to the north; its height eleven feet nine inches, the breadth of its sides three feet, and the pedestal is seven feet square. Before it, at a distance of twelve feet, is a colossal altar. It is of good workmanship, and has been painted red, though scarcely any vestige of the paint remains, and the surface is time-worn. The two engravings given opposite represent the front and back view. The former appears to represent the portrait of a king or hero, perhaps erected into a deity. It is judged to be a portrait, from certain marks of individuality in the features, also observable in most of the others, and its sex is ascertained by the beard, as in the Egyptian monuments, though this has a mustache, which is not found in Egyptian portraits.

The back of this idol, again, presents an entirely different subject, consisting of tablets, each containing two figures oddly grouped together, ill-formed, in some cases with hideous heads, while in others the natural countenance is preserved. The ornaments, diadems, and dresses are interesting, but what these personages are doing or suffering it is impossible to make out. This statue had suffered so much from the action of time and weather, that it was not always easy to make out the characters, the light being in all cases very bad, and coming through irregular openings among the branches of trees.

The stone of which all these altars and statues are made is a soft grit-stone from the quarries before referred to. At the quarries we observed many blocks with hard flint-stones distributed through them, which had been rejected by the workmen after they were quarried out. The back of this monument had contained two. Between the second and third tablets the flint has been picked out, and the sculpture is blurred ; the other, in the last row but one from the bottom, remains untouched. An inference from this is, that the sculptor had no instruments with which he could cut so hard a stone, and, consequently, that iron was unknown. We had, of course, directed our searches and inquiries particularly to this point, but did not find any pieces of iron or other metal, nor could we hear of any having ever been found there. Don Miguel had a collection of chay or flint stones, cut in the shape of arrow-heads, which *he* thought, and Don Miguel was no fool, were the instruments employed. They were sufficiently hard to scratch into the stone. Perhaps by men accustomed to the use of them, the whole of these deep relief ornaments might have been scratched, but the chay stones themselves looked as if they had been cut by metal.

The engraving opposite represents the altar as it stands before the last monument. It is seven feet square and four feet high, richly sculptured on all its sides. The front represents a death's head. The top is sculptured, and contains grooves, perhaps for the passage of the blood of victims, animal or human, offered in sacrifice. The trees in the engraving give an idea of the forest in which these monuments are buried.

F. Catherwood.

S. H. Gumber.

IDOL AND ALTAR.

F. Catherwood.

S.H. Gimber.

FALLEN IDOL.

At the distance of one hundred and twenty feet north is the monument marked O, which, unhappily, is fallen and broken. In sculpture it is the same with the beautiful half-buried monument before given, and, I repeat it, in workmanship equal to the best remains of Egyptian art. The fallen part was completely bound to the earth by vines and creepers, and before it could be drawn it was necessary to unlace them, and tear the fibres out of the crevices. The paint is very perfect, and has preserved the stone, which makes it more to be regretted that it is broken. The altar is buried, with the top barely visible, which, by excavating, we made out to represent the back of a tortoise.

The next engravings exhibit the front, back, and one of the sides of monument N, distant twenty feet from the last. It is twelve feet high, four feet on one side, three feet four inches on the other, and stands on a pedestal seven feet square, with its front to the west. There is no altar visible; probably it is broken and buried. The front view seems a portrait, probably of some deified king or hero. The two ornaments at the top appear like the trunk of an elephant, an animal unknown in that country. The crocodile's head is seven feet from it, but appears to have no connexion with it. This is four feet out of the ground, and is given in the plate as one of the many fragments found among the ruins.

The back presents an entirely different subject from the front. At the top is a figure sitting cross-legged, almost buried under an enormous headdress, and three of the compartments contain tablets of hieroglyphics.

Not to multiply engravings, I have omitted side views, as they are, in general, less interesting. This is particularly beautiful. The tablets of hieroglyphics are very distinct.

F. Catherwood.   A. L. Dick.

FRONT OF IDOL.

BACK OF IDOL.

F. Catherwood.   S.H Gimber.

SIDE OF IDOL.

At the distance of twenty-eight feet in the same direction is the statue marked M, which is fallen, and lies on its back, with a tree across it nearly lengthwise, leaving visible only the outline, feet, and sandals, both of which are well sculptured. The following engraving is a representation of it.

Opposite is a circular altar with two grooves on the top, three feet high, and five feet six inches in diameter, an engraving of which is here given.

The next three engravings are the front, back, and side view of the monument marked L, distant seventy-two feet north from the last, with its front toward the west, twelve feet high, three feet in front, two feet eight inches on the side, and the pedestal is six feet square. Before it, at a distance of eleven feet, is an altar very much defaced, and buried in the earth.

The front view is a portrait. The back is entirely made up of hieroglyphics, and each tablet has two hieroglyphics joined together, an arrangement which afterward we observed occasionally at Palenque. The side presents a single row of hieroglyphics, joined in the same manner. The tablets probably contain the history of the king or hero delineated, and the particular circumstances or actions which constituted his greatness.

I have now given engravings of all the most interesting monuments of Copan, and I repeat, they are accurate and faithful representations. I have purposely abstained from all comment. If the reader can derive from them but a small portion of the interest that we did, he will be repaid for whatever he may find unprofitable in these pages.

Of the moral effect of the monuments themselves, standing as they do in the depths of a tropical forest, silent and solemn, strange in design, excellent in sculpture, rich in ornament, different from the works of any other people, their uses and purposes, their whole history so entirely unknown, with hieroglyphics explaining all, but perfectly unintelligible, I shall not pretend to convey any idea. Often the imagination was pained in gazing at them. The tone which pervades the ruins is that of deep solemnity. An imaginative mind might

STONE IDOL (*front view*).

F. Catherwood.   A.L.Dick.

STONE IDOL (*back view*).

STONE IDOL (*side view*).

be infected with superstitious feelings. From constantly calling them by that name in our intercourse with the
Indians, we regarded these solemn memorials as "idols"
—deified kings and heroes—objects of adoration and
ceremonial worship. We did not find on either of the
monuments or sculptured fragments any delineations of
human, or, in fact, any other kind of sacrifice, but had
no doubt that the large sculptured stone invariably
found before each "idol" was employed as a sacrificial
altar. The form of sculpture most frequently met with
was a death's head, sometimes the principal ornament,
and sometimes only accessory; whole rows of them on
the outer wall, adding gloom to the mystery of the
place, keeping before the eyes of the living death and
the grave, presenting the idea of a holy city—the Mecca or Jerusalem of an unknown people.

In regard to the age of this desolate city I shall not
at present offer any conjecture. Some idea might perhaps be formed from the accumulations of earth and the
gigantic trees growing on the top of the ruined structures, but it would be uncertain and unsatisfactory.
Nor shall I at this moment offer any conjecture in regard to the people who built it, or to the time when or
the means by which it was depopulated, and became
a desolation and ruin; whether it fell by the sword, or
famine, or pestilence. The trees which shroud it may
have sprung from the blood of its slaughtered inhabitants; they may have perished howling with hunger;
or pestilence, like the cholera, may have piled its streets
with dead, and driven forever the feeble remnants from
their homes; of which dire calamities to other cities we
have authentic accounts, in eras both prior and subse-
quent to the discovery of the country by the Spaniards. One thing I believe, that its history is graven

on its monuments. No Champollion has yet brought to them the energies of his inquiring mind. Who shall read them?

> "Chaos of ruins! who shall trace the void,
> O'er the dim fragments cast a lunar light,
> And say 'here *was* or is,' where all is doubly night?"

In conclusion, I will barely remark, that if this is the place referred to by the Spanish historian as conquered by Hernando de Chaves, which I almost doubt, at that time its broken monuments, terraces, pyramidal structures, portals, walls, and sculptured figures were entire, and all were painted; the Spanish soldiers must have gazed at them with astonishment and wonder; and it seems strange that a European army could have entered it without spreading its fame through official reports of generals and exaggerated stories of soldiers. At least, no European army could enter such a city now without this result following; but the silence of the Spaniards may be accounted for by the fact that these conquerors of America were illiterate and ignorant adventurers, eager in pursuit of gold, and blind to everything else; or, if reports were made, the Spanish government, with a jealous policy observed down to the last moment of her dominion, suppressed everything that might attract the attention of rival nations to her American possessions.

CHAPTER VIII.

HAVING decided that, under the circumstances, it was
best to separate, we lost no time in acting upon the conclusion. I had difficulty in coming to a right understanding with my muleteer, but at length a treaty was
established. The mules were loaded, and at two
o'clock I mounted. Mr. C. accompanied me to the
edge of the woods, where I bade him farewell, and
left him to difficulties worse than we had apprehended.
I passed through the village, crossed the river, and,
leaving the muleteer on the bank, rode to the hacienda
of Don Gregorio ; but I was deprived of the satisfaction which I had promised myself at parting, of pouring upon him my indignation and contempt, by the consideration that Mr. Catherwood was still within the
reach of his influence ; and even now my hand is stay-
ed by the reflection that when Mr. C., in great distress,
robbed by his servant, and broken down by fever, took
refuge in his house, the don received him as kindly as
his bearish nature would permit. My only comfort
was in making the lordly churl foot up an account of
sixpences and shillings for eggs, milk, meat, &c., to the
amount of two dollars, which I put into his hands. I
afterward learned that I had elevated myself very much
in his estimation, and in that of the neighbourhood

generally, by my handsome conduct in not going off
without paying.*

My good understanding with the muleteer was of
short duration. At parting, Mr. C. and I had divided
our stock of plates, knives and forks, spoons, &c.,
and Augustin had put my share in the basket which had
carried the whole, and these, being loose, made such a
clattering that it frightened the mule. The beast ran
away, setting us all off together with a crashing noise,
till she threw herself among the bushes. We had a
scene of terrible confusion, and I escaped as fast as I
could from the hoarse and croaking curses of the muleteer.

For some distance the road lay along the river. The
Copan has no storied associations, but the Guadalquiv-
er cannot be more beautiful. On each side were mountains, and at every turn a new view. We crossed a
high range, and at four o'clock again came down upon
the river, which was here the boundary-line of the State
of Honduras. It was broad and rapid, deep, and broken by banks of sand and gravel. Fording it, I again
entered the State of Guatimala. There was no village, not even a house in sight, and no difficulty about
passport. Late in the afternoon, ascending a little eminence, I saw a large field with stone fences, and bars,
and cattle-yard, that looked like a Westchester farm.
We entered a gate, and rode up through a fine park to
a long, low, substantial-looking hacienda. It was the
house of Don Clementino, whom I knew to be the kins-
man of Don Gregorio, and the one of all others I would

---

* On Mr. Catherwood's second visit, finding the rancho of Don Miguel deserted, he rode to Don Gregorio's. The don had in the mean time been to Esquipulas, and learned our character from the cura; and it is due to him to say, that he
received Mr. C. kindly, and made many inquiries after me. The rest of the family were as cordial as before.

have avoided, but also the very one at which the muleteer had determined to contrive a halt. The family
consisted of a widow with a large family of children,
the principal of whom were Don Clementino, a young
man of twenty-one, and a sister of about sixteen or
seventeen, a beautiful fair-haired girl. Under the shed
was a party of young people in holyday dresses, and
five or six mules, with fanciful saddles, were tied to the
posts of the piazza. Don Clementino was jauntily
dressed in white jacket and trousers, braided and embroidered, a white cotton cap, and over it a steeple-
crowned glazed hat, with a silver cord twisted round as
a band, a silver ball with a sharp piece of steel as a
cockade, and red and yellow stripes under the brim.
He had the consequential air and feelings of a boy who
had suddenly become the head of an establishment, and
asked me, rather superciliously, if I had finished my visit to the " idols ;" and then, without waiting for an answer, if I could mend an accordion ; then, if I could
play on the guitar ; then to sell him a pair of pocket-
pistols which had been the admiration of Don Gregorio's household ; and, finally, if I had anything to sell.
With this young gentleman I should have been more
welcome as a pedler than an ambassador from any
court in Europe, though it must be admitted that I
was not travelling in a very imposing way. Finding
I had nothing to make a bargain for, he picked up a
guitar, danced off to his own music, and sat down on
the earthen floor of the piazza to play cards.

Within, preparations were going on for a wedding at
the house of a neighbour, two leagues distant, and a
little before dark the young men and girls appeared
dressed for the journey. All were mounted, and, for
the first time, I admired exceedingly the fashion of the

country in riding. My admiration was called forth by
the sister of Don Clementino and the happy young gal-
lant who escorted her. Both rode the same mule and
on the same saddle. She sat sidewise before him; his
right arm encircled her waist; at starting, the mule was
restiff, and he was obliged, from necessity, to support
her in her seat, to draw her close to himself; her ear
invited a whisper; and when she turned her face toward him her lips almost touched his. I would have
given all the honours of diplomacy for his place.

Don Clementino was too much of a coxcomb to set
off in this way; he had a fine mule gayly caparisoned,
swung a large basket-hilted sword through a strap in
the saddle, buckled on a pair of enormous spurs, and,
mounting, wound his poncha around his waist, so that
the hilt of the sword appeared about six inches above it;
giving the animal a sharp thrust with his spurs, he drove
her up the steps, through the piazza, and down the other
side, and asked me if I wanted to buy her. I declined;
and, to my great satisfaction, he started to overtake the
others, and left me alone with his mother, a respectable-looking, gray-haired old lady, who called together
all the servants and Indian children for vesper prayers.
I am sorry to say it, but for the first time I was reminded that it was Sunday. I stood in the door, and it was
interesting to see them all kneeling before the figure of
the Virgin. An old gray-nosed mule walked up the
piazza, and, stopping by my side, put his head in the
door, when, more forward than I, he walked in, gazed
a moment at the figure of the Virgin, and, without disturbing anybody, walked out again.

Soon after I was called in to supper, which consisted
of fried beans, fried eggs, and tortillas. The beans and
eggs were served on heavy silver dishes, and the tortil-

las were laid in a pile by my side. There was no plate, knife, fork, or spoon. Fingers were made before forks ; but bad habits make the latter, to a certain degree, necessary. Poultry, mutton, beef, and the like, do not come amiss to fingers, but beans and fried eggs were puzzling. How I managed I will not publish ; but, from appearances afterward, the old lady could not have supposed that I had been at all at a loss. I slept in an outbuilding constructed of small poles and thatched, and for the whole paid eighteen and three quarter cents. I gave a pair of earrings to a woman whom I supposed to be a servant, but who, I found, was only a visiter, and who went away at the same time that I did.

At a distance of two leagues from the hacienda we passed the house of the wedding-party. The dancing was not yet over, and I had a strong fancy to see again the fair-haired sister of Don Clementino. Having no better excuse, I determined to call him out and " talk mule." As I rode up, the doorway and the space thence to the middle of the room were filled with girls, all dressed in white, with the roses in their hair faded, and the brightness of their eyes somewhat dimmed by a night's dissipation. The sister of Don Clementino was modest and retiring, and, as if she suspected my object, shrank back from observation, while he made all open a way for him and his guitar. I had no idea of buying his mule, but made him an offer, which, to my surprise and regret at the time, he accepted ; but virtue is its own reward, and the mule proved a most faithful animal.

Mounted on my new purchase, we commenced ascending the great Sierra, which divides the streams of the Atlantic from those that empty into the Pacific Ocean. The ascent was rugged and toilsome, but in two hours we reached the top. The scenery was wild and grand, I have no doubt; but the fact is, it rained very hard all the time; and while I was floundering among mud-holes I would have given the chance of the sublime for a good Macadamized road. Mr. Catherwood, who crossed on a clear day, says that the view from the top, both ways, was the most magnificent he saw in the country. Descending, the clouds were lifted, and I looked down upon an almost boundless plain, running from the foot of the Sierra, and afar off saw, standing alone in the wilderness, the great church of Esquipulas, like the Church of the Holy Sepulchre in Jerusalem, and the Caaba in Mecca, the holiest of temples. My muleteer was very anxious to stop at a collection of huts on this side of the town, and told me first that the place was occupied by Carrera's soldiers, and then that he was ill. I had a long and magnificent descent to the foot of the Sierra. The plain reminded me of the great waste-places of Turkey and Asia Minor, but was more beautiful, being bounded by immense mountains. For three hours the church was our guide. As we approached, it stood out more clearly defined against mountains whose tops were buried in the clouds.

Late in the afternoon we entered the town and rode up to the convent. I was a little nervous, and presented my passport as a letter of introduction; but could I have doubted the hospitality of a padre? Don Gregorio's reception made me feel more deeply the welcome of the cura of Esquipulas. None can know the value of hospitality but those who have felt the want of it, and they can never forget the welcome of strangers in a strange land.

The whole household of the cura turned out to assist, and in a few minutes the mules were munching corn in

ESQUIPULAS.

F. Catherwood.

the yard, while I was installed in the seat of honour in the convent. It was by far the largest and best building in the place. The walls were three or four feet thick; a large portico extended in front; the entrance was by a wide hall, used as a sleeping-place for servants, and communicating with a courtyard in the rear; on the left was a large sala or reception-room, with lofty windows and deep recesses; on one side of the wall was a long wooden settee, with a high back, and arms at each end; before it was a massive unpolished mahogany table, and above hung a painting of our Saviour; against the wall were large antiquated chairs, the backs and seats covered with leather, and studded with nails having large brass heads.

The cura was a young man, under thirty, of delicate frame, and his face beamed with intelligence and refinement of thought and feeling. He was dressed in a long black bombazet gown, drawn tight around the body, with a blue border around the neck, and a cross was suspended to his rosary. His name was *Jesus* Maria Guttierrez. It was the first time I had ever heard that name applied to a human being, and even in him it seemed a profanation.

On a visit to him, and breaking the monotony of his secluded life, was an old schoolfellow and friend, Colonel San Martin, of Honduras, who had been wounded in the last battle against Morazan, and was staying at the convent to recover his health and strength. His case showed the distracted state of the country. His father was of the same politics with himself, and his brother was fighting on the other side in the battle in which he was wounded.

They gave me disagreeable information in regard to my road to Guatimala. Carrera's troops had fallen back from the frontiers of San Salvador, and occupied the whole line of villages to the capital. They were mostly Indians, ignorant, intemperate, and fanatic, who could not comprehend my official character, could not read my passport, and, in the excited state of the country, would suspect me as a stranger. They had already committed great atrocities; there was not a curate on the whole road; and to attempt traversing it would be to expose myself to robbery and murder. I was very loth to protract my journey, but it would have been madness to proceed; in fact, no muleteer would undertake to go on with me, and I was obliged to turn my eyes to Chiquimula and the road I had left. The cura said I must be guided by him. I put myself in his hands, and at a late hour lay down to rest with the strange consciousness of being a welcome guest.

I was awaked by the sound of the matin bell, and accompanied the cura to mass. The church for everyday use was directly opposite the convent, spacious and gloomy, and the floor was paved with large square bricks or tiles. Rows of Indian women were kneeling around the altar, cleanly dressed, with white mantillas over their heads, but without shoes or stockings. A few men stood up behind or leaned against the walls.

We returned to breakfast, and afterward set out to visit the only object of interest, the great church of the pilgrimage, the Holy Place of Central America. Every year, on the fifteenth of January, pilgrims visit it, even from Peru and Mexico; the latter being a journey not exceeded in hardship by the pilgrimage to Mecca. As in the East, " it is not forbidden to trade during the pilgrimage ;" and when there are no wars to make the roads unsafe, eighty thousand people have assembled among the mountains to barter and pay homage to " our Lord of Esquipulas."

The town contains a population of about fifteen hundred Indians. There was one street nearly a mile long, with mud houses on each side ; but most of the houses were shut, being occupied only during the time of the fair. At the head of this street, on elevated ground, stood the great church. About half way to it we crossed a bridge over a small stream, one of the sources of the great Lempa. It was the first stream I had seen that emptied into the Pacific Ocean, and I saluted it with reverence. Ascending by a flight of massive stone steps in front of the church, we reached a noble platform a hundred and fifty feet broad, and paved with bricks a foot square. The view from this platform of the great plain and the high mountains around was magnificent ; and the church, rising in solitary grandeur in a region of wildness and desolation, seemed almost the work of enchantment. The façade was rich with stucco ornaments and figures of saints larger than life ; at each angle was a high tower, and over the dome a spire, rearing aloft in the air the crown of that once proud power which wrested the greatest part of America from its rightful owners, ruled it for three centuries with a rod of iron, and now has not within it a foot of land or a subject to boast of.

We entered the church by a lofty portal, rich in sculptured ornaments. Inside was a nave with two aisles, separated by rows of pilasters nine feet square, and a lofty dome, guarded by angels with expanded wings. On the walls were pictures, some drawn by artists of Guatimala, and others that had been brought from Spain ; and the recesses were filled with statues, some of which were admirably well executed. The pulpit was covered with gold leaf, and the altar protected by an iron railing with a silver balustrade, ornamented with six silver pillars about two feet high, and two angels standing as guardians on the steps. In front of the altar, in a rich shrine, is an image of the Saviour on the cross, " our Lord of Esquipulas," to whom the church is consecrated, famed for its power of working miracles. Every year thousands of devotees ascend the steps of his temple on their knees, or laden with a heavy cross, who are not permitted to touch the sacred image, but go away contented in obtaining a piece of riband stamped with the words " Dulce nombre de Jesus."

We returned to the convent, and while I was sitting with Colonel San Martin the curate entered, and, closing the door, asked me if my servant was faithful. Augustin's face was an unfortunate letter of recommendation. Colonel M'Donald, Don Francisco, and, as I afterward heard, General Cascara, distrusted him. I told the cura all I knew of him, and mentioned his conduct at Comotan; but he still cautioned me to beware of him. Soon after, Augustin, who seemed to suspect that he had not made a very favourable impression, asked me for a dollar to pay for a confession. My intelligent friend was not free from the prejudices of education; and though he could not at once change his opinion so warmly expressed, he said that Augustin had been well brought up.

In the course of the day I had an opportunity of seeing what I afterward observed throughout all Central America: the life of labour and responsibility passed by the cura in an Indian village, who devotes himself faithfully to the people under his charge. Besides officiating in all the services of the church, visiting the

sick, and burying the dead, my worthy host was looked
up to by every Indian in the village as a counsellor,
friend, and father. The door of the convent was always open, and Indians were constantly resorting to
him : a man who had quarrelled with his neighbour ; a
wife who had been badly treated by her husband ; a
father whose son had been carried off as a soldier ; a
young girl deserted by her lover : all who were in trouble or affliction, came to him for advice and consolation,
and none went away without it. And, besides this, he
was principal director of all the public business of the
town ; the right hand of the alcalde ; and had been
consulted whether or not I ought to be considered a
dangerous person. But the performance of these multifarious duties, and the excitement and danger of the
times, were wearing away his frame. Four years before he gave up the capital, and took upon himself this
curacy, and during that time he had lived a life of labour, anxiety, and peril ; cut off from all the delights
of social intercourse that make labour welcome, beloved by the Indians, but without any to sympathize
with him in his thoughts and feelings. Once the troops
of Morazan invaded the town, and for six months he
lay concealed in a cave of the mountains, supported by
Indians. Lately the difficulties of the country had increased, and the cloud of civil war was darker than
ever. He mourned, but, as he said, he had not long to
mourn ; and the whole tone of his thoughts and conversation was so good and pure, that it seemed like a
green spot in a sandy desert. We sat in the embrasure
of a large window ; within, the room was already dark.
He took a pistol from the window-sill, and, looking at
it, said, with a faint smile, that the cross was his protection ; and then he put his thin hand in mine, and

told me to feel his pulse. It was slow and feeble, and seemed as if every beat would be the last; but he said it was always so; and, rising suddenly, added that this was the hour of his private devotions, and retired to his room. I felt as if a good spirit had flitted away.

My anxiety to reach Guatimala would not permit me long to enjoy the cura's hospitality. I intended to discharge my muleteer; but, unable to replace him immediately, and unwilling to lose another day, I was obliged to retain him. The usual course was to leave Esquipulas in the afternoon, and ride four leagues; but, having seven mules and only four cargoes, I determined to make these four leagues and the next day's journey also in one. Early in the morning I started. When I bade farewell, the priest and the soldier stood side by side, pictures of Christian humility and man's pride, and both recommended me to God at parting.

We crossed the plain; the mountains of Esquipulas seemed to have gained in grandeur; in half an hour commenced ascending the Mountain of Quezaltepeque, thickly wooded, and, like that of Mico, muddy and full of gullies and deep holes. Heavy clouds were hanging over it, and as we ascended it rained hard; but before reaching the top the clouds were lifted, the sun shone, and the plain of Esquipulas, with the great Sierra behind, covered with lofty pines, and clouds chasing each other over its sides, all blended together, made one of the grandest spectacles I ever beheld; and the great church still presented itself for the farewell view of the pilgrim. But the gleam of sunshine did not last long, and again the rain poured; for a while I had great satisfaction in seeing the muleteer drenched and hearing him grumble; but an unaccountable fit of good-humour came over me, and I lent him my bear's skin greatcoat. At intervals the sun shone, and we saw at a great distance below us the village of Quezaltepeque. The descent was very precipitous, and the mud-holes and gullies were very deep; and the clouds which hung over the mountain were typical of my fortune. Mr. Catherwood, who followed on this road about three weeks afterward, heard from the Padre of Quezaltepeque that a plan had been formed to murder and rob me, on the supposition that I had a large amount of money about my person, which laudable project was defeated by my crossing in the morning instead of the afternoon, as is usually done.

We passed through Quezaltepeque without dismounting. It is usual, in dividing the stages to Guatimala, to make an afternoon's journey to this place and sleep. It was now but eleven o'clock, clear and bright as a September day at home. Leaving the village, we crossed a beautiful stream, at which some women were washing. Very soon we ascended again, and on the top of the mountain came to an abrupt precipice, forming the side of a deep ravine. We descended by a narrow path on the very edge of the precipice, part of the way on a narrow protruding ledge, and in other places by a path built against the rock to the bottom of the ravine. On the other side rose another precipitous wall. The ravine was deep and narrow, and wild to sublimity. The stream ran through it over a rocky bed, and for some distance the road lay in this bed. We ascended by a steep and difficult path to the top of the other side of the ravine, and rode for some distance along its edge. The opposite side was a perpendicular mass of limestone rock, black with exposure, and in some places were patches of grass on a brown ground, lighted up occasionally by brief gleams of sunshine. We descended again to the very bottom of the ravine, and, crossing the stream, ascended almost immediately a narrow path built along the side of the precipice to the top, being on the same side from which we started. It is impossible to give any idea of the wildness of this double crossing of the ravine. It terminated abruptly, and at the extreme end, on a point, was a small hacienda, on one side looking directly up this awful opening, and on the other upon a soft valley.

At three o'clock we struck the rituello of San Jacinto. On the opposite side was a fine table of land, with mountains rising beyond, and covered to the top with noble pines. There was no cultivation, and the whole country was in primeval wildness. At five o'clock we crossed the stream and entered the village of San Jacinto. It consisted of a collection of huts, some made of poles and some plastered with mud. The church was of the same simple construction. On each side was an arbour thatched with leaves of Indian corn, and at the corners were belfries, with three bells each. In front were two gigantic Ceiba trees, the roots of which ran along even with the ground more than a hundred feet, and the branches spread to an equal extent.

The village was under the care of the cura of Quezaltepeque, who was then at San Jacinto. I rode up to his house and presented the letter of the cura of Esquipulas. My muleteer, without unloading the mules, threw himself down on the piazza, and, with my greatcoat on his unthankful body, began abusing me for killing him with long marches. I retorted; and before the padre had time to recover from his surprise at our visit, he was confounded by our clamour.

But he was a man who could bear a great deal, being above six feet, broad shouldered, and with a protuber-

ance in front that required support to keep it from falling. His dress consisted of a shirt and pair of pantaloons, with button-holes begging for employment; but
he had a heart as big as his body, and as open as his
wearing apparel; and when I told him I had ridden
from Esquipulas that day, he said I must remain a week
to recruit. As to going the next day, he would not
hear of it; and, in fact, very soon I found that it was
impossible without other aid, for my abominable muleteer filled up the measure of his iniquities by falling ill
with a violent fever.

At my earnest solicitation, the padre endeavoured to
procure me mules for the next day, and during the evening we had a levee of villagers. The man upon whom
he principally relied said that it was dangerous travelling; that two Ingleses had been arrested in Honduras,
and had escaped, but their muleteers and servants were
murdered. I could perhaps have thrown some light
upon this story, but did not think it worth while to
know anything about such suspicious characters. The
padre was distressed that he could not serve me, but at
length said that a man of my rank and character (I had
shown him my passport, and Augustin had fired the Balize guns) ought to have every facility, and he would
provide for me himself; and he ordered a man to go
early in the morning to his hacienda for mules; after
which, fatigued with such unusual efforts, he threw his
gigantic body into a hammock, and swung himself to
sleep.

The household of the padre consisted of two young
men, one deaf and dumb, and the other a fool. The
former possessed extraordinary vivacity and muscular
powers, and entertained the padre by his gesticulations,
stories, and sleight-of-hand tricks, and particularly with

a steel puzzle. There was something intensely interesting in the kindness with which the padre played with him, and the earnestness with which he hung around his gigantic master. At times the young man became so excited that it seemed as if he would burst in the effort to give utterance to his thoughts; but all ended in a feeble sound, which grated upon my nerves, and seemed to knit him more closely to the good-hearted padre. The latter was continually changing the puzzle, but the ingenuity of the lad could not be defeated. The poor simpleton meanwhile looked on with admiration. The padre offered him half a dollar if he could open it, and both he and the deaf and dumb lad laughed at the awkward attempts of the simpleton. The padre finished with a warm panegyric upon the worth of both, which the deaf and dumb boy seemed to understand and thank him for, but which he that had ears seemed not to hear.

The padre insisted on my taking his own cartaret, which was unusually neat, and had a moscheto-netting. It was my best bed since I left Colonel M'Donald's at Balize. Before I was up he stood over me with a flask of agua ardiente. Soon after came chocolate, with a roll of sweet bread; and finding that it was impossible to get away that day, I became a willing victim to his hospitality. At nine o'clock we had breakfast; at twelve, fruit; at two, dinner; at five, chocolate and sweet bread; and at eight, supper, with constant intermediate invitations to agua ardiente, which the padre, with his hand on that prominent part of his own body, said was good for the stomach. In everything except good feeling he was the complete antipodes of the cura of Esquipulas. I had had some suspicion that my muleteer was not as unwell as he pretended; but his neglect of the padre's good fare convinced me that he was really in a bad way. I gave him some medicine, but I believe he suspected me, and was afraid to take it.

At twelve o'clock the mules sent for by the padre arrived, with a strapping young ladino as muleteer ; but they were not in a condition to set off that day. In the afternoon I took a long walk on the bank of the river, and, returning, stopped under one of the Ceiba trees, where a travelling merchant was displaying his wares, consisting of two trunks of striped cottons, beads, horn combs, scissors, &c. His mule was tied by a long rope, and a pair of pistols lay on one of the boxes.

Passing on, I met a party of women, dressed in white, with red shawls over the tops of their heads. I have seen enough of fancy colours in women to remove some prejudices, but retain an oldfashioned predilection for white faces; and here I remarked that the whitest women were the prettiest, though the padre did not agree with me entirely. Under the shed of a deserted house near by was an old Indian with ten or twelve Indian girls, teaching them the catechism. They were dressed in red plaid cotton, drawn round the waist and tied in a knot on the left side, and a white handkerchief over the shoulders. Other parties were out in different places, organizing for a village fête in honour of some saint ; and toward evening, while sitting with the padre, now dressed in his long black gown, a procession advanced, headed by the oldest man in the village, with white hair and beard, and a lame man and two or three associates playing on violins. Before reaching the house they set off five or six rockets, and then all went up and saluted the padre, kissing the back of his hand; the women went inside, carrying bundles wrapped in clean white napkins ; and when I

went in to take my chocolate, I found the table piled
up with cakes and confectionary. Afterward all went
to the church for vesper prayers. I could but think,
what afterward impressed itself upon me more and
more in every step of my journey in that country, blessed is the village that has a padre.

During the day, the deaf and dumb boy had contrived several times to make me understand that he
wished to accompany me, and in the evening the padre
concluded to make him happy by giving him a journey
to Guatimala. Early in the morning the convent was
in commotion. The good padre was unused to fitting
out an expedition for Guatimala. Many things were
wanting besides the mules, and the village was laid
under contribution. During the bustle, a single soldier
entered the village, and created an alarm that he was
the pioneer of others come to quarter upon them. The
padre told him who I was, and that the guard must not
molest me. At length all was ready; a large concourse
of people, roused by the requisitions of the padre, were
at the door, and among them two men with violins.
The padre directed his own gigantic energies particularly to the eatables ; he had put up chocolate, bread,
sausages, and fowl; a box of cakes and confectionary ;
and, as the finale, the deaf and dumb lad came out of
the house, holding at arm's length above his head the
whole side of an ox, with merely the skin taken off and
the ribs cracked, which was spread as a wrapper over
one of the cargoes, and secured by a netting. A large
pot, with the bottom upward, was secured on the top
of another cargo. The padre took a kind leave of me,
and a most affectionate one of the deaf and dumb lad ;
and at nine o'clock, with violins playing, and a turn-
out that would have astonished my city friends, I made

another start for the capitol. A low groan from the
piazza reminded me of my muleteer. I dismounted,
and, at the moment of parting, exchanged a few words
of kindness. His brawny figure was prostrated by fever; at times he had vexed me almost beyond endu-
rance; but, with all my malice against him, I could not
have wished him in a worse condition. The boy sat
by his side, apparently softened by the illness of his
master, and indifferent as to my going.

For the first time in a long while we had a level
road. The land was rich and productive; brown sugar
sold for three cents a pound, and white lump, even under their slow process of making it, for eight cents,
and indigo could be raised for two shillings a pound.
I was riding quietly, when four soldiers sprang into the
road almost at my mule's head. They were perfectly
concealed until I approached, and their sudden appearance was rather footpad-like. They could not read my
passport, and said that they must conduct me to Chiquimula. My road lay a little off from that town; and,
fortunately, while under escort, the soldier whom I had
seen in San Jacinto overtook us, satisfied them, and released me. A short distance beyond I recognised the
path by which we turned off to go to Copan. Three
weeks had not elapsed, and it seemed an age. We
passed by the old church of Chiquimula, and, winding
up the same zigzag path by which we had descended,
crossed the mountain, and descended to the plain of
Zacapa and the Motagua River, which I hailed as an
old acquaintance. It was growing late, and we saw
no signs of habitation. A little before dark, on the top
of a small eminence on the right, we saw a little boy,
who conducted us to the village of San Rosalie, beautifully situated on a point formed by the bend of the river.

The village consisted of a miserable collection of huts;
before the door of the best was a crowd of people, who
did not ask us to stop, and we rode up to one of the
poorest. All we wanted was sacate* for the mules.
The stores of the padre were abundant for me, and the
deaf and dumb lad cut a few ribs from the side of the
ox, and prepared supper for himself and the muleteer.

While supping we heard a voice of lamentation from
the house before which the crowd was assembled. After dark I walked over, and found that they were mourning over the dead. Inside were several women; one
was wringing her hands, and the first words I distinguished were, " Oh, our Lord of Esquipulas, why have
you taken him away ?" She was interrupted by the
tramp of horses' hoofs, and a man rode up, whose figure
in the dark I could not see, but who, without dismounting, in a hoarse voice said that the priest asked six dollars to bury the corpse. One of the crowd cried out,
" Shame! shame!" and others said they would bury it
in el campo, the field. The horseman, in the same
hoarse voice, said that it was the same if buried in the
road, the mountain, or the river, the priest must have
his fee. There was a great outcry; but the widow, in a
weeping tone, declared that the money must be paid,
and then renewed her exclamations: " My only help,
my consolation, my head, my heart; you who was so
strong, who could lift a ceroon of indigo :" " you said
you would go and buy cattle;" " I said, ' yes; bring me
fine linen and jewelry.'" The words, and the piercing
tone of distress, reminded me of a similar scene I had
once beheld on the banks of the Nile. By invitation
of one of the friends I entered the house. The corpse

* Sacate means any kind of grass or leaves for mules. The best is sacate
de maize, or the stalks and leaves of Indian corn.

lay on the ground, in a white cotton dress extending from the neck to the feet. It was that of a young man, not more than twenty-two, with the mustache just budding on his upper lip, tall, and but a month before so strong that he could "lift a ceroon of indigo." He had left home to buy cattle, returned with a fever, and in a week was dead. A bandage was tied under his chin to hold up his jaw; his thin wrists were secured across his breast; and his taper fingers held a small crucifix made of corn-husks stitched together. On each side of his head was a lighted candle, and ants, which burden the ground, were swarming over his face. The widow did not notice me, but the mother and two young sisters asked me if I had no remedios; if I could not cure him; if I could have cured him if I had seen him before.

I left the bereaved family and withdrew. The man who had asked me to enter met me at the door, and gave me a seat among the friends. He inquired about my country, where it was, and whether the customs were like theirs; and very soon, but for the lamentations of the widow, many would have forgotten that a few yards from them lay a dead friend.

I remained with them an hour, and then returned to my hut. The piazza was full of hogs; the interior was a perfect piggery, full of fleas and children; and the woman, with a cigar in her mouth, and the harshest voice I ever heard, still brought in child after child, and piled them up on the floor. My men were already asleep outside; and borrowing an undressed ox-hide, I spread it on the floor at the end of the house; upon this I laid my pellon, and upon that I laid myself. The night before I had slept under a moscheto netting! Oh, padre of San Jacinto, that a man of my "rank and character" should come to this! The woman was sleepless; a dozen times she came out to smoke a cigar or to drive away the hogs; and her harsh voice, and the screams from the house of mourning, made me rejoice when the cocks crew for morning.

CHAPTER IX.

Chimalapa.—The Cabildo.—A Scene of Revelry.—Gustatoya.—A Hunt for Robbers.—Approach to Guatimala.—Beautiful Scenery.—Volcanoes of Agua and Fuego.—First View of the City.—Entry into the City.—First Impressions.—The Diplomatic Residence.—Parties in Central America.—Murder of Vicepresident Flores.—Political State of Guatimala.—An embarrassing Situation.—The Constituent Assembly.—Military Police.

At peep of day I bathed in the Motagua. In the mean time the deaf and dumb boy prepared chocolate, and the corpse of the young man was borne to its final resting-place. I went over to the desolate house, bade farewell to the mourners, and resumed my journey. Again we had on our right the Motagua River and the mountains of Vera Paz. The road was level; it was excessively hot, and we suffered from thirst. At noon we stopped two hours at the village of Fisioli. Late in the afternoon we came upon a table of land covered with trees bearing a flower, looking like apple-trees in blossom, and cactus or tunos, with branches from three to fifteen feet long. I was in advance; and having been in the saddle all day, and wishing to relieve my mule, I dismounted and walked. A man overtook me on horseback, who touched me by telling me that my mule was tired. The mule, unused to being led, pulled back, and my new acquaintance followed, whipping her; and remembering the fable, and that I could not please everybody, I mounted, and we rode into Chimalapa together.

It was a long, straggling village, with a large church, but there was no cura, and I rode to the cabildo. This, besides being the town-house, is a sort of caravansary or stopping-place for travellers, being a remnant of Oriental usages still existing in Spain, and introduced into her former American possessions. It was a large building, situated on the plaza, plastered and whitewashed. At one end the alcalde was holding a sort of court, and at the other were the gratings of a prison. Between them was a room about thirty feet by twenty, with naked walls, and destitute of chair, bench, or table. The luggage was brought in, the hammock hung up, and the alcalde sent me my supper. Hearing the sound of a drum and violin, I walked to the house whence it issued, which was crowded with men and women smoking, lounging in hammocks, dancing, and drinking agua ardiente, in celebration of a marriage. The night before I had been present at a death-scene. This was an exhibition of disgusting revelry, and the prominent vagabond was disposed to pick a quarrel with me ; seeing which, I quietly walked back to the cabildo, shut the door, and betook myself to my hammock.

We started early. Leaving the town, for some distance on each side was a fence made of a rail upon crotches four feet high, and filled with long pieces of tunos. The road was the same as we had found it on the preceding day, level, and abounding with the cactus. Again it was desperately hot, and in the afternoon we saw at the foot of a high mountain a cluster of cocoanut-trees, glittering in the sunbeams like plates of silver, and concealing the town of Gustatoya. At four o'clock we entered the town, beautifully situated, overlooking a valley in the rear of the square waving with Indian corn, and rode up to the house of the brother of Donna Bartola, our hostess of Gualan, to whom I was recommended by her.

I had a good supper of eggs, frigoles, chocolate, tortillas, and was lying in a hammock with my boots off when

the alcalde entered with a sword under his arm, followed by my host and several other persons, and told me
that a party of robbers was out after me; that he had
men on their traces, and wished to borrow my arms
and servants. The latter I was willing enough to lend,
for I knew they would find their way back; but the former, I thought, were more secure under my own eye.
Being on the main road, I considered it so safe that I
had that day taken off the caps of my pistols and gun;
but, drawing on my boots, recapping and distributing
my surplus arms, we sallied forth. The muleteer would
not go, but the deaf and dumb lad, with a face of fire,
drew his machete and followed.

It was pitchy dark, and on first going out from the
light I could not see at all, but stumbled along after my
companions, who moved swiftly and without noise
through the plaza, and along the whole length of the
town. In the suburbs we approached a hut which
stood alone, with the side toward us, closed, but the
light of a fire issued from both ends; and here it was
supposed the robbers were, unconscious of pursuit or
suspicion. After a brief consultation, it was agreed
that the party should separate, and one half enter at
each end; and the alcalde's charge was to shoot the
villains rather than let them escape. Stealing toward
the hut, we rushed in at the same time from the opposite sides, and captured an old woman, who sat on the
ground replenishing the fire. She was not surprised at
our visit, and, with a bitter laugh, said the birds had
flown. At that moment we heard the report of a musket, which was recognised as the signal of the men
who had been stationed to watch them. All rushed
out; another report hurried us on faster, and very soon
we reached the foot of a mountain. As we ascended,

the alcalde said that he saw a man crawling on his hands and feet up the side of the mountain, and, snatching my double-barrelled gun, fired at him as coolly as he would have done at a woodcock ; all scattered in pursuit, and I was left with Augustin and the deaf and dumb boy.

Moving on, but not very fast, and looking back occasionally to the distant lights in the village, with an unknown mountain before me and a dark night, I began to think that it was about enough for me to defend myself when attacked ; although the affair was got up on my account, it was straining a point for me to pass the night in helping to rid the town of its robbers.   Next I reflected that, if the gentlemen we were in pursuit of should take it into their heads to double, my cap and white dress made me conspicuous, and it might be awkward to meet them at this place ; and, in order to gain time for consideration what it was best to do, I walked back toward the town, and had not fully made up my mind when I reached the plaza.

Here I stopped, and in a few minutes a man passed, who said that he had met two of the robbers on the main road, and that they had told him they would catch me in the morning.   They had got it into their heads that I was an aiddecamp of Carrera, returning from Balize with a large amount of money to pay the troops. In about an hour the alcalde and his posse comitatus returned.   I had no idea of being robbed by mistake ; and, knowing the facility with which the robbers might go ahead and take a long shot at me, I asked the alcalde to furnish me with two men to go in advance and keep a lookout ; but I was heartily sick of the country and the excitement of its petty alarms.

Daylight dispelled the gloom which night had cast

over my spirits. Leaving Gustatoya, for some distance
I rode through a cultivated country, and the fields were
divided by fences. Very soon I forgot all apprehensions of robbers, and, tired of the slow pace of the cargo-mules, rode on, leaving them far behind. At eleven
o'clock I entered a ravine so wild that I thought it could
not be the main road to Guatimala ; there were no
mule-tracks visible ; and, returning, I took another
road, the result of which was that I lost my way, and
rode the whole day alone. I could gain no certain
intelligence of Augustin and the muleteer, but continued on in the belief that they were before me. Push-
ing on rapidly, at dark I rode up to a hacienda on one
side of the road, at which I was very kindly received
by the proprietor, who was a mulatto, and, to my great
surprise, I learned that I had advanced to within one
long day's journey of Guatimala. He made me anxious, however, about the safety of my luggage ; but for
that night I could do nothing. I lay down opposite
a large household altar, over which was a figure of the
Virgin. At about ten o'clock I was roused by the arrival of Augustin and the muleteer. Besides their apprehensions about me, they had had their own difficulties ; two of the mules broke down, and they were
obliged to stop and let them rest, and feed them.

Early the next morning, leaving the luggage with
the muleteer (which, by-the-way, was at that time a
very imprudent proceeding), and taking merely a
change of apparel, I set out with Augustin. Almost
immediately we commenced ascending a rugged mountain, very steep, and commanding at every step a wild
and magnificent view ; and from the top saw, at a great
distance below us, in the hollow of an amphitheatre of
mountains, the village of El Puente, the ground around

which was white, and trodden hard by caravans of mules. We descended to the village, and crossed the bridge, which was laid on a stone arch, thrown across a ravine with a cataract foaming through it; at this point we were completely encircled by mountains, wild to sublimity, and reminding me of some of the finest parts of Switzerland. On the other side of the bridge we commenced ascending another mountain. The road was winding, and, when very high up, the view of the village and bridge at the immense distance below was surpassingly fine. Descending a short distance, we passed a village of huts, situated on the ridge of the mountain, commanding on both sides a view of an extensive valley four or five thousand feet below us. Continuing on this magnificent ridge, we descended upon a table of rich land, and saw a gate opening into grounds which reminded me of park scenery in England, undulating, and ornamented with trees. In the midst of this stood the hacienda of San José, a long, low stone building, with a corridor in front; it was one of those situations which, when least expected, touch a tender chord, call up cherished associations, make a traveller feel as though he could linger around it forever, and particularly welcome to us, as we had not breakfasted.

It was a hacienda de ganados, or cattle-hacienda, and had hundreds of cattle roaming over it; but all that it could give us to eat was eggs, tortillas, and beans softened in hot water; the last being about equal to a basket of fresh chips. This over, we made a last push for Guatimala. The road lay over a table of land, green and rich as a European lawn, ornamented with trees, and with features of scenery peculiarly English; muleteers who had left the city at midnight, and had al-

ready finished their day's work, were lying under the
shade of the trees, with their saddles and cargoes piled
up like walls, and their mules pasturing near. Along
the table was a line of huts, and if adorned instead of
being deformed by the hand of man, this would be a
region of poetic beauty. Indians, men and women,
with loads on their backs, every party with a bundle of
rockets, were returning from the " Capitol," as they
proudly called it, to their villages among the mountains. All told us that two days before Carrera had re-
entered the city with his soldiers.

When we were yet two leagues from the city Augustin's horse gave out. I was anxious to have a view of the
city before dark, and rode on. Late in the afternoon,
as I was ascending a small eminence, two immense volcanoes stood up before me, seeming to scorn the earth,
and towering to the heavens. They were the great
volcanoes of Agua and Fuego, forty miles distant, and
nearly fifteen thousand feet high, wonderfully grand and
beautiful. In a few moments the great plain of Guatimala appeared in view, surrounded by mountains, and
in the centre of it the city, a mere speck on the vast expanse, with churches, and convents, and numerous turrets, cupolas, and steeples, and still as if the spirit of
peace rested upon it ; with no storied associations, but
by its own beauty creating an impression on the mind
of a traveller which can never be effaced. I dismounted and tied my mule. As yet the sun lighted up the
roofs and domes of the city, giving a reflection so daz-
zling that I could only look at them by stealth. By degrees, its disk touched the top of the Volcano del Agua ;
slowly the whole orb sank behind it, illuminating the
background with an atmosphere fiery red. A rich gold-
en cloud rolled up its side and rested on the top, and

while I gazed the golden hues disappeared, and the glory of the scene was gone.

Augustin came along with his poor horse hobbling after him, and a pistol in his hand. He had been told on the way that Carrera's soldiers were riotous, and that there were many ladrones about the suburbs of the city, and he was in the humour to fire upon any one who asked a question. I made him put up his pistols, and we both mounted. An immense ravine was still between us and the city. It was very dark when we reached the bottom of this ravine, and we were almost trodden down by a caravan of loaded mules coming out. Rising on the other side to the top, we entered the outer gate, still a mile and a half from Guatimala. Inside were miserable huts, with large fires before them, surrounded by groups of drunken Indians and vagabond soldiers, firing their muskets at random in the air. Augustin told me to spur; but his poor horse could not keep up, and we were obliged to move on at a walk. As yet I did not know where to stop; there was no hotel in Guatimala. What's the use of a hotel in Guatimala? Who ever goes to Guatimala? was the answer of a gentleman of that place to my inquiries on this subject. I had several letters of introduction, and one was to Mr. Hall, the English vice-consul; and, fortunately, resolved to throw myself upon his hospitality.

We picked up a ragged Indian, who undertook to conduct us to his house, and under his guidance entered the city at the foot of a long straight street. My country-bred mule seemed astonished at the sight of so many houses, and would not cross the gutters, which were wide, and in the middle of the street. In spurring her over one, she gave a leap that, after her hard journey, made me proud of her; but she broke her bridle, and I was obliged to dismount and lead her. Augustin's poor beast was really past carrying him, and he followed on foot, whipping mine, the guide lending a hand before and behind. In this way we traversed the streets of Guatimala. Perhaps no diplomatist ever made a more unpretending entry into a capitol. Our stupid Indian did not know where Mr. Hall lived; there were hardly any people in the streets to inquire of, and I was an hour hauling my mule over the gutters and grumbling at the guide before I found the house. I knocked some time without receiving any answer. At length a young man opened the shutter of a balconied window, and told me that Mr. Hall was not at home. This would not serve my turn. I gave my name, and he retired; and in a few minutes the large door was unlocked, and Mr. Hall himself received me. He gave me as a reason for not opening sooner, that the soldiers had mutinied that day for want of pay, and threatened to sack the city. Carrera had exerted himself in trying to pacify them, and had borrowed fifty dollars from his (Mr. Hall's) neighbour, a French merchant; but the inhabitants were greatly alarmed; and when I knocked at his door he was afraid that the soldiers were beginning to put their threat in execution. Mr. H. had taken down his staff, because on their last entry, when he had his flag flying, the soldiers had fired upon it, calling it a bandera de guerra. They were mostly Indians from the villages, ignorant and insolent, and a few days before he had his hat knocked off by a sentinel because he did not raise it in passing, for which his complaint was then before the government.* The whole city was kept in a state of awe. No one ven-

---

* It is due to Carrera to say, that by his orders the soldier received two hundred lashes.

tured out at night, and Mr. Hall wondered how I had been able to wander through the streets without being molested. All this was not very agreeable, but it could not destroy my satisfaction in reaching Guatimala. For the first time since I entered the country, I had a good bed and a pair of clean sheets. It was two months that day since I embarked from New-York, and only one since I entered the country, but it seemed at least a year.

The luxury of my rest that night still lingers in my recollections, and the morning air was the most pure and invigorating I ever breathed. Situated in the " Tierras templadas," or temperate regions, on a table-land five thousand feet above the sea, the climate of Guatimala is that of perpetual spring, and the general aspect reminded me of the best class of Italian cities. It is laid out in blocks of from three to four hundred feet square, the streets parallel and crossing each other at right angles. The houses, made to resist the action of earthquakes, are of only one story, but very spacious, with large doors and windows, protected by iron balconies. In the centre of the city stands the Plaza, a square of one hundred and fifty yards on each side, paved with stone, with a colonnade on three sides ; on one of these stands the old vice-regal palace and hall of the Audiencia ; on another are the cabildo and other city buildings ; on the third the custom-house and palace of the ci-devant Marquisate of Aycinena ; and on the fourth side is the Cathedral, a beautiful edifice, in the best style of modern architecture, with the archiepiscopal palace on one side, and the College de Infantes on the other. In the centre is a large stone fountain, of imposing workmanship, supplied with pipes from the mountains about two leagues distant ; and the area is used as a market-place. The churches and convents correspond with the beauty of the Plaza, and their costliness and grandeur would attract the attention of tourists in Italy or old Spain.

The foundation of the city was laid in 1776, a year memorable in our own annals, and when our ancestors thought but little of the troubles of their neighbours. At that time the old capital, twenty-five miles distant, shattered and destroyed by earthquakes, was abandoned by its inhabitants, and the present was built in the rich valley of Las Vaccas, in a style commensurate with the dignity of a captain-generalship of Spain. I have seldom been more favourably impressed with the first appearance of any city, and the only thing that pained me in a two hours' stroll through the streets was the sight of Carrera's ragged and insolent-looking soldiers; and my first idea was, that in any city in Europe or the United States, the citizens, instead of submitting to be lorded over by such barbarians, would rise *en masse* and pitch them out of the gates.

In the course of the morning I took possession of the house that had been occupied by Mr. De Witt, our late chargé d'affaires. If I had been favourably impressed with the external appearance of the houses, I was charmed with the interior. The entrance was by a large double door, through a passage paved with small black and white stones, into a handsome patio or courtyard paved in like manner. On the sides were broad corridors paved with square red bricks, and along the foot of the corridors were borders of flowers. In front, on the street, and adjoining the entrance, was an anteroom with one large balconied window, and next to it a sala or parlour, with two windows. At the farther end a door opened from the side into the comedor or

dining-room, which had a door and two windows opening upon the corridor. At the end of the dining-room
was a door leading to a sleeping-room, with door and
one window, and then another room of the same size,
all with doors and windows opening upon the corridor.
The building and corridor were continued across the
foot of the lot; in the centre were rooms for servants,
and in the corners were a kitchen and stable, completely hidden from sight, and each furnished with a
separate fountain. This is the plan of all the houses in
Guatimala; others are much larger; that of the Aycinena family, for instance, covered a square of two hundred feet; but mine combined more beauty and comfort than any habitation I ever saw.

At two o'clock my luggage arrived, and I was most
comfortably installed in my new domicil. The sala or
reception-room was furnished with a large bookcase,
containing rows of books with yellow bindings, which
gave me twinging recollections of a law-office at home;
the archives of the legation had quite an imposing aspect; and over Mr. De Witt's writing-table hung another memorial of home : a fac-simile of the Declaration
of Independence.

My first business was to make arrangements for sending a trusty escort for Mr. Catherwood, and, this over,
it was incumbent upon me to look around for the government to which I was accredited.

From the time of the conquest Guatimala had remained in a state of profound tranquillity as a colony
of Spain. The Indians submitted quietly to the authority of the whites, and all bowed to the divine right of
the Romish Church. In the beginning of the present
century a few scattering rays of light penetrated to the
heart of the American Continent · and in 1823 the

Kingdom of Guatimala, as it was then called, declared its independence of Spain, and, after a short union with Mexico, constituted itself a republic under the name of the United States of Central America. By the articles of agreement the confederacy was composed of five states, viz., Guatimala, San Salvador, Honduras, Nicaragua, and Costa Rica. Chiapas had the privilege of entering if it should think proper, but it never did. Quezaltenango, a district of Guatimala, was afterward erected into a separate state, and added.

The monster party-spirit was rocked in the very cradle of their independence, and a line of demarcation was at once drawn between the Aristocratic and Democratic parties. The local names of these at first confused me, the former being called the Central or Servile, and the latter the *Federal* or Liberal, or *Democratic* party. Substantially they were the same with our own Federal and Democratic parties. The reader will perhaps find it difficult to understand that in any country, in a political sense, Federal and Democratic can mean the same thing, or that when I speak of a Federalist I mean a Democrat; and, to prevent confusion in referring to them hereafter, I shall call the Aristocratic the Central, and the Democratic the Liberal party. The former, like our own Federal party, was for consolidating and centralizing the powers of the general government, and the latter contended for the sovereignty of the states. The Central party consisted of a few leading families, which, by reason of certain privileges of monopoly for importations under the old Spanish government, assumed the tone of nobles, sustained by the priests and friars, and the religious feeling of the country. The latter was composed of men of intellect and energy, who threw off the yoke of the Romish

Church, and, in the first enthusiasm of emancipated minds, tore away at once the black mantle of superstition, thrown, like a funeral pall, over the genius of the people. The Centralists wished to preserve the usages of the colonial system, and resisted every innovation and every attack, direct or indirect, upon the privileges of the Church, and their own prejudices or interests. The Liberals, ardent, and cherishing brilliant schemes of reform, aimed at an instantaneous change in popular feelings and customs, and considered every moment lost that did not establish some new theory or sweep away some old abuse. The Centralists forgot that civilization is a jealous divinity, which does not admit of partition, and cannot remain stationary. The Liberals forgot that civilization requires a harmony of intelligence, of customs, and of laws. The example of the United States and of their free institutions was held up by the Liberals ; and the Centralists contended that, with their ignorant and heterogeneous population, scattered over a vast territory, without facilities of communication, it was a hallucination to take our country as a model. At the third session of Congress the parties came to an open rupture, and the deputies of San Salvador, always the most Liberal state in the confederacy, withdrew.

Flores, the vice-chief of the State of Guatimala, a Liberal, had made himself odious to the priests and friars by laying a contribution upon the convent at Quezaltenango ; and while on a visit to that place the friars of the convent excited the populace against him, as an enemy to religion. A mob gathered before his house, with cries of " Death to the heretic !" Flores fled to the church ; but as he was entering the door a mob of women seized him, wrested a stick from his hands, beat him with it, tore off his cap, and dragged him by the hair. He escaped from these furies and ran up into the pulpit. The alarm-bell was sounded, and all the rabble of the town poured into the plaza. A few soldiers endeavoured to cover the entrance to the church, but were assailed with stones and clubs; and the mob, bearing down all opposition, forced its way into the church, making the roof ring with cries of "Death to the heretic!" Rushing toward the pulpit, some tried to unhinge it, others to scale it; others struck at the unhappy vice-chief with knives tied to the ends of long poles; while a young fiend, with one foot on the mouldings of the pulpit and the other elevated in the air, leaned over and seized him by the hair. The curate, who was in the pulpit with him, frightened at the tempest he had assisted to raise, held up the Holy of Holies, and begged the mob to spare him, promising that he should leave the city immediately. The unhappy Flores, on his knees, confirmed these promises; but the friars urged on the mob, who became so excited with religious phrensy, that, after kneeling before the figure of the Saviour, exclaiming, "We adore thee, oh Lord, we venerate thee," they rose up with the ferocious cry, "but for thy honour and glory this blasphemer, this heretic, must die!" They dragged him from the pulpit across the floor of the church, and in the cloisters threw him into the hands of the fanatic and furious horde, when the women, like unchained furies, with their fists, sticks, and stones, beat him to death. His murderers stripped his body, leaving it, disfigured and an object of horror, exposed to the insults of the populace, and then dispersed throughout the city, demanding the heads of Liberals, and crying "Viva la Religion, y mueran los heregos del Congresso." About the same time

religious fanaticism swept the state, and the Liberal
party was crushed in Guatimala.

But the state of San Salvador, from the beginning
the leader in Liberal principles, was prompt in its efforts of vengeance, and on the sixteenth of March, 1827,
its army appeared within the outer gates of Guatimala, threatening the destruction of the capital; but religious fanaticism was too strong; the priests ran through
the streets exhorting the people to take up arms, the
friars headed mobs of women, who, with drawn knives,
swore destruction to all who attempted to overturn
their religion, and the San Salvadoreans were defeated and driven back. For two years the parties were
at open war. In 1829 the troops of San Salvador, under General Morazan, who had now become the head
of the Liberal party, again marched upon Guatimala,
and, after three days' fighting, entered it in triumph.
All the leaders of the Central party, the Aycinenas,
the Pavons, and Peñoles, were banished or fled, the
convents were broken up, the institution of friars abolished, the friars themselves put on board vessels and
shipped out of the country, and the archbishop, antici-
pating banishment, or perhaps fearing a worse fate,
sought safety in flight.

In 1831 General Morazan was elected president of
the republic; at the expiration of the term he was re-
elected; and for eight years the Liberal party had the
complete ascendancy. During the latter part of his
term, however, there was great discontent, particularly
on account of forced loans and exactions for the support of government, or, as the Centralists said, to gratify the rapacity of unscrupulous and profligate office-
holders. The Church party was always on the alert.
The exiles in the United States and Mexico, and on the

frontier, with their eyes always fixed upon home, kept up constant communications, and fostered the growing discontents. Some of them, in a state of penury abroad, ventured to return, and these not being molested, others soon followed. At this time came on the rising of Carrera, which was at first more dreaded by the Centralists than the Liberals, but suddenly, and to their own utter astonishment, placed the former nominally at the head of government.

In May preceding my arrival the term of the president, senators, and deputies had expired, and no elections had been held to supply their places. The vice-president, who had been elected during an unexpired term, was the only existing officer of the Federal Government. The states of Guatimala, Honduras, Nicaragua, and Costa Rica had declared themselves independent of the Federal Government. The states of San Salvador and Quezaltenango sustained the Federal Government, and Morazan, as commander-in-chief of the Federal forces, had defeated Ferrera, and established troops in Honduras, which gave the Liberal party the actual control of three states.

Virtually, then, the states stood " three and three." Where was my government ? The last Congress, before its dissolution, had recommended that panacea for political ills, a convention to amend the Constitution. The governments of England and France were represented near that of Central America by consuls general. Neither had any treaty; England could not procure one except upon a surrender of all claim to the Island of Roatan, in the Bay of Honduras, and to Balize. One had been drawn up with France, but, though pressed with great earnestness by the consul general of that country, the senate refused to ratify it.

Ours was the only government that had any treaty with
Central America, and, up to the time of Mr. De Witt's
departure from the country, we were represented by a
chargé d'affaires. The British consul-general had published a circular denying the existence of the general
government; the French consul was not on good
terms with either party; and my arrival, and the course
I might take, were a subject of some interest to politicians.

There was but one side to politics in Guatimala.
Both parties have a beautiful way of producing unanim-
ity of opinion, by driving out of the country all who do
not agree with them. If there were any Liberals, I did
not meet them, or they did not dare to open their lips.
The Central party, only six months in power, and still
surprised at being there, was fluttering between arro-
gance and fear. The old families, whose principal
members had been banished or politically ostracized,
and the clergy, were elated at the expulsion of the
Liberal party, and their return to what they considered
their natural right to rule the state; they talked of re-
calling the banished archbishop and friars, restoring the
privileges of the Church, repairing the convents, revi-
ving monastic institutions, and making Guatimala what
it had once been, the jewel of Spanish America.

One of my first visits of ceremony was to Señor Rivera Paz, the chief of the state. I was presented by
Mr. Henry Savage, who had formerly acted as United
States consul at Guatimala, and was the only American resident, to whom I am under many obligations for
his constant attentions. The State of Guatimala, having declared its independence of the Federal government, was at that time governed by a temporary body
called a Constituent Assembly. On the last entry of

Carrera into the city, in March preceding my arrival, Salazar, the chief of the state, fled, and Carrera, on horseback, knocked at the door of Señor Rivera Paz before daylight, and, by his individual pleasure, installed him as chief. It was a fortunate choice for the people of Guatimala. He was about thirty-eight, gentleman-ly in his appearance and manners, and, in all the trying positions in which he was afterward placed, exhibited more than ordinary prudence and judgment.

I had been advised that it would be agreeable to the government of Guatimala for me to present my creden-tials to the chief of that state, and afterward to the chiefs of the other states, and that the states separately would treat of the matters for which I was accredited to the general government. The object of this was to preclude a recognition on my part of the power which was, or claimed to be, the general government. The suggestion was of course preposterous, but it showed the dominion of party-spirit with men who knew bet-ter. Señor Rivera Paz expressed his regret at my hap-pening to visit the country at such an unfortunate pe-riod, and assured me of the friendly disposition of that state, and that it would do all in its power to serve me. During my visit I was introduced to several of the lead-ing members of the administration, and I left with a favourable opinion of Rivera Paz, which was never sha-ken in regard to him personally.

In the evening, in company with Mr. Hall, I attend-ed the last meeting of the Constituent Assembly. It was held in the old Hall of Congress ; the room was large, hung with portraits of old Spaniards distinguish-ed in the history of the country, and dimly lighted. The deputies sat on a platform at one end, elevated about six feet, and the president on an elevation in a

large chair, two secretaries at a table beneath, and on
the wall were the arms of the republic, the groundwork
of which was three volcanoes, emblematic, I suppose,
of the combustible state of the country. The deputies
sat on each side, about thirty being present, nearly half
of whom were priests, with black gowns and caps ; and
by the dull light the scene carried me back to the dark
ages, and seemed a meeting of inquisitors.

The subject under discussion was a motion to revive
the old law of tithes, which had been abolished by the
Liberal party. The law was passed unanimously ; but
there was a discussion upon a motion to appropriate a
small part of the proceeds for the support of hospitals
for the poor. The priests took part in the discussion,
and with liberal sentiments ; a lay member, with big
black whiskers, opposed it, saying that the Church
stood like a light in darkness ; and the Marquis Aycinena, a priest and the leading member of the party,
said that " what was raised for God should be given
to God alone." There was another discussion upon the
point whether the law should operate upon cattle then
in being or to be born thereafter ; and, finally, as to the
means of enforcing it. One gentleman contended that
coercive measures should not be used, and, with a fine
burst of eloquence, said that reliance might be placed
upon the religious feelings of the people, and that the
poorest Indian would come forward and contribute his
mite ; but the Assembly decided that the law should be
enforced by Las leyes antiguas de los Espagnoles, the
old laws of the Spaniards, the severities of which had
been one of the great causes of revolution in all Spanish countries. There was something horrible in this
retrograde legislation. I could hardly realize that, in
the nineteenth century, men of sense, and in a country

through the length and breadth of which free principles were struggling for the ascendancy, would dare fasten on the people a yoke which, even in the dark ages, was too galling to be borne. The tone of debate was respectable, but calm and unimpassioned, from the entire absence of any opposition party. The Assembly purported to be a popular body, representing the voice of the people. It was a time of great excitement, and the last night of its session; and Mr. Hall and I, four men and three boys, were the only listeners.

As it was not safe to be in the streets after eight o'clock, the Assembly was adjourned, and, after a short session the next morning, assembled at a state breakfast. The place of meeting was in the old library, a venerable room, containing a valuable collection of rare old Spanish books and manuscripts, among which had lately been discovered the two missing volumes of Fuentes, and where I promised myself much satisfaction. The only guests were Mr. Hall, the French consul general, Colonel Monte Rosa, an aid of Carrera, and myself. Carrera was invited, but did not come. The table was profusely ornamented with flowers and fruits. There was very little wine drunk, no toasts, and no gayety. There was not a gray-haired man at table; all were young, and so connected that it seemed a large family party; more than half had been in exile, and if Morazan returned to power they would all be scattered again.

I had been but three days in Guatimala, and already the place was dull. The clouds which hung over the political horizon weighed upon the spirits of the inhabitants, and in the evening I was obliged to shut myself up in my house alone. In the uncertainty which hung over my movements, and to avoid the trouble of housekeeping for perhaps but a few weeks, I dined and supped at the house of the señora, an interesting young widow who owned mine (her husband had been shot in a private revolution of his own getting up), and lived nearly opposite. The first evening I remained there till nine o'clock; but as I was crossing on my return home a fierce " Quien vive ?" " who goes ?" came booming up the street. In the dark I could not see the sentinel, and did not know the password. Fortunately, and what was very unusual, he repeated the challenge two or three times, but so fiercely that the tones of his voice went through me like a musket-ball, and probably in a moment more the ball itself would have followed, but an old lady rushed out of the house I had left, and, with a lantern in her hand, screamed " Patria Libra."

Though silent, I was not idle; and when in a safe place thanked her from across the street, hugging close the inside of my doorway. Since Carrera's entry, he had placed sentinels to preserve the peace of the city, which was very quiet before he came, and his peace-officers kept it in a constant state of alarm. These sentinels were Indians, ignorant, undisciplined, and insolent, and fond of firing their muskets. They were ordered to challenge " Quien Vive ?" " Who goes ?" " Que gente ?" " What people ?" " Quel Regimento ?" " What regiment ?" and then fire. One fellow had already obeyed his orders literally, and, hurrying through the three questions, without waiting for answers, fired, and shot a woman. The answers were, " Patria Libra," " Country free ;" " Paisáno," " Countryman ;" and " Paz," " Peace."

This was a subject of annoyance all the time I was in Guatimala. The streets were not lighted; and hearing the challenge, sometimes at the distance of a square, in a ferocious voice, without being able to see the sentinel, I always imagined him with his musket at his shoulder, peering through the darkness to take aim. I felt less safe by reason of my foreign pronunciation; but I never met any one, native or stranger, who was not nervous when within reach of the sentinel's challenge, or who would not go two squares out of the way to avoid it.

CHAPTER X.

Hacienda of Narengo.—Lazoing.—Diplomatic Correspondence.—Formulas.—
Fête of La Concepcion.—Taking the Black Veil.—A Countrywoman.—Re-
nouncing the World.—Fireworks, &c.—Procession in honour of the Virgin.—
Another Exhibition of Fireworks.—A fiery Bull.—Insolent Soldiery.

THE next day, in company with Mr. Savage, I rode
to Narengo, a small hacienda of the Aycinena family,
about seven miles from the city. Beyond the walls all
was beautiful, and in the palmy days of Guatimala the
Aycinenas rolled to the Narengo in an enormous car-
riage, full of carving and gilding, in the style of the
grandees of Spain, which now stands in the courtyard
of the family-house as a memorial of better days. We
entered by a large gate into a road upon their land,
undulating and ornamented with trees, and by a large
artificial lake, made by damming up several streams.
We rode around the borders of the lake, and entered a
large cattle-yard, in the centre of which, on the side of
a declivity, stood the house, a strong stone structure,
with a broad piazza in front, and commanding a beautiful view of the volcanoes of the Antigua.

The hacienda was only valuable from its vicinity to
Guatimala, being what would be called at home a
country-seat; and contained only seven thousand acres
of land, about seventy mules, and seven hundred head
of cattle. It was the season for marking and number-
ing the cattle, and two of the Señores Aycinena were
at the hacienda to superintend the operations. The
cattle had been caught and brought in; but, as I had
never seen the process of lazoing, after dinner a hun-

dred head, which had been kept up two days without food, were let loose into a field two or three miles in circumference. Eight men were mounted, with iron spurs an inch long on their naked heels, and each with a lazo in hand, which consisted of an entire cow's hide cut into a single cord about twenty yards long; one end was fastened to the horse's tail, which was first wrapped in leaves to prevent its being lacerated, and the rest was wound into a coil, and held by the rider in his right hand, resting on the pommel of the saddle. The cattle had all dispersed; we placed ourselves on an elevation commanding a partial view of the field, and the riders scattered in search of them. In a little while thirty or forty rushed past, followed by the riders at full speed, and very soon were out of sight. We must either lose the sport or follow; and in one of the doublings, taking particularly good care to avoid the throng of furious cattle and headlong riders, I drew up to the side of two men who were chasing a single ox, and followed over hill, through bush, brush, and underwood; one rider threw his lazo beautifully over the horns of the ox, and then turned his horse, while the ox bounded to the length of the lazo, and, without shaking horse or rider, pitched headlong to the ground.

At this moment a herd swept by, with the whole company in full pursuit. A large yellow ox separated from the rest, and all followed him. For a mile he kept ahead, doubled, and dodged, but the horsemen crowded him down toward the lake; and, after an ineffectual attempt to bolt, he rushed into the water. Two horsemen followed and drove him out, and gave him a start, but in a few moments the lazo whizzed over his head, and, while horse and rider stood like marble, the ox again came with a plunge to the ground. The riders scat-

t°red, and one horse and rider rolled over in such a
way that I thought every bone in his body was broken;
but the sport was so exciting that I, who at the beginning was particularly careful to keep out of harm's way,
felt very much disposed to have my own horse's tail tied
up and take a lazo in my hand. The effect of the sport
was heightened by the beauty of the scene, with the
great volcanoes of Agua and Fuego towering above us,
and toward evening throwing a deep shade over the
plain. It was nearly dark when we returned to the
house. With that refinement of politeness, which I
believe is exclusively Spanish, the gentlemen escorted
us some distance on our road. At dark we reached
Guatimala, and, to our great satisfaction, learned at the
gate that the soldiers were confined to the barracks.

The news of my arrest and imprisonment, with great
exaggeration of circumstance, had reached Guatimala
before me, and I was advised that the state government intended making me a communication on the subject. I waited several days, and, not receiving any,
made a formal complaint, setting forth the facts, and
concluding that I did not attempt to suggest what
ought to be done, but felt satisfied that the government
would do what was consistent with its own honour and
the rights of a friendly nation. In a few days I received an answer from the secretary of state, conveying the regrets of the president for the occurrence, and
stating that, before receiving my note, the government
had taken the measures which it deemed proper in the
premises. As this was very indefinite, and as I bore
considerable anger against the parties, and, moreover,
as I heard out of doors something about these "measures," and considered it necessary, for the protection
of Americans who were or might be in that country,

not to suffer an outrage that had become notorious to be treated lightly, I addressed a farther note to the secretary, asking specifically whether the officer and alcalde referred to had been punished, and if so, in what way. To this I received for answer that, in the circumstances in which the country was placed by means of an extraordinary popular revolution, and the distrust prevailing in the frontier villages, the local authorities were more suspicious than usual in the matter of passports, and that the outrage, " el atropellamento," which I had suffered, had its origin in the orders of a military officer, " un official militar," who suspected that I and my companion were " enemies," and that General Cascara, as soon as he was informed of the circumstances, had removed him from his command; the reply went on to say that the government, much to its regret, from the difficult circumstances in which the country was placed, had not the power to give that security to travellers which it desired, but would issue preventive orders to the local authorities to secure me in my farther travels.

I had understood that General Cascara had removed the officer, but the intelligence was hardly received in Guatimala before Carrera ordered him to be restored; and I afterward saw in a San Salvador paper that he had threatened to shoot General Cascara if his degradation was not revoked. In farther communications with the secretary and the chief of the state, they confessed their inability to do anything; and being satisfied that they desired it even more than myself, I did not consider it worth while to press the subject; as indeed, in strictness, I had no right to call upon the state government. The general government had not the least particle of power in the state, and I mention the circumstance to show the utter feebleness of the administration, and the wretched condition of the country generally. It troubled me on one account, as it showed the difficulty and danger of prosecuting the travels I had contemplated.

From the moment of my arrival I was struck with the devout character of the city of Guatimala. At matins and vespers the churches were all open, and the people, particularly the women, went regularly to prayers. Every house had its figure of the Virgin, the Saviour, or some tutelary saint, and on the door were billets of paper with prayers. "La verdadera sangre de Cristo, nuestro redentor que solo representada en Egipto libro a los Israelitas de un brazo fuerte y poderoso, libre nos de la peste, guerra, y muerte repentina. Amen." "The true blood of Christ our Redeemer, which alone, exhibited in Egypt, freed the Israelites from a strong and powerful arm, deliver us from pestilence, war, and sudden death. Amen."

"O Maria, concebida sin pecado, rogad por nosotros, que recurrimos a vos." "O Virgin, conceived without sin, pray for us, that we may have recourse to thee."

"Ave Maria, gracia plena, y la santissima Trinidad nos favorezca." "Hail Mary, full of grace, and may the Holy Spirit favour us."

"El dolce nombre de Jesus,
Sea con nosotros. Amen."

On the first Sunday after my arrival was celebrated the fête of La Concepcion, a fête always honoured in the observances of the Catholic Church, and this day more important from the circumstance that a probationer in the convent of La Concepcion intended to take the black veil. At break of day the church bells rang

throughout the city, cannon were fired in the plaza,
and rockets and fireworks set off at the corners of the
streets. At nine o'clock crowds of people were hurrying to the Church of La Concepcion. Before the door,
and extending across the streets, were arches decorated
with evergreens and flowers. The broad steps of the
church were strewed with pine leaves, and on the platform were men firing rockets. The church was one of
the handsomest in Guatimala, rich with gold and silver
ornaments, pictures, and figures of saints, and adorned
with arches and flowers. The Padre Aycinena, the
vice-president of the state, and the leading member of
the Constituent Assembly, was the preacher of the day,
and his high reputation attracted a large concourse of
people. The pulpit was at one end of the church, and
the great mass of the people were anxious to hear the
sermon. This left the other end comparatively vacant, and I placed myself on a step of the nearest
altar, directly in front of the grating of the convent.
At the close of the sermon there was a discharge of
rockets and crackers from the steps of the church, the
smoke of which clouded the interior, and the smell of
powder was stronger than that of the burning incense.
The floor was strewed with pine leaves, and covered
with kneeling women, with black mantas drawn close
over the top of the head, and held together under the
chin. I never saw a more beautiful spectacle than
these rows of kneeling women, with faces pure and
lofty in expression, lighted up by the enthusiasm of religion ; and among them, fairer than most and lovely as
any, was one from my own land ; not more than twenty-two, married to a gentleman belonging to one of the
first families of Guatimala, once an exile in the United
States. In a new land and among a new people, she

had embraced a new faith; and, with the enthusiasm of a youthful convert, no lady in Guatimala was more devout, more regular at mass, or more strict in all the discipline of the Catholic Church than the Sister Susannah.

After the fireworks there was a long ceremony at the altar, and then a general rush toward the other extremity of the church. The convent was directly adjoining, and in the partition wall, about six feet from the floor, was a high iron grating, and about four feet beyond it another, at which the nuns attended the services of the church. Above the iron grating was a wooden one, and from this in a few minutes issued a low strain of wild Indian music, and presently a figure in white, with a long white veil and a candle in her right hand, and both arms extended, walked slowly to within a few feet of the grating, and then as slowly retired. Presently the same low note issued from the grating below, and we saw advancing a procession of white nuns, with long white veils, each holding in her hand a long lighted candle. The music ceased, and a chant arose, so low that it required intent listening to catch the sound. Advancing two and two with this low chant to within a few feet of the grating, the sisters turned off different ways. At the end of the procession were two black nuns, leading between them the probationer, dressed in white, with a white veil and a wreath of roses round her head. The white nuns arranged themselves on each side, their chant ceased, and the voice of the probationer was heard alone, but so faint that it seemed the breathing of a spirit of air. The white nuns strewed flowers before her, and she advanced between the two black ones. Three times she stopped and kneeled, continuing the same low

chant, and the last time the white nuns gathered
around her, strewing flowers upon her head and in her
path.   Slowly they led her to the back part of the chapel, and all kneeled before the altar.

At this time a strain of music was heard at the other
end of the church; a way was cleared through the
crowd, and a procession advanced, consisting of the
principal priests, clothed in their richest robes, and
headed by the venerable provesor, an octogenarian
with white hair, and tottering on the verge of the grave,
as remarkable for the piety of his life as for his venerable appearance.   A layman bore on a rich frame a gold
crown and sceptre studded with jewels.   The procession advanced to a small door on the right of the grating, and the two black nuns and the probationer appeared in the doorway.   Some words passed between
her and the provesor, which I understood to be an examination by him whether her proposed abandonment
of the world was voluntary or not.   This over, the provesor removed the wreath of roses and the white veil,
and put on her head the crown and in her hand the
sceptre.   The music sounded loud notes of triumph,
and in a few moments she reappeared at the grating
with the crown and sceptre, and a dress sparkling with
jewels.   The sisters embraced her, and again threw
roses upon her.   It seemed horrible to heap upon her
the pomp and pleasures of the world, at the moment
when she was about to bid farewell to them forever.
Again she kneeled before the altar; and when she rose
the jewels and precious stones, the rich ornaments with
which she was decorated, were taken from her, and she
returned to the bishop, who took away the crown and
sceptre, and put on her head the black veil.   Again she
appeared before the grating; the last, the fatal step was

not yet taken; the black veil was not drawn. Again the nuns pressed round, and this time they almost devoured her with kisses.

I knew nothing of her story. I had not heard that the ceremony was to take place till late in the evening before, and I had made up my mind that she was old and ugly; but she was not, nor was she faded and worn with sorrow, the picture of a broken heart; nor yet a young and beautiful enthusiast; she was not more than twenty-three, and had one of those good faces which, without setting men wild by their beauty, bear the impress of a nature well qualified for the performance of all duties belonging to daughter, and wife, and mother, speaking the kindliness and warmth of a woman's heart. It was pale, and she seemed conscious of the important step and the solemn vows she was taking, and to have no pangs; and yet who can read what is passing in the human breast?

She returned to the provesor, who drew over her face a black veil; and music rose in bursts of rejoicing, that one who was given to the world to take a share in its burdens had withdrawn herself from it. Immediately commenced the hum of restrained voices; and working my way through the crowd, I joined a party of ladies, one of whom was my fair countrywoman. She was from a small country town in Pennsylvania, and the romance of her feelings toward convents and nuns had not yet worn off. On Carrera's first invasion she had taken refuge in the convent of La Concepcion, and spoke with enthusiasm of the purity and piety of the nuns, describing some as surpassing in all the attributes of woman. She knew particularly the one who had just taken the veil, and told me that in a few days she would appear at the grating of the convent to embrace her friends and bid them farewell, and promised to take me and procure me a share in the distribution.

During this time rockets were fired from the steps, and in the street, immediately in front, was a frame of fireworks thirty feet high, which the whole crowd waited on the steps and in the street to see set off. Everybody spoke of the absurdity of such an exhibition by daylight, but they said it was the custom. The piece was complicated in its structure, and in the centre was a large box. There was a whizzing of wheels, a great smoke, and occasionally a red flash; and as the extremities burned out, for the finale, with a smart cracking, the box flew open, and when the smoke cleared away, discovered the figure of a little black nun, at which all laughed and went away.

In the afternoon was the procession in honour of the Virgin. Although Guatimala was dull, and, by the convulsions of the times, debarred all kinds of gayety, religious processions went on as usual, and it would have been an evidence of an expiring state to neglect them. All the streets through which the procession was to pass were strewed with pine leaves, and crossing them were arches decorated with evergreens and flowers; the long balconied windows were ornamented with curtains of crimson silk, and flags with fanciful devices. At the corners of the streets were altars, under arbours of evergreens as high as the tops of the houses, adorned with pictures and silver ornaments from the churches, and the whole covered with flowers. Rich as the whole of Central America is in natural productions, the valley of Guatimala is distinguished for the beauty and variety of its flowers; and for one day the fields were stripped of their clothing to beautify the city. I have seen great fêtes in Europe, got up with lavish expenditure of money, but never anything so simply beautiful. My stroll through the streets before the procession was the most interesting part of the day. All the inhabitants, in their best dresses, were there : the men standing at the corners, and the women, in black mantillas, seated in long rows on each side ; the flags and curtains in the balconied windows, the green of the streets, the profusion of flowers, the vistas through the arches, and the simplicity of manners which permitted ladies of the first class to mingle freely in the crowd and sit along the street, formed a picture of beauty that even now relieves the stamp of dulness with which Guatimala is impressed upon my mind.

The procession for which all these beautiful preparations were made opened with a single Indian, old, wrinkled, dirty, and ragged, bareheaded, and staggering under the load of an enormous bass-drum, which he carried on his back, seeming as old as the conquest, with every cord and the head on one side broken ; another Indian followed in the same ragged costume, with one ponderous drumstick, from time to time striking the old drum. Then came an Indian with a large whistle, corresponding in venerableness of aspect with the drum, on which, from time to time, he gave a fierce blast, and looked around with a comical air of satisfaction for applause. Next followed a little boy about ten years old, wearing a cocked hat, boots above his knees, a drawn sword, and the mask of a hideous African. He was marshalling twenty or thirty persons, not inaptly called the Devils, all wearing grotesque and hideous masks, and ragged, fantastic dresses ; some with reed whistles, some knocking sticks together ; and the principal actors were two pseudo-women, with broad-brimmed European hats, frocks high in the necks, waists

across the breast, large boots, and each with an old guitar, waltzing and dancing an occasional fandango.
How it happened that these devils, who, of course, excited laughter in the crowd, came to form part of a religious procession, I could not learn. The boys followed them, just as they do the military with us on a fourth
of July; and, in fact, with the Guatimala boys, there is
no good procession without good Devils.

Next, and in striking contrast, came four beautiful
boys, six or eight years old, dressed in white frocks and
pantalettes, with white gauze veils over wreaths of roses,
perfect emblems of purity; then four young priests,
bearing golden candlesticks, with wax candles lighted;
and then four Indians, carrying on their shoulders the
figure of an angel larger than life, with expanded wings
made of gauze, puffed out like a cloud, and intended to
appear to float in air, but dressed more after the fashion
of this world, with the frock rather short, and the *sus-
penders* of the stockings of pink riband. Then, borne
as before, on the shoulders of Indians, larger than life,
the figure of Judith, with a drawn sword in one hand,
and in the other the gory head of Holofernes. Then
another angel, with a cloud of silk over her head, and
then the great object of veneration, La Virgina de la
Concepcion, on a low hand-barrow, richly decorated
with gold and silver and a profusion of flowers, and
protected by a rich silken canopy, upborne on the ends
of four gilded poles. Priests followed in their costly
dresses, one under a silken canopy, holding up the
Host, before the imaginary splendour of which all fell
on their knees. The whole concluded with a worse
set of devils than those which led the procession, being
about five hundred of Carrera's soldiers, dirty and ragged, with fanaticism added to their usual expression of

ferocity, and carrying their muskets without any order ; the officers dressed in any costume they could command ; a few, with black hat and silver or gold band, like footmen, carried their heads very high. Many were lame from gunshot wounds badly cured; and a gentleman who was with me pointed out several who were known to have committed assassinations and murders, for which, in a country that had any government, they would have been hung. The city was at their mercy, and Carrera was the only man living who had any control over them.

At the head of the street the procession filed off in the cross streets, and the figure of the Virgin was taken from its place and set up on the altar. The priests kneeled before it and prayed, and the whole crowd fell on their knees. I was at the corner near the altar, which commanded a view of four streets, and rising a little on one knee, saw in all the streets a dense mass of kneeling figures, rich men and beggars, lovely women and stupid-looking Indians, fluttering banners and curtains in balconied windows, and the figures of angels in their light gauze drapery seeming to float in air ; while the loud chant of the crowd, swollen by the deep chorus of the soldiers' voices, produced a scene of mingled beauty and deformity at once captivating and repulsive. This over, all rose, the Virgin was replaced on her throne, and the procession again moved. At the next altar I turned aside and went to the square in front of the Church of San Francisco, the place fixed for the grand finale of the honours to the Virgin, the exhibition of fireworks !

At dark the procession entered the foot of a street leading to the square. It approached with a loud chant, and at a distance nothing was visible but a long

train of burning candles, making the street light as day.
The devils were still at its head, and its arrival in the
square was announced by a discharge of rockets. In
a few minutes the first piece of fireworks was set off
from the balustrade of the church ; the figures on the
roof were lighted by the glare, and, though not built
expressly for that purpose, the church answered exceedingly well for the exhibition.

The next piece was on the ground of the square, a
national one, and as much a favourite in the exhibition
of fireworks as the devils in a religious procession, called the Toros, or Bull, being a frame covered with paste-
board, in the form of a bull, covered on the outside with
fireworks ; into this figure a man thrust his head and
shoulders, and, with nothing but his legs visible, rushed
into the thickest of the crowd, scattering on all sides
streams of fire. I was standing with a party of ladies
and several members of the Constituent Assembly, the
latter of whom were speaking of an invasion of troops
from Quezaltenango, and the sally of Carrera to repel
them. As the toros came at us, we retreated till we
could go no farther ; the ladies screamed, and we
bravely turned our backs ; and holding down our
heads, sheltered them from the shower of fire. All
said it was dangerous, but it was the custom. There
was more cheerfulness and gayety than I had yet seen
in Guatimala, and I felt sorry when the exhibition was
over.

All day I had felt particularly the influence of the
beautiful climate ; the mere breathing of the air was a
luxury, and the evening was worthy of such a day.
The moonbeams were lighting up the façade of the
venerable church, and showing in sadness a rent made
by an earthquake from top to bottom. As we walked

home, the streets were lighted with a brilliancy almost unearthly; and the ladies, proud of their moonlight, almost persuaded me that it was a land to love.

Continuing on our way, we passed a guardhouse, where a group of soldiers were lying at full length, so as to make everybody pass off the walk and go round them. Perhaps three or four thousand people, a large portion ladies, were turned off. All felt the insolence of these fellows, and I have no doubt some felt a strong disposition to kick them out of the way; but, though young men enough passed to drive the whole troop out of the city, no complaint was made, and no notice whatever taken of it. In one of the corridors of the plaza another soldier lay on his back crosswise, with his musket by his side, and muttering to everybody that passed, "Tread on me if you dare, and you'll see!" and we all took good care not to tread on him. I returned to my house, to pass the evening in solitude; and it was melancholy to reflect that, with the elements of so much happiness, Guatimala was made so miserable.

CHAPTER XI.

THE next three or four days I passed in receiving and paying visits, and in making myself acquainted with the condition of the country. Among the most interesting visiters was the venerable provesor, since the banishment of the archbishop the head of the church, who, by a late bull of the pope, had been appointed bishop; but, owing to the troubled times, had not yet been ordained. A friend in Baltimore had procured for me a letter from the archbishop in that city, to whom I here acknowledge my obligations, recommending me to all his brother ecclesiastics in Central America. The venerable provesor received this letter as from a brother in the Church, and upon the strength of it, afterward, when I set out for Palenque, gave me a letter of recommendation to all the curas under his charge. During the day my time passed agreeably enough; but the evenings, in which I was obliged to keep within doors, were long and lonely. My house was so near the plaza that I could hear the sentinels' challenge, and from time to time the report of a musket. These reports, in the stillness of night, were always startling. For some time I did not know the cause; but at length learned that cows and mules

straggled about the city, which, heard moving at a
distance and not answering the challenge, were fired
upon without ceremony.

There was but one paper in Guatimala, and that a
weekly, and a mere chronicler of decrees and political
movements. City news passed by word of mouth.
Every morning everybody asked his neighbour what
was the news. One day it was that an old deaf woman,
who could not hear the sentinel's challenge, had been
shot; another, that Asturias, a rich old citizen, had
been stabbed; and another morning the report circulated that thirty-three nuns in the convent of Santa
Teresa had been poisoned. This was a subject of excitement for several days, when the nuns all recovered,
and it was ascertained that they had suffered from the
unsentimental circumstance of eating food that did not
agree with them.

On Friday, in company with my fair countrywoman,
I visited the convent of La Concepcion for the purpose of embracing a nun, or rather *the* nun, who had
taken the black veil. The room adjoining the parlato-
ria of the convent was crowded, and she was standing
in the doorway with the crown on her head and a doll
in her hand. It was the last time her friends could see
her face; but this puerile exhibition of the doll detract-
ed from the sentiment. It was an occasion that addressed itself particularly to ladies; some wondered
that one so young should abandon a world to them
beaming with bright and beautiful prospects; others,
with whom the dreams of life had passed, looked upon
her retirement as the part of wisdom. They embraced
her, and retired to make room for others. Before our
turn came there was an irruption of those objects of
my detestation, the eternal soldiers, who, leaving their

muskets at the door, forced their way through the crowd, and presenting themselves, though respectfully, for an embrace, retired. By her side was a black nun, with a veil so thick that not a lineament of her face could be seen, whom my countrywoman had known during her seclusion in the convent, and described as young, of exceeding beauty and loveliness, and around whom she threw a charm which almost awakened a spirit of romance. I would have made some sacrifice for one glimpse of her face. At length our turn came; my fair companion embraced her, and, after many farewell words, recommended me as her countryman. I never had much practice in embracing nuns; in fact, it was the first time I ever attempted such a thing; but it came as natural as if I had been brought up to it. My right arm encircled her neck, her right arm mine; I rested my head upon her shoulder, and she hers upon mine; but a friend's grandmother never received a more respectful embrace. "Stolen joys are always dearest;" there were too many looking on. The grating closed, and the face of the nun will never be seen again.

That afternoon Carrera returned to the city. I was extremely desirous to know him, and made an arrangement with Mr. Pavon to call upon him the next day. At ten o'clock the next morning Mr. Pavon called for me. I was advised that this formidable chief was taken by external show, and put on the diplomatic coat, with a great profusion of buttons, which had produced such an effect at Copan, and which, by-the-way, owing to the abominable state of the country, I never had an opportunity of wearing afterward, and the cost of which was a dead loss.

Carrera was living in a small house in a retired street.

Sentinels were at the door, and eight or ten soldiers basking in the sun outside, part of a body-guard, who had been fitted out with red bombazet jackets and tartan plaid caps, and made a much better appearance than any of his soldiers I had before seen. Along the corridor was a row of muskets, bright and in good order. We entered a small room adjoining the sala, and saw Carrera sitting at a table counting money.

Ever since my arrival in the country this name of terror had been ringing in my ears. Mr. Montgomery, to whom I have before referred, and who arrived in Central America about a year before me, says, " An insurrection, I was told, had taken place among the Indians, who, under the directions of a man called Carrera, were ravaging the country and committing all kinds of excesses. Along the coast, and in some of the departments, tranquillity had not been disturbed; but in the interior there was no safety for the traveller, and every avenue to the capital was beset by parties of brigands, who showed no mercy to their victims, especially if they were foreigners ;" and in referring to the posture of affairs at his departure he adds, " It is probable, however, that while this is being written, the active measures of General Morazan for putting down the insurrection have been successful, and that the career of this rebel hero has been brought to a close." But the career of the " rebel hero" was not brought to a close; the " man called Carrera" was now absolute master of Guatimala ; and, if I am not deceived, he is destined to become more conspicuous than any other leader who has yet risen in the convulsions of Spanish America.

He is a native of one of the wards of Guatimala. His friends, in compliment, call him a mulatto ; I, for the same reason, call him an Indian, considering that the better blood of the two. In 1829 he was a drummer-boy in Colonel Aycinena's regiment. When the Liberal or Democratic party prevailed, and General Morazan entered the city, Carrera broke his drum and retired to the village of Matasquintla. Here he entered into business as a pig-driver, and for several years continued in this respectable occupation, probably as free as one of his own pigs from any dreams of future greatness. The excesses of political parties, severe exactions for the support of government, encroachments upon the property of the Church, and innovations, particularly the introduction of the Livingston Code, establishing trial by jury, and making marriage a civil contract, created discontent throughout the country. The last gave great offence to the clergy, who exercised an unbounded influence over the minds of the Indians. In 1837 the cholera, which, in its destructive march over the habitable world, had hitherto spared this portion of the American continent, made its terrible appearance, and, besides strewing it with dead, proved the immediate cause of political convulsions. The priests persuaded the Indians that the foreigners had poisoned the waters. Galvez, who was at that time the chief of the state, sent medicines into all the villages, which, being ignorantly administered, sometimes produced fatal consequences; and the priests, always opposed to the Liberal party, persuaded the Indians that the government was endeavouring to poison and destroy their race. The Indians became excited all over the country; and in Matasquintla they rose in mass, with Carrera at their head, crying "Viva la Religion, y muerte a los Etrangeros!" The first blow was struck by murdering the judges appointed under the Livingston Code. Galvez sent a commission, with detachments of cavalry and a white flag, to hear their complaints; but while conferring with the insurgents they were surrounded, and almost all of them cut to pieces. The number of the disaffected increased to more than a thousand, and Galvez sent against them six hundred troops, who routed them, plundered and burned their villages, and, among other excesses, the last outrage was perpetrated upon Carrera's wife. Roused to fury by this personal wrong, he joined with several chiefs of villages, vowing never to lay down his arms while an officer of Morazan remained in the state. With a few infuriated followers he went from village to village, killing the judges and government officers, when pursued escaping to the mountains, begging tortillas at the haciendas for his men, and sparing and protecting all who assisted him. At this time he could neither read nor write; but, urged on and assisted by some priests, particularly one Padre Lobo, a notorious profligate, he issued a proclamation, having his name stamped at the foot of it, against strangers and the government, for attempting to poison the Indians, demanding the destruction of all foreigners excepting the Spaniards, the abolition of the Livingston Code, a recall of the archbishop and friars, the expulsion of heretics, and a restoration of the privileges of the Church and old usages and customs. His fame spread as a highwayman and murderer; the roads about Guatimala were unsafe; all travelling was broken up; the merchants were thrown into consternation by intelligence that the whole of the goods sent to the fair at Esquipulas had fallen into his hands (which, however, proved untrue); and very soon he became so strong that he attacked villages and even towns.

The reader will bear in mind that this was in the

State of Guatimala. The Liberal party was dominant, but at this critical moment a fatal division took place among its members; Barundia, a leading member, disappointed of a high office for a profligate relative, deserted the administration, and appeared in the Assembly at the head of the opposition. Party distraction and the rising of Carrera stirred up all who were dissatisfied with the government; and the citizens of the Antigua, about twenty-five miles distant, sent in a petition for a decree of amnesty for political offences, allowing exiles to return, and a redress of other grievances. A deputation of the Assembly was sent to confer with them, which returned unsuccessful, and the Antiguans threatened to march against Guatimala.

On Sunday, the twentieth of February (1838), proclamations of the Antiguanos were found strewed in the streets, and there was a general alarm that the Antiguanos were on their march to attack the city. The troops of the general government (less than five hundred in number) and the militia were mustered; cannon placed at the corners of the square, and sentinels in the streets; and General Prem published a bando, calling upon all citizens to take up arms. Galvez, the chief of the state, mounted his horse, and rode through the streets, endeavouring to rouse the citizens, and giving out that Morazan was on his march, and had defeated three hundred of Carrera's gang. On Monday all business was suspended. Galvez, in great perplexity, reinstated some officers who had been dismissed, and appointed Mexia, a Spaniard, lieutenant-colonel; which gave such disgust that Prem and all the officers sent in their resignations. Galvez begged and implored them to continue, reconciling himself to each individually; and at length, on his revoking the commission of Mexia, they

consented. At two o'clock it was rumoured that Carrera had joined the Antiguanos. Prem published a decree that all males from fourteen to sixty, except priests
and persons labouring under physical imbecility, should
take up arms. At nine o'clock at night there was an
alarm that a party of Carrera's gang was at the Ayce-
tuna. The square was garrisoned, and sentinels and
cannons placed at the corners of the streets. To add
to the excitement, during the night the provesor died,
and news was received that the Livingston Code had
been publicly burned at Chiquimula, and that the town
had declared against Galvez. On Wednesday morning fossés were commenced at the corners of the public square; but on Thursday the Marquis of Aycinena,
the leader of the Central party, by a conference with
the divided Liberals, succeeded in inducing a majority
of deputies to sign a convention of amnesty, which gave
general satisfaction, and the next day the city was perfectly quiet.

At midday this calm proved the forerunner of a
dreadful storm. The troops of the Federal government, the only reliable force, revolted, and with bayonets fixed, colours flying, and cannon in front, left the
barracks and marched into the plaza. They refused to
ratify the convention by which, it was represented to
them, Galvez was to be deposed, and Valenzuela, the
vice-chief, and a tool of Barundia, appointed in his
stead. They refused to serve under any of the opposition, and said they could give protection, and had no
occasion to ask it. Deputies were cited to attend a
meeting of the Assembly, but they were afraid to con-
vene. The officers had a conference with the soldiers;
and Merino, a sergeant, drew up a document requiring
the President Morazan to be sent for, and Galvez to

remain chief until his arrival. This was assented to. Deputies were sent requesting Morazan to come to Guatimala, and also to the Antigua, to explain the circumstances of violating the convention; but they were unsuccessful, and the same night the alarm-bell announced the approach of eight hundred men to attack the city. The militia were called to arms, but only about forty appeared. At half past five Galvez formed the government troops, and, accompanied by Prem, marched from the plaza to meet the rebels; but before he reached the gate a conspiracy broke out among the troops, and with the cry "Viva el General Merino, y muera el Gefe del Estado, qui nos ha vendido—fuego, muchachos!" "Live General Merino, and die the chief of the state, who has sold us—fire, boys," the infantry fired upon the etat major. A ball passed through Prem's hat; Galvez was thrown from his horse, but escaped, and took refuge behind the altar of the Church of La Concepcion. Yañez succeeded in dispersing the troops with his cavalry, and returned to the square, leaving fifteen dead in the street. Merino, with about a hundred and twenty men, took possession of the small field-piece of the battalion, and stationed himself in the square of Guadaloupe. Parties of the dispersed troops remained out all night, firing their muskets, and keeping the city in a state of alarm; but Yañez saved it from plunder by patrolling with his cavalry. In the morning Merino asked permission to march into the plaza. His number had increased by the return of straggling parties; and on forming in the plaza he and three or four of the ringleaders were ordered to leave the ranks, and sent to prison in the convent of San Domingo, where, on Monday afternoon, he was tied to a stake in his cell and shot. His grave at the foot of the stake, and blood

spattered on the wall, were among the curiosities shown
to me in Guatimala.

On Sunday morning the bells again sounded the
alarm ; the rebels were at the old gate, and commissioners were sent out to treat with them. They demanded an evacuation of the plaza by the soldiers ; but
the soldiers answered, indignantly, that the rebels
might come and take the square. Prem softened this
into an answer that they could not surrender to rebels,
and at about half past twelve at night the attack commenced. The rebels scattered in the suburbs, wasting
powder and bullets, and in the morning Yañez, with
seventy cavalry, made a sally, and, routing three hundred of them, returned into the plaza with lances reek-
ing with blood. Probably, if he had been seconded by
the citizens, he would have driven them all back to the
Antigua.

On Wednesday Carrera joined the rebels. He had
sent his emissaries to the villages, rousing the Indians,
and promising them the plunder of Guatimala ; and on
Thursday, with a tumultuous mass of half-naked savages, men, women, and children, estimated at ten or
twelve thousand, presented himself at the gate of the
city. The Antiguanos themselves were struck with consternation, and the citizens of Guatimala were thrown
into a state bordering on distraction. Commissioners
were again sent out to treat with him, from whom he
demanded the deposition of Galvez, the chief of the
state, the evacuation of the plaza by the Federal troops,
and a free passage into the city. Probably, even at this
time, if the Federal troops had been supported by the
citizens they could have resisted the entry ; but the
consternation, and the fear of exasperating the rebellious hordes, were so great, that nothing was thought of

but submission.   The Assembly met in terror and distraction, and the result was an assent to all that was demanded.

At five o'clock the small band of government troops evacuated the plaza.   The infantry, amounting to three hundred, marched out by the Calle Real, or Royal-street.   The cavalry, seventy in number, exclusive of officers, on their march through another street, met an aiddecamp of Carrera, who ordered them to lay down their arms.   Yañez answered that he must first see his general; but the dragoons, suspecting some treachery on the part of Valenzuela, became panic-struck, and fled.   Yañez, with thirty-five men, galloped through the city, and escaped by the road to Mixco; the rest rushed back into the plaza, threw down their lances in disgust, dismounted and disappeared, when not a single man was left under arms.

In the mean time Carrera's hordes were advancing. The commandant of the Antiguans asked him if he had his masses divided into squares or companies; he answered, "No entiendo nada de eso.   Todo es uno." "I don't understand anything of that.   It is all the same."   Among his leaders were Monreal and other known outlaws, criminals, robbers, and murderers. He himself was on horseback, with a green bush in his hat, and hung round with pieces of dirty cotton cloth, covered with pictures of the saints.   A gentleman who saw them from the roof of his house, and who was familiar with all the scenes of terror which had taken place in that unhappy city, told me that he never felt such consternation and horror as when he saw the entry of this immense mass of barbarians; choking up the streets, all with green bushes in their hats, seeming at a distance like a moving forest; armed with rusty muskets, old pistols, fowling-pieces, some with locks and some without; sticks formed into the shape of muskets, with tin-plate locks; clubs, machetes, and knives tied to the ends of long poles; and swelling the multitude were two or three thousand women, with sacks and alforgas for carrying away the plunder. Many, who had never left their villages before, looked wild at the sight of the houses and churches, and the magnificence of the city. They entered the plaza, vociferating "Viva la religion, y muerte a los etrangeros!" Carrera himself, amazed at the immense ball he had set in motion, was so embarrassed that he could not guide his horse. He afterward said that he was frightened at the difficulty of controlling this huge and disorderly mass. The traitor Barundia, the leader of the opposition, the Catiline of this rebellion, rode by his side on his entry into the plaza.

At sundown the whole multitude set up the Salve, or Hymn to the Virgin. The swell of human voices filled the air, and made the hearts of the inhabitants quake with fear. Carrera entered the Cathedral; the Indians, in mute astonishment at its magnificence, thronged in after him, and set up around the beautiful altar the uncouth images of their village saints. Monreal broke into the house of General Prem, and seized a uniform coat, richly embroidered with gold, into which Carrera slipped his arms, still wearing his straw hat with its green bush. A watch was brought him, but he did not know the use of it. Probably, since the invasion of Rome by Alaric and the Goths, no civilized city was ever visited by such an inundation of barbarians.

And Carrera alone had power to control the wild elements around him. As soon as possible some of the authorities sought him out, and in the most abject terms

begged him to state on what conditions he would evac-
uate the city. He demanded the deposition of Galvez,
the chief of the state, all the money, and all the arms
the government could command. The priests were the
only people who had any influence with him, and words
cannot convey any idea of the awful state of suspense
which the city suffered, dreading every moment to hear
the signal given for general pillage and massacre. The
inhabitants shut themselves up in their houses, which,
being built of stone, with iron balconies to the windows, and doors several inches thick, resisted the assaults of straggling parties; but atrocities more than
enough were committed, as it seemed, preliminary to a
general sacking. The vice-president of the republic
was murdered ; the house of Flores, a deputy, sacked,
his mother knocked down by a villain with the butt of
a musket, and one of his daughters shot in the arm with
two balls.

The house of Messrs. Klee, Skinner, & Co., the
principal foreign merchants in Guatimala, which was
reported to contain ammunition and arms, was several
times attacked with great ferocity ; having strong balconied windows, and the door being secured by bales
of merchandise piled up within, it resisted the assaults
of an undisciplined mob, armed only with clubs, muskets, knives, and machetes. The priests ran through
the streets bearing the crucifix, in the name of the Virgin and saints restraining the lawless Indians, stilling
the wildness of passion, and saving the terrified inhabitants. And I cannot help mentioning one whose name
was in everybody's mouth, Mr. Charles Savage, at that
time United States consul, who, in the midst of the
most furious assault upon Mr. Klee's house, rushed
down the street under a shower of bullets, knocking up

bayonets and machetes, drove the mob back from the door, and, branding them as robbers and murderers, with his white hair streaming in the wind, poured out such a torrent of indignation and contempt, that the Indians, amazed at his audacity, desisted. After this, with an almost wanton exposure of life, he was seen in the midst of every mob. To the astonishment of everybody, he was not killed; and the foreign residents presented him a unanimous letter of thanks for his fearless and successful exertions in the protection of life and property.

Pending the negotiation, Carrera, dressed in Prem's uniform, endeavoured to restrain his tumultuous followers; but several times he said that he could not himself resist the temptation to sack Klee's house, and those of the other Ingleses. There was a strange dash of fanaticism in the character of this lawless chieftain. The battle-cry of his hordes was "Viva la religion!" The palace of the archbishop had been suffered to be used as a theatre by the Liberals; Carrera demanded the keys, and, putting them in his pocket, declared that, to prevent any future pollution, it should not be opened again until the banished archbishop returned to occupy it.

At length the terms upon which he consented to withdraw were agreed upon, viz., eleven thousand dollars in silver, ten thousand to be distributed among his followers, and one thousand for his own share; a thousand muskets, and a commission as lieutenant-colonel for himself. The amount of money was small as the price of relief from such imminent danger, but it was an immense sum in the eyes of Carrera and his followers, few of whom were worth more than the rags on their backs and the stolen arms in their hands; and it was not easily raised; the treasury was bankrupt, and the money was not very cheerfully contributed by the citizens. The madness of consenting to put in the hands of Carrera a thousand muskets was only equalled by the absurdity of making him a lieutenant-colonel.

On the afternoon of the third day the money was paid, the muskets delivered, and Carrera was invested with the command of the province of Mita, a district near Guatimala. The joy of the inhabitants at the prospect of his immediate departure was without bounds; but at the last moment an awful rumour spread, that the wild bands had evinced an uncontrollable eagerness, before leaving, to sack the city. A random discharge of muskets in the plaza confirmed this rumour, and the effect was dreadful. An hour of terrible suspense followed, but at five o'clock they filed off in straggling crowds from the plaza. At the Plaza de Toros they halted, and, firing their muskets in the air, created another panic. A rumour was revived that Carrera had demanded four thousand dollars more, and that, unless he received it, he would return and take it by force. Carrera himself did actually return, and demanded a fieldpiece, which was given him; and at length, leaving behind him a document requiring the redress of certain grievances, to the unspeakable joy of all the inhabitants he left the city.

The delight of the citizens at being relieved from the pressure of immediate danger was indeed great, but there was no return of confidence, and, unhappily, no healing of political animosities. Valenzuela was appointed chief of the state; the Assembly renewed its distracted sessions; Barundia, as the head of the now ministerial party, proposed to abolish all the unconstitutional decrees of Galvez; money was wanted, and recourse had to the old system of forced loans. This exasperated the moneyed men; and in the midst of discord and confusion news was received that Quezaltenango, one of the departments of Guatimala, had seceded, and declared itself a separate state. At this time, too, the government received a letter from Carrera, stating that he had been informed, since his arrival at Matasquintla, that people spoke ill of him in the capital, and if they continued to do so he had four thousand men, and would return and put things right. From time to time he sent a message to the same effect by some straggling Indian who happened to pass through his village. Afterward it was reported that his followers had renounced his authority and commenced operations on their own account, threatening the city with another invasion, determined, according to their proclamations, to exterminate the whites and establish a government of pardos libres, " free tigers," and enjoy in their own right the lands which had devolved upon them by their emancipation from the dominion of the whites. To the honour of Guatimala, a single spark of spirit broke forth, and men of all classes took up arms; but it was a single flash, and soon died away. Again intelligence arrived that Carrera himself had sent out his emissaries to summon his hordes for another march upon the city. Several families received private information and advice to seek safety in flight. Hundreds of people did so, and the roads were crowded with processions of mules, horses, and Indians loaded with luggage. On Sunday everybody was going, and early on Monday morning guards were placed at the barriers. Hundreds of passports were applied for and refused. Again a decree was published that all should take up arms. The militia were again mus-

tered. At ten o'clock on Tuesday night it was said
that Carrera was at Palencia, at eleven that he had
gone to suppress an insurrection of his own bandits,
and on Wednesday night that he was at a place called
Canales. On Sunday, the fourth of March, a review
took place of about seven hundred men. The Antigua sent three hundred and fifty muskets, and ammunition, which they did not consider it prudent to keep, as
there had been cries of " muera Guatimala, y viva Carrera !" and placards bearing the same ominous words
had been posted on the walls. At this time a letter
was received from Carrera by the government, advising them to disband their troops, and assuring them
that he was collecting forces only to destroy a party of
four hundred rebels, headed by one Galvez (the former chief of the state, whom he had deposed), and requesting two cannon and more ammunition. At another time, probably supposing that the government
must be interested in his fortunes, he sent word that he
had narrowly escaped being assassinated. Monreal
had taken advantage of an opportunity, seduced his
men, tied him to a tree, and was in the very act of
having him shot, when his brother Sotero Carrera
rushed in, and ran Monreal through with his bayonet.
The government now conceived the project of inducing
his followers, by the influence of the priests, to surrender their arms on paying them five dollars apiece ; but
very soon he was heard of stronger than ever, occupying all the roads, sending in imperious proclamations to
the government, and at length the news came that he
was actually marching upon the city.

At this time, to the unspeakable joy of the inhabitants, General Morazan, the president of the republic,
arrived from San Salvador, with fifteen hundred men.

But even yet party spirit was dominant. General Morazan encamped a few leagues from the city, hesitating to enter it or to employ the forces of the general government in putting down a revolution in the state except with the consent of the state government. The state government was jealous of the federal government, tenacious of prerogatives it had not the courage to defend, and demanded from the president a plan of his campaign; passed a decree offering Carrera and his followers fifteen days to lay down their arms, which General Morazan would not permit to be published at his headquarters; two days afterward annulled it, and authorized the president of the republic to act as circumstances might require.

During this time one of Morazan's piquets had been cut off and the officers murdered, which created a great excitement among his soldiers; but, anxious to avoid shedding more blood, he sent into the city for the Canonigo Castillo and Barundia, deputing them as commissioners to persuade the bandits to surrender their arms, even offering to pay fifteen dollars a head rather than come to extremities. The commissioners found Carrera at one of his old haunts among the mountains of Matasquintla, surrounded by hordes of Indians living upon tortillas. The traitor Barundia had been received by Morazan's soldiers with groans; his poor jaded horse was tied up at Morazan's camp a day and a half without a blade of grass; and, as a farther reward of his treason, Carrera refused to meet him under a roof, because, as he said, he did not wish to plunge his new lance, a present from a priest, into Barundia's breast.

The meeting took place in the open air, and on the top of a mountain. Carrera refused to lay down his arms unless all his former demands were complied with, and unless also the Indian capitation tax was reduced to one third of its amount ; but he softened his asperity against foreigners to the demand that only those not married should be expelled the country, and that thereafter they should be permitted to traffic only, and not to radicate in it. The atrocious priest Padre Lobo, his constant friend and adviser, was with him. The arguments of the Canonigo Castillo, particularly in regard to the folly of charging the government with an attempt to poison the Indians, were listened to with much attention by them, but Carrera broke up the conference by asserting vehemently that the government had offered him twenty dollars a head for every Indian he poisoned.

All hope of compromise was now at an end, and General Morazan marched immediately to Matasquintla ; but before he reached it Carrera's bands had disappeared among the mountains. He heard of them in another place, devastating the country, desolating villages and towns, and again, before his troops could reach them, the muskets were concealed, and the Indians either in the mountains or quietly working in the fields. Mr. Hall, the British vice-consul, received a letter from eleven British subjects at Salama, a distance of three days' journey, stating that they had been seized at night by a party of Carrera's troops, stripped of everything, confined two nights and a day without food, and sentenced to be shot, but finally ordered to leave the country, which they were then doing, destitute of everything, and begging their way to the port. A few nights after, at ten o'clock, the cannon of alarm was sounded in the city, and it was reported that Carrera was again at the gates. All this time party strife was as violent as ever ; the Centralists trembling

with apprehension, but in their hearts rejoicing at the
distraction of the country under the administration of
the Liberals, and that one had risen up capable of in-
spiring them with terror ; and the divided Liberals ha-
ting each other with a more intense hate even than the
Centralists bore to them ; but the excitement became so
great that all the parties drew up separate petitions to
General Morazan, representing the deplorable state of
insecurity in the city, and begging him to enter and
provide for its safety. Separate sets of deputies hurried to anticipate each other at General Morazan's
headquarters, and pay court to him by being the first to
ask his protection. General Morazan had become acquainted with the distracted condition of the city, and
was in the act of mounting his horse when the deputies
arrived. On Sunday he entered with an escort of two
hundred soldiers, amid the ringing of bells, firing of
cannon, and other demonstrations of joy. The same
day the merchants, with the Marquis of Aycinena and
others of the Central party, presented a petition representing the dreadful state of public feeling, and requesting Morazan to depose the state authorities and assume
the reins of government, and to convoke a Constituent
Assembly, as the only means of saving Guatimala from
utter ruin. In the evening deputies from the different
branches of the Liberal party had long conferences
with the president. Morazan answered all that he
wished to act legally, would communicate with the Assembly the next day, and be governed by their decision. The proceedings in the Assembly are too afflict-
ing and disgraceful to dwell upon. So far as I can understand the party strife of that time, after wading
through papers and pamphlets emanating from both
sides, General Morazan conducted himself with probi-

ty and honour. The Centralists made a desperate effort to attach him to them, but he would not accept the offered embrace, nor the sycophantic service of men who had always opposed him; nor would he sustain what he believed to be wrong in his own partisans.

In the mean time Carrera was gaining ground; he had routed several detachments of the Federal troops, massacred men, and increased his stock of ammunition and arms. At length all agreed that something must be done; and at a final meeting of the Assembly, with a feeling of desperation, it was decreed without debate,

1. That the state government should retire to the Antigua.

2. That the president, in person or by delegate, should govern the *district* according to article 176 of the Constitution.

Amid these scenes within the city, and rumours of worse from without, on Sunday night a ball was given to Morazan; but the Centralists, displeased at his not acceding to their overtures, did not attend. Galvez, the chief deposed by Carrera, made his first appearance since his deposition, and danced the whole time.

Though Morazan was irresolute in the cabinet, he was all energy in the field; and being now invested with full power, sustained his high reputation as a skilful soldier. The bulletin of the army for May and June exhibits the track of Carrera, devastating villages and towns, and the close pursuit of the government troops, beating him wherever they found him, but never able to secure his person. In the mean time, party jealousies continued, and the state government was in a state of anarchy. The Assembly could not meet, because, the state party not attending, it was incumbent on the vice-chief to retire, and the oldest counsellor to take his place. But there was no such person; the term of the council had expired, and no new elections had been held; and while Morazan was dispersing the wild bands of Carrera, and relieving the Guatimalians from the danger which had brought them to their knees before him, the old jealousies revived, and incendiary publications were issued, charging him with exhausting the country in supporting idle soldiers, and keeping the city in subjection by bayonets.

About the first of July General Morazan considered Guatimala relieved from all external danger, and returned to San Salvador, leaving troops in different towns under the command of Carvallo, and appointing Carlos Salazar commandant in the city. Carrera was supposed to be completely put down; and to bring things to a close, Carvallo published the following

"NOTICE.

"The person or persons who may deliver the criminal Rafael Carrera, dead or alive (if he does not present himself voluntarily under the last pardon), shall receive a reward of fifteen hundred dollars and two cabellerias of land, and pardon for any crime he has committed.

"The general-in-chief,

"*Guatimala, July* 20, 1838.   J. N. CARVALLO."

But the "criminal" Carrera, the proscribed outlaw, was not yet put down. One by one, he surprised the detachments of Federal troops; and while the city exhibited the fierceness of party spirit, forced loans, complaints of the expense of maintaining idle soldiers, plans to abolish the state government and form a provisional junta, its actual prostration, and the organizing of a Constituent Assembly with M. Rivera Paz at the head, Carrera, with still increasing numbers, attacked Amatitan, took the Antigua, and, barely waiting to sack a few houses, stripped it of cannon, muskets, and ammunition, and again marched against Guatimala, proclaiming his intention to raze every house to the ground, and murder every white inhabitant.

The consternation in the city cannot be conceived. General Morazan was again solicited to come. A line in pencil was received from him by a man who carried it sewed up in the sleeve of his coat, urging the city to defend itself and hold out for a few days; but the danger was too imminent; Salazar, at the head of the Federal troops (the idle soldiers complained of), marched out at two o'clock in the morning, and, aided by a thick fog, came upon Carrera suddenly at Villa Nueva, killed four hundred and fifty of his men, and completely routed him, Carrera himself being badly wounded in the thigh. The city was saved from destruction, and the day after Morazan entered with a thousand men. The shock of the immense danger they had escaped was not yet over; on the morrow it might return; party jealousies were scared away; all looked to General Morazan as the only man who could effectually save them from Carrera, and, in turn, begged him to accept the office of dictator.

About the same time Guzman, the general of Quezaltenango, arrived, with seven hundred men, and General Morazan made formidable arrangements to enclose and crush the Cachurecos. The result was the same as before: Carrera was constantly beaten, but as constantly escaped. His followers were scattered, his best men taken and shot, and he himself was penned up and almost starved on the top of a mountain, with a cordon of soldiers around its base, and only escaped by the remissness of the guard. In three months, chased from place to place, his old haunts broken up, and hemmed in on every side, he entered into a treaty with Guzman, by which he agreed to deliver up one thousand muskets, and disband his remaining followers. In executing the treaty, however, he delivered only four hundred muskets, and those old and worthless; and this breach of the convention was winked at by Guzman, little dreaming of the terrible fate reserved for himself at Carrera's hands.

This over, Morazan deposed Rivera Paz, restored Salazar, and returned to San Salvador, first laying heavy contributions on the city to support the expense of the war, and taking with him all the soldiers of the Federal Government, belying one of the party cries against him, that he was attempting to retain an influence in the city by bayonets. Guzman returned to Quezaltenango, and the garrison consisted only of seventy men.

The contributions and the withdrawal of the troops from the city created great dissatisfaction with Morazan, and at this time the political horizon became cloudy throughout the republic. The Marquis of Aycinena, who had been banished by Morazan, and had resided several years in the United States, studying our institutions, by a series of articles which were widely circulated, purporting to illustrate our constitution and laws, hurried on the crisis; Honduras and Costa Rica declared their independence of the general government: all this came back upon Guatimala, and added fuel to the already flaming fire of dissension.

On the 24th of March, 1839, Carrera issued a bulletin from his old quarters in Matasquintla, in which, referring to the declaration of independence by the States, he says: "When those laws came to my hands, I read them and returned to them very often; as a loving mother clasps in her arms an only son whom she

believed lost, and presses him against her heart, so did
I with the pamphlet that contained the declaration; for
in it I found the principles that I sustain and the reforms
I desire." This was rather figurative, as Carrera could
not at that time read; but it must have been quite
new to him, and a satisfaction to find out what principles he sustained. Again he threatened to enter the
city. All was anarchy and distraction in the councils,
and on the twelfth of April his hordes appeared before
the gates. All were aghast, but there was no rising to
repel him. Morazan was beyond the reach of their
voice, and they who had been loudest in denouncing
him for attempting to control the city by bayonets now
denounced him for leaving them to the mercy of Carrera. All who could hid away their treasures and fled;
the rest shut themselves up in their houses, barring
their doors and windows, and at two o'clock in the
morning, routing the guard, he entered with fifteen hundred men. Salazar, the commandant, fled, and Carrera, riding up to the house of Rivera Paz, knocked at
the door, and reinstalled him chief of the state. His
soldiers took up their quarters in the barracks, and
Carrera established himself as the guardian of the city;
and it is due to him to say that he acknowledged his
own incompetency to govern, and placed men at the
disposition of the municipality to preserve the peace.
The Central party was thus restored to power. Carrera's fanaticism bound him to the Church party; he
was flattered by his association and connexion with the
aristocracy, was made brigadier-general, and presented with a handsome uniform; and, besides empty honours, he had the city barracks and pay for his men,
which was better than Indian huts and foraging expeditions; the last, too, being a resource for pastime. The

league had continued since the April preceding my arrival. The great bond of union was hatred of Morazan and the Liberals. The Centralists had their Constituent Assembly, abolished the laws made by the Liberals, revived old Spanish laws and old names for the courts of justice and officers of government, and passed any laws they pleased so that they did not interfere with him. Their great difficulty was to keep him quiet. Unable to remain inactive in the city, he marched toward San Salvador, for the ostensible purpose of attacking General Morazan. The Centralists were in a state of great anxiety; Carrera's success or his defeat was alike dangerous to them. If defeated, Morazan might march directly upon the city, and take signal vengeance upon them; if successful, he might return with his barbarians so intoxicated by victory as to be utterly uncontrollable. A little circumstance shows the position of things. Carrera's mother, an old woman well-known as a huckster on the plaza, died. Formerly it was the custom with the higher classes to bury in vaults constructed within the churches; but from the time of the cholera, all burials, without distinction, were forbidden in the churches, and even within the city, and a campo santo was established outside the town, in which all the principal families had vaults. Carrera signified his pleasure that his mother should be buried in the Cathedral! The government charged itself with the funeral, issued cards of invitation, and all the principal inhabitants followed in the procession. No efforts were spared to conciliate and keep him in good temper; but he was subject to violent bursts of passion, and, it was said, had cautioned the members of the government at such moments not to attempt to argue with him, but to let him have his own

way. Such was Carrera, at the time of my visit more
absolute master of Guatimala than any king in Europe
of his dominions, and by the fanatic Indians called el
Hico de Dios, the Son of God, and nuestro Señor, our
Lord.

When I entered the room he was sitting at a table
counting sixpenny and shilling pieces. Colonel Monte
Rosa, a dark Mestitzo, in a dashing uniform, was sitting
by his side, and several other persons were in the room.
He was about five feet six inches in height, with
straight black hair, an Indian complexion and expression, without beard, and did not seem to be more than
twenty-one years old. He wore a black bombazet
roundabout jacket and pantaloons. He rose as we entered, pushed the money on one side of the table, and,
probably out of respect to my coat, received me with
courtesy, and gave me a chair at his side. My first
remark was an expression of surprise at his extreme
youth ; he answered that he was but twenty-three years
old ; certainly he was not more than twenty-five ; and
then, as a man conscious that he was something extraordinary, and that I knew it, without waiting for any
leading questions, he continued, that he had begun (he
did not say what) with thirteen men armed with old
muskets, which they were obliged to fire with cigars ;
pointed to eight places in which he had been wounded,
and said that he had three balls then in his body. At
this time he could hardly be recognised as the same
man who, less than two years before, had entered Guatimala with a horde of wild Indians, proclaiming death
to strangers. Indeed, in no particular had he changed
more than in his opinion of foreigners, a happy illustration of the effect of personal intercourse in breaking
down prejudices against individuals or classes. He

had become personally acquainted with several, one of whom, an English doctor, had extracted a ball from his side; and his intercourse with all had been so satisfactory, that his feelings had undergone an entire revulsion; and he said that they were the only people who never deceived him. He had done, too, what I consider extraordinary; in the intervals of his hurried life he had learned to write his name, and had thrown aside his stamp. I never had the fortune to be presented to any legitimate king, nor to any usurper of the prerogatives of royalty except Mohammed Ali. Old as he was, I gave him some good advice; and it grieves me that the old lion is now shorn of his mane. Considering Carrera a promising young man, I told him that he had a long career before him, and might do much good to his country; and he laid his hand upon his heart, and with a burst of feeling that I did not expect, said he was determined to sacrifice his life for his country. With all his faults and his crimes, none ever accused him of duplicity, or of saying what he did not mean; and, perhaps, as many self-deceiving men have done before him, he believes himself a patriot.

I considered that he was destined to exercise an important, if not a controlling influence on the affairs of Central America; and trusting that hopes of honourable and extended fame might have some effect upon his character, I told him that his name had already reached my country, and that I had seen in the newspapers an account of his last entry into Guatimala, with praises of his moderation and exertions to prevent atrocities. He expressed himself pleased that his name was known, and such mention made of him among strangers; and said he was not a robber and murderer, as he was called by his enemies. He seemed intelligent and capable of improvement, and I told him that he ought to travel into other countries, and particularly, from its contiguity, into mine. He had a very indefinite notion as to where my country was; he knew it only as El Norte, or the North; inquired about the distance and facility for getting there, and said that, when the wars were over, he would endeavour to make El Norte a visit. But he could not fix his thoughts upon anything except the wars and Morazan; in fact, he knew of nothing else. He was boyish in his manners and manner of speaking, but very grave; he never smiled, and, conscious of power, was unostentatious in the exhibition of it, though he always spoke in the first person of what he had done and what he intended to do. One of the hangers-on, evidently to pay court to him, looked for a paper bearing his signature to show me as a specimen of his handwriting, but did not find one. My interview with him was much more interesting than I had expected; so young, so humble in his origin, so destitute of early advantages, with honest impulses, perhaps, but ignorant, fanatic, sanguinary, and the slave of violent passions, wielding absolutely the physical force of the country, and that force entertaining a natural hatred to the whites. At parting he accompanied me to the door, and in the presence of his villanous soldiers made me a free offer of his services. I understood that I had the good fortune to make a favourable impression; and afterward, but, unluckily, during my absence, he called upon me in full dress and in state, which for him was an unusual thing.

At that time, as Don Manuel Pavon told me, he professed to consider himself a brigadier-general, subject to the orders of the government. He had no regular

allowance for the maintenance of himself and troops ;
he did not like keeping accounts, and called for money
when he wanted it ; and, with this understanding, in
eight months he had not required more than Morazan
did in two.   He really did not want money for himself,
and as a matter of policy he paid the Indians but little.
This operated powerfully with the aristocracy, upon
whom the whole burden of raising money devolved.
It may be a satisfaction to some of my friends to know
that this lawless chief is under a dominion to which
meeker men are loth to submit ; his wife accompa-
nies him on horseback in all his expeditions, influenced
by a feeling which is said to proceed sometimes from
excess of affection ; and I have heard that it is no unimportant part of the business of the chief of the state
to settle family jars.

As we were returning to my house, we met a gentleman who told Mr. Pavon that a party of soldiers
was searching for a member of the Assembly who was
lying under the displeasure of Carrera, but a personal
friend of theirs ; and as we passed on we saw a file
of soldiers drawn up before his door, while others were
inside searching the house.   This was done by Carrera's orders, without any knowledge on the part of the
government.

CHAPTER XII.

In consequence of the convulsions and danger of the times, the city was dull, and there was no gayety in private circles; but an effort had been made by some enterprising ladies to break the monotony, and a party, to which I was invited, was formed for that afternoon to Mixco, an Indian village about three leagues distant, at which the festival of its patron saint was to be celebrated the next day with Indian rites.

At four o'clock in the afternoon I left my door on horseback, to call on Don Manuel Pavon. His house was next to that of the proscribed deputy, and a line of soldiers was drawn around the whole block, with the purpose of preventing an escape, while every house was searched. I always gave these gentlemen a wide berth when I could, but it was necessary to ride along the whole line; and as I passed the house of the deputy, with the door closed and sentinels before it, I could but think of his distressed family, in agony lest his hiding-place should be discovered.

Don Manuel was waiting for me, and we rode to the house of one of the ladies of the party, a young widow whom I had not seen before, and who, in her riding-dress, made a fine appearance. Her horse was ready, and when she had kissed the old people good-by we carried her off. The women-servants, with familiarity

and affection, followed to the door, and continued farewell greetings and cautions to take good care of herself, which the lady answered as long as we were
within hearing. We called at two or three other
houses, and then all assembled at the place of rendez-
vous. The courtyard was full of horses, with every variety of fanciful mountings. Although we were going
only nine miles, and to a large Indian village, it was
necessary to carry beds, bedding, and provisions. A
train of servants large enough to carry stores for a small
military expedition was sent ahead, and we all started.
Outside the gate all the anxieties and perils which
slumbered in the city were forgotten. Our road lay
over an extensive plain, seeming, as the sun went down
behind the volcanoes of Agua and Fuego, a beautiful
bowling-green, in which our party, preceded by a long
file of Indians with loads on their backs, formed a
picture. I was surprised to find that the ladies were
not good horsewomen. They never ride for pleasure,
and, on account of the want of accommodation on the
road, seldom travel.

It was after dark when we reached the borders of
a deep ravine separating the plain from Mixco. We
descended, and, rising on the other side, emerged from
the darkness of the ravine into an illuminated street,
and, at two or three horses' lengths, into a plaza blazing with lights and crowded with people, nearly all
Indians in holyday costume. In the centre of the plaza
was a fine fountain, and at the head of it a gigantic
church. We rode up to the house that had been provided for the ladies, and, leaving them there, the gentlemen scattered to find lodgings for themselves. The
door of every house was open, and the only question
asked was whether there was room. Some of the

young men did not give themselves this trouble, as
they were disposed to make a night of it; and Mr. P.
and I, having secured a place, returned to the house occupied by the ladies.   In one corner was a tienda about
ten feet square, partitioned off and shelved, which served
as a place for their hats and shawls.   The rest of the
room contained merely a long table and benches.   In a
few moments the ladies were ready, and we all sallied
out for a walk.   All the streets and passages were brill-
iantly illuminated, and across some were arches decorated with evergreens and lighted, and at the corners were
altars under arbours of branches adorned with flowers.
The spirit of frolic seemed to take possession of our file-
leaders, who, as the humour prompted them, entered
any house, and after a lively chat left it, contriving to
come out just as the last of the party were going in.   In
one house they found a poncha rolled up very carefully,
with the end of a guitar sticking out.   The proprietor
of the house only knew that it belonged to a young man
from Guatimala, who had left it as an indication of his
intention to pass the night there.   One of the young
men unrolled the poncha, and some loaves of bread
fell out, which he distributed, and with half a loaf in
his mouth struck up a waltz, which was followed by a
quadrille; the good people of the house seemed pleased at this free use of their roof, and shaking hands all
around, with many expressions of good-will on both
sides, we left as unceremoniously as we had entered.
We made the tour of all the principal streets, and as
we returned to the plaza the procession was coming out
of the church.

The village procession in honour of its patron saint
is the great pride of the Indian, and the touchstone of
his religious character.   Every Indian contributes his

labour and money toward getting it up, and he is most
honoured who is allowed the most important part in it.
This was a rich village, at which all the muleteers of
Guatimala lived; and nowhere had I seen an Indian
procession so imposing. The church stood on an elevation at the head of the plaza, its whole façade rich in
ornaments illuminated by the light of torches; and the
large platform and the steps were thronged with women
in white. A space was cleared in the middle before
the great door, and with a loud chant the procession
passed out of the doorway. First came the alcalde and
his alguazils, all Indians, with rods of office in one hand
and lighted wax candles, six or eight feet long, in the
other; then a set of devils, not as playful as the devils
of Guatimala, but more hideous, and probably better
likenesses, according to the notions of the Indians; then
came, borne aloft by Indians, a large silver cross, richly
chased and ornamented, and followed by the curate,
with a silken canopy held over his head on the ends of
long poles borne by Indians. As the cross advanced
all fell on their knees, and a stranger would have been
thought guilty of an insult upon their holy religion who
omitted conforming to this ceremony. Then came figures of saints larger than life, borne on the shoulders
of Indians; and then a figure of the Virgin, gorgeously
dressed, her gown glittering with spangles. Then followed a long procession of Indian women dressed in
costume, with a thick red cord twisted in the hair, so as
to look like a turban, all carrying lighted candles. The
procession passed through the illuminated streets, under
the arches, and stopping from time to time before the
altars, made the tour of the village, and in about an
hour, with a loud chant, ascended the steps of the
church. Its re-entry was announced by a discharge of

rockets, after which all gathered in the plaza for the exhibition of fireworks.

It was some time before these were ready, for those who had figured in the procession, particularly the devils, were to be the principal managers. Our party was well known in Mixco ; and though the steps of the church were crowded, one of the best places was immediately vacated for us. From their nearness to Guatimala, the people of Mixco knew all the principal families of the former place, and were glad to see so distinguished a party at their festa ; and the familiar but respectful way in which they were everywhere treated, manifested a simplicity of manners, and a kindliness of feeling between the rich and the poor, which to me was one of the most interesting parts of the whole fête.

The exhibition began with the Toros ; the man who played the bull gave universal satisfaction ; scattering and putting to flight the crowd in the plaza, he rushed up the steps of the church, and, amid laughing and screaming, went out. Flying pigeons and other pieces followed ; and the whole concluded with the grand national piece of the Castle of San Felippe, which was a representation of the repulse of an English fleet. A tall structure represented the castle, and a little brig perched on the end of a stick, like a weathercock, the fleet. The brig fired a broadside, and then, by a sudden jerk, turned on a pivot and fired another ; and long after, until she had riddled herself to pieces, the castle continued pouring on all sides a magnanimous stream of fire.

When all was over we returned to the posada. A cloth was spread over the long table, and in a few minutes, under the direction of the ladies, covered with the pic-nic materials brought from Guatimala.

The benches were drawn up to the table, and as many as could find seats sat down. Before supper was over there was an irruption of young men from Guatimala, with glazed hats, ponchas, and swords, and presenting a rather disorderly appearance ; but they were mostly juveniles, brothers and cousins of the ladies. With their hats on, they seated themselves at the vacated tables, and, as soon as they had finished eating, hurried off the plates, piled the tables away in a corner, one on the top of the other, and the candles on the top of all, the violins struck up, and gentlemen and ladies, lighting cigars and cigarillos, commenced dancing. I am sorry to say that generally the ladies of Central America, not excepting Guatimala, smoke, married ladies puros, or all tobacco, and unmarried cigars, or tobacco wrapped in paper or straw. Every gentleman carries in his pocket a silver case, with a long string of cotton, steel and flint, taking up nearly as much space as a handkerchief, and one of the offices of gallantry is to strike a light ; by doing it well, he may help to kindle a flame in a lady's heart ; at all events, to do it bunglingly would be ill-bred. I will not express my sentiments on smoking as a custom for the sex. I have recollections of beauteous lips profaned. Nevertheless, even in this I have seen a lady show her prettiness and refinement, barely touching the straw to her lips, as it were kissing it gently and taking it away. When a gentleman asks a lady for a light, she always removes the cigar from her lips. Happily, the dangerous proximity which sometimes occurs between gentlemen in the street is not in vogue. The dancing continued till two o'clock, and the breaking up was like the separation of a gay

family party. The young men dispersed to sleep or to
finish the night with merriment elsewhere, and Don
Manuel and I retired to the house he had secured for us.

We were in our hammocks, talking over the affairs
of the night, when we heard a noise in the street, a
loud tramping past the door, and a clash of swords.
Presently Mr. P.'s servant knocked for admission, and
told us that a man had been killed a few doors off by a
sword-cut across the head. Instead of going out to
gratify an idle curiosity, like prudent men we secured
the door. The tramping passed up the street, and
presently we heard reports of firearms. The whole
place seemed to be in an uproar. We had hardly lain
down again before there was another knock at the door.
Our host, a respectable old man, with his wife, slept in
a back room, and, afraid of rioters, they had a consultation about opening it. The former was unwilling to
do so, but the latter, with a mother's apprehensions,
said that she was afraid some accident had happened to
Chico. The knocking continued, and Raffael, a known
companion of their son, cried out that Chico was
wounded. The old man rose for a light, and, apprehending the worst, the mother and a young sister burst
into tears. The old man sternly checked them, said
that he had always cautioned Chico against going out at
night, and that he deserved to be punished. The sister ran and opened the door, and two young men entered. We could see the glitter of their swords, and that
one was supporting the other ; and, just as the old man
procured a light, the wounded man fell on the ground.
His face was ghastly pale, and spotted with blood ; his
hat cut through the crown and rim as smoothly as if done
with a razor, and his right hand and arm were wound

in a pocket-handerchief, which was stained with blood.
The old man looked at him with the sternness of a Roman, and told him that he knew this would be the consequence of his running out at night ; the mother and
sister cried, and the young man, with a feeble voice,
begged his father to spare him. His companion carried him into the back room ; but before they could
lay him on the bed he fell again and fainted. The
father was alarmed, and when he recovered, asked
him whether he wished to confess. Chico, with a
faint voice, answered, As you please. The old man
told his daughter to go for the padre, but the uproar
was so great in the street that she was afraid to venture
out. In the mean time we examined his head, which,
notwithstanding the cut through his hat, was barely
touched ; and he said himself that he had received the
blow on his hand, and that it was cut off. There was no
physician nearer than Guatimala, and not a person who
was able to do anything for him. I had had some
practice in medicine, but none in surgery ; I knew,
however, that it was at all events proper to wash and
cleanse the wound, and with the assistance of Don
Manuel's servant, a young Englishman whom Don
Manuel had brought from the United States, laid him
on a bed. This servant had had some experience in
the brawls of the country, having killed a young man in
a quarrel growing out of a love affair, and been confined to the house seven months by wounds received in
the same encounter. With his assistance I unwound
the bloody handkerchief ; as I proceeded I found my
courage failing me, and as, with the last coil, a dead
hand fell in mine, a shudder and a deep groan ran
through the spectators, and I almost let the hand drop.

It was cut off through the back above the knuckles, and the four fingers hung merely by the fleshy part of the thumb. The skin was drawn back, and showed on each side four bones protruding like the teeth of a skeleton. I joined them together, and as he drew up his arm they jarred like the grating of teeth. I saw that the case was beyond my art. Possibly the hand might have been restored by sewing the skin together ; but I believed that the only thing to be done was to cut it off entirely, and this I was not willing to do. Unable to give any farther assistance, I wound it up again in the handkerchief. The young man had a mild and pleasing countenance ; and as thankful for my ineffectual attempt as if I had really served him, told me not to give myself any more trouble, but return to bed ; his mother and sister, with stifled sobs, hung over his head ; his father retained the sternness of his manner, but it was easy to see that his heart was bleeding ; and to me, a stranger, it was horrible to see a fine young man mutilated for life in a street-brawl.

As he told the story himself, he was walking with some of his friends, when he met one of the Spinosas from Guatimala, also with a party of friends. The latter, who was known as a bully, approached them with an expression in Spanish about equivalent to the English one, " I'll give it to you." Chico answered, " No you won't," and immediately they drew their swords. Chico, in attempting to ward off a stroke, received it on the edge of his right hand. In passing through all the bones, its force was so much broken that it only cut the crown and rim of his hat. The loss of his hand had no doubt saved his life; for, if the whole force of the stroke had fallen on his head, it must have killed him ; but the unfortunate young man, instead of being thankful for his escape, swore vengeance against Spinosa. The latter, as I afterward learned, swore that the next time Chico should not escape with the loss of his hand; and, in all probability, when they meet again one of them will be killed.

All this time the uproar continued, shifting its location, with occasional reports of firearms ; an aunt was wringing her hands because her son was out, and we had reason to fear a tragical night. We went to bed, but for a long time the noise in the street, the groans of poor Chico, and the sobbing of his mother and sister kept us from sleeping.

We did not wake till nearly ten o'clock. It was Sunday; the morning was bright and beautiful, the arches and flowers still adorned the streets, and the Indians, in their clean clothes, were going to Sunday mass. None except the immediate parties knew or cared for the events of the night. Crossing the plaza, we met a tall, dashing fellow on horseback, with a long sword by his side, who bowed to Mr. Pavon, and rode on past the house of Chico. This was Spinosa. No one attempted to molest him, and no notice whatever was taken of the circumstance by the authorities.

The door of the church was so crowded that we could not enter ; and passing through the curate's house, we stood in a doorway on one side of the altar. The curate, in his richest vestments, with young Indian assistants in sacerdotal dresses, their long black hair and sluggish features contrasting strangely with their garb and occupations, was officiating at the altar. On the front steps, with their black mantons drawn over their heads, and their eyes bent on the ground, were the dancers of our party the preceding night; kneeling along the whole floor of the immense church was a dense

mass of Indian women, with red headdresses ; and leaning against the pillars, and standing up in the background, were Indians wrapped in black chamars.

We waited till mass was over, and then accompanied
the ladies to the house and breakfasted. Sunday though
it was, the occupations for the day were a cockfight in
the morning and bullfight in the afternoon. Our party
was increased by the arrival of a distinguished family
from Guatimala, and we all set out for the former. It
was in the yard of an unoccupied house, which was already crowded ; and I noticed, to the honour of the Indians and the shame of the better classes, that they
were all Mestitzoes or white men, and, always excepting Carrera's soldiers, I never saw a worse looking or
more assassin-like set of men. All along the walls of
the yard were cocks tied by one leg, and men running
about with other cocks under their arms, putting them
on the ground to compare size and weight, regulating
bets, and trying to cheat each other. At length a match
was made ; the ladies of our party had seats in the corridor of the house, and a space was cleared before them.
The gaffs were murderous instruments, more than two
inches long, thick, and sharp as needles, and the birds
were hardly on the ground before the feathers of the
neck were ruffled and they flew at each other. In less
time than had been taken to gaff them, one was lying
on the ground with its tongue hanging out, and the
blood running from its mouth, dead. The eagerness
and vehemence, noise and uproar, wrangling, betting,
swearing, and scuffling of the crowd, exhibited a dark
picture of human nature and a sanguinary people. I
owe it to the ladies to say, that in the city they never
are present at such scenes. Here they went for no
other reason that I could see than because they were

away from home, and it was part of the fête. We must make allowances for an education and state of society every way different from our own. They were not wanting in sensibility or refinement; and though they did not turn away with disgust, they seemed to take no interest in the fight, and were not disposed to wait for a second.

Leaving the disgusting scene, we walked around the suburbs, one point of which commands a noble view of the plain and city of Guatimala, with the surrounding mountains, and suggests a wonder that, amid objects so grand and glorious, men can grow up with tastes so grovelling. Crossing the plaza, we heard music in a large house belonging to a rich muleteer; and entering, we found a young harpist, and two mendicant friars with shaved crowns, dressed in white, with long white mantles and hoods, of an order newly revived in Guatimala, and drinking agua ardiente. Mantas and hats were thrown off, tables and seats placed against the wall, and in a few moments my friends were waltzing; two or three cotillons followed, and we returned to the posada, where, after fruit of various kinds had been served, all took seats on the back piazza. A horse happened to be loose in the yard, and a young man, putting his hands on the hind quarters, jumped on his back. The rest of the young men followed suit, and then one lifted the horse up by his fore legs; when he dropped him another took him up, and all followed, very much to the astonishment of the poor animal. Then followed standing on the piazza and jumping over each other's heads; then one leaned down with his hands resting on the piazza, and another mounted on his back, and the former tried to shake him off without letting go his hands. Other feats followed, all impromptu, and each

more absurd than the one before it; and the whole
concluded with a bullfight, in which two young men
mounted on the backs of other two as matadors, and
one, with his head between his shoulders, ran at them
like a bull. Though these amusements were not very
elegant, all were so intimate with each other, and there
was such a perfect abandonment, that the whole went
off with shouts of laughter.

This over, the young men brought out the ladies'
mantas, and again we sallied for a walk; but, reaching
the plaza, the young men changed their minds; and
seating the ladies, to whom I attached myself, in the
shade, commenced prisoner's base. All who passed
stopped, and the villagers seemed delighted with the
gayety of our party. The players tumbled each other
in the dust, to the great amusement of the lookers-on;
and this continued till we saw trays coming across the
plaza, which was a sign of dinner. This over, and
thinking that I had seen enough for one Sunday, I determined to forego the bullfight; and in company with
Don Manuel and another prominent member of the Assembly, and his family, I set out on my return to the
city. Their mode of travelling was primitive. All
were on horseback, he himself with a little son behind
him; his daughter alone; his wife on a pillion, with a
servant to support her; a servant-maid with a child in
her arms, and a servant on the top of the luggage. It
was a beautiful afternoon, and the plain of Guatimala,
with its green grass and dark mountains, was a lovely
scene. As we entered the city we encountered a religious procession, with priests and monks all bearing
lighted candles, and preceded by men throwing rockets. We avoided the plaza on account of the soldiers,
and in a few minutes I was in my house, alone.

CHAPTER XIII.

On Tuesday, the seventeenth of December, I set out on an excursion to La Antigua Guatimala and the Pacific Ocean. I was accompanied by a young man who lived opposite, and wished to ascend the Volcano de Agua. I had discharged Augustin, and with great difficulty had procured a man who knew the route. Romaldi had but one fault : he was married ; like some other married men, he had a fancy for roving ; but his wife set her face against this propensity ; she said that I was going to El Mar, the sea, and might carry him off, and she would never see him again, and the affectionate woman wept at the bare idea ; but upon my paying the money into her hands before going, she consented. My only luggage was a hammock and pair of sheets, which Romaldi carried on his mule, and each had a pair of alforgas. At the gate we met Don José Vidaury, whom I had first seen in the president's chair of the Constituent Assembly, and who was going to visit his hacienda at the Antigua. Though it was only five or six hours' distant, Señor Vidaury, being a very heavy man, had two led horses, one of which he insisted on my mounting ; and when I expressed my admiration of the animal, he told me, in the usual phrase of Spanish courtesy, that the horse was mine. It was done in the same spirit in which a Frenchman, who had been entertained hospitably in a country house in England, offered himself to seven of the daughters, merely for the compliment. And my worthy friend would have been very much astonished if I had accepted his offer.

The road to Mixco I have already described. In the village I stopped to see Chico. His hand had been cut off, and he was doing well. Leaving the village, we ascended a steep mountain, from the top of which we had a fine view of the village at its foot, the plain and city of Guatimala, and the Lake of Amatitan, enclosed by a belt of mountains. Descending by a wild and rugged road, we reached a plain, and saw on the left the village of San Pablo, and on the right, at some distance, another village. We then entered a piece of woodland, and first ascending, then again descended by the precipitous side of a mountain, with a magnificent ravine on our right, to a beautiful stream. At this place mountains rose all around us; but the banks of the stream were covered with delicate flowers, and parrots with gay plumage were perched on the trees and flying over our heads, making, in the midst of gigantic scenery, a fairy spot. The stream passed between two ranges of mountains so close together that there was barely room for a single horsepath by its side. As we continued the mountains turned to the left, and on the other side of the stream were a few openings, cultivated with cochineal, into the very hollow of the base. Again the road turned and then ran straight, making a vista of more than a mile between the mountains, at the end of which was the Antigua, standing in a delightful valley, shut in by mountains and hills that always retain their verdure, watered by two rivers that supply numerous fountains, with a climate in which heat

or cold never predominates ; yet this city, surrounded
by more natural beauty than any location I ever saw,
has perhaps undergone more calamities than any city
that was ever built. We passed the gate and rode
through the suburbs, in the opening of the valley, on
one side of which was a new house that reminded me
of an Italian villa, with a large cochineal plantation extending to the base of the mountain. We crossed a
stream bearing the poetical name of El Rio Pensativo;
on the other side was a fine fountain, and at the corner
of the street was the ruined church of San Domingo, a
monument of the dreadful earthquakes which had prostrated the old capital, and driven the inhabitants from
their home.

On each side were the ruins of churches, convents,
and private residences, large and costly, some lying in
masses, some with fronts still standing, richly ornamented with stucco, cracked and yawning, roofless,
without doors or windows, and trees growing inside
above the walls. Many of the houses have been re-
paired, the city is repeopled, and presents a strange appearance of ruin and recovery. The inhabitants, like
the dwellers over the buried Herculaneum, seemed to
entertain no fears of renewed disaster. I rode up
to the house of Don Miguel Manrique, which was occupied by his family at the time of the destruction of
the city, and, after receiving a kind welcome, in company with Señor Vidaury walked to the plaza. The
print opposite will give an idea, which I cannot, of
the beauty of this scene. The great volcanoes of
Agua and Fuego look down upon it; in the centre is
a noble stone fountain, and the buildings which face it,
especially the palace of the captain general, displaying
on its front the armorial bearings granted by the Em-

F. Catherwood

H. Jordan

GREAT SQUARE OF THE ANTIGUA GUATIMALA.

CRATER OF THE VOLCANO DE AGUA (*see p. 271*).

peror Charles the Fifth to the loyal and noble city, and surmounted by the Apostle St. James on horseback, armed, and brandishing a sword ; and the majestic but roofless and ruined cathedral, three hundred feet long, one hundred and twenty broad, nearly seventy high, and lighted by fifty windows, show at this day that La Antigua was once one of the finest cities of the New World, deserving the proud name which Alvarado gave it, the city of St. James of Gentlemen.

This was the second capital of Guatimala, founded in 1542 on account of the destruction of the first by a water volcano. Its history is one of uninterrupted disasters. " In 1558 an epidemic disorder, attended with a violent bleeding at the nose, swept away great numbers of people ; nor could the faculty devise any method to arrest the progress of the distemper. Many severe shocks of earthquake were felt at different periods; the one in 1565 seriously damaged many of the principal buildings; those of 1575, 76, and 77 were not less ruinous. On the 27th of December, 1581, the population was again alarmed by the volcano, which began to emit fire ; and so great was the quantity of ashes thrown out and spread in the air, that the sun was entirely obscured, and artificial light was necessary in the city at midday."

" The years 1585 and 6 were dreadful in the extreme. On January 16th of the former, earthquakes were felt, and they continued through that and the following year so frequently, that not an interval of eight days elapsed during the whole period without a shock more or less violent. Fire issued incessantly, for months together, from the mountain, and greatly increased the general consternation. The greatest damage of this series took place on the 23d of December,

1586, when the major part of the city again became a heap of ruins, burying under them many of the unfortunate inhabitants; the earth shook with such violence that the tops of the high ridges were torn off, and deep chasms formed in various parts of the level ground.

" In 1601 a pestilential distemper carried off great numbers. It raged with so much malignity that three days generally terminated the existence of such as were affected by it."

" On the 18th of February, 1651, about one o'clock, afternoon, a most extraordinary subterranean noise was heard, and immediately followed by three violent shocks, at very short intervals from each other, which threw down many buildings and damaged others; the tiles from the roofs of the houses were dispersed in all directions, like light straws by a gust of wind ; the bells of the churches were rung by the vibrations; masses of rock were detached from the mountains; and even the wild beasts were so terrified, that, losing their natural instinct, they quitted their retreats, and sought shelter from the habitations of men."

" The year 1686 brought with it another dreadful epidemic, which in three months swept away a tenth part of the inhabitants." ... " From the capital the pestilence spread to the neighbouring villages, and thence to the more remote ones, causing dreadful havoc, particularly among the most robust of the inhabitants."

" The year 1717 was memorable ; on the night of August 27th the mountain began to emit flames, attended by a continued subterranean rumbling noise. On the night of the 28th the eruption increased to great violence, and very much alarmed the inhabitants. The images of saints were carried in procession, public prayers were put up, day after day ; but the terrifying eruption still continued, and was followed by frequent shocks, at intervals, for more than four months. At last, on the night of September 29th, the fate of Gua-timala appeared to be decided, and inevitable destruc-tion seemed to be at hand. Great was the ruin among the public edifices ; many of the houses were thrown down, and nearly all that remained were dreadfully in-jured ; but the greatest devastation was seen in the churches."

" The year 1773 was the most melancholy epoch in the annals of this metropolis ; it was then destroyed, and, as the capital, rose no more from its ruins." ... "About four o'clock, on the afternoon of July 29, a tremendous vibra-tion was felt, and shortly after began the dreadful con-vulsion that decided the fate of the unfortunate city." ... " On the 7th September there was another, which threw down most of the buildings that were damaged on the 29th of July ; and on the 13th December, one still more violent terminated the work of destruction." ... " The people had not well recovered from the conster-nation inflicted by the events of the fatal 29th of July, when a meeting was convoked for the purpose of col-lecting the sense of the inhabitants on the subject of the removal." ... " In this meeting it was determined all the public authorities should remove provisionally to the little village of La Hermita, until the valleys of Ja-lapa and Las Vacas could be surveyed, and until the king's pleasure could be ascertained on the subject." ... " On the 6th of September the governor and all the tribunals withdrew to La Hermita ; the surveys of the last-mentioned places being completed, the inhabitants were again convoked, to decide upon the transfer. This congress was held in the temporary capital, and lasted from the 12th to the 16th of January, 1774 : the

report of the commissioners was read, and, by a plu-
rality of votes, it was resolved to make a formal translation of the city of Guatimala to the Valley of Las
Vacas.   The king gave his assent to this resolution on
the 21st of July, 1775 ; and, by a decree of the 21st of
September following, approved most of the plans that
were proposed for carrying the determination into effect ; granting very liberally the whole revenue arising
from the customs, for the space of ten years, toward
the charges of building, &c.   In virtue of this decree,
the ayuntamiento was in due form established in the
new situation on the 1st of January, 1776 ; and on the
29th of July, 1777, a proclamation was issued in Old
Guatimala, commanding the population to remove to
the new city within one year, and totally abandon the
remains of the old one."

Such is the account given by the historian of Guatimala concerning the destruction of this city ; besides
which, I saw on the spot Padre Antonio Croques, an
octogenarian, and the oldest canonigo in Guatimala,
who was living in the city during the earthquake which
completed its destruction.   He was still vigorous in
frame and intellect, wrote his name with a free hand
in my memorandum-book, and had vivid recollections
of the splendour of the city in his boyhood, when, as he
said, carriages rolled through it as in the streets of Ma-
drid.   On the fatal day he was in the Church of San
Francisco with two padres, one of whom, at the moment of the shock, took him by the hand and hurried
him into the patio ; the other was buried under the ruins of the church.   He remembered that the tiles flew
from the roofs of the houses in every direction ; the
clouds of dust were suffocating, and the people ran to
the fountains to quench their thirst.   The fountains

were broken, and one man snatched off his hat to dip
for water. The archbishop slept that night in his car-
riage in the plaza. He described to me the ruins of individual buildings, the dead who were dug from under
them, and the confusion and terror of the inhabitants ;
and though his recollections were only those of a boy,
he had material enough for hours of conversation.

In company with the cura we visited the interior of
the Cathedral. The gigantic walls were standing, but
roofless ; the interior was occupied as a burying-
ground, and the graves were shaded by a forest of
dahlias and trees seventy or eighty feet high, rising
above the walls. The grand altar stood under a cupo-
la supported by sixteen columns faced with tortoise-
shell, and adorned with bronze medallions of exquisite
workmanship. On the cornice were once placed statues of the Virgin and the twelve apostles in ivory ;
but all these are gone ; and more interesting than the
recollections of its ancient splendour or its mournful
ruins was the empty vault where once reposed the
ashes of Alvarado the Conqueror.

Toward evening my young companion joined me,
and we set out for Santa Maria, an Indian village at
two leagues' distance, situated on the side of the Volcano de Agua, with the intention of ascending the
next day to the summit. As we entered the valley, the
scene was so beautiful I did not wonder that even earthquakes could not make it desolate. At the distance of
a league we reached the village of San Juan Obispo,
the church and convent of which are conspicuous from
below, and command a magnificent view of the valley
and city of the Antigua. At dark we reached the village of Santa Maria, perched at a height of two thousand feet above the Antigua, and seven thousand feet

above the level of the Pacific. The church stands in a
noble court with several gates, and before it is a gigantic white cross. We rode up to the convent, which
is under the charge of the cura of San Juan Obispo,
but it was unoccupied, and there was no one to receive
us except a little talkative old man, who had only arrived that morning. Very soon there was an irruption
of Indians, with the alcalde and his alguazils, who
came to offer their services as guides up the mountain.
They were the first Indians I had met who did not speak
Spanish, and their eagerness and clamour reminded me
of my old friends the Arabs. They represented the
ascent as very steep, with dangerous precipices, and the
path extremely difficult to find, and said it was necessary for each of us to have sixteen men with ropes to
haul us up, and to pay twelve dollars for each man.
They seemed a little astonished when I told them that
we wanted two men each, and would give them half a
dollar apiece, but fell immediately to eight men for
each, and a dollar apiece; and, after a noisy wrangling, we picked out six from forty, and they all retired.
In a few minutes we heard a violin out of doors, which
we thought was in honour of us; but it was for the little
old man, who was a titritero or puppet-player, and intended giving an exhibition that night. The music
entered the room, and a man stationed himself at the
door to admit visiters. The price of admission was
three cents, and there were frequent wranglings to have
one cent taken off, or two admitted for three cents.
The high price preventing the entrance of common
people, the company was very select, and all sat on
the floor. The receipts, as I learned from the door-
keeper, were upward of five shillings. Romaldi, who
was a skilful amateur, led the orchestra, that is, the

other fiddler. The puppet was in an adjoining room, and when the door opened it disclosed a black chamar hanging as a curtain, the rising of which discovered the puppet-player sitting at a table with his little figures before him. The sports of the puppets were carried on with ventriloquial conversations, in the midst of which I fell asleep.

We did not get off till seven o'clock the next morning. The day was very unpromising, and the whole mountain was covered with clouds. As yet the side of the volcano was cultivated. In half an hour the road became so steep and slippery that we dismounted, and commenced the ascent on foot. The Indians went on before, carrying water and provisions, and each of us was equipped with a strong staff. At a quarter before eight we entered the middle region, which is covered with a broad belt of thick forest ; the path was steep and muddy, and every three or four minutes we were obliged to stop and rest. At a quarter before nine we reached a clearing, in which stood a large wooden cross. This was the first resting-place, and we sat down at the foot of the cross and lunched. A drizzling rain had commenced, but, in the hope of a change, at half past nine we resumed our ascent. The path became steeper and muddier, the trees so thickly crowded together that the sun never found its way through them, and their branches and trunks covered with green excrescences. The path was made and kept open by Indians, who go up in the winter-time to procure snow and ice for Guatimala. The labour of toiling up this muddy acclivity was excessive, and very soon my young companion became fatigued, and was unable to continue without help. The Indians were provided with ropes, one of which was tied around his waist, and two Indians went

before with the rope over the shoulders. At half past
ten we were above the region of forest, and came out
upon the open side of the volcano. There were still
scattering trees, long grass, and a great variety of curious plants and flowers, furnishing rich materials for
the botanist. Among them was a plant with a red
flower, called the arbol de las manitas, or hand-plant,
but more like a monkey's paw, growing to the height
of thirty or forty feet, the inside a light vermilion colour, and outside vermilion with stripes of yellow. My
companion, tired with the toil of ascending, even with
the aid of the rope, at length mounted an Indian's
shoulders. I was obliged to stop every two or three
minutes, and my rests were about equal to the actual
time of walking. The great difficulty was on account
of the wet and mud, which, in ascending, made us lose
part of every step. It was so slippery that, even with
the staff, and the assistance of branches of trees and
bushes, it was difficult to keep from falling. About
half an hour before reaching the top, and perhaps one
thousand or fifteen hundred feet from it, the trees became scarce, and seemed blasted by lightning or withered by cold. The clouds gathered thicker than before,
and I lost all hope of a clear day. At half an hour before twelve we reached the top and descended into the
crater. A whirlwind of cloud and vapour was sweeping around it. We were in a perspiration ; our clothes
were saturated with rain and mud ; and in a few moments the cold penetrated our very bones. We attempted to build a fire, but the sticks and leaves were wet,
and would not burn. For a few moments we raised a
feeble flame, and all crouched around it ; but a sprinkling of rain came down, just enough to put it out. We
could see nothing, and the shivering Indians begged me

to return. On rocks near us were inscriptions, one of which bore date in 1548; and on a cut stone were the words,

Alexandro Ldvert,
De San Petersbrgo;
Edvardo Legh Page,
De Inglaterra;
Jose Croskey,
De Fyladelfye,
Bibymos aqui unas Boteas
De Champana, el dia 26
de Agosto de 1834.

It seemed strange that three men from such distant and different parts of the world, St. Petersburgh, England, and *Philadelphia*, had met to drink Champagne on the top of this volcano. While I was blowing my fingers and copying the inscription, the vapour cleared away a little, and gave me a view of the interior of the crater. It was a large oval basin, the area level and covered with grass. The sides were sloping, about one hundred or one hundred and fifty feet high, and all around were masses of rock piled up in magnificent confusion, and rising to inaccessible peaks. There is no tradition of this mountain having ever emitted fire, and there is no calcined matter or other mark of volcanic eruption anywhere in its vicinity. The historical account is, that in 1541 an immense torrent, not of fire, but of water and stones, was vomited from the crater, by which the old city was destroyed. Father Remesal relates that on this occasion the crown of the mountain fell down. The height of this detached part was one league, and from the remaining summit to the plain was a distance of three leagues, which he affirms he measured in 1615. The area, by my measurement, is eighty-three paces long and sixty wide. According to Torquemada (and such is the tradition according to Padre Alcantra,

of Ciudad Vieja), this immense basin, probably the crater of an extinct volcano, with sides much higher than
they are now, became filled with water by accumulations
of snow and rain.   There never was any eruption of water, but one of the sides gave way, and the immense body
of fluid rushed out with horrific force, carrying with it
rocks and trees, inundating and destroying all that opposed its progress.   The immense barranca or ravine
by which it descended was still fearfully visible on the
side of the mountain.   The height of this mountain has
been ascertained by barometrical observation to be fourteen thousand four hundred and fifty feet above the level
of the sea.   The edge of the crater commands a beautiful view of the old city of Guatimala, thirty-two surrounding villages, and the Pacific Ocean; at least so
I am told, but I saw nothing of it.   Nevertheless, I did
not regret my labour; and though drenched with rain
and plastered with mud, I promised myself in the month
of February, when the weather is fine, to ascend again,
prepared for the purpose, and pass two or three days in
the crater.

   At one o'clock we began our descent. It was rapid, and
sometimes dangerous, from the excessive steepness and
slipperiness, and the chance of pitching head foremost
against the trunk of a tree.   At two o'clock we reached the cross; and I mention, as a hint for others, that,
from the pressure of heavy water-proof boots upon the
doigts du pied, I was obliged to stop frequently; and,
after changing the pressure by descending sidewise
and backward, catching at the branches of trees, I was
obliged to pull off my boots and go down barefooted,
ankle deep in mud.   My feet were severely bruised by
the stones, and I could hardly walk at all, when I met
one of the Indians pulling my horse up the mountain

to meet me.   At four o'clock we reached Santa Maria, at five the Antigua, and at a quarter past I was in bed.

The next morning I was still asleep when Señor Vidaury rode into the courtyard to escort me on my journey. Leaving Romaldi to follow, I was soon mounted ; and emerging from the city, we entered the open plain, shut in by mountains, and cultivated to their base with cochineal. At about a mile's distance we turned in to the hacienda of Señor Vidaury. In the yard were four oxen grinding sugarcane, and behind was his nopal, or cochineal plantation, one of the largest in the Antigua. The plant is a species of cactus, set out in rows like Indian corn, and, at the time I speak of it, was about four feet high. On every leaf was pinned with a thorn a piece of cane, in the hollow of which were thirty or forty insects. These insects cannot move, but breed, and the young crawl out and fasten upon the leaf ; when they have once fixed they never move ; a light film gathers over them, and as they feed the leaves become mildewed and white. At the end of the dry season some of the leaves are cut off and hung up in a storehouse for seed, the insects are brushed off from the rest and dried, and are then sent abroad to minister to the luxuries and elegances of civilized life, and enliven with their bright colours the *salons* of London, Paris, and St. Louis in Missouri. The crop is valuable, but uncertain, as an early rain may destroy it ; and sometimes all the workmen of a hacienda are taken away for soldiers at the moment when they are most needed for its culture. The situation was ravishingly beautiful, at the base and under the shade of the Volcano de Agua, and the view was bounded on all sides by mountains of perpetual green ; the morning air was soft and balmy, but pure and refreshing. With good government and laws, and one's friends around, I never saw a more beautiful spot on which man could desire to pass his allotted time on earth.

Resuming our ride, we came out upon a rich plain covered with grass, on which cattle and horses were pasturing, between the bases of the two great volcanoes; and on the left, at a distance, on the side of the Volcano de Agua, saw the Church of Ciudad Vieja, the first capital of Guatimala, founded by Alvarado the Conqueror. I was now on classic ground. The fame of Cortez and his exploits in Mexico spread among the Indian tribes to the south, and the Kachiquel kings sent an embassy offering to acknowledge themselves vassals of Spain. Cortez received the ambassadors with distinction, and sent Pedro de Alvarado, an officer distinguished in the conquest of New Spain, to receive the submission of the native kings, and take possession of Guatimala. On the thirteenth of November, 1523, Alvarado left the city of Mexico with three hundred Spaniards, and a large body of Tlascaltecas, Cholotecas, Chinapas, and other auxiliary Mexican Indians, fought his way through the populous provinces of Soconusco and Tonala, and on the fourteenth of May, by a decisive victory over the Quiché Indians, he arrived at the capital of the Kachiquel kingdom, now known as the village of Tecpan Guatimala. After remaining a few days to recover from their fatigues, the conquering army continued their route by the villages on the coast, overcoming all that disputed their progress; and on the 24th of July, 1524, arrived at a place called by the Indians Almolonga, meaning, in their language, a spring of water (or the mountain from which water flows), situated at the base of the Volcano de Agua. The situation, says Remesal, pleased them so much by its fine climate, the beauty of the meadows, delightfully watered by running streams, and particularly from its lying between two lofty mountains, from one of which descended runs of water in every direction, and from the summit of the other issued volumes of smoke and fire, that they determined to build a city which should be the capital of Guatimala.

On the twenty-fifth of July, the festival of St. James, the patron of Spain, the soldiers, with martial music, splendid armour, waving plumes, horses superbly caparisoned in trappings glittering with jewels and plates of gold, proceeded to the humble church which had been constructed for that purpose, where Juan Godines, the chaplain to the army, said mass. The whole body invoked the protection of the apostle, and called by his name the city they had founded. On the same day Alvarado appointed alcaldes, regidors, and the chief alguazil. The appearance of the country harmonized with the romantic scenes of which it had been the theatre ; and as I rode over the plain I could almost imagine the sides of the mountains covered with Indians, and Alvarado and his small band of daring Spaniards, soldiers and priests, with martial pride and religious humility, unfurling the banners of Spain and setting up the standard of the cross.

As we approached the town its situation appeared more beautiful ; but very early in its history dreadful calamities befell it. " In 1532 the vicinity of the city was ravaged, and the inhabitants thrown into consternation by a lion of uncommon magnitude and ferocity, that descended from the forests on the mountain called the Volcan de Agua, and committed great devastation among the herds of cattle. A reward of twenty-five gold dollars, or one hundred bushels of wheat, was offered by the town council to any person that could kill it; but the animal escaped, even from a general hunting-party of the whole city, with Alvarado at the head of it. After five or six months' continual depredations, he was killed on the thirtieth of July by a herdsman, who received the promised reward. The next great disaster was a fire that happened in February, 1536, and caused great injury; as the houses were at that time nearly all thatched with straw, a large portion of them was destroyed before it could be extinguished. The accident originated in a blacksmith's shop; and, to prevent similar misfortunes in future, the council prohibited the employment of forges within the city.

"The most dreadful calamity that had as yet afflicted this unfortunate place occurred on the morning of September 11, 1541. It had rained incessantly, and with great violence, on the three preceding days, particularly on the night of the tenth, when the water descended more like the torrent of a cataract than rain; the fury of the wind, the incessant appalling lightning, and the dreadful thunder, were indescribable." . . . "At two o'clock on the morning of the eleventh, the vibrations of the earth were so violent that the people were unable to stand; the shocks were accompanied by a terrible subterranean noise, which spread universal dismay; shortly afterward, an immense torrent of water rushed down from the summit of the mountain, forcing away with it enormous fragments of rocks and large trees, which, descending upon the ill-fated town, overwhelmed and destroyed almost all the houses, and buried a great number of the inhabitants under the ruins; among the many, Doña Beatrice de la Cueba, the widow of Pedro Alvarado, lost her life."

All the way down the side of the volcano we saw the seams and gullies made by the torrents of water which had inundated the city. Again we crossed the beautiful stream of El Rio Pensativo, and rode up to the convent. It stands adjoining the gigantic and venerable church of the Virgin. In front was a high stone wall; a large gate opened into a courtyard, at the extremity and along the side of which were the spacious corridors of the convent, and on the left the gigantic wall of the church, with a door of entry from one end of the corridor. The patio was sunk about four feet below the level of the corridor, and divided into parterres, with beds of flowers, and in the centre was a large white circular fountain, with goldfish swimming in it, and rising out of it, above a jet d'eau, an angel with a trumpet and flag.

Señor Vidaury had advised Padre Alcantra of my intended visit, and he was waiting to receive us. He was about thirty-three, intelligent, educated, and energetic, with a passion for flowers, as was shown by the beautiful arrangements of the courtyard. He had been banished by Morazan, and only returned to his curacy about a year before. On a visit to him was his friend and neighbour Don Pepe Astegueta, proprietor of a cochineal hacienda, and a man of the same stamp and character. They were among the few whom I met who took any interest in the romantic events connected with the early history of the country. After a brief rest in the convent, with a feeling more highly wrought than any that had been awakened in me except by the ruins of Copan, we visited a tree standing before the church and extending wide its branches, under whose shade, tradition says, Alvarado and his soldiers first encamped; the fountain of Almolonga, or, in the Indian language, the mountain from which water flows, which first induced him to select this spot as the site for the capital; and the ruined cathedral, on the spot where Juan Godines first said mass. The fountain is a large natural basin of clear and beautiful water, shaded by trees, under which thirty or forty Indian women were washing. The walls of the cathedral were standing, and in one corner was a chamber filled with the sculls and bones of those destroyed by the inundation from the volcano.

After breakfast we visited the church, which was very large, and more than two hundred years old; its altar is rich in ornaments of gold and silver, among which is a magnificent crown of gold, studded with diamonds and emeralds, presented by one of the Philips to the Virgin, to whom the church was consecrated. Returning to the house, I found that Padre Alcantra had prepared for me a visit from a deputation of Indians, consisting of the principal chiefs and women, descendants of caciques of the Mexican auxiliaries of Alvarado, calling themselves, like the Spaniards, Conquistadores, or Conquerors; they entered, wearing the same costumes which their ancestors had worn in the time of Cortez, and bearing on a salver covered with velvet a precious book bound in red velvet, with silver corners and clasp, containing the written evidence of their rank and rights. It was written on parchment, dated in 1639, and contained the order of Philip the First, acknowledging them as conquerors, and exempting them, as such, from the tribute paid by the native Indians. This exemption continued until the revolution of 1825, and even yet they call themselves descendants of the conquerors, and the head of the Indian aristocracy. The interest which I felt in these memorials of the conquerors was increased in no small degree by the beauty and comfort of the convent, and Padre Alcantra's kindness. In the afternoon we walked down to the bridge across the Rio Pensativo. The plain on which the Spanish soldiers had glittered in armour was shaded by the high volcanoes, and the spirit of romance rested upon it.

The day which I passed at the "old city" is one of those upon which I look back with pleasure. Señor Vidaury and Don Pepe remained with us all day. Afterward, when Padre Alcantra had again been obliged to fly from the convent at the approach of an invading army, and we had all passed through the crash of the revolution, on leaving Guatimala to return home I diverged from my road to pay them a visit, and they were the last friends to whom I said farewell.

In the morning, with great regret, I left Ciudad Vieja. Padre Alcantra and Don Pepe accompanied me, and, to help me on my journey, the latter lent me a noble mule, and the padre an excellent servant. The exit from this mountain-girt valley was between the two great volcanoes of Agua and Fuego, rising on each side nearly fifteen thousand feet high; and from between the two, so unexpectedly to me as almost to induce a burst of enthusiasm, we overlooked an immense plain, and saw the Pacific Ocean. At a league's distance we reached the village of Alotenango, where, among Indian huts, stood another gigantic church, roofless, and ruined by an earthquake, and where, with the hope, in which I was not disappointed, of seeing them again, I took leave of the cura and Don Pepe. The road between the two great volcanoes was singularly interesting; one with its base cultivated, girt by a belt of thick forests, and verdant to the very summit; the other with

three bare and rugged peaks, covered with dried lava
and ashes, shaken by the strife of the elements within,
the working of internal fires, and emitting constantly a
pale blue smoke.   The road bears marks of the violent
convulsions to which it has been subject.   In one place
the horse-path lies through an immense chasm, rent
asunder by a natural convulsion, over which huge stones,
hurled in every direction, lay in the wildest confusion;
in another it crosses a deep bed of ashes, and cinders,
and scorified lava; and a little farther on strata of de-
composed vegetable matter cover the volcanic substan-
ces, and high shrubs and bushes have grown up, forming a thick shady arbour, fragrant as the fields of Araby
the Blessed.   At every step there was a strange contrast
of the horrible and beautiful.   The last eruption of the
Volcan del Fuego took place about twelve years ago,
when flames issued from the crater and ascended to a
great height; immense quantities of stones and ashes
were cast out, and the race of monkeys inhabiting the
neighbouring woods was almost extirpated; but it can
never burst forth again; its crater is no longer el Boca
del Infierno, or the Mouth of the Infernal Regions, for,
as a very respectable individual told me, it has been
blessed by a priest.

After a beautiful ride under a hot sun, but shaded
nearly all the way, at three o'clock we reached Escuintla, where was another magnificent church, roofless,
and again with its rich façade cracked by an earthquake.
Before it were two venerable Ceiba trees, and the platform commanded a splendid panoramic view of the volcanoes and mountains of the Antigua.

In the streets were soldiers and drunken Indians.   I
rode to the house of the corregidor, Don Juan Dios de
Guerra, and, with Romaldi for a guide, I walked down

to the banks of a beautiful stream, which makes Escuintla, in the summer months of January and February, the great watering-place of Guatimala. The bank was high and beautifully shaded, and, descending to the river through a narrow passage between perpendicular rocks, in a romantic spot, where many a Guatimala lover has been hurried, by the charming influences around, into a premature outpouring of his hopes and fears, I sat down on a stone and washed my feet.

Returning, I stopped at the church. The front was cracked from top to bottom by an earthquake, and the divided portions stood apart, but the towers were entire. I ascended to the top, and looked down into the roofless area. On the east the dark line of forest was broken by the curling smoke of a few scattered huts, and backed by verdant mountains, by the cones of volcanoes, with their tops buried in the clouds, and by the Rock of Mirandilla, an immense block of bare granite held up among the mountain tops, riven and blasted by lightning. On the west the setting sun illuminated a forest of sixty miles, and beyond shed its dying glories over the whole Pacific Ocean.

At two o'clock, under a brilliant moonlight, and with a single guide, we started for the Pacific. The road was level and wooded. We passed a trapiche or sugar-mill, worked by oxen, and before daylight reached the village of Masagua, four leagues distant, built in a clearing cut out of the woods, at the entrance of which we stopped under a grove of orange-trees, and by the light of the moon filled our pockets and alforgas with the shining fruit. Daylight broke upon us in a forest of gigantic trees, from seventy-five to a hundred feet high, and from twenty to twenty-five feet in circumference, with creepers winding around their trunks and

hanging from the branches. The road was merely a
path through the forest, formed by cutting away shrubs
and branches. The freshness of the morning was delightful. We had descended from the table of land
called the tierras templadas, and were now in the tierras callientes ; but at nine o'clock the glare and heat of
the sun did not penetrate the thick shade of the woods.
In some places the branches of the trees, trimmed by
the machete of a passing muleteer, and hung with a
drapery of vines and creepers, bearing red and purple
flowers, formed for a long distance natural arches more
beautiful than any ever fashioned by man ; and there
were parrots and other birds of beautiful plumage flying
among the trees ; among them Guacamayas, or great
macaws, large, clothed in red, yellow, and green, and
when on the wing displaying a splendid plumage. But
there were also vultures and scorpions, and, running
across the road and up the trees, innumerable iguanas
or lizards, from an inch to three feet long. The road
was a mere track among the trees, perfectly desolate,
though twice we met muleteers bringing up goods from
the port. At the distance of twelve miles we reached
the hacienda of Narango, occupied by a major-domo,
who looked after the cattle of the proprietor, roaming
wild in the woods ; the house stood alone in the midst
of a clearing, built of poles, with a cattle-yard in front;
and I spied a cow with a calf, which was a sign of milk.
But you must catch a cow before you can milk her.
The major-domo went out with a lazo, and, playing
upon the chord of nature, caught the calf first, and then
the cow, and hauled her up by the horns to a post.
The hut had but one waccal, or drinking-shell, made
of a gourd, and it was so small that we sat down by the
cow so as not to lose much time. We had bread, choc-

olate, and sausages, and, after a ride of twenty-four miles, made a glorious breakfast ; but we exhausted the poor cow, and I was ashamed to look the calf in the face.

Resuming our journey, at a distance of nine miles we reached the solitary hacienda of Overo. The whole of this great plain was densely wooded and entirely un-cultivated, but the soil was rich, and capable of main-taining, with very little labour, thousands of people. Beyond Overo the country was open in places, and the sun beat down with scorching force. At one o'clock we crossed a rustic bridge, and through the opening in the trees saw the river Michetoya. We followed along its bank, and very soon heard breaking on the shore the waves of the great Southern Ocean. The sound was grand and solemn, giving a strong impression of the immensity of those waters, which had been rolling from the creation, for more than five thousand years, unknown to civilized man. I was loth to disturb the impression, and rode slowly through the woods, listening in pro-found silence to the grandest music that ever fell upon my ear. The road terminated on the bank of the river, and I had crossed the Continent of America.

On the opposite side was a long sandbar, with a flagstaff, two huts built of poles and thatched with leaves, and three sheds of the same rude construction; and over the bar were seen the masts of a ship, riding on the Pacific. This was the port of Istapa. We shouted above the roar of the waves, and a man came down to the bank, and loosing a canoe, came over for us. In the mean time, the interest of the scene was somewhat broken by a severe assault of moschetoes and sandflies. The mules suffered as much as we ; but I could not take them across, and was obliged to tie them

under the trees. Neither Romaldi nor my guide could
be prevailed upon to remain and watch them ; they said
it would be death to sleep there. The river is the outlet of the Lake of Amatitan, and is said to be navigable
from the Falls of San Pedro Martyr, seventy miles from
its mouth ; but there are no boats upon it, and its banks
are in the wildness of primeval nature. The crossing-
place was at the old mouth of the river. The sandbar
extends about a mile farther, and has been formed since
the conquest. Landing, I walked across the sand to
the house or hut of the captain of the port, and a few
steps beyond saw the object of my journey, the boundless waters of the Pacific. When Nunez de Balboa,
after crossing swamps and rivers, mountains and woods,
which had never been passed but by straggling Indians,
came down upon the shores of this newly-discovered
sea, he rushed up to the middle in the waves with his
buckler and sword, and took possession of it in the
name of the king his master, vowing to defend it in
arms against all his enemies. But Nunez had the assurance that beyond that sea " he would find immense
stores of gold, out of which people did eat and drink."
I had only to go back again. I had ridden nearly sixty
miles ; the sun was intensely hot, the sand burning, and
very soon I entered the hut and threw myself into a
hammock. The hut was built of poles set up in the
sand, thatched with the branches of trees ; furnished
with a wooden table, a bench, and some boxes of merchandise, and swarming with moschetoes. The captain
of the port, as he brushed them away, complained of
the desolation and dreariness of the place, its isolation
and separation from the world, its unhealthiness, and
the misery of a man doomed to live there ; and yet he

feared the result of the war, a change of administration, and being turned out of office!

Toward evening, rested and refreshed, I walked out upon the shore. The port is an open roadstead, without bay, headland, rock, or reef, or anything whatever to distinguish it from the line of the coast. There is no light at night, and vessels at sea take their bearings from the great volcanoes of the Antigua, more than sixty miles inland. A buoy was anchored outside of the breakers, with a cable attached, and under the sheds were three large launches for embarking and disembarking cargoes. The ship, which was from Bordeaux, lay off more than a mile from the shore. Her boat had landed the supercargo and passengers, since which she had had no communication with the land, and seemed proudly independent of so desolate a place. Behind the sandbar were a few Indian huts, and Indians nearly naked were sitting by me on the shore. Yet this desolate place was once the focus of ambitious hopes, high aspirations, lust of power and gold, and romantic adventure. Here Alvarado fitted out his armament, and embarked with his followers to dispute with Pizarro the riches of Peru. The sun was sinking, and the red globe touched the ocean; clouds were visible on its face, and when it disappeared, ocean and land were illuminated with a ruddy haze. I returned to the hut and threw myself into my hammock. Could it be that I was again so far from home, and that these were the waves of the great Southern Ocean breaking on my ears?

CHAPTER XIV.

AT three o'clock Romaldi woke me to set out on my return. The moonbeams were glancing over the water, and the canoe was ready. I bade farewell to my host as he lay in his hammock, and crossed the river. Here I found an unexpected difficulty. My spare mule had broken her halter, and was nowhere to be seen. We beat about among the woods till daylight, and concluding that she must have taken the only path open, and set out for home on her own account, we saddled and rode on to Overo, a distance of twenty miles. But no stray mule had passed the hacienda, and I stopped and sent Romaldi back to the port.

Very soon I became tired of waiting at the miserable hacienda, saddled my mule, and started alone. The road was so shaded that I did not stop for the noonday heat. For twenty-one miles farther the road was perfectly desolate, the only sound being occasionally the crash of a falling tree. At the village of Masagua I rode up to a house, at which I saw a woman under the shed, and, unsaddling my mule, got her to send a man out to cut sacate, and to make me some chocolate. I was so pleased with my independence that I almost resolved to travel altogether by myself, without servant or change of apparel. In half an hour I resumed my

ESQUINTLA.

F. Catherwood.

journey. Toward sundown I met drunken Indians coming out from Escuintla, and, looking back over the great plain, saw the sun fast sinking into the Pacific. Some time after dark I rode up to the house of the corregidor, having performed in the two days a hundred and ten miles. Unfortunately, there was no sacate for my mule. This article is brought into the towns by the Indians daily, and every person buys just enough for the night, and no more. There was not a spare lock of grass in the place. With a servant of the corregidor's I made an exploring expedition through the town, and by an affecting appeal to an old woman, enforced by treble price, bought from under their very noses the portion of two mules, and left them supperless.

I waited till two o'clock the next day for Romaldi and the mule, and, after a vain endeavour to procure a guide to the falls of San Pedro Martyr, set out alone direct for Guatimala. At the distance of two leagues, ascending a steep hill, I passed a trapiche or sugar-mill, in a magnificent situation, commanding a full view of the plain I had crossed and the ocean beyond. Two oxen were grinding sugarcane, and under a shed was a large boiling caldron for making panela, a brown sugar, in lumps of about two pounds each, an enormous quantity of which is consumed in the country. Here the humour seized me to make some inquiries about the falls of San Pedro Martyr. A man out at elbows, and every other mentionable and unmentionable part of his body, glad to get rid of regular work, offered to conduct me. I had passed, a league back, the place where I ought to have turned off; and proceeding onward to the village of San Pedro, he turned off to the right, and went back almost in the same direction by a narrow path descending through thick woods choked with bushes, and in a ravine reached the Michetoya River, which I had crossed at Istapa. It was narrow and rapid, breaking wildly over a stony bed, with a high mountain on the opposite side. Following it, we reached the cataract, consisting of four streams separated by granite rock, partly concealed by bushes, and precipitated from a height of about two hundred feet, forming with the wild scenery around a striking and romantic view. A little below it were a sugar-mill worked by water, and an uncommonly fine hacienda, which commanded a view of the falls, and at which I was very much disposed to pass the night. The major-domo, a black man, was somewhat surprised at my visit; but when he learned that I did not come to see the mill, but only the falls, he seemed to suspect that I was no better than I should be ; and when I asked him if I could reach San Cristoval before dark, he answered that I could if I started immediately. This was not exactly an invitation to stay, and I left him. It shows the want of curiosity and indolence of the people, that, though these falls are but a pleasant afternoon's ride from Escuintla, which for two months is thronged with visiters from Guatimala, nobody ever visits them.

Hurrying back by the same wild path, we reached the main road, and, as it was late, I hired my guide to go on with me to San Cristoval. We passed through the village of San Pedro, which was a collection of miserable huts, with an estanco or place for the sale of agua ardiente, and thronged with half-intoxicated Indians. As we advanced, clouds began to gather around the mountains, and there was every appearance of heavy rain. I had no cloak or greatcoat, and, being particularly apprehensive of fevers and rheumatisms, after riding about a mile I returned to San Pedro. The most respectable citizens of the place were reeling round the estanco, and urged me to stop; but my guide said they were a bad set, and advised me to return and pass the night at the sugar-mill. Presuming that he knew the people of whom he spoke better than I did, I was no way inclined to disregard his caution. It was after dark when we reached the trapiche; some of the workmen were sitting around a fire smoking; others were lying asleep under a shed, and I had but to

> " Look around and choose *my* ground,
> And take my rest."

I inquired for the major-domo, and was escorted to a mud house, where in the dark I heard a harsh voice, and presently, by the light of a pine stick, saw an old and forbidding face corresponding, and by its side that of a young woman, so soft and sweet that it seemed to appear expressly for the sake of contrast; and these two were one. I was disposed to pity her; but the old major-domo was a noble fellow in heart, and she managed him so beautifully that he never suspected it. He was about going to bed, but sent men out to cut sacate, and both he and his wife were pleased that accident had brought me to their hut. The workmen sympathized in their humour, and we sat for two hours around a large table under the shed, with two candles sticking up in their own tallow. They could not comprehend that I had been to the top of the Volcano de Agua, and then ridden down to the coast merely to see the Pacific. A fine, open-faced young man had a great desire to travel, only he did not like to go away from home. I offered to take him with me and give him good wages. The subject was discussed aloud. It was an awful thing to go away from home, and among strangers, where no one would care for him. His house was the outside of the major-domo's hut, but his home was in the hearts of his friends, and perhaps some of them would be dead before he return- ed. The wife of the major-domo seemed a good spirit in tempering the hearts and conduct of these wild and half-naked men. I promised to give him money to pay his expenses home when he should wish to return, and he agreed to go with me. At three o'clock the old ma- jor-domo was shouting in my ears. I was not familiar with my own name with the don prefixed, and thought he had " waked up the wrong passenger." The courage of the young man who wished to travel failed him, and he did not make his appearance ; in the expectation of his going my guide did not come, and I set out alone. Before daylight I passed for the third time through the village of San Pedro, and a little beyond overtook a bundle on horseback, which proved to be a boy and a woman, with one poncha over both.

The River Michetoya was foaming and breaking in a long succession of rapids on our right, and we rode on together to San Cristoval. I rode up to the convent, pounced upon the cura at the witching hour of break- fast, mounted again, and rode around the base of the Volcano de Agua, with its cultivated fields and belt of forest and verdure to the top. Opposite was another volcano, its sides covered with immense forests. Be- tween the two I passed a single trapiche belonging to a convent of Dominican friars, entered a large and beautiful valley, passed hot springs, smoking for more than a mile along the road, and entered among the no- pals or cochineal plantations of Amatitan. On both sides were high clay fences, and the nopals were more extensive than those of the Antigua, and more valuable,

as, though only twenty-five miles from it, the climate is
so different that they produce two crops in each season.

Approaching the town, I remembered that Mr. Handy, who had travelled from the United States through
Texas and Mexico with a caravan of wild animals, had
told me in New-York of an American in his employ,
who had left him at this place to take charge of a cochineal plantation, and I was curious to see how he looked
and flourished in such employment. I had forgotten
his name, but, inquiring on the road for an American
del Norte, was directed to the nopal of which he had
charge. It was one of the largest in the place, and contained four thousand plants. I rode up to a small building in the middle of the plantation, which looked like a
summer-house, and was surrounded by workmen, one of
whom announced me as a " Spaniard," as the Indians
generally call foreigners. Dismounting and giving
my mule to an Indian, I entered and found Don Hen-
riques sitting at a table with an account-book before him,
settling accounts with the workmen. He was dressed
in the coton or jacket of the country, and had a very
long beard ; but I should have recognised him anywhere as an American. I addressed him in English,
and he stared at me, as if startled by a familiar sound,
and answered in Spanish. By degrees he comprehend-
ed the matter. He was under thirty, from Rhinebeck
Landing, on the Hudson River, where his father keeps
a store, and his name was Henry Pawling; had been a
clerk in New-York, and then in Mexico. Induced by
a large offer and a strong disposition to ramble and see
the country, he accepted a proposal from Mr. Handy.
His business was to go on before the caravan, hire a
place, give notice, and make preparations for the exhibition of the animals. In this capacity he had travelled

all over Mexico, and from thence to Guatimala. It was
seven years since he left home, and since parting with
Mr. Handy he had not spoken a word of his own language; and as he spoke it now it was more than half
Spanish. I need not say that he was glad to see me.
He conducted me over the plantation, and explained the
details of the curious process of making cochineal. He
was somewhat disappointed in his expectations, and
spoke with great feeling of home; but when I offered to
forward letters, said he had resolved never to write to
his parents again, nor to inform them of his existence
until he retrieved his fortunes, and saw a prospect of returning rich. He accompanied me into the town of
Amatitan; and as it was late, and I expected to return
to that place, I did not visit the lake, but continued direct for Guatimala.

The road lay across a plain, with a high, precipitous,
and verdant wall on the left. At a distance of a league
we ascended a steep hill to the table-land of Guatimala.
I regret that I cannot communicate to the reader the
highest pleasure of my journey in Central America, that
derived from the extraordinary beauty of scenery constantly changing. At the time I thought this the most
delightful ride I had had in the country. On the way I
overtook a man and his wife on horseback, he with a
game-cock under his arm, and she with a guitar; a little
boy was hidden away among bedding on a luggage-
mule, and four lads were with them on foot, each with
a game-cock wrapped in matting, with the head and tail
only visible. They were going to Guatimala to pass
the Christmas holydays, and with this respectable party
I entered the gate of the city, on the eighth day after
my departure. I found a letter from Mr. Catherwood,
dated at Esquipulas, advising me that he had been rob-

bed by his servant, taken ill, had left the ruins, gone to
Don Gregorio's, and was then on his journey to Guatimala. My messenger had passed through Copan, and
gone on he did not know where. I was in great distress, and resolved, after a day's rest, to set off in search
of him.

I dressed myself and went to a party at Señor Zeba-
dours, formerly minister to England, where I surprised
the Guatimaltecos by the tour I had made, and particularly by having come alone from Istapa. Here I met
Mr. Chatfield, her Britannic majesty's consul general,
and Mr. Skinner, who had arrived during my absence.
It was Christmas Eve, the night of El Nascimiento, or
birth of Christ. At one end of the sala was a raised
platform, with a green floor, and decorated with branches of pine and cypress, having birds sitting upon them,
and looking-glass, and sandpaper, and figures of men
and animals, representing a rural scene, with an arbour,
and a wax doll in a cradle ; in short, the grotto of Beth-
lehem and the infant Saviour. Always, at this season
of the year, every house in Guatimala has its nascimiento, according to the wealth and taste of the proprietor,
and in time of peace the figure of the Saviour is adorned
with family jewels, pearls, and precious stones, and at
night every house is open, and the citizens, without acquaintance or invitation, or distinction of rank or persons, go from house to house visiting ; and the week of
El Nascimiento is the gayest in the year ; but, unfortunately, at this time it was observed only in form; the
state of the city was too uncertain to permit general
opening of houses and running in the streets at night.
Carrera's soldiers might enter.

The party was small, but consisted of the élite of
Guatimala, and commenced with supper, after which

followed dancing, and, I am obliged to add, smoking. The room was badly lighted, and the company, from the precarious state of the country, not gay; but the dancing was kept up till twelve o'clock, when the ladies put on their mantas, and we all went to the Cathedral, where were to be performed the imposing ceremonies of the Christmas Eve. The floor of the church was crowded with citizens, and a large concourse from the villages around. Mr. Savage accompanied me home, and we did not get to bed till three o'clock in the morning.

The bells had done ringing, and Christmas mass had been said in all the churches before I awoke. In the afternoon was the first bullfight of the season. My friend Vidaury had called for me, and I was in the act of going to the Plaza de Toros, when there was a loud knock at the porte cochère, and in rode Mr. Catherwood, armed to the teeth, pale and thin, most happy at reaching Guatimala, but not half so happy as I was to see him. He was in advance of his luggage, but I dressed him up and carried him immediately to the Plaza de Toros.

It stands near the church of El Calvario, at the end of the Calle Real, in shape and form like the Roman amphitheatre, about three hundred and fifty feet long and two hundred and fifty broad, capable of containing, as we supposed, about eight thousand people, at least one fourth of the population of Guatimala, and was then crowded with spectators of both sexes and all classes, the best and the vilest in the city, sitting together indiscriminately; and among them were conspicuous the broad-brimmed, turned-up, and sharp-pointed hat and black gown of the priest.

The seats commenced about ten feet above the area, with a corridor and open wooden fence in front to protect the spectators, astride which sat Carrera's disorderly soldiers to keep order. At one end, underneath the corridor, was a large door, through which the bull was to be let in. At the other end, separated by a partition from the part occupied by the rest of the spectators, was a large box, empty, formerly intended for the captain general and other principal officers of government, and now reserved for Carrera. Underneath was a military band, composed mostly of Indians. Notwithstanding the collection of people, and the expectation of an animating sport, there was no clapping or stamping, or other expression of impatience and anxiety for the performance to begin. At length Carrera entered the captain general's box, dressed in a badly-fitting blue military frock-coat, embroidered with gold, and attended by Monte Rosa and other officers, richly dressed, the alcalde and members of the municipality. All eyes were turned toward him, as when a king or emperor enters his box at the theatre in Europe. A year before he was hunted among the mountains, under a reward for his body, " dead or alive," and nine tenths of those who now looked upon him would then have shut the city against him as a robber, murderer, and outcast.

Soon after the matadores entered, eight in number, mounted, and each carrying a lance and a red poncha ; they galloped round the area, and stopped with their lances opposite the door at which the bull was to enter. The door was pulled open by a padre, a great cattle-proprietor, who owned the bulls of the day, and the animal rushed out into the area, kicking up his heels as if in play, but at sight of the line of horsemen and lances turned about and ran back quicker than he entered. The padre's bull was an ox, and, like a sensible beast, would rather run than fight ; but the door was closed

upon him, and perforce he ran round the area, looking
up to the spectators for mercy, and below for an outlet
of escape. The horsemen followed, "prodding" him
with their lances; and all around the area, men and boys
on the fence threw barbed darts with ignited fireworks
attached, which, sticking in his flesh and exploding on
every part of his body, irritated him, and sometimes
made him turn on his pursuers. The matadores led
him on by flaring ponchas before him, and as he pressed them, the skill of the matadore consisted in throwing the poncha over his horns so as to blind him, and
then fixing in his neck, just behind his jaw, a sort of
balloon of fireworks; when this was done successfully
it created shouts of applause. The government, in an
excess of humanity, had forbidden the killing of bulls,
and restricted the fight to worrying and torturing. Consequently, it was entirely different from the bullfight in
Spain, and wanted even the exciting interest of a fierce
struggle for life, and the chance of the matadore being
gored to death or tossed over among the spectators.
But, watching the earnest gaze of thousands, it was
easy to imagine the intense excitement in a martial age,
when gladiators fought in the arena before the nobility
and beauty of Rome. Our poor ox, after being tired
out, was allowed to withdraw. Others followed, and
went through the same round. All the padre's bulls
were oxen. Sometimes a matador on foot was chased
to the fence under a general laugh of the spectators.
After the last ox had run his rounds, the matadores
withdrew, and men and boys jumped over into the arena in such numbers that they fairly hustled the ox.
The noise and confusion, the flaring of coloured ponchas, the running and tumbling, attacking and retreat-
ing, and clouds of dust, made this the most stirring

scene of any; but altogether it was a puerile exhibition, and the better classes, among whom was my fair countrywoman, regarded it merely as an occasion for meeting acquaintances.

In the evening we went to the theatre, which opened for the first time. A large building had been commenced in the city, but in one of the revolutions it had been demolished, and the work was abandoned. The performance was in the courtyard of a house. The stage was erected across one of the corners; the patio was the pit, and the corridor was divided by temporary partitions into boxes; the audience sent beforehand, or servants brought with them, their own seats. We had invitations to the box of Señor Vidaury. Carrera was there, sitting on a bench a little elevated against the wall of the house, and at the right hand of Rivera Paz, the chief of the state. Some of his officers were with him in their showy uniforms, but he had laid his aside, and had on his black bombazet jacket and pantaloons, and was very unpretending in his deportment. I considered him the greatest man in Guatimala, and made it a point to shake hands with him in passing. The first piece was Saide, a tragedy. The company consisted entirely of Guatimaltecos, and their performance was very good. There was no change of scenery; when the curtain fell, all lighted cigars, ladies included, and, fortunately, there was an open courtyard for the escape of the smoke. When the performance was over, the boxes waited till the pit was emptied. Special care had been taken in placing sentinels, and all went home quietly.

During the week there was an attempt at gayety, but all was more or less blended with religious solemnities. One was that of the Novena, or term of nine days'

praying to the Virgin. One lady, who was distinguished for the observance of this term, had an altar built
across the whole end of the sala, with three steps, decorated with flowers, and a platform adorned with look-
ing-glasses, pictures, and figures, in the centre of which
was an image of the Virgin richly dressed, the whole
ornamented in a way impossible for me to describe, but
that may be imagined in a place where natural flowers
are in the greatest profusion, and artificial ones made
more perfect than in Europe, and where the ladies have
extraordinary taste in the disposition of them. When
I entered the gentlemen were in an anteroom, with
hats, canes, and small swords ; and in the sala the ladies, with female servants cleanly dressed, were on
their knees praying; in front of the fairy altar was one
who seemed a fairy herself ; and while her lips moved,
her bright eye was roving, and she looked more worthy
of being kneeled to than the pretty image before her,
and as if she thought so too.

In regard to my official business I was perfectly at a
loss what to do. In Guatimala all were on one side ;
all said that there was no Federal Government; and
Mr. Chatfield, the British consul general, whose opinion I respected more, concurred, and had published a
circular, denying its existence. But the Federal Government claimed to be in existence ; and the bare suggestion of General Morazan's marching against Guatimala excited consternation. Several times there were
rumours to that effect, and one that he had actually determined to do so ; that not a single priest would be
spared, and that the streets would run with blood.
The boldest partisans trembled for their lives. Morazan had never been beaten ; Carrera had always run
before him ; they had no faith in his being able to de-

fend them, and could not defend themselves. At all events, I had as yet heard only one side, and did not consider myself justified in assuming that there was no government. I was bound to make " diligent search," and then I might return, in legal phrase, " cepi corpus," or " non est inventus," according to circumstances.

For this purpose I determined to go to San Salvador, which was formerly, and still claimed to be, the capital of the Confederation and the seat of the Federal Government, or, rather, to Cojutepeque, to which place the government had been then lately transferred, on account of earthquakes at San Salvador. This project was not without its difficulties. One Rascon, with an insurgent and predatory band, occupied an intervening district of country, acknowledging neither party, and fighting under his own flag. Mr. Chatfield and Mr. Skinner had come by sea, a circuitous route, to avoid him, and Captain De Nouvelle, master of a French ship lying at the port of San Salvador, arrived in Guatimala almost on a run, having ridden sixty miles the last day over a mountainous country, who reported horrible atrocities, and three men murdered near San Vicente, on their way to the fair at Esquipulas, and their faces so disfigured that they could not be recognised. Immediately on his arrival he sent a courier to order his ship up to Istapa, merely to take him back, and save him from returning by land. I had signified my intention to the state government, which was dissatisfied with my going to San Salvador at all, but offered me an escort of soldiers, suggesting, however, that if we met any of Morazan's there would certainly be a fight. This was not at all pleasant. I was loth to travel a third time the road to Istapa, but, under the circumstances, accepted

Captain De Nouvelle's invitation to take a passage in his ship.

Meanwhile I passed my time in social visiting. In our own city the aristocracy is called by the diplomatic corps at Washington the aristocracy of streets. In Guatimala it is the aristocracy of houses, as certain families live in the houses built by their fathers at the foundation of the city, and they are really aristocratic old mansions. These families, by reason of certain monopolies of importation, acquired under the Spanish dominion immense wealth and rank as "merchant princes." Still they were excluded from all offices and all part in the government. At the time of the revolution one of these families was noble, with the rank of marquisate, and its head tore off the insignia of his rank, and joined the revolutionary party. Next in position to the officers of the crown, they thought that, emancipated from the yoke of Spain, they would have the government in their own hands; and so they had, but it was only for a short time. The principles of equal rights began to be understood, and they were put aside. For ten years they had been in obscurity, but accidentally they were again in power, and at the time of my visit ruled in social as well as political life. I do not wish to speak harshly of them, for they were the only people who constituted society; my intercourse was almost exclusively with them; my fair countrywoman was one of them; I am indebted to them for much kindness; and, besides, they are personally amiable; but I speak of them as public men. I did not sympathize with them in politics.

To me the position of the country seemed most critical, and from a cause which in all Spanish America had never operated before. At the time of the first invasion a few hundred Spaniards, by superior bravery and skill, and with more formidable arms, had conquered the whole Indian population. Naturally peaceable, and kept without arms, the conquered people had remained quiet and submissive during the three centuries of Spanish dominion. In the civil wars following the independence they had borne but a subordinate part; and down to the time of Carrera's rising they were entirely ignorant of their own physical strength. But this fearful discovery had now been made. The Indians constituted three fourths of the inhabitants of Guatimala; were the hereditary owners of the soil; for the first time since they fell under the dominion of the whites, were organized and armed under a chief of their own, who chose for the moment to sustain the Central party. I did not sympathize with that party, for I believed that in their hatred of the Liberals they were courting a third power that might destroy them both; consorting with a wild animal which might at any moment turn and rend them in pieces. I believed that they were playing upon the ignorance and prejudices of the Indians, and, through the priests, upon their religious fanaticism; amusing them with fêtes and Church ceremonies, persuading them that the Liberals aimed at a demolition of churches, destruction of the priests, and hurrying back the country into darkness; and in the general heaving of the elements there was not a man of nerve enough among them, with the influence of name and station, to rally round him the strong and honest men of the country, reorganize the shattered republic, and save them from the disgrace and danger of truckling to an ignorant uneducated Indian boy.

Such were my sentiments; of course I avoided expressing them; but because I did not denounce their

opponents, some looked coldly upon me. With them
political differences severed all ties. Our worst party
abuse is moderate and mild compared with the terms in
which they speak of each other. We seldom do more
than call men ignorant, incompetent, dishonest, dishon-
ourable, false, corrupt, subverters of the Constitution,
and bought with British gold; there a political oppo-
nent is a robber, an assassin; it is praise to admit that
he is not a bloodthirsty cutthroat. We complain that
our ears are constantly offended and our passions roused by angry political discussions. There it would have
been delightful to hear a good, honest, hot, and angry
political dispute. I travelled in every state, and I never heard one; for I never met two men together who
differed in political opinions. Defeated partisans are
shot, banished, run away, or get a moral lockjaw, and
never dare express their opinions before one of the dominant party. We have just passed through a violent
political struggle; twenty millions of people have been
divided almost man to man, friend against friend,
neighbour against neighbour, brother against brother,
and son against father; besides honest differences of
opinion, ambition, want, and lust of power and office
have roused passions sometimes to fierceness. Two
millions of men highly excited have spoken out their
thoughts and sentiments fearlessly and openly. They
have all been counted, and the first rule in arithme-
tic has decided between them; and the defeated party
are still permitted to live in the country; their wives
and children are spared; nay, more, they may grumble in the streets, and hang out their banners of defiance, of continued and determined opposition: and,
more than all, the pillars of the republic are not sha-
ken! Among a million of disappointed men, never,

with all the infirmities of human passion, has one breathed resistance to the Constitution and laws. The world has never presented such a spectacle, such a proof of the capacity of the people for self-government. Long may it continue! May the tongue wither that dares preach resistance to the ballot-boxes; and may the moral influence of our example reach our distracted sister republics, staying the sword of persecution in the hands of victors, and crushing the spirit of revolution in a defeated party.

January 1, 1840. This day, so full of home associations—snow, and red noses, and blue lips out of doors, and blazing fires and beauteous faces within— opened in Guatimala like a morning in spring. The sun seemed rejoicing in the beauty of the land it shone upon. The flowers were blooming in the courtyards, and the mountains, visible above the tops of the houses, were smiling in verdure. The bells of thirty-eight churches and convents proclaimed the coming of another year. The shops were shut as on a Sunday; there was no market in the plaza. Gentlemen well dressed, and ladies in black mantas, were crossing it to attend grand mass in the Cathedral. Mozart's music swelled through the aisles. A priest in a strange tongue proclaimed morality, religion, and love of country. The floor of the church was thronged with whites, Mestitzoes, and Indians. On a high bench opposite the pulpit sat the chief of the state, and by his side Carrera, again dressed in his rich uniform. I leaned against a pillar opposite and watched his face; and if I read him right, he had forgotten war and the stains of blood upon his hands, and his very soul was filled with fanatic enthusiasm; exactly as the priests would have him. I did verily believe that he was honest in his impulses, and

would do right if he knew how. They who undertake
to guide him have a fearful responsibility. The service
ended, a way was cleared through the crowd. Carrera,
accompanied by the priests and the chief of the state,
awkward in his movements, with his eyes fixed on the
ground, or with furtive glances, as if ill at ease in being
an object of so much attention, walked down the aisle.
A thousand ferocious-looking soldiers were drawn up
before the door. A wild burst of music greeted him,
and the faces of the men glowed with devotion to their
chief. A broad banner was unfurled, with stripes of
black and red, a device of a death's head and legs in
the centre, and on one side the words " Viva la religion!" and on the other " Paz o muerte a los Liber-
ales!" Carrera placed himself at their head, and with
Rivera Paz by his side, and the fearful banner floating in the air, and wild and thrilling music, and the
stillness of death around, they escorted the chief of the
state to his house. How different from Newyear's Day
at home!

Fanatic as I knew the people to be in religion, and
violent in political animosities, I did not believe that such
an outrage would be countenanced as flaunting in the
plaza of the capital a banner linking together the support
of religion and the death or submission of the Liberal
party. Afterward, in a conversation with the chief of
the state, I referred to this banner. He had not noticed
it, but thought that the last clause was " Paz o muerte
a los qui no lo quieron," "to those who do not wish it."
This does not alter its atrocious character, and only
adds to fanaticism what it takes from party spirit. I
think, however, that I am right; for on the return of the
soldiers to the plaza, Mr. C. and I followed it, till, as
we thought, the standard-bearer contracted its folds ex-

pressly to hide it, and some of the officers looked at us so suspiciously that we withdrew.

For the sake of home associations, I called on my fair countrywoman; dined at Mr. Hall's, and in the afternoon went to the cockpit, a large circular building handsomely proportioned, with a high seat for the judges, who rang a bell as a signal for the fight, when commenced a clamour: "I offer five dollars!" "I offer twenty," &c.; and I am happy to say that in this crowded den I saw but one man whom I had ever seen before; from there I went to the bullfight, and then to the theatre. The reader will admit that I made a brilliant beginning to the year 1840.

CHAPTER XV.

Hunt for a Government.—Diplomatic Difficulties.—Departure from Guatimala. —Lake of Amatitan.—Attack of Fever and Ague.—Overo.—Istapa.—A French Merchant Ship.—Port of Acajutla.—Illness.—Zonzonate.—The Government found.—Visit to the Volcano of Izalco.—Course of the Eruptions.—Descent from the Volcano.

ON Sunday, the fifth of January, I rose to set out in search of a government. Don Manuel Pavon, with his usual kindness, brought me a packet of letters of introduction to his friends in San Salvador. Mr. Catherwood intended to accompany me to the Pacific. We had not packed up, the muleteer had not made his appearance, and my passport had not been sent. Captain De Nouvelle waited till nine o'clock, and then went on in advance. In the midst of my confusion I received a visit from a distinguished canonigo. The reverend prelate was surprised at my setting out on that day. I was about pleading my necessities as an excuse for travelling on the Sabbath; but he relieved me by adding that there was to be a dinner-party, a bullfight, and a play, and he wondered that I could resist such temptations. At eleven o'clock the muleteer came, with his mules, his wife, and a ragged little son; and Mr. Savage, who was always my help through the little vexations attendant upon doing anything in that country, as well as in more important matters, returned from the Government House with word that my passport had been sent to me. I knew that the government was displeased with my purpose of going to the capitol. The night before it had been currently reported that I intended to present my credentials at San Salvador, and recognise the existence of the Federal Government; newspapers received the same night by the courier from Mexico were burdened with accounts of an invasion of that country by the Texans. I had before received a piece of information that was new to me, and of which it was considered diplomatic that I should profess ignorance, viz., that, though not so avowed, the Texans were supported and urged on by the government of the United States. We were considered as bent upon the conquest of Mexico; and, of course, Guatimala would come next. The odium of our ambitious pretensions increased the feeling of coldness and distrust toward me, arising from my not having attached myself to the dominant party. In general I was considered as the successor of Mr. De Witt. It was known among politicians that proceedings were pending for the renewal of a treaty, and that our government had a claim for the destruction of property of our citizens in one of the revolutions of the country; but some imagined that the special object of my mission was very deep, and in favour of the party at San Salvador. When Mr. Savage returned without any passport, suspecting that there was an intention to embarrass me and make me lose the opportunity of going by sea, I went immediately to the Government House, where I received the same answer that had been given to Mr. Savage. I requested another, but the secretary of state objected, on the ground that none could be made out on that day. There were several clerks in the office, and I urged my pressing necessity, the actual departure of Captain De Nouvelle, my seasonable application, and the promise that it should be sent to my house. After an unpleasant parley, one was given me, but without assigning me any official character. I pointed out the omission, and the secretary said that I had not presented

my credentials. I answered that my credentials were
to the general government, and not to that of the State
of Guatimala, which alone he represented ; but he persisted that it was not the custom of his government to
recognise an official character unless he presented his
credentials. *His* government had been in existence
about six months, and during that time no person
claiming to be official had been near the country. I
put into his hands my passport from my own government, reminded him that I had been arrested and imprisoned once, assured him that I should at all events
set out for San Salvador, and wished to know definitive-
ly whether he would give me such a passport as I had
a right to ask for. After much hesitation, and with a
very bad grace, he interlined before the official title the
words *con el caracter*. I make great allowance for party
feeling in a country where political divisions are matters
of life and death, more particularly for Don Joaquim
Durand, whose brother, a priest, was shot a short time
before by the Morazan party ; but this attempt to embarrass my movements, by depriving me of the benefit of official character, excited a feeling of indignation which I
did not attempt to conceal. To refuse accepting the passport altogether, or to wait a day for remonstrance, would
cause me to lose my passage by sea, and make it necessary to undertake a dangerous journey by land, or
abandon going to the capitol ; which, I believe, was
precisely what was wished. I was resolved not to be
prevented by any indirect means. I only needed a
passport to the port—the best they could give I did not
value very highly—in San Salvador it would be utterly worthless ; and with the uncourteous paper thus un-
graciously bestowed, I returned to the house, and at

two o'clock we started. It was the hottest hour of the day, and when we passed the gate the sun was scorching. Late as it was, our muleteer had not finished his leave-taking. His wife and little son accompanied him; and at some distance outside we were obliged to stop in the hot sun and wait till they came up. We were extremely glad when they exchanged their last embraces, and the wife and son turned off for their home in Mixco.

Notwithstanding the lateness of the hour, we diverged from the regular road for the purpose of passing by the Lake of Amatitan, but it was dark when we reached the top of the high range of mountains which bounds that beautiful water. Looking down, it seemed like a gathering of fog in the bottom of a deep valley. The descent was by a rough zigzag path on the side of the mountain, very steep, and, in the extreme darkness, difficult and dangerous. We felt happy when we reached the bank of the lake, though still a little above it. The mountains rose round it like a wall, and cast over it a gloom deeper than the shade of night. We rode for some distance with the lake on our left, and a high and perpendicular mountain-side on our right. A cold wind had succeeded the intense heat of the day, and when we reached Amatitan I was perfectly chilled. We found the captain in the house he had indicated. It was nine o'clock, and, not having touched anything since seven in the morning, we were prepared to do justice to the supper he had provided for us.

To avoid the steep descent to the lake with the cargo-mules, our muleteer had picked up a guide for us on the road, and gone on himself direct ; but, to our surprise, he had not yet arrived. While at supper we

heard an uproar in the street, and a man ran in to tell
us that a mob was murdering our muleteer. The captain, a frequent visiter to the country, said it was probably a general machete fight, and cautioned us against
going out. While in the corridor, hesitating, the uproar was hurrying toward us; the gate burst open, and
a crowd rushed in, dragging with them our muleteer,
that respectable husband and father, with his machete
drawn, and so tipsy that he could hardly stand, but
wanted to fight all the world. With difficulty we got
him entangled among some saddle-gear, when he dropped down, and, after vain efforts to rise, fell asleep.

I woke the next morning with violent headache and
pain in all my bones. Nevertheless, we started at daylight, and rode till five o'clock. The sun and heat increased the pain in my head, and for three hours before
reaching Escuintla I was in great suffering. I avoided going to the corregidor's, for I knew that his sleeping apartment was open to all who came, and I wanted
quiet; but I made a great mistake in stopping at the
house of the captain's friend. He was the proprietor
of an estanco or distillery for making agua ardiente,
and gave us a large room directly back of a store, and
separated from it by a low board partition open over
the top; and this store was constantly filled with noisy,
wrangling, and drinking men and women. My bed
was next to the partition, and we had eight or ten men
in our room. All night I had a violent fever, and in
the morning I was unable to move. Captain De Nouvelle regretted it, but he could not wait, as his ship was
ready to lie off and on without coming to anchor. Mr.
Catherwood had me removed to a storeroom filled with
casks and demijohns, where, except from occasional

entries to draw off liquor, I was quiet; but the odour was sickening.

In the afternoon the fever left me, and we rode to Masaya, a level and shady road of four leagues, and, to our surprise and great satisfaction, found the captain at the house at which I had stopped on my return from Istapa. He had advanced two leagues beyond, when he heard of a band of robbers at some distance farther on, and returned to wait for company, sending, in the mean time, to Escuintla for a guard of soldiers. We afterward learned that they were a body of exiles who had been expelled from Guatimala, and were crossing from Quezaltenango to San Salvador; but, being in desperate circumstances, they were dangerous persons to meet on the road.

The hut at which we stopped was hardly large enough for the family that occupied it, and our luggage, with two hammocks and a cartaret, drove them into a very small space. Crying children are said to be healthy; if so, the good woman of the house was blessed: besides this, a hen was hatching a brood of chickens under my head. During the night a party of soldiers entered the village, in pursuance of the captain's requisition, and passed on to clear the road. We started before daylight; but as the sun rose my fever returned, and at eleven o'clock, when we reached Overo, I could go no farther.

I have before remarked that this hacienda is a great stopping-place from Istapa and the salt-works; and unfortunately for me, several parties of muleteers, in apprehension of the robbers, had joined together, and starting at midnight, had already finished their day's labour. In the afternoon a wild boar was hunted, which our muleteer, with my gun, killed. There was a great feast in cooking and eating him, and the noise racked my brain. Night brought no relief. Quiet was all I wanted, but that it seemed impossible to have ; besides which, the rancho was more than usually abundant in fleas. All night I had violent fever. Mr. Catherwood, who, from not killing any one at Copan, had conceived a great opinion of his medical skill, gave me a powerful dose of medicine, and toward morning I fell asleep.

At daylight we started, and arrived at Istapa at nine o'clock. Captain De Nouvelle had not yet gone on board. Two French ships were then lying off the port: the Belle Poule and the Melanie, both from Bordeaux, the latter being the vessel of Captain De Nouvelle. He had accounts to arrange with the captain of the Belle Poule, and we started first for his vessel.

I have before remarked that Istapa is an open roadstead, without bay, headland, rock, reef, or any protection whatever from the open sea. Generally the sea is, as its name imports, pacific, and the waves roll calmly to the shore ; but in the smoothest times there is a breaker, and to pass this, as a part of the fixtures of the port, an anchor is dropped outside, with a buoy attached, and a long cable passing from the buoy is secured on shore. The longboat of the Melanie lay hard ashore, stern first, with a cable run through a groove in the bows, and passing through the sculling-hole in the stern. She was filled with goods, and among them we took our seats. The mate sat in the stern, and, taking advantage of a wave that raised the bows, gave the order to haul. The wet rope whizzed past, and the boat moved till, with the receding wave, it struck heavily on the sand. Another wave and another haul, and she swung clear of the bottom ; and meeting the coming, and hauling fast on the receding wave, in a few minutes we passed the breakers, the rope was thrown out of the groove, and the sailors took to their oars.

It was one of the most beautiful of those beautiful days on the Pacific. The great ocean was as calm as a lake; the freshness of the morning still rested upon the water, and already I felt revived. In a few minutes we reached the Belle Poule, one of the most beautiful ships that ever floated, and considered a model in the French commercial marine. The whole deck was covered with an awning, having a border trimmed with scarlet, and fluttering in the wind. The quarter-deck was raised, protected by a fanciful awning, furnished with settees, couches, and chairs, and on a brass railing in front sat two beautiful Peruvian parrots. The door of the cabin was high enough to admit a tall man without stooping. On each side were four staterooms, and the stern was divided into two chambers for the captain and supercargo, each with a window in it, and furnished with a bed (not a berth), a sofa, books, drawers, writing-desk, everything necessary for luxurious living on shipboard; just the comforts with which one would like to circumnavigate the world. She was on a trading voyage from Bordeaux, with an assorted cargo of French goods; had touched at the ports in Peru, Chili, Panama, and Central America, and left at each place merchandise to be sold, and the proceeds to be invested in the products of the country; and was then bound to Mazatlan, on the coast of Mexico, whence she would return and pick up her cargo, and in two years return to Bordeaux. We had a déjeuner à la fourchette, abounding in Paris luxuries, with wines and café, as in Paris, to which, fortunately for the ship's stores, I did not bring my accustomed vigour; and there was style in everything, even to the name of the steward, who was called the maître d'hôtel.

At two o'clock we went on board the Melanie. She was about the same size, and if we had not seen the Belle Poule first, we should have been delighted with her. The comfort and luxury of these " homes on the sea" were in striking contrast with the poverty and misery of the desolate shore. The captain of the Belle Poule came on board to dine. It was a pleasure to us to see the delight with which these two Bordeaux men and their crews met on this distant shore. Cape Horn, Peru, and Chili were the subjects of conversation, and we found on board a file of papers, which gave us the latest news from our friends in the Sandwich Islands. Mr. C. and the captain of the Belle Poule remained on board till we got under way. We bade them good-by over the railing; the evening breeze filled our sails; for a few moments we saw them, a dark spot on the water; the wave sank, and we lost sight of them entirely.

I remained on deck but a short time. I was the only passenger, and the maître d'hôtel made me a bed with settees directly under the stern windows, but I could not sleep. Even with windows and doors wide open the cabin was excessively warm; the air was heated, and it was full of moschetoes. The captain and mates slept on deck. I was advised not to do so, but at twelve o'clock I went out. It was bright starlight; the sails were flapping against the mast; the ocean was like a sheet of glass, and the coast dark and irregular, gloomy, and portentous with volcanoes. The great bear was almost upon me, the north star was lower than I had ever seen it before, and, like myself, seemed waning. A young sailor of the watch on deck

spoke to me of the deceitfulness of the sea, of shipwrecks, of the wreck of an American vessel which he
had fallen in with on his first cruise in the Pacific, and
of his beautiful and beloved France. The freshness of
the air was grateful; and while he was entertaining me,
I stretched myself on a settee and fell asleep.

The next day I had a recurrence of fever, which
continued upon me all day, and the captain put me under ship's discipline. In the morning the maître d'hôtel
stood by me with cup and spoon, "Monsieur, un vom-
itif," and in the afternoon, " Monsieur, une purge."
When we arrived at Acajutla I was unable to go
ashore. As soon as we cast anchor the captain landed, and before leaving for Zonzonate engaged mules
and men for me. The port of Acajutla is not quite so
open as that of Istapa, having on the south a slight
projecting headland of rock. In the offing were a
goelette brig for a port in Peru, a Danish schooner for
Guayaquil, and an English brig from London. All the
afternoon I sat on the upper deck. Some of the sailors
were asleep and others playing cards. In sight were
six volcanoes; one constantly emitting smoke, and another flames. At night the Volcano of Izalco seemed a
steady ball of fire.

The next morning the mate took me ashore in the
launch. The process was the same as at Istapa, and
we were detained some time by the boat of the English
vessel occupying the cable. As soon as we struck, a
crowd of Indians, naked except a band of cotton cloth
around the loins and passing between the legs, backed
up against the side of the boat. I mounted the shoulders of one of them; as the wave receded he carried
me several paces onward, then stopped and braced
himself against the coming wave. I clung to his neck,

but was fast sliding down his slippery sides, when he deposited me on the shore of San Salvador, called by the Indians " Cuscatlan," or the land of riches. Alvarado, on his voyage to Peru, was the first Spaniard who ever set foot upon this shore, and as I took special care to keep my feet from getting wet, I could but think of the hardy frames as well as iron nerves of the conquerors of America.

The mate and sailors took leave of me and returned to the ship. I walked along the shore and up a steep hill. It was only eight o'clock, and already excessively hot. On the bank fronting the sea were the ruins of large warehouses, occupied as receptacles for merchandise under the Spanish dominion, when all the ports of America were closed against foreign vessels. In one corner of the ruined building was a sort of guardroom, where a few soldiers were eating tortillas, and one was cleaning his musket. Another apartment was occupied by the captain of the port, who told me that the mules engaged for me had got loose, and the muleteers were looking for them. Here I had the pleasure to meet Dr. Drivin, a gentleman from the Island of St. Lucia, who had a large sugar hacienda a few leagues distant, and was at the port to superintend the disembarcation of machinery for a mill from the English brig. While waiting for the mules he conducted me to a hut where he had two Guayaquil hammocks hung, and feeling already the effect of my exertions, I took possession of one of them.

The woman of the rancho was a sort of ship's husband; and there being three vessels in port, the rancho was encumbered with vegetables, fruit, eggs, fowls, and ship's stores. It was close and hot, but very soon I required all the covering I could get. I had a violent ague, followed by a fever, in comparison with which all I had suffered before was nothing. I called for water till the old woman was tired of giving it to me, and went out and left me alone. I became lightheaded, wild with pain, and wandered among the miserable huts with only the consciousness that my brain was scorching. I have an indistinct recollection of speaking English to some Indian women, begging them to get me a horse to ride to Zonzonate; of some laughing, others looking at me with pity, and others leading me out of the sun, and making me lie down under the shade of a tree. At three o'clock in the afternoon the mate came ashore again. I had changed my position, and he found me lying on my face asleep, and almost withered by the sun. He wanted to take me back on board the ship, but I begged him to procure mules and take me to Zonzonate, within the reach of medical assistance. It is hard to feel worse than I did when I mounted. I passed three hours of agony, scorched by the intense heat, and a little before dark arrived at Zonzonate, fortunate, as Dr. Drivin afterward told me, in not having suffered a stroke of the sun. Before entering the town and crossing the bridge over the Rio Grande, I met a gentleman well mounted, having a scarlet Peruvian pellon over his saddle, with whose appearance I was struck, and we exchanged low bows. This gentleman, as I afterward learned, was the government I was looking after.

I rode to the house of Captain De Nouvelle's brother, one of the largest in the place, where I had that comfort, seldom known in Central America, a room to myself, and everything else necessary. For several days I remained within doors. The first afternoon I

went out I called upon Don Manuel de Aguila, formerly
chief of the State of Costa Rica, but about a year before driven out by a revolution and banished for life.
At his house I met Don Diego Vigil, the vice-president
of the republic, the same gentleman whom I had met
on the bridge, and the only existing officer of the Federal Government. From observation and experience
in my own country, I had learned never to take the
character of a public man from his political enemy;
and I will not soil this page with the foul aspersions
which men of veracity, but blinded by party prejudice,
threw upon the character of Señor Vigil. He was
about forty-five, six feet high, thin, and suffering from
a paralytic affection, which almost deprived him of the
use of both legs; in dress, conversation, and manners,
eminently a gentleman. He had travelled more extensively in his own country than most of his countrymen, and knew all the objects of interest; and with a
politeness which I appreciated, made no reference to my
position or my official character.

His business at Zonzonate showed the wretched state
of the country. He had come expressly to treat with
Rascon, the head of the band which had prevented my
coming from Guatimala by land. Chico Rascon, as he
was familiarly called in Zonzonate, was of an old and
respectable family, who had spent a large fortune in
dissipation in Paris, and returning in desperate circumstances, had turned patriot. About six months before
he had made a descent upon Zonzonate, killed the
garrison to a man, robbed the custom-house, and retreated to his hacienda. He was then on a visit in the
town, publicly, by appointment with Señor Vigil, and
demanded, as the price of disbanding his troops, a
colonel's commission for himself, other commissions for

some of his followers, and four thousand dollars in money. Vigil assented to all except the four thousand dollars in money, but offered instead the credit of the State of San Salvador, which Rascon agreed to accept. Papers were drawn up, and that afternoon was appointed for their execution; but, while Vigil was waiting for him, Rascon and his friends, without a word of notice, mounted their horses and rode out of town. The place was thrown into great excitement, and in the evening I saw the garrison busily engaged in barricading the plaza, in apprehension of another attack.

The next day I made a formal call upon Señor Vigil. I was in a rather awkward position. When I left Guatimala in search of a government, I did not expect to meet it on the road. In that state I had heard but one side; I was just beginning to hear the other. If there was any government, I had *treed* it. Was it the real thing or was it not? In Guatimala they said it was not; here they said it was. It was a knotty question. I was in no great favour in Guatimala, and in endeavouring to play a safe game I ran the risk of being hustled by all parties. In Guatimala they had no right to ask for my credentials, and took offence because I did not present them; here, if I refused, they had a right to consider it an insult. In this predicament I opened my business with the vice-president, and told him that I was on my way to the capital, with credentials from the United States; but that, in the state of anarchy in which I found the country, was at a loss what to do; I was desirous to avoid making a false step, and anxious to know whether the Federal Government really existed, or whether the Republic was dissolved. Our interview was long and interesting, and the purport of his answer was, that the government did exist de facto and de jure; he himself

was legally elected vice-president; the act of the four
states in declaring themselves independent was unconstitutional and rebellious; the union could not be dissolved except by a convention of deputies from all the
states; the government had the actual control in three
states, one had been reduced to subjection by arms, and
very soon the Federal party would have the ascendancy
in the others. He was familiar with the case of South
Carolina, and said that our Congress had sustained the
right of the general government to coerce states into
subjection, and they were in the same position. I referred to the shattered condition of the government; its
absolute impotence in other states; the non-existence of
senate and other co-ordinate branches, or even of a secretary of state, the officer to whom my credentials were
addressed; and he answered that he had in his suite an
acting secretary of state, confirming what had been told
me before, that the " Government" would, at a moment's notice, make any officer I wanted; but I owe it
to Señor Vigil to say, that, after going over fully the
whole ground of the unhappy contest, and although at
that critical juncture the recognition of the Federal Government by that of the United States would have been
of moment to his party, and not to recognise it was dis-
respectful and favoured the cause of the rebellious or independent states, he did not ask me to present my credentials. The Convention, which was expected to compose the difficulties of the Republic, was then about as-
sembling in Honduras. The deputies from St. Salvador
had gone to take their seats, and it was understood that
I should await the decision of this body. The result of
my interview with the vice-president was much more
agreeable than I expected. I am sure that I left him
without the least feeling of ill-will on his part; but my

great perplexity whether I had any government was not yet brought to a close.

In the mean time, while the political repairs were going on, I remained in Zonzonate recruiting. The town is situated on the banks of the Rio Grande, which is formed by almost innumerable springs, and in the Indian language its name means four hundred springs of water. It stands in one of the richest districts of the rich State of San Salvador, and has its plaza, with streets at right angles, and white houses of one story, some of them very large ; but it has borne its share of the calamities which have visited the unfortunate Republic. The best houses are deserted, and their owners in exile. There are seven costly churches and but one cura.

I was unable to undertake any journey by land, and feeling the enervating effect of the climate, swung all day in a hammock. Fortunately, the proprietors of the brig which I had seen at Acajutla, bound for Peru, changed her destination, and determined to send her to Costa Rica, the southernmost state of the Confederacy. At the same time, a man offered as a servant, very highly recommended, and whose appearance I liked ; and I resolved to have the benefit of the sea voyage, and, in returning by land, explore the canal route between the Atlantic and Pacific by the Lake of Nicaragua, a thing which I had desired much, but despaired of being able to accomplish.

Before leaving I roused myself for an excursion. The window of my room opened upon the Volcano of Izalco. All day I heard at short intervals the eruptions of the burning mountain, and at night saw the column of flame bursting from the crater, and streams of fire rolling down its side. Fortunately, Mr. Blackburn, a Scotch merchant, for many years resident in Peru, arrived, and agreed to accompany me. The next morning before five o'clock we were in the saddle. At the distance of a mile we forded the Rio Grande, here a wild river, and riding through a rich country, in half an hour reached the Indian village of Naguisal, a lovely spot, and literally a forest of fruits and flowers. Large trees were perfectly covered with red, and at every step we could pluck fruit. Interspersed among these beautiful trees were the miserable huts of Indians, and lying on the ground, or at some lazy work, were the miserable Indians themselves. Continuing another league through the same rich country, we rose upon a table of land, from which, looking back, we saw an immense plain, wooded, and extending to the shore, and beyond, the boundless waters of the Pacific. Before us, at the extreme end of a long street, was the church of Izalco, standing out in strong relief against the base of the volcano, which at that moment, with a loud report like the rolling of thunder, threw in the air a column of black smoke and ashes, lighted by a single flash of flame.

With difficulty we obtained a guide, but he was so tipsy that he could scarcely guide himself along a straight street; and he would not go till the next day, as he said it was so late that we should be caught on the mountain at night, and that it was full of tigers. In the mean time the daughter of our host found another, and, stowing four green cocoanuts in his alforgas, we set out. Soon we came out upon an open plain, and without a bush to obstruct the view, saw on our left the whole volcano from its base to its top. It rose from near the foot of a mountain, to a height perhaps of three thousand feet, its sides brown and barren, and all around for miles the earth was covered with lava. Being in a state of eruption, it was impossible to ascend

it, but behind it is a higher mountain, which commands
a view of the burning crater.   The whole volcano was
in full sight, spouting into the air a column of black
smoke and an immense body of stones, while the earth
shook under our feet.   Crossing the plain, we commenced ascending the mountain.   At eleven o'clock we
sat down by the bank of a beautiful stream to breakfast.   My companion had made abundant provision, and
for the first time since I left Guatimala I felt the keen-
ness of returning appetite.   In half an hour we mounted, and soon after twelve o'clock entered the woods,
having a very steep ascent by a faint path, which we
soon lost altogether.   Our guide changed his direction
several times, and at length got lost, tied his horse, and
left us to wait while he searched the way.   We knew
that we were near the volcano, for the explosions sounded like the deep mutterings of dreadful thunder.   Shut
up as we were in the woods, these reports were awful.
Our horses snorted with terror, and the mountain quaked
beneath our feet.   Our guide returned, and in a few
minutes we came out suddenly upon an open point,
higher than the top of the volcano, commanding a view
of the interior of the crater, and so near it that we saw
the huge stones as they separated in the air, and fell pat-
tering around the sides of the volcano.   In a few minutes our clothes were white with ashes, which fell around
us with a noise like the sprinkling of rain.

The crater had three orifices, one of which was inactive ; another emitted constantly a rich blue smoke ;
and after a report, deep in the huge throat of the third
appeared a light blue vapour, and then a mass of thick
black smoke, whirling and struggling out in enormous
wreaths, and rising in a dark majestic column, lighted
for a moment by a sheet of flame ; and when the smoke

dispersed, the atmosphere was darkened by a shower of stones and ashes. This over, a moment of stillness followed, and then another report and eruption, and these continued regularly, at intervals, as our guide said, of exactly five minutes, and really he was not much out of the way. The sight was fearfully grand. We refreshed ourselves with a. draught of cocoanut milk, thought how this grandeur would be heightened when the stillness and darkness of night were interrupted by the noise and flame, and forthwith resolved to sleep upon the mountain.

The cura of Zonzonate, still in the vigour of life, told me that he remembered when the ground on which this volcano stands had nothing to distinguish it from any other spot around. In 1798 a small orifice was discovered puffing out small quantities of dust and pebbles. He was then living at Izalco, and, as a boy, was in the habit of going to look at it; and he had watched it, and marked its increase from year to year, until it had grown into what it is now. Captain De Nouvelle told me he could observe from the sea that it had grown greatly within the last two years. Two years before its light could not be seen at night on the other side of the mountain on which I stood. Night and day it forces up stones from the bowels of the earth, spouts them into the air, and receives them upon its sides. Every day it is increasing, and probably it will continue to do so until the inward fires die, or by some violent convulsion the whole is rent to atoms.

Old travellers are not precluded occasional bursts of enthusiasm, but they cannot keep it up long. In about an hour we began to be critical and even captious. Some eruptions were better than others, and some were comparatively small affairs. In this frame of mind we summed up our want of comforts for passing the night on the mountain, and determined to return. Mr. Blackburn and I thought that we could avoid the circuit of the mountain by descending directly to the base of the volcano, and crossing it, reach the camino real; but our guide said it was a tempting of Providence, and refused to accompany us. We had a very steep descent on foot, and in some places our horses slid down on their haunches. An immense bed of lava, stopped in its rolling course by the side of the mountain, filled up the wide space between us and the base of the volcano. We stepped directly upon this black and frightful bed, but we had great difficulty in making our horses follow. The lava lay in rolls as irregular as the waves of the sea, sharp, rough, and with huge chasms, difficult for us and dangerous for the horses. With great labour we dragged them to the base and around the side of the volcano. Massive stones, hurled into the air, fell and rolled down the sides, so near that we dared not venture farther. We were afraid of breaking our horses' legs in the holes into which they were constantly falling, and turned back. On the lofty point from which we had looked down into the crater of the volcano sat our guide, gazing, and, as we could imagine, laughing at us. We toiled back across the bed of lava and up the side of the mountain, and when we reached the top both my horse and I were almost exhausted. Fortunately, the road home was down hill. It was long after dark when we passed the foot of the mountain and came out upon the plain. Every burst of the volcano sent forth a pillar of fire; in four places were steady fires, and in one a stream of fire was rolling down its side. At eleven o'clock we reached Zonzonate, besides toiling around the base of the volcano, having ridden up-

ward of fifty miles ; and such had been the interest of
the day's work, that, though my first effort, I never suffered from it.

The arrangements for my voyage down the Pacific
were soon made.   The servant to whom I referred was
a native of Costa Rica, then on his way home, after a
long absence, with a cargo of merchandise belonging to
himself. He was a tall, good-looking fellow, dressed
in a Guatimala jacket or coton, a pair of Mexican leather trousers, with buttons down the sides, and a steeple-
crowned, broad-brimmed, drab wool hat, altogether far
superior to any servant I saw in the country ; and I
think if it had not been for him I should not have un-
dertaken the journey.   The reader will perhaps be
shocked to hear that his name was *Jesus*, pronounced
in Spanish 'Hezoos, by which latter appellation, to avoid
what might be considered profanity, I shall hereafter
call him.

CHAPTER XVI.

On Monday, the twenty-second of January, two
hours before daylight, we started for the port. 'Hezoos
led the way, carrying before him all my luggage, rolled
up in a baquette, being simply a cowhide, after the
fashion of the country. At daylight we heard behind
us the clattering of horses' hoofs, and Don Manuel
de Aguila, with his two sons, overtook us. Before the
freshness of the morning was past we reached the port,
and rode up to the old hut which I hàd hoped never to
see again. The hammock was swinging in the same
place. The miserable rancho seemed destined to be the
abode of sickness. In one corner lay Señor D'Yriarte,
my captain, exhausted by a night of fever, and unable
to sail that day.

Dr. Drivin was again at the port. He had not yet
disembarked his machinery; in fact, the work was suspended by a mutiny on board the English brig, the
ringleader of which, as the doctor complained to me,
was an American. I passed the day on the seashore.
In one place, a little above high-water mark, almost
washed by the waves, were rude wooden crosses, marking the graves of unhappy sailors who had died far from
their homes. Returning, I found at the hut Captain
Jay, of the English brig, who also complained to me
of the American sailor. The captain was a young

man, making his first voyage as master ; his wife, whom he had married a week before sailing, accompanied him. He had had a disastrous voyage of eight months from London ; in doubling Cape Horn his crew were all frostbitten and his spars carried away. With only one man on deck he had worked up to Guayaquil, where he incurred great loss of time and money in making repairs, and shipped an entirely new crew. At Acajutla he found that his boats were not sufficient to land the doctor's machinery, and was obliged to wait until a raft could be constructed. In the mean time his crew mutinied, and part of them refused to work. His wife was then at the doctor's hacienda ; and I noticed that, while writing her a note with pencil, his sunburned face was pale, and large drops of perspiration stood on his forehead. Soon after he threw himself into the hammock, and, as I thought, fell asleep ; but in a few minutes I saw the hammock shake, and, remembering my own shaking there, thought it was at its old tricks of giving people the fever and ague ; but very soon I saw that the poor captain was in convulsions. Excepting Captain D'Yriarte, who was lying against the wall perfectly helpless, I was the only man in the hut ; and as there was danger of his throwing himself out of the hammock, I endeavoured to hold him in ; but with one convulsive effort he threw me to the other side of the hut, and hung over the side of the hammock, with one hand entangled in the cords, and his head almost touching the ground. The old woman said that the devil had taken possession of him, and ran out of doors screaming. Fortunately, this brought in a man whom I had not seen before, Mr. Warburton, an engineer who had come out to set up the machinery, and who was himself a machine of many horse-power, having a pair of shoulders that

seemed constructed expressly for holding men in convulsions. At first he was so shocked that he did not
know what to do. I told him that the captain was to be
held, whereupon, opening his powerful arms, he closed
them around the captain's with the force of a hydraulic
press, turning the legs over to me. These legs were a
pair of the sturdiest that ever supported a human body;
and I verily believe that if the feet had once touched
my ribs, they would have sent me through the wall of
the hut. Watching my opportunity, I wound the hammock around his legs, and my arms around the hammock. In the mean time he broke loose from Mr. Warburton's hug, who, taking the hint from me, doubled his
part in with the folds of the hammock, and gave his
clinch from the outside. The captain struggled, and,
worming like a gigantic snake, slipped his head out of
the top of the hammock, and twisted the cords around his
neck, so that we were afraid of his strangling himself.
We were in utter despair, when two of his sailors rushed in, who, being at home with ropes, extricated his
head, shoved him back into the hammock, wrapped it
around him as before, and I withdrew completely exhausted.

The two recruits were Tom, a regular tar of about
forty, and the cook, a black man, and particular friend
of Tom, who called him Darkey. Tom undertook the
whole direction of securing the captain; and although Dr.
Drivin and several Indians came in, Tom's voice was
the only one heard, and addressed only to " Darkey."
" Stand by his legs, Darkey!" " Hold fast, Darkey!"
" Steady, Darkey!" but all together could not hold
him. Turning on his face and doubling himself inside,
he braced his back, and drove both legs through the
hammock, striking his feet violently against the ground;

his whole body passed through. His struggles were dreadful. Suddenly the mass of bodies on the floor rolled against Captain D'Yriarte's bed, which broke down with a crash, and with a fever upon him, he was obliged to scramble out of the way. In the interval of one of the most violent struggles we heard a strange idiotic noise, which seemed like an attempt to crow. The Indians who crowded the hut laughed, and Dr. Drivin was so indignant at their heartlessness that he seized a club and drove them all out of doors. An old naked African, who had been a slave at Balize, and had lost his language without acquiring much of any other, returned with a bunch of feathers, which he wished to stick in the captain's nose and set fire to, saying it was the remedy of his country; but the doctor showed him his stick, and he retreated.

The convulsions continued for three hours, during which time the doctor considered the captain's situation very critical. The old woman persisted that the devil was in him, and would not give him up, and that he must die; and I could not but think of his young wife, who was sleeping a few miles off, unconscious of the calamity that threatened her. The fit was brought on, as the doctor said, by anxiety and distress of mind occasioned by his unfortunate voyage, and particularly by the mutiny of his crew. At eleven o'clock he fell asleep, and now we learned the cause of the strange noise which had affected us so unpleasantly. Tom was just preparing to go on board the vessel, when the African ran down to the shore and told him that the captain was at the hut drunk. Tom, being himself in that state, felt that it was his duty to look after the captain; but he had just bought a parrot, for which he had paid a dollar, and, afraid to trust him in other hands, hauled his baggy shirt a foot more out of his trousers, and thrust the parrot into his bosom, almost smothering it with his neckcloth. The parrot, indignant at this confinement, was driving his beak constantly into Tom's breast, which was scarified and covered with blood; and once, when Tom thought it was going too far, he put his hand inside and pinched it, which produced the extraordinary sounds we had heard.

In a little while Tom and Darkey got the Indians to relieve them, and went out to drink the captain's health. On their return they took their places on the ground, one on each side of their commander. I threw myself into the broken hammock; and Dr. Drivin, charging them, if the captain awoke, not to say anything that could agitate him, went off to another hut.

It was not long before the captain, raising his head, called out, " What the devil are you doing with my legs?" which was answered by Tom's steady cry, " Hold on, Darkey!" Darkey and an Indian were holding the captain's legs, two Indians his arms, and Tom was spread over his body. The captain looked perfectly sensible, and utterly amazed at being pinned to the ground. " Where am I?" said he. Tom and Darkey had agreed not to tell him what had happened; but, after the most extraordinary lying on the part of Tom, while the captain was looking at him and us in utter amazement, the poor fellow became so entangled, that, swearing the doctor might stay and tell his own stories, he began where he and Darkey came in, and found the captain kicking in the hammock; and the captain was given to understand that if it had not been for him and Darkey he would have kicked his own brains out. I relieved Tom's story from some obscurity, and a general and noisy conversation followed,

which was cut short by poor Captain D'Yriarte, who
had not had a wink of sleep all night, and begged us to
give him a chance.

In the morning, while I was taking chocolate with
Doctor Drivin, the mate came to the hut with the mutinous American sailor in the custody of four soldiers,
to make a complaint to me. The sailor was a young
man of twenty-eight, short, well-made, and very good-
looking, and his name was Jemmy. He, too, complained to me; wanted to leave the brig, and said that
he would stop on a barren rock in the midst of the
ocean rather than remain on board. I told him I was
sorry to find an American sailor a ringleader in mutiny, and represented to him the distress and danger in
which it had placed the captain. Doctor Drivin had
had some sharp passages with him on board the brig,
and, after a few words, started up and struck him.
Jemmy fell back in time to avoid the full blow, and, as
if by no means unused to such things, continued to fall
back and ward off; but when pressed too hard, he broke
loose from the soldiers, and tore off his jacket for a regular fight. I had no idea of favouring a mutinous sail-
or, but still less of suffering an American to be mal-
treated by odds, and hauled off the soldiers. In a
moment the doctor's passion was over, and he discontinued his attack, whereupon Jemmy surrendered himself to the soldiers, who carried him, as I supposed, to
the guardhouse. I waited a little while, and, going
down, saw Jemmy sitting on the ground in front of the
quartel, with both legs in the stocks above the knees.
He was keenly alive to the disgrace of his situation,
and my blood boiled. I hurried to the captain of the
port, and complained warmly of his conduct as high-
handed and insufferable, and insisted that Jemmy must

be released, or I would ride to San Salvador on the instant and make a complaint against him. Doctor Drivin joined me, and Jemmy was released from the stocks, but put under guard in the quartel. This will probably never reach the eyes of any of his friends, but I will not mention his name. He was from the little town of Esopus, on the Hudson. In 1834 he sailed from New-York in the sloop-of-war Peacock for the Pacific station; was transferred to the North Carolina, and regularly discharged at Valparaiso; entered the Chilian naval service, and after plenty of fighting and no prize-money, shipped on board this brig. I represented that he was liable to be tried for mutiny, and had only escaped the stocks by my happening to be at the port; that I could do nothing more for him; and he might be kept on shore till the vessel sailed, and carried on board in irons. It was a critical moment in the young man's life; and, as one destitute of early opportunities, and whom necessity had probably doomed to a wayward life, and, moreover, as a countryman, I was anxious to save him from the effects of headstrong passion. The captain said he was the best sailor on board; and as he was short of hands, I procured from him a promise that, if Jemmy would return to his duty, he would take no notice of what had passed, and would give him his discharge at the first port where he could procure a substitute.

Fortunately, in the afternoon Captain D'Yriarte was sufficiently recovered to sail, and before going on board my vessel I took Jemmy to his. She was the dirtiest vessel I ever saw, and her crew a fair sample of the villanous sailors picked up in the ports of the Pacific. Among them, and as bad as any in appearance, was another countryman, Jemmy's American accomplice.

I did not wonder that Jemmy was discontented ; I left him on board in a bad condition, but, unfortunately, I afterward heard of him in a worse.

A few strokes of the oar brought me on board our vessel, and, as before, with the evening breeze we got under way. The vessel in which I embarked was called La Cosmopolita. She was a goelette brig, and the only vessel that bore on the Pacific the Central American flag. She was built in England for a collier, and called the Britannia. By some accident she reached the Pacific Ocean, was bought by the State of San Salvador when at war with Guatimala, and called by that state's Indian name of Cuscatlan. Afterward she was sold to an Englishman, who called her Eugenia ; and by him to Captain D'Yriarte, who called her La Cosmopolita.

My first night on board was not particularly agreeable. I was the only cabin passenger ; but, besides the bugs that always infest an old vessel, I had in my berth moschetoes, spiders, ants, and cockroaches. Yet there is no part of my tour upon which I look back with so much quiet satisfaction as this voyage on the Pacific. I had on board Gil Blas and Don Quixote in the original, and all day I sat under an awning, my attention divided between them and the great range of gigantic volcanoes which stud the coast. Before this became tedious we reached the Gulf of Papajayo, the only outlet by which the winds of the Atlantic pass over to the Pacific. The dolphin, the most beautiful fish that swims, played under our bows and stern, and accompanied us slowly alongside. But the sailors had no respect for his golden back. The mate, a murderous young Frenchman, stood for hours with a harpoon in his hand, drove it into several, and at length brought one on board. The king of the sea seemed conscious of his fallen state ; his beautiful colours faded, and he became spotted, and at last heavy and lustreless, like any other dead fish.

We passed in regular succession the volcanoes of San Salvador, San Vicente, San Miguel, Telega, Momotombo, Managua, Nindiri, Masaya, and Nicaragua, each one a noble spectacle, and all together forming a chain with which no other in the world can be compared ; indeed, this coast has well been described as "bristling with volcanic cones." For two days. we lay with sails flapping in sight of Cape Blanco, the upper headland of the Gulf of Nicoya. On the afternoon of the thirty-first we entered the gulf. On a line with the point of the cape was an island of rock, with high, bare, and precipitous sides, and the top covered with verdure. It was about sunset ; for nearly an hour the sky and sea seemed blazing with the reflection of the departing luminary, and the island of rocks seemed like a fortress with turrets. It was a glorious farewell view. I had passed my last night on the Pacific, and the highlands of the Gulf of Nicoya closed around us.

Early in the morning we had the tide in our favour, and very soon leaving the main body of the gulf, turned off to the right, and entered a beautiful little cove, forming the harbour of Caldera. In front was the range of mountains of Aguacata, on the left the old port of Pont Arenas, and on the right the Volcano of San Pablo. On the shore was a long low house set upon piles, with a tile roof, and near it were three or four thatched huts and two canoes. We anchored in front of the houses, and apparently without exciting the attention of a soul on shore.

All the ports of Central America on the Pacific are

unhealthy, but this was considered deadly. I had entered without apprehension cities where the plague was raging, but here, as I looked ashore, there was a death-like stillness that was startling. To spare me the necessity of sleeping at the port, the captain sent the boat ashore with my servant, to procure mules with which I could proceed immediately to a hacienda two leagues beyond.

Our boat had hardly started before we saw three men coming down to the shore, who presently put off in a canoe, met our boat, turned her back, and boarded us themselves. They were two paddles and a soldier, the latter of whom informed the captain that, by a late decree, no passenger was permitted to land without the special permission of the government, for which it was necessary to send an application to the capital, and wait on board for an answer. He added that the last vessel was full of passengers, who were obliged to remain twelve days before the permission was received. I was used to vexations in travelling, but I could not bear this quietly. The captain made a bold attempt in my favour by saying that he had no passengers; that he had on board the Minister of the United States, who was making the tour of Central America, and who had been treated with courtesy in Guatimala and San Salvador, and that it would be an indignity for the government of Costa Rica not to permit his landing. He wrote to the same effect to the captain of the port, who, on the return of the soldier, came off himself. I was almost sick with vexation, and the captain of the port finished two glasses of wine before I had courage to introduce the subject. He answered with great courtesy, regretting that the law was imperative, and that he had no discretion. I replied that the law was intended to prevent the entrance of seditious persons, emigrés, and expulsados from other states, who might disturb the peace of Costa Rica, but that it could not contemplate a case like mine, at the same time laying great stress upon my official character. Fortunately for me, he had a high sense of the respect due to that character, and, though holding a petty office, had a feeling of pride that his state should not be considered wanting in courtesy to an accredited stranger. For a long time he was at a loss what to do; but finally, after much deliberation, he requested me to wait till morning, when he would despatch a courier to advise the government of the circumstances, and would take upon himself the responsibility of permitting me to land. Fearful of some accident or some change of purpose, and anxious to get my feet on shore, I suggested that, in order to avoid travelling in the heat of the day, it would be better to sleep on shore, to be ready for an early start, to which he assented.

In the afternoon the captain took me ashore. At the first house we saw two candles lighted to burn at the body of a dead man. All whom we saw were ill, and all complained that the place was fatal to human life. In fact, it was almost deserted; and, notwithstanding its advantages as a port, government, a few days afterward, issued an order for breaking it up, and removing back to the old port of Pont Arenas. The captain was still suffering from fever and ague, and would not on any account remain after dark. I was so rejoiced to find myself on shore, that if I had met a death's head at every step it would hardly have turned me back.

The last stranger at the port was a distinguished American. His name was Handy; I had first heard of him at the Cape of Good Hope, hunting giraffes, afterward met him in New-York, and regretted exceedingly

to miss him here.   He had travelled from the United
States through Texas, Mexico, and Central America,
with an elephant and two dromedaries as his file leaders !   The elephant was the first ever seen in Central
America, and I often heard of him in the Pueblos under
the name of El Demonio.   Six days before, Mr. Handy,
with his interesting family, had embarked for Peru, and
perhaps he is at this moment crossing the pampas to
Brazil.

Determined not to lose sight of my friend the captain
of the port, with my luggage at my heels I walked
down the beach for the custom-house.   It was a frame
building, about forty feet long, and stood at a little distance above high-water mark, on piles about six feet
above ground.   It was the gathering-place of different
persons in the employ of the government, civil and military, and of two or three women employed by them.
The military force consisted of the captain of the port
and the soldier who boarded us, so that I had not much
fear of being sent back at the point of the bayonet.
During the evening a new difficulty arose about my servant ; but, considering myself tolerably secure, I insisted
that he was my suite, and obtained permission for him to
accompany me.   My host gave me a bedstead, with a
bull's hide for a bed.   It was a warm night, and I placed
it opposite an open door, and looked out upon the water of the gulf.   The waves were breaking gently upon
the shore, and it was beautiful to see the Cosmopolita
riding quietly at her anchor, without even 'Hezoos or the
luggage in her.

At two o'clock in the morning we rose, and before
three we started.   The tide was low, and for some distance we rode along the shore by moonlight.   At daylight we overtook the courier sent to give advice of my

coming; in an hour crossed the river of Jesus Maria, and at seven o'clock stopped to breakfast at the hacienda of the same name.

It was a miserable shell, with an arbour of branches around it, but had an appearance of cleanliness and comfort; and 'Hezoos told me that the proprietor had on it two thousand head of cattle, and owned all the land over which we had ridden from the sea. 'Hezoos was quite at home; and, as he afterward told me, he had once wanted to marry one of the daughters; but the father and mother objected, because he was not good enough. He added that they were surprised at seeing him return in such prosperous circumstances, and that the daughter told him she had always refused to marry any one else on account of her affection for him.

While breakfasting, the mother told me of a sick daughter, asked me for remedios, and finally requested me to go in and see her. The door opened from the shed, and all the apertures in the room were carefully closed, so as to exclude even a breath of air. The invalid lay in a bed in one corner, with a cotton covering over it like a moscheto-netting, but lower, and pinned close all around; and when the mother raised the covering, I encountered a body of hot and unwholesome air that almost overcame me. The poor girl lay on her back, with a cotton sheet wound tightly around her body; and already she seemed like one laid out for burial. She was not more than eighteen; the fever had just left her, her eye still sparkled, but her face was pale, and covered with spots, seams, and creases of dirt. She was suffering from intermitting fever, that scourge which breaks down the constitution and carries to the grave thousands of the inhabitants of Central America; and, according to the obstinate prejudice of

the country, her face had not been washed for more
than two months ! I had often been disgusted with the
long beards and unwashed faces of fever and ague subjects, and the ignorance and prejudice of the people
on medical subjects ; in illustration of which, Dr. Drivin
told me of a case of practice by an old quack woman,
who directed her patient, a rich cattle proprietor, to be
extended on the ground naked every morning, and a
bullock to be slaughtered over him, so that the blood
could run warm upon his body. The man submitted
to the operation more than a hundred times, and was
bathed with the blood of more than a hundred bullocks ;
afterward he underwent a much more disgusting process, and, strange to say, he lived.

But to return : in general my medical practice was
confined to men, and with them I considered myself a
powerful practitioner. I did not like prescribing for
women ; and in this case I struck at all the prejudices
of the country, and cheapened my medical skill by di-
recting, first, that the poor girl's face should be washed ;
but I saved myself somewhat by making a strong point
that it should be washed with warm water. Whether
they thanked me or not I do not know, but I had my
reward, for I saw a lovely face, and long afterward I
remembered the touching expression of her eyes, as she
turned toward me, and listened to the advice I gave her
mother.

At ten we resumed our journey. The land was level
and rich, but uncultivated. We passed several miserable cattle haciendas, the proprietors of which lived in
the towns, and kept men on the estate, from time to
time, to gather and number the cattle, which roamed
wild in the woods. At eleven we passed the hacienda
of San Felippe, belonging to a Welshman engaged in

mining. It was in a large clearing, and a fine situation, and its cleanliness, neatness, and good fences showed that the Welshman had not forgotten what he had learned at home.

We crossed the river Surubris and the Rio Grande or Machuca, and reached the hacienda of San Mateo, situated in the Boca of the mountain of Aguacate, and from this place we began to ascend. The road had been much improved lately, but the ascent was steep, wild, and rugged. As we toiled up the ravine, we heard before us a loud noise, that sounded like distant thunder, but regular and continued, and becoming louder as we advanced; and at length we came out on a small clearing, and saw on the side of the mountain a neat frame building of two stories, with a light and graceful balcony in front; and alongside was the thundering machine which had startled us by its noise. Strangers from the other side of the Atlantic were piercing the sides of the mountain, and pounding its stones into dust to search for gold. The whole range, the very ground which our horses spurned with their hoofs, contained that treasure for which man forsakes kindred and country.

I rode up to the house and introduced myself to Don Juan Bardh, the superintendent, a German from Friesburg. It was about two o'clock, and excessively hot. The house was furnished with chairs, sofa, and books, and had in my eyes a delightful appearance; but the view without was more so. The stream which turned the immense pounding-machine had made the spot, from time immemorial, a descansadera, or resting-place for muleteers. All around were mountains, and directly in front one rose to a great height, receding, and covered to the top with trees.

Don Juan Bardh had been superintendent of the Quebrada del Ingenio for about three years. The Company
which he represented was called the Anglo Costa Rican
Economical Mining Company. It had been in operation these three years without losing anything, which
was considered doing so well that it had increased its
capital, and was about continuing on a larger scale.
The machine, which had just been set up, was a new
German patent, called a *Machine for extracting Gold*
by the Zillenthal Patent Self-acting Cold Amalgamation
Process (I believe that I have omitted nothing), and its
great value was that it required no preliminary process,
but by one continued and simple operation extracted
the gold from the stone. It was an immense wheel of
cast iron, by which the stone, as it came from the mountain, was pounded into powder ; this passed into troughs
filled with water, and from them into a reservoir containing vases, where the gold detached itself from the
other particles, and combined with the quicksilver with
which the vases were provided.

There were several mines under Don Juan's charge,
and after dinner he accompanied me to that of Cor-
rallio, which was the largest, and, fortunately, lay on
my road. After a hot ride of half an hour, ascending
through thick woods, we reached the spot.

According to the opinion of the few geologists who
have visited that country, immense wealth lies buried
in the mountain of Aguacate ; and so far from being
hidden, the proprietors say, its places are so well marked that all who search may find. The lodes or min-
eral veins run regularly north and south, in ranges of
greenstone porphyry with strata of basaltic porphyry, and
average about three feet in width. In some places side-
cuts or lateral excavations are made from east to west,

and in others shafts are sunk until they strike the vein. The first opening we visited was a side-cut four feet wide, and penetrating two hundred and forty feet before it struck the lode; but it was so full of water that we did not enter. Above it was another cut, and higher still a shaft was sunk. We descended the shaft by a ladder made of the trunk of a tree, with notches cut in it, until we reached the vein, and followed it with a candle as far as it was worked. It was about a yard wide, and the sides glittered—but it was not with gold; they were of quartz and feldspar, impregnated with sulphuret of iron, and gold in such small particles as to be invisible to the naked eye. The most prominent objects in these repositories of wealth were naked workmen with pickaxes, bending and sweating under heavy sacks of stones.

It was late in the afternoon when I came out of the shaft. Don Juan conducted me by a steep path up the side of the mountain, to a small table of land, on which was a large building occupied by miners. The view was magnificent: below was an immense ravine; above, perched on a point, like an eagle's nest, the house of another superintendent; and on the opposite side the great range of the mountains of Candelaria. I waited till my mules came up, and with many thanks for his kindness, bade Don Juan farewell.

As we continued ascending, every moment the view became more grand and beautiful; and suddenly, from a height of six thousand feet, I looked down upon the Pacific, the Gulf of Nicoya, and, sitting like a bird upon the water, our brig, La Cosmopolita. And here, on the very highest points, in the wildest and most beautiful spots that ever men chose for their abodes, were the huts of the miners. The sun touched the sea, lighted up the surface of the water, and softened the rugged mountains; it was the most beautiful scene I ever saw, and this loveliest view was the last; for suddenly it became dark, and very soon the darkest night I ever knew came on. As we descended, the woods were so thick that even in the daytime they shut out the light, and in some places the road was cut through steep hills higher than our heads, and roofed over by the dense foliage. 'Hezoos was before me, with a white hat and jacket, and had a white dog running by his side, but I could not see the outline of his figure. The road was steep but good, and I did not pretend to direct the mule. In one of the darkest passages 'Hezoos stopped, and, with a voice that made the woods ring, cried out " a lion," " a lion." I was startled, but he dismounted and lighted a cigar. This was cool, I thought; he relieved me by telling me that the lion was a different animal from the roarer of the African desert, small, frightened by a shout, and only ate children. Long as it seemed, our whole descent did not occupy three hours, and at ten o'clock we reached the house in the Boca de la Montagna. It was shut, and all were asleep; but we knocked hard, and a man opened the door, and, before we could ask any questions, disappeared. Once inside, however, we made noise enough to wake everybody, and got corn for the mules and a light. There was a large room open to all comers, with three bedsteads, all occupied, and two men were sleeping on the floor. The occupant of one of the beds, after eying me a few moments, vacated it, and I took his place. The reader must not suppose that I am perfectly unscrupulous; he took all his bedclothes, viz., his chamar, with him. The bed and all its furniture consisted of an untanned bull's hide.

CHAPTER XVII.

THE next morning we entered an open, rolling, and undulating country, which reminded me of scenes at home. At nine o'clock we came to the brink of a magnificent ravine, and winding down by a steep descent of more than fifteen hundred feet, the mountains closed around us and formed an amphitheatre. At the bottom of the ravine was a rough wooden bridge crossing a narrow stream running between perpendicular rocks a hundred and fifty feet high, very picturesque, and reminding me of Trenton Falls.

We ascended by a steep road to the top of the ravine, where a long house stood across the road, so as to prevent all passing except directly through it. It is called La Garita, and commands the road from the port to the capital. Officers are stationed here to take an account of merchandise and to examine passports. The one then in command had lost an arm in the service of his country, i. e., in a battle between his own town and another fifteen miles off, and the place was given to him as a reward for his patriotic services.

As we advanced the country improved, and for a league before entering Alihuela it was lined on both sides with houses three or four hundred yards apart, built of sundried bricks, whitewashed, and the fronts of some were ornamented with paintings. Several had chalked in red on each side of the door the figure of a soldier, with his musket shouldered and bayonet fixed, large as life and stiff as a martinet. But all imperfections were hidden by rows of trees on both sides of the road, many of them bearing beautiful flowers, which in some places completely imbowered the houses. The fields were cultivated with sugarcane, and every house had its little trapiche or sugarmill; and there were marks of carriage-wheels, and very soon we heard a vehicle approaching. The creaking of its wheels made almost as much noise as the Zillenthal Patent Cold Amalgamating Machine in the mountain of Aguacate. They were made of a cut, about ten or twelve inches thick, from the trunk of a Guanacaste tree, with a hole in the centre, which played upon the axle almost ad libitum, and made the most mournful noise that can be conceived. The body was constructed of sugarcane; it was about four feet high, and drawn by oxen fastened by the horns instead of the neck.

At the entry of Alihuela I stopped to inquire for one bearing a name immortal in the history of the Spanish conquest. It was the name of Alvarado. Whether he was a descendant or not I do not know, nor did he; and strange to say, though I met several bearing that name, not one attempted to trace his lineage to the conqueror. Don Ramon Alvarado, however, was recommended to me for qualities which allied him in character with his great namesake. He was the courier of the English Mining Company for Serapequea and the River St. Juan, one of the wildest roads in all Central America.

Next to the advantage of the sea voyage, my principal object in leaving Zonzonate was to acquire some information in regard to the canal route between the

Atlantic and Pacific by means of the Lake of Nicaragua and the River San Juan, and my business with Alvarado was to secure him as a guide to the port of San Juan. In half an hour all these arrangements were made, the day fixed, and half the contract-money paid. In the mean time 'Hezoos was busily engaged in drawing a black glazed covering over my hat, and fixing in it an American eagle which I had taken off on shipboard.

There are four cities in Costa Rica, all of which lie within the space of fifteen leagues; yet each has a different climate and different productions. Including the suburbs, Alihuela contains a population of about 10,000. The plaza was beautifully situated, and the church, the cabildo, and the houses fronting it were handsome. The latter were long and low, with broad piazzas and large windows, having balconies made of wooden bars. It was Sunday, and the inhabitants, cleanly dressed, were sitting on the piazzas, or, with doors wide open, reclining in hammocks, or on high-backed wooden settees inside. The women were dressed like ladies, and some were handsome, and all white. A respectable-looking old man, standing in the door of one of the best houses, called out "Amigo," "friend," and asked us who we were, whence we came, and whither we were going, recommending us to God at parting ; and all along the street we were accosted in the same friendly spirit.

At a distance of three leagues we passed through Heredia without dismounting. I had ridden all day with a feeling of extraordinary satisfaction; and if such were my feelings, what must have been those of 'Hezoos ? He was returning to his country, with his love for it increased by absence and hardship away from home. All the way he met old acquaintances

and friends. He was a good-looking fellow, dashing-
ly dressed, and wore a basket-hilted Peruvian sword
more than six feet long. Behind him was strapped a
valise of scarlet cloth, with black borders, part of the
uniform of a Peruvian soldier. It would have been curious to remember how many times he told his story:
of military service and two battles in Peru; of impress-
ment for the navy and desertion; a voyage to Mexico,
and his return to Guatimala by land; and always concluded by inquiring about his wife, from whom he had
not heard since he left home, "la povera" being regularly his last words. As we approached his home his
tenderness for la povera increased. He could not procure any direct intelligence of her; but one good-na-
tured friend suggested that she had probably married
some one else, and that he would only disturb the
peace of the family by his return.

A league beyond Heredia we came to another great
ravine. We descended, and crossed a bridge over
the Rio Segondo. A few months before, this river
had risen suddenly and without any apparent cause,
swept away a house and family near the bridge, and
carried with it consternation and death. But little is
known of the geography of the interior of the country,
and it is supposed that a lake had burst its bounds.
Rising upon the other side, 'Hezoos pointed out the scene
of the battle in which the officer at La Garita had lost
his arm, and in which he himself had taken part, and,
being a San José man, he spoke of the people of the
other town as an Englishman in Lord Nelson's time
would of a Frenchman.

On the top of the ravine we came upon a large table
of land covered with the rich coffee-plantations of San
José. It was laid out into squares of two hundred feet,

enclosed by living fences of trees bearing flowers, with
roads sixty feet wide; and, except the small horsepath,
the roads had a sod of unbroken green. The deep
green of the coffee-plantations, the sward of the roads,
and the vistas through the trees at all the crossroads
were lovely; at a distance on each side were mountains, and in front, rising above all, was the great Volcano of Cartago. It was about the same hour as when,
the day before, from the top of the mountain of Aguacate, I had looked down into great ravines and over
the tops of high mountains, and seen the Pacific Ocean.
This was as soft as that was wild; and it addressed itself to other senses than the sight, for it was not, like
the rest of Central America, retrograding and going to
ruin, but smiling as the reward of industry. Seven
years before the whole plain was an open waste.

At the end of this table of land we saw San José on
a plain below us. On the top of the hill we passed a
house with an arch of flowers before the door, indica-
ting that within lay one waiting to receive the last sac-
rament before going to his final account in another
world. Descending, we saw at a distance a long procession, headed by a cross with the figure of the Saviour crucified. It approached with the music of violins and a loud chorus of voices, and was escorting the
priest to the house of the dying man. As it approached, horsemen pulled off their hats and pedestrians fell
on their knees. We met it near a narrow bridge at the
foot of the hill. The sun was low, but its last rays
were scorching to the naked head. The priest was
carried in a sedan chair. We waited till he passed,
and taking advantage of a break in the procession,
crossed the bridge, passed a long file of men and longer of women, and being some distance ahead, I put on

my hat. A fanatic fellow, with a scowl on his face,
cried out, " quittez el sombrero," " take off your hat."
I answered by spurring my horse, and at the same moment the whole procession was thrown into confusion.
A woman darted from the line, and 'Hezoos sprang from
his horse and caught her in his arms, and hugged and
kissed her as much as decency in the public streets
would allow. To my great surprise, the woman was
only his cousin, and she told him that his wife, who was
the principal milliner in the place, was on before in the
procession. 'Hezoos was beside himself; ran back, returned, caught his horse, and dragged the beast after
him ; then mounting and spurring, begged me to hurry
on and let him go back to his wife. Entering the town,
we passed a respectable-looking house, where four or
five well-dressed women were sitting on the piazza.
They screamed, 'Hezoos drove his mule up the steps,
and throwing himself off, embraced them all around.
After a few hurried words, he embraced them all over
again. Some male friends attempted to haul him off,
but he returned to the women. In fact, the poor fellow
seemed beside himself, though I could not but observe
that there was method in his madness; for, after two
rounds with the very respectable old ladies, he abandoned them, and dragging forward a very pretty young
girl with his arms around her waist, and kissing her
every moment, told me she was the apprentice of his
wife ; and though at every kiss he asked her questions
about his wife, he did not wait for answers, and the
kisses were repeated faster than the questions. During
all this time I sat on my horse looking on. Doubtless
it was very pleasant for him, but I began to be impa-
tient ; seeing which, he tore himself away, mounted,
and, accompanied by half a dozen of his friends, he

again led the way. As we advanced his friends increased. It was rather vexatious, but I could not disturb him in the sweetest pleasures in life, the welcome of friends after a long absence. Crossing the plaza, two or three soldiers of his old company, leaning on the railing of the quartel, cried out companero, and, with the sergeant at their head, passed over and joined us. We crossed the plaza with fifteen or twenty in our suite, or, rather, in his suite, some of whom, particularly the sergeant, in compliment to him, were civil to me.

While he had so many friends to welcome him, I had none. In fact, I did not know where I should sleep that night. In the large towns of Central America I was always at a loss where to stop. Throughout the country the traveller finds no public accommodation save the cabildo and a jar of water. Everything else he must carry with him, or purchase on the spot—if he can. But in the large towns he has not this resource, for it is not considered respectable to stop at the cabildo. I had letters of recommendation, but it was excessively disagreeable to present one from the back of a mule with my luggage at my heels, as it was, in fact, a draught at sight for board and lodging.

'Hezoos had told me that there was an old chapiton, i. e., a person from Spain, in whose house I could have a room to myself, and pay for it; but, unfortunately, time had made its changes, and the old Spaniard had been gone so long that the occupants of his house did not know what had become of him. I had counted upon him with so much certainty that I had not taken out my letters of recommendation, and did not even know the names of the persons to whom they were addressed. The cura was at his hacienda, and his house

shut up; a padre who had been in the United States
was sick, and could not receive any one; my servant's
friends all recommended different persons, as if I had
the whole town at my disposal; and principally they
urged me to honour with my company the chief of the
state. In the midst of this street consultation, I longed
for a hotel at a hundred dollars a day, and the government for paymaster. 'Hezoos, who was all the time in
a terrible hurry, after an animated interlude with some
of his friends, spurred his mule and hurried me back,
crossed a corner of the plaza, turned down a street to
the right, stopped opposite a small house, where he dismounted, and begging me to do the same, in a moment the saddles were whipped off and carried inside.
I was ushered into the house, and seated on a low chair
in a small room where a dozen women, friends of 'Hezoos and his wife, were waiting to welcome him to his
home. He told me that he did not know where his
house was, or that it had an extra room, till he learned it from his friends; and carrying my luggage into
a little dark apartment, said that I could have that to
myself, and that he, and his wife, and all his friends
would wait upon me, and that I could be more comfortable than in any house in San José. I was excessively
tired, having made three days' journey in two, worn
out with the worry of searching for a resting-place, and
if I had been younger, and had no character to lose, I
should not have given myself any farther trouble; but,
unfortunately, the dignity of office might have been
touched by remaining in the house of my servant; and,
besides, I could not move without running against a
woman; and, more than all, 'Hezoos threw his arms
around any one he chose, and kissed her as much as
he pleased. In the midst of my irresolution "la pove-

ra" herself arrived, and half the women in the procession, amateurs of tender scenes, followed. I shall not attempt to describe the meeting. 'Hezoos, as in duty bound, forsook all the rest, and notwithstanding all that he had done, wrapped her little figure in his arms as tightly as if he had not looked at a woman for a month; and la povera lay in his arms as happy as if there were no pretty cousins or apprentices in the world.

All this was too much for me : I worked my way out of doors, and after a consultation with the sergeant, ordered my horse to be saddled, and riding a third time across the plaza, stopped before the convent of Don Antonio Castro. The woman who opened the door said that the padre was not at home. I answered that I would walk in and wait, and ordered my luggage to be set down on the portico. She invited me inside, and I ordered the luggage in after me. The room occupied nearly the whole front of the convent, and besides some pictures of saints, its only furniture was a large wooden table, and a long, high-backed, wooden-bottomed settee. I laid my pistols and spurs upon the table, and stretching myself upon the settee, waited to welcome the padre to his house.

It was some time after dark when he returned. He was surprised, and evidently did not know what to do with me, but seemed to recognise the principle that possession is nine points of the law. I saw, however, that his embarrassment was not from want of hospitality, but from a belief that he could not make me comfortable. In Costa Rica the padres are poor, and I afterward learned that there it is unusual for a stranger to plant himself upon one. I have since thought that the Padre Castro must have considered me particularly cool; but, at all events, his nephew coming in soon after, they forthwith procured me chocolate. At each end of the long room was a small one, one occupied by the padre and the other by his nephew. The latter vacated his; and with a few pieces from the padre's, they fitted me up so well, that when I lay down I congratulated myself upon my forcible entry; and probably before they had recovered from their surprise I was asleep.

My arrival was soon known, and the next morning I received several invitations to the houses of residents— one from the lady of Don Manuel de Aguila; but I was so well pleased with the convent that I was not disposed to leave it. As a matter of course, I soon became known to all the foreign residents, who, however, were but four; Messrs. Steiples and Squire, a German and an Englishman, associated in business; Mr. Wallenstein, German; and the fourth was a countryman, Mr. Lawrence, from Middletown, Connecticut. All lived with Mr. Steiples; and I had immediately a general invitation to make his house my home.

San José is, I believe, the only city that has grown up or even improved since the independence of Central America. Under the Spanish dominion Cartago was the royal capital; but, on the breaking out of the revolution, the fervour of patriotism was so hot, that it was resolved to abolish this memorial of colonial servitude, and establish the capital at San José. Their local advantages are perhaps equal. Cartago is nearer the Atlantic, and San José the Pacific; but they are only six leagues apart. The buildings in San José are all republican; there is not one of any grandeur or architectural beauty; and the churches are inferior to many erected by the Spaniards in the smallest villages. Nevertheless, it exhibited a development of resources and an appearance of business unusual in this lethargic country; and there was one house in the plaza which showed that the owner had been abroad, and had returned with his mind so liberalized as to adopt the improvements of other countries, and build differently from the custom of his fathers and the taste of his neighbours.

My first visit of ceremony was to Señor Carillo, the Gefe del Estado. The State of Costa Rica enjoyed at that time a degree of prosperity unequalled by any in the disjointed confederacy. At a safe distance, without wealth enough to excite cupidity, and with a large tract of wilderness to protect it against the march of an invading army, it had escaped the tumults and wars which desolated and devastated the other states. And yet, but two years before, it had had its own revolution : a tumultuous soldiery entered the plaza, and shouting A bas De Aguila, Viva Carillo, my friend Don Manuel was driven out by bayonets and banished from the state, and Carillo installed in his place; he appointed his father-in-law, a quiet, respectable old man, vice-chief; called the soldiery, officers, civil and military, into the plaza, and all went through the solemn farce of swearing fealty to the Constitution. The time fixed by the Constitution for holding new elections came, but they were not permitted to be held; having tried this once and failed, he does not mean to run the risk of another ; and probably he will hold on till he is turned out by the same force that put him in. In the mean time, he uses prudent precautions : does not permit emigrés, nor revolutionists, nor suspected persons from other states to enter his dominions; has sealed up the press, and imprisons or banishes, under pain of death if they return, all who speak loud against the government.

He was about fifty, short and stout, plain, but careful in his dress, and with an appearance of dogged resolution in his face. His house was republican enough, and had nothing to distinguish it from that of any other citizen; in one part his wife had a little store, and in the other was his office for government business. It was not larger than the counting-room of a third-rate merchant, and he had three clerks, who at the moment of my entering were engaged writing, while he, with his coat off, was looking over papers. He had heard of my coming, and welcomed me to Costa Rica. Though the law under which I came near being detained at the port was uppermost in my mind, and I am sure was not forgotten by him, neither of us referred to it. He inquired particularly about Guatimala; and, though sympathizing in the policy of that state, had no good opinion of Carrera. He was uncompromising in his hostility to General Morazan and the Federal Government, and, in fact, it seemed to me that he was against any general government, and strongly impressed with the idea that Costa Rica could stand alone; doubtless believing that the state, or, which is the same thing, he himself, could disburse the revenues better than any other authority. Indeed, this is the rock on which all the politicians of Central America split : there is no such thing as national feeling. Every state would be an empire ; the officers of state cannot brook superiors ; a chief of the state cannot brook a president. He had not sent deputies to the Convention, and did not intend to do so ; but said that Costa Rica would remain neutral until the other states had settled their difficulties. He spoke with much interest of the improvement of the roads, particularly to the ports on the Atlantic and Pacific, and expressed great satisfaction at

the project of the British government, which I mentioned to him, of sending steamboats to connect the West
India Islands with the American coast, which, by touching at the port of San Juan, could bring his secluded
capital within eighteen or twenty days of New-York.
In fact, usurper and despot as he is, Carillo works hard
for the good of the state, and for twelve hundred dollars a year, with perquisites, and leave to be his own
paymaster. In the mean time, all who do not interfere
with him are protected. A few who cannot submit to
despotism talk of leaving the country; but the great
mass are contented, and the state prospers. As for
myself, I admire him. In that country the alternative
is a strong government or none at all. Throughout his
state I felt a sense of personal security, which I did not
enjoy in any other. For the benefit of travellers, may
he live a thousand years !

In the afternoon I dined with the foreign residents at
the house of Mr. Steiples. This gentleman is an instance of the vicissitudes of fortune. He is a native of
Hanover. At fifteen he left college and entered the
Prussian army; fought at Dresden and Leipsic; and at
the battle of Waterloo received a ball in his brain, from
which, unfortunately, only within the month preceding,
he lost the use of one eye. Disabled for three years by
his wound, on his recovery, with three companions, he
sailed for South America, and entered the Peruvian
army, married a Hica del Sol, Daughter of the Sun,
turned merchant, and came to San José, where he was
then living in a style of European hospitality. I shall
lose all reputation as a sentimental traveller, but I cannot help mentioning honourably every man who gave
me a good dinner; and with this determination I shall
offend the reader but once more.

Early the next morning, accompanied by my countryman Mr. Lawrence, and mounted on a noble mule
lent me by Mr. Steiples, I set off for Cartago. We left
the city by a long, well-paved street, and a little beyond
the suburbs passed a neat coffee-plantation, which reminded me of a Continental villa. It was the property
of a Frenchman, who died just as he completed it ; but
his widow had provided another master for his house
and father for his children. On both sides were mountains, and in front was the great Volcano of Cartago.
The fields were cultivated with corn, plantains, and potatoes. The latter, though indigenous, and now scattered all over Europe, is no longer the food of the natives,
and but rarely found in Spanish America. The Cartago
potatoes are of good flavour, but not larger than a hick-
ory nut, doubtless from the want of care in cultivating
them. We passed a Campo Santo, a square enclosure
of mud-walls whitewashed, and came to an Indian village, the first I had seen in Costa Rica, and much better
than any in the other states, the houses being of tejas,
more substantial, and the inhabitants having clothes on.

Half way between San José and Cartago we reached
the village of Tres Rios. From this place the road was
more broken, without fences, and the land but little cultivated.

Entries have been found in the records of Cartago
dated in 1598, which show it to be the oldest city in
Central America. Coming from San José, its appearance was that of an ancient city. The churches were
large and imposing ; the houses had yard-walls as high
as themselves ; and its quiet was extraordinary. We
rode up a very long street without seeing a single person, and the cross-streets, extending to a great distance

both ways, were desolate. A single horseman crossing at some distance was an object to fix our attention.

The day before we had met at San José Dr. Brayley, the only foreign resident in Cartago, who had promised to procure a guide, and make arrangements for ascending the Volcano of Cartago; and we found that, besides doing all that he had promised, he was himself prepared to go with us. While dinner was preparing, Mr. L. and I visited another countryman, Mr. Lovel, a gentleman whom I knew in New-York. He had brought with him a newly-married wife, a young lady from New-York, whom, to my surprise and with great pleasure, I recognised as an acquaintance : very slight, it is true ; but the merest personal knowledge, so far from home, was almost enough to constitute an intimacy. She had encountered many hardships, and her home was indeed in a strange land ; but she bore all with the spirit of a woman who had given up all for one, and was content with the exchange. Their house was situated on one side of the plaza, commanding a view of the volcano almost from its base to its top, and, though one of the best in the place, the rent was only six dollars per month.

Immediately after dinner we set out to ascend the volcano. It was necessary to sleep en route, and Mr. Lovel furnished me with a poncha from Mexico for a covering, and a bear's skin from the Rocky Mountains for a bed.

Passing down the principal street, we crossed in front of the Cathedral, and immediately began to ascend. Very soon we reached a height which commanded a view of a river, a village, and an extensive valley not visible from the plain below. The sides of the volcano are particularly favourable for cattle; and while the plains below were unappropriated, all the way up were potreros or pasture-grounds, and huts occupied by persons who had charge of the cattle.

Our only anxiety was lest we should lose our way. A few months before my companions had attempted to ascend with Mr. Handy, but, by the ignorance of their guide, got lost; and after wandering the whole night on the sides of the volcano, returned without reaching the top. As we ascended the temperature became colder. I put on my poncha; before we reached our stopping-place my teeth were chattering, and before dismounting I had an ague. The situation was most wild and romantic, hanging on the side of an immense ravine; but I would have exchanged its beauties for a blazing coal fire. The hut was the highest on the mountain, built of mud, with no opening but the door and the cracks in the wall. Opposite the door was a figure of the Virgin, and on each side was a frame for a bed; on one of them my friends spread the bear's skin, and tumbling me upon it, wrapped me up in the poncha. I had promised myself a social evening; but who can be sure of an hour of pleasure ? I was entirely unfit for use; but my friends made me some hot tea; the place was perfectly quiet; and, upon the whole, I had as comfortable a chill and fever as I ever experienced.

Before daylight we resumed our journey; the road was rough and precipitous; in one place a tornado had swept the mountain, and the trees lay across the road so thickly as to make it almost impassable; we were obliged to dismount, and climb over some and creep under others. Beyond this we came into an open region, where nothing but cedar and thorns grew; and here I saw whortleberries for the first time in Central America.

In that wild region there was a charm in seeing anything that was familiar to me at home, and I should
perhaps have become sentimental, but they were hard
and tasteless. As we rose we entered a region of
clouds ; very soon they became so thick that we could
see nothing ; the figures of our own party were barely
distinguishable, and we lost all hope of any view from
the top of the volcano. Grass still grew, and we ascended till we reached a belt of barren sand and lava ;
and here, to our great joy, we emerged from the region
of clouds, and saw the top of the volcano, without a
vapour upon it, seeming to mingle with the clear blue
sky; and at that early hour the sun was not high enough
to play upon its top.

Mr. Lawrence, who had exerted himself in walking,
lay down to rest, and the doctor and I walked on. The
crater was about two miles in circumference, rent and
broken by time or some great convulsion; the fragments stood high, bare, and grand as mountains, and
within were three or four smaller craters. We ascended on the south side by a ridge running east and west
till we reached a high point, at which there was an immense gap in the crater impossible to cross. The lofty
point on which we stood was perfectly clear, the atmosphere was of transparent purity, and looking beyond
the region of desolation, below us, at a distance of perhaps two thousand feet, the whole country was covered
with clouds, and the city at the foot of the volcano was
invisible. By degrees the more distant clouds were
lifted, and over the immense bed we saw at the same
moment the Atlantic and Pacific Oceans. This was
the grand spectacle we had hoped, but scarcely expected to behold. My companions had ascended the volcano several times, but on account of the clouds had

only seen the two seas once before. The points at
which they were visible were the Gulf of Nicoya and
the harbour of San Juan, not directly opposite, but
nearly at right angles to each other, so that we saw
them without turning the body. In a right line over
the tops of the mountains neither was more than twenty miles distant, and from the great height at which we
stood they seemed almost at our feet. It is the only
point in the world which commands a view of the two
seas ; and I ranked the sight with those most interesting occasions, when from the top of Mount Sinai I looked out upon the Desert of Arabia, and from Mount Hor
I saw the Dead Sea.*

There is no history or tradition of the eruption of this
volcano ; probably it took place long before the country
was discovered by Europeans. This was one of the
occasions in which I regretted the loss of my barometer, as the height of the mountain has never been measured, but is believed to be about eleven thousand feet.

We returned to our horses, and found Mr. Lawrence
and the guide asleep. We woke them, kindled a fire,
made chocolate, and descended. In an hour we reached the hut at which we had slept, and at two o'clock
Cartago.

Toward evening I set out with Mr. Lovel for a stroll.
The streets were all alike, long and straight, and there
was nobody in them. We fell into one which seemed
to have no end, and at some distance were intercepted
by a procession coming down a cross street. It was
headed by boys playing on violins ; and then came a
small barrow tastefully decorated, and strewed with

* I have understood from several persons who have crossed the isthmus from
Chagres to Panama, that there is no point on the road from which the two seas
are visible.

flowers. It was a bier carrying the body of a child to the cemetery. We followed, and passing it at the gate, entered through a chapel, at the door of which sat three or four men selling lottery-tickets, one of whom asked us if we wished to see the grave of our countryman. We assented, and he conducted us to the grave of a young American whom I had known by sight, and several members of whose family I knew personally. He died about a year before my visit, and his funeral was attended with mournful circumstances. The vicar refused him burial in consecrated ground. Dr. Brayley, who was the only European resident in Cartago, and at whose house he died, rode over to San José, and making a strong point of the treaty existing between the United States and Central America, obtained an order from the government for his burial in the cemetery. Still the fanatic vicar, acting, as he said, under a higher power, refused. A messenger was sent to San José, and two companies of soldiers were ordered to the doctor's house to escort the body to the grave. At night men were stationed at its side to watch that it was not dug up and thrown out. The next day the vicar, with the cross and images of saints, and all the emblems of the church, and a large concourse of citizens, moved in solemn procession to the cemetery, and formally reconsecrated the ground which had been polluted by the burial of a heretic. The grave is the third from the corridor.

In the corridor, and in an honoured place among the principal dead of Cartago, lay the body of another stranger, an Englishman named Bailey. The day before his death the alcalde was called in to draw his will, who, according to the customary form, asked him if he was a Christian. Mr. Bailey answered yes; and the alcalde wrote him Catolico Romano Apostolico Christiano.   Mr. Bailey himself did not contemplate this; he knew the difficulty in the case of my countryman about six months before ; and wishing to spare his friends a disagreeable and, perhaps, unsuccessful controversy, had already indicated a particular tree under which he wished to be buried.   Before the will was read to him he died.   His answer to the alcalde was considered evidence of his orthodoxy ; his friends did not interfere, and he was buried under the special direction of the priests, with all the holiest ceremonies of the Church. It was the greatest day ever known in Cartago.   The funeral was attended by all the citizens.   The procession started from the door of the church, headed by violins and drums ; priests followed, with all the crosses, figures of saints, and banners that had been accumulating from the foundation of the city.   At the corners of the plaza and of all the principal streets, the procession stopped to sing hallelujahs, to represent the joy in Heaven over a sinner that repents.

While standing in the corridor we saw pass the man who had accompanied the bier, with the child in his arms.   He was its father, and with a smile on his face was carrying it to its grave.   He was followed by two boys playing on violins, and others were laughing around. The child was dressed in white, with a wreath of roses around its head ; and as it lay in its father's arms it did not seem dead, but sleeping.   The grave was not quite ready, and the boys sat on the heap of dirt thrown out, and played the violin till it was finished.   The father then laid the child carefully in its final resting-place, with its head to the rising sun ; folded its little hands across its breast, and closed its fingers around a small wooden crucifix ; and it seemed, as they thought it was, happy at escaping the troubles of an uncertain world. There were no tears shed ; on the contrary, all were cheerful ; and though it appeared heartless, it was not because the father did not love his child, but because he and all his friends had been taught to believe, and were firm in the conviction, that, taken away so young, it was transferred immediately to a better world. The father sprinkled a handful of dirt over its face, the grave-digger took his shovel, in a few moments the little grave was filled up, and preceded by the boy playing on his violin, we all went away together.

The next morning, with great regret, I took leave of my kind friends and returned to San José.

It is my misfortune to be the sport of other men's wives. I lost the best servant I had in Guatimala because his wife was afraid to trust him with me, and on my return I found 'Hezoos at the convent waiting for me. While putting my things in order, without looking me in the face, he told me of the hardships his wife, " la povera," had suffered during his absence, and how difficult it was for a married woman to get along without her husband. I saw to what he was tending ; and feeling, particularly since the recurrence of my fever and ague, the importance of having a good servant in the long journey I had before me, with the selfishness of a traveller I encouraged his vagabond propensities, by telling him that in a few weeks he would be tired of home, and would not have so good an opportunity of getting away. This seemed so sensible that he discontinued his hints and went off contented.

At three o'clock I felt uncertain in regard to my chill, but, determined not to give way, dressed myself, and went to dine with Mr. Steiples. Before sitting down, the blueness of my lips, and a tendency to use superfluous syllables, betrayed me; and my old enemy shook me all the way back to the convent, and into bed. Fever followed, and I lay in bed all next day, receiving many visits at the door, and a few inside. One of the latter was from 'Hezoos, who returned stronger than before, and coming to the point, said that he himself was anxious to go with me, but his wife would not consent. I felt that if she had fairly taken the field against me it was all over, but told him that he had made a contract, and was already overpaid; and sent her a pair of gold earrings to keep her quiet.

For four days in succession I had a recurrence of chill and fever. Every kindness was shown me in the convent, friends visited me, and Dr. Brayley came over from Cartago to attend me, but withal I was desponding. The day fixed for setting out with Alvarado arrived. It was impossible to go; Dr. Brayley advised me that it would be unwise, while any tendency to the disease remained, to undertake it. There were six days of desert travelling to the port of San Juan, without a house on the road, but mountains to cross and rivers to ford. The whole party was to go on foot except myself; four extra men would be needed to pass my mule over some difficult places, and there was always more or less rain. San Juan was a collection of miserable shanties, and from that place it was necessary to embark in a bungo for ten or fifteen days on an unhealthy river. Besides all this, I had the alternative to return by the Cosmopolita to Zonzonate, or to go to Guatimala by land, a journey of twelve hundred miles, through a country destitute of accommodations for travellers, and dangerous from the convulsions of civil war. At night, as I lay alone in the convent, and by the light of a small candle saw the bats flying along the roof, I felt gloomy, and would have been glad to be at home.

Still I could not bear the idea of losing all I came for. The land-route lay along the coast of the Pacific, and for three days was the same as to the port. I determined to go by land, but, by the advice of Dr. Brayley, to start in time for the vessel; and in the hope that I would not have another chill, I bought two of the best mules in San José, one being that on which I had ascended the Volcano of Cartago, and the other a macho, not more than half broke, but the finest animal I ever mounted.

To return to 'Hezoos. The morning after I gave him the earrings he had not come, but sent word that he had the fever and ague. The next day he had it much worse, and satisfied that I must lose him, I sent him word that if he would procure me a good substitute I would release him. This raised him from bed, and in the afternoon he came with his substitute, who had very much the air of being the first man he had picked up in the street. His dress was a pair of cotton trousers, with a shirt outside, and a high, bell-crowned, narrow-brimmed black straw hat; and all that he had in the world was on his back. His hair was cut very close except in front, where it hung in long locks over his face; in short, he was the *beau ideal* of a Central American loafer. I did not like his looks, but I was at the time under the influence of fever, and told him I could give him no answer. He came again the next day at a moment when I wanted some service; and by degrees, though I never hired him, he quietly engaged me as his master.

The morning before I left, Don Augustin Gutierres called upon me, and seeing this man at the door, ex-

pressed his surprise, telling me that he was the town
blackguard, a drunkard, gambler, robber, and assassin;
that the first night on the road he would rob, and perhaps
murder me. Shortly after Mr. Lawrence entered, who
told me that he had just heard the same thing. I discharged him at once, and apparently not much to his
surprise, though he still continued round the convent, as
he said, in my employ. It was very important for me
to set out in time for the vessel, and I had but that day
to look out for another. 'Hezoos was astonished at the
changes time had made in the character of his friend.
He said that he had known him when a boy, and had
not seen him in many years till the day he brought him
to me, when he had stumbled upon him in the street.
Not feeling perfectly released, after a great deal of running he brought me another, whose name was Nicolas.
In any other country I should have called him a mulatto; but in Central America there are so many different
shades that I am at a loss how to designate him. He
was by trade a mason. Hezoos had encountered him
at his work, and talked him into a desire to see Guatimala and Mexico, and come back as rich as himself.
He presented himself just as he left his work, with his
shirt-sleeves rolled up above his elbows, and his trousers above his knees : a rough diamond for a valet; but
he was honest, could take care of mules, and make
chocolate. I did not ask more. He was married, too;
and as his wife did not interfere with me, I liked him
the better for it.

In the afternoon, being the last before I started, in
company with Mr. Lawrence I visited the coffee-plantations of Don Mariano Montealegre. It was a lovely
situation, and with great good taste, Don Mariano lived
there a great part of the year. He was at his factory,

and his son mounted his horse and accompanied us. It was a beautiful walk, but in that country gentlemen never walk.

The cultivation of coffee on the plains of San José has increased rapidly within a few years. Seven years before the whole crop was not more than five hundred quintals, and this year it was supposed that it would amount to more than ninety thousand. Don Mariano was one of the largest planters, and had three cafétals in that neighbourhood; that which we visited contained twenty-seven thousand trees, and he was preparing to make great additions the next year. He had expended a large sum of money in buildings and machinery; and though his countrymen said he would ruin himself, every year he planted more trees. His wife, La Senora, was busily engaged in superintending the details of husking and drying the grains. In San José, by-the-way, all the ladies were what might be called good business-men, kept stores, bought and sold goods, looked out for bargains, and were particularly knowing in the article of coffee.

CHAPTER XVIII.

On the thirteenth day of February I mounted for
my journey to Guatimala. My equipage was reduced
to articles of the last necessity : a hammock of striped
cotton cloth laid over my pellon, a pair of alforgas,
and a poncha strapped on behind. Nicolas had strung
across his alvarda behind a pair of leather cohines, in
shape like buckets, with the inner side flat, containing
biscuit, chocolate, sausages, and dolces, and in front,
on the pommel, my wearing apparel rolled up in an ox-
hide, after the fashion of the country. During my
whole stay at the convent the attentions of the padre
were unremitted. Besides the services he actually ren-
dered me, I have no doubt he considers that he saved
my life; for during my sickness he entered my room
while I was preparing to shave, and made me desist
from so dangerous an operation. I washed my face by
stealth, but his kindness added another to the list of obligations I was already under to the padres of Central
America.

I felt great satisfaction at being able once more to re-
sume my journey, pleased with the lightness of my
equipage, the spirit of my mules, and looked my journey of twelve hundred miles boldly in the face. All at
once I heard a clattering behind, and Nicolas swept by
me on a full run. My macho was what was called es-

pantosa, or scary, and started. I had very little strength, and was fairly run away with. If I had bought my beasts for racing I should have had no reason to complain; but, unluckily, my saddle turned, and I came to the ground, fortunately clearing the stirrups, and the beast ran, scattering on the road pistols, holsters, saddle-cloths, and saddle, and continued on bare-backed toward the town. To my great relief, some muleteers intercepted him, and saved my credit as a horseman in San José. We were more than an hour in recovering scattered articles and repairing broken trappings.

For three days my road was the same that I had travelled in entering Costa Rica. The fourth morning I rose without any recurrence of fever. Mr. Lawrence had kindly borne me company from San José, and was still with me; he had relieved me from all trouble, and had made my journey so easy and comfortable that, instead of being wearied, I was recruited, and abandoned all idea of returning by sea.

At seven o'clock we started, and in half an hour reached Esparza. From this place to Nicaragua, a distance of three hundred miles, the road lay through a wilderness; except the frontier town of Costa Rica, there were only a few straggling haciendas, twenty, thirty, and forty miles apart. I replenished my stock of provisions, and my last purchase was a yard and a half of American cotton from a Massachusetts factory, called by the imposing name of Manta del Norte.

In half an hour we crossed the Barranca, a broad, rapid, and beautiful river, but which lost in my eyes all its beauty, for here Mr. Lawrence left me. Since the day of my arrival at San José he had been almost constantly with me, had accompanied me in every excursion, and during my sickness had attended me constant-

ly. He was a native of Middletown in Connecticut,
about fifty years old, and by trade a silversmith, and
with the exception of a single return visit, had been
nineteen years from home. In 1822 he went to Peru,
where, besides carrying on his legitimate business upon
a large scale, his science and knowledge of the precious metals brought him into prominent public positions. In 1830 he sold a mint to the government
of Costa Rica, and was offered the place of its director. Business connected with the mint brought him
to Costa Rica, and during his absence he left his affairs in the hands of a partner, who mismanaged them
and died. Mr. L. returned to Peru, but without en-
gaging in active business, and in the mean time the
mint purchased of him was worn out, and another im-
ported from Europe, so complicated that no one in
Costa Rica could work it. Offers were made to Mr.
L. of such a nature, that, connected with mining purposes of his own, they induced him to return. Don
Manuel de Aguila was then Gefe del Estado, and on
Mr. L.'s arrival at the port he met Don Manuel banished and flying from the state. The whole policy of
the government was changed. Mr. L. remained quietly in San José, and when I left intended to establish
himself at Pont Arenas, to traffic with the pearl fisher-
men. Such is, in brief, the history of one of our many
countrymen scattered in different parts of the world,
and it would be a proud thing for the country if all sustained as honourable a reputation as his. We exchanged adieus from the backs of our mules, and, not
to be sentimental, lighted our cigars. Whether we
shall ever meet again or not is uncertain.

I was again setting out alone. I had travelled so
long with companions or in ships, that when the mo-

ment for plunging into the wilderness came, my courage almost failed me. And it was a moment that required some energy; for we struck off immediately into one of the wildest paths that I met on the whole of that desolate journey. The trees were so close as to darken it, and the branches so low that it was necessary to keep the head constantly bent to avoid hitting them. The noise of the locusts, which had accompanied us since we reached the mountain of Aguacate, here became startling. Very soon families of monkeys, walking heavily on the tops of the trees, disturbed these noisy tenants of the woods, and sent them flying around us in such swarms that we were obliged to beat them off with our hats. My macho snorted and pulled violently on the bit, dragging me against the trees; and I could not help thinking, if this is the outset, what will be the end?

Parting with Mr. Lawrence advanced the position of Nicolas. Man is a talking animal; Nicolas was particularly so, and very soon I knew the history of his life. His father was a muleteer, and he seemed constructed for the same rough business; but after a few journeys to Nicaragua he retired in disgust, married, and had two children. The trying moment of his life was when compelled to serve as a soldier. His great regret was that he could not read or write, and his astonishment that he worked hard and yet could not get on. He wanted to go with me to Mexico, to go to my country, to be away two years, and to return with a sum of money in hand, as 'Hezoos had done. He knew that General Morazan was a great man, for when he visited Costa Rica there was a great firing of cannons and a ball. He was a poor man himself, and did not know what the wars were about; and supposed that

Don Manuel de Aguila was expelled because Carillo wanted to be chief.

We continued in the woods till about two o'clock, when, turning off by a path to the right, we reached a clearing, on one side of which was the hacienda of Aranjuez. The entrance to the house was by a ladder from the outside, and underneath was a sort of store-house. It was occupied by a major-domo, a Mestitzo, and his wife. Near it was the cucinera, where the wife and another woman were at work. The major-domo was sitting on the ground doing nothing, and two able-bodied men were helping him.

The major-domo told us that he had a good potrero for the mules, and the house promised a good resting-place for me. Outside, and extending all around, was a rough board piazza, one side of which commanded a view of the ocean. I seated myself on this side, and very soon Nicolas brought me my dinner. It consisted of tortillas, rice cooked with lard, which he brought in a shell, and salt in his hands. I finished with a cup of chocolate, and could not but think of the blessings wasted by this major-domo. In the same situation, one of our backwoodsmen, with his axe, his wife, and two pairs of twins, would in a few years surround himself with all the luxuries that good land can give.

After dinner I led the mules to a stream, on the banks of which were tufts of young grass, and while I was sitting here two wild turkeys flew over my head and lighted on a tree near by. I sent Nicolas for my gun, and soon had a bird large enough for a household dinner, which I sent immediately to the house to be converted into provender. At sundown I returned, and then discovered a deficiency in my preparations which I felt during the whole journey, viz., of candles. A light was manufactured by filling a broken clay vessel with grease, and coiling in it some twisted cotton, with one end sticking out about an inch. The workmen on the hacienda took advantage of the light, and brought out a pack of cards. The wife of the major-domo joined them, and seeing no chance of a speedy termination of the game, I undressed myself and went to bed. When they finished the woman got into a bed 'directly opposite mine, and before lying down lighted another cigar. The men did the same on the floor, and till the cigars went out continued discussing the game. The major-domo was already asleep in the hammock. All night the wife of the major-domo smoked, and the men snuffled and snored. At two o'clock I rose and went out of doors. The moon was shining, and the freshness of the morning air was grateful. I woke Nicolas, and paying the major-domo as he lay in his hammock, at three o'clock we resumed our journey. I was charmed with this place when we reached it, and disgusted when we left. The people were kind and of as good disposition as the expectation of pay could make them, but their habits were intolerable.

The freshness of the morning air restored my equanimity; the moon shed a glorious light over the clearing, and lighted up the darkness of the forest. We heard only the surge of monkeys, as, disturbed by our noise, they moved on the tops of the trees.

At eight o'clock we reached the River Lagartos, breaking rapidly over a bed of white sand and gravel, clear as crystal, and shaded by trees, the branches of which met at the fording-place, and formed a complete arbour. We dismounted, took off the saddles from our mules and tied them to a tree, kindled a fire on the bank, and breakfasted. Wild scenes had long lost the

charm of novelty, but this I would not have exchanged
for a déjeuner à la fourchette at the best restaurant of
Paris.   The wild turkey was not more than enough for
my household, which consisted of Nicolas.

Resuming our journey, in two hours we emerged
from the woods, and came into an open country in
sight of the Cerros of Collito, a fine bare peak, standing alone, conical, and covered with grass to the top.
At twelve o'clock we reached the rancho of an Indian.
On one side was a group of orange-trees loaded with
fruit, and in front a shed thatched with leaves of Indian
corn.   An old Indian woman was sitting in the door,
and a sick Indian was lying asleep under the shed.   It
was excessively hot, and riding under the shed, I dismounted, threw myself into a ragged hammock, and
while quenching my thirst with an orange fell asleep.
The last that I remembered was seeing Nicolas drive
into the hut a miserable half-starved chicken.   At two
o'clock he woke me, and set before me the unfortunate
little bird, nearly burned up, the expense of which,
with oranges ad libitum, was six and a quarter cents,
which the old woman wished to commute for a charge
of gunpowder.   I was very poor in this, and would
rather have given her a dollar, but could not help adding the charge of gunpowder to the coin.

At two o'clock we set off again.   We had already
made a day's journey, but I had a good resting-place
for the night in view.   It was excessively hot, but very
soon we reached the woods again.   We had not gone
far before a deer crossed our path.   It was the first I
had seen in the country, which was almost destitute of
all kinds of game.   Indeed, during my whole journey,
except at the wild turkey, I had fired but twice, and then
merely to procure curious birds; and most unfortunate-

ly, in pursuance of my plan of encumbering myself as little as possible, I had with me but a few charges of duck-shot and half a dozen pistol balls. Very soon I saw two deer together, and within reach of a ball. Both barrels of my gun were loaded with duck. I dismounted and followed them into the woods, endeavouring to get within reach. In the course of an hour I saw perhaps a dozen, and in that hour fired away my last duck-shot. I was resolved not to use my pistol balls, and as both barrels were empty, kept quiet. As the evening approached the deer increased, and I am safe in saying I saw fifty or sixty, and many within rifle-shot. Occasionally cattle peeped at us through the trees as wild as the deer. The sun was getting low when we came out into a large clearing, on one side of which stood the hacienda of Santa Rosa. The house stood on the right, and directly in front, against the side of a hill, was a large cattle-yard, enclosed by a hard clay wall, divided into three parts, and filled with cows and calves. On the left was an almost boundless plain, interspersed with groves of trees; and as we rode up a gentleman in the yard sent a servant to open the gate. Don Juan José Bonilla met me at the porch, and before I had time to present my letter, welcomed me to Santa Rosa.

Don Juan was a native of Cartago, a gentleman by birth and education, and of one of the oldest families in Costa Rica. He had travelled over his own country, and what was very unusual in that region, had visited the United States, and though labouring under the disadvantage of not speaking the language, spoke with great interest of our institutions. He had been an active member of the Liberal party; had laboured to carry out its principles in the administration of the government, and to save his country from the disgrace of falling back into despotism. He had been persecuted, heavy contributions had been laid upon his property, and four years before he had withdrawn from Cartago and retired to this hacienda. But political animosity never dies. A detachment of soldiers was sent to arrest him, and, that no suspicion might be excited, they were sent by sea, and landed at a port on the Pacific within the bounds of his own estate. Don Juan received an intimation of their approach, and sent a servant to reconnoitre, who returned with intelligence that they were within half a day's march. He mounted his horse to escape, but near his own gate was thrown, and his leg badly broken. He was carried back insensible, and when the soldiers arrived they found him in bed ; but they made him rise, put him on horseback, hurried him to the frontiers of the state, and left him, communicating to him his sentence of banishment, and death if he returned. The boundary-line of the State of Costa Rica is a river in the midst of a wilderness, and he was obliged to travel on horseback to Nicaragua, a journey of four days. He had never recovered the use of his leg, which was two or three inches shorter than the other. He remained two years in exile ; and on the election of Don Manuel de Aguila as chief of the state, returned. On the expulsion of Don Manuel he retired again to his hacienda, and was then busily engaged in making repairs for the reception of his family ; but he did not know at what moment another order might come to expel him from his home.

While sitting at the supper-table we heard a noise over our heads, which seemed to me like the opening of the roof. Don Juan threw his eyes to the ceiling, and suddenly started from his chair, threw his arms around the neck of a servant, and with the fearful

words "temblor!" "temblor!" "an earthquake!"
"an earthquake!" all rushed for the doors. I sprang
from my chair, made one bound across the room, and
cleared the piazza. The earth rolled like the pitching
of a ship in a heavy sea. My step was high, my feet
barely touched the ground, and my arms were thrown
up involuntarily to save myself from falling. I was the
last to start, but, once under way, I was the last to stop.
Half way across the yard I stumbled over a man on his
knees, and fell. I never felt myself so feeble a thing
before. At this moment I heard Don Juan calling to
me. He was leaning on the shoulder of his servant,
with his face to the door, crying to me to come out of
the house. It was pitchy dark; within was the table at
which we had sat, with a single candle, the light of
which extended far enough to show a few of the kneeling figures, with their faces to the door. We looked
anxiously in, and waited for the shock which should
prostrate the strong walls and lay the roof on the ground.
There was something awful in our position, with our
faces to the door, shunning the place which at all other
times offers shelter to man. The shocks were continued perhaps two minutes, during which time it required
an effort to stand firm. The return of the earth to
steadiness was almost as violent as the shock. We
waited a few minutes after the last vibration, when Don
Juan said it was over, and, assisted by his servant, entered the house. I had been the last to leave it, but I
was the last to return; and my chair lying with its back
on the floor, gave an intimation of the haste with which
I had decamped. The houses in Costa Rica are the
best in the country for resisting these shocks, being,
like the others, long and low, and built of adobes, or
undried bricks, two feet long and one broad, made of

clay mixed with straw to give adhesion, and laid when soft, with upright posts between, so that they are dried by the sun into one mass, which moves with the surface of the earth.

Before the evening was over I forgot the earthquake in a minor trouble. The uncultivated grounds of Central America teem with noxious insects. Riding all day in the woods, and striking my head against the branches of trees, had brought ticks down upon me in such numbers that I brushed them off with my hand. I had suffered so much during the day, that twice I was obliged to strip at a stream and tear them out of my flesh; but this gave me only temporary relief; lumps of irritation were left; and in the midst of serious disquisitions with Don Juan, it was not polite, but I was obliged to use my nails violently and constantly. I was fain to entreat of him that he would go out and give me the room to myself. He retired, and in a moment all my clothes were out of doors, and I tore the vipers out by the teeth; but Don Juan sent to my relief a deaf and dumb boy, who, by touching them with a ball of black wax, drew them from their burrowing-places without any pain; yet they left behind wounds from which I did not recover in a long time.

Early in the morning two horses were at the door, and two servants in attendance for a ride. Don Juan mounted the same horse which he had ridden in his exile, and was attended by the same servants. Heretofore I had always heard constant complaints of servants, and to do them justice, I think they are the worst I ever knew; but Don Juan's were the best in the world, and it was evident that they thought he was the best master.

The estate of Don Juan covered as much ground as

a German principality, containing two hundred thousand acres, and was bounded on one side, for a long distance, by the Pacific Ocean. But a small portion of it was cultivated, not more than enough to raise maize for the workmen, and the rest was a roaming-ground for cattle. More than ten thousand were wandering over it, almost as wild as the deer, and never seen except as they crossed a path in the woods, or at the season of lazoing them for the purpose of taking an account of the increase.

We had not gone far before we saw three deer all close together, and not far from us. It was exceedingly vexatious, the first time I was in a country where there was anything to shoot at, to be so wholly unprovided, and I had no chance of supplying myself till I was out of that region. Don Juan was incapacitated for sporting by his lameness; in fact, deer-shooting was not considered sporting, and venison not fit to eat. In the course of an hour we saw more than twenty.

I had set out on this long journey without any cargo-mule, from the difficulty of procuring one that could keep pace with the riding-beasts; but we had felt the inconvenience of being encumbered with luggage; and, besides Don Juan's kindness to me at his house, he furnished me with one which he had broken expressly for his own use in rapid journeys between Cartago and the hacienda, and which he warranted me, with a light load, would trot and keep up with mine.

Late in the afternoon I left his hospitable dwelling. Don Juan, with his deaf and dumb boy, accompanied me a league on the way, when we dismounted and took leave of each other. My new mule, like myself, was very reluctant to leave Don Juan, and seemed to have a sentiment that she should never see her old master

again.   Indeed, it was so difficult to get her along, that
Nicolas tied her by the halter to his mule's tail, after a
manner common in the country, and thus leading her
along, I followed at her heels.   The deer were more
numerous than I had yet seen them, and I now looked
at them only as animating a beautiful landscape.   At
dark we began to have apprehensions about the road.
There was a difficult mountain-pass before us, and Nicolas wanted to stop and wait till the moon rose ; but as
that would derange the journey for the next day, I pushed on for more than an hour through the woods.   The
mules stumbled along in the dark, and very soon we
lost all traces of a path ; while trying to find it, we
heard the crash of a falling tree, which in the darkness
sounded appalling, and made us hesitate to enter the
woods.   I determined to wait for the moon, and dismounted.   Peering into the darkness, I saw a glimmer-
ing light on the left.   We shouted with all our strength,
and were answered by a pack of barking dogs, and
moving in that direction, reached a hut where three or
four workmen were lying on the ground, who were at
first disposed to be merry and impertinent when we
asked for a guide to the next hacienda ; but one of them
recognised my cargo-mule, said that he had known it
since he was a child (rather doubtful praise of my new
purchase), and was at length induced to make us an
offer of his services.   A horse was brought, large, wild,
and furious, as if never bitted ; snorting, rearing, and
almost making the ground shake at every tread ; and
before the rider was fairly on his back he was tearing
in the dark across the plain.   Making a wide sweep,
he returned, and the guide, releasing the cargo-mule
from that of Nicolas, tied her to the tail of his horse,
and then led the way.   Even with the drag of the car-

go-mule it was impossible for him to moderate his pace, and we were obliged to follow at a most unhappy rate. It was the first piece of bad road we had met with, having many sharp turns, and ascents and descents, broken and stony. Fortunately, while we were in the woods, the moon rose, touched with a silvery light the tops of the trees, and when we reached the bank of the river it was almost as light as day. Here my guide left me, and I lost all confidence in the moon, for by her deceitful light I slipped into his hand a gold piece instead of a silver one, without either of us knowing it.

As we ascended the bank after crossing the stream, the hacienda was in full sight. The occupants were in bed, but Don Manuel, to whom I was recommended by Don Juan, rose to receive me. On the bank of the river, near the house, was a large sawmill, the first I had seen in the country, built, as Don Manuel told me, by an American, who afterward straggled to Guatimala, and was killed in some popular insurrection.

At daylight the next morning, as the workmen on the hacienda were about going to work, we set off again. In an hour we heard the sound of a horn, giving notice of the approach of a drove of cattle. We drew up into the woods to let them pass, and they came with a cloud of dust, the faces of the drivers covered, and would have trampled to death anything that impeded their progress.

At eleven o'clock we entered the village of Bagases. We had made tremendous journeys, and it was the first time in four days we had seen anything but single haciendas, but we rode through without stopping, except to ask for a cup of water.

Late in the afternoon we came into a broad avenue and saw marks of wheels. At dusk we reached the river which runs by the suburbs of Guanacaste, the frontier town of Costa Rica. The pass was occupied by an ox-cart, with four stubborn oxen, which would not go ahead and could not go back. We were detained half an hour, and it was dark when we entered. We passed through the plaza, before the door of the church, which was lighted up for vespers, and rode to a house at which I had been directed to stop. Nicolas went in to make preliminary inquiries, and returning, told me to dismount, and unloaded the luggage-mule. I went in, took off my spurs, and stretched myself on a bench. Soon it struck me that my host was not particularly glad to see me. Several children came in and stared, and then ran back into another room; and in a few minutes I received the compliments of the lady of the house, and her regret that she could not accommodate me. I was indignant at Nicolas, who had merely asked whether such a person lived there, and without more ado had sent me in. I left the house, and with the halter of my macho in one hand and spurs in the other, and Nicolas following with the mules, sought the house of the commandant. I found him standing on the piazza, with the key in his hand, and all his household stuff packed up outside, only waiting till the moon rose to set out for another post. I believe he regretted that he could not accommodate me, nor could he refer me to any other house; but he sent his servant to look for one, and I waited nearly an hour, up for a bidder.

In the mean time I made inquiries about my road. I did not wish to continue on the direct route to Nicaragua, but to go first to the port of San Juan on the Pacific, the proposed termination of the canal to connect the Atlantic and Pacific Oceans. The command-

ant regretted that I had not come one day sooner. He
mentioned a fact of which I was aware before, that Mr.
Bailey, an English gentleman, had been employed by
the government to survey the canal route, and had resided some time at the post, and added that since his
departure it was perfectly desolate; no one ever visited it, not a person in the place knew the road to it,
and, unluckily, a man who had been in Mr. Bailey's
employ had left that morning for Nicaragua. Most
fortunately, on inquiry, the man was found to be still in
the place, and he, too, intended setting out as soon as
the moon rose. I had no inducement to remain; nobody seemed very anxious for the honour of my company, and I would have gone on immediately if the
mules had been able to continue; but I made an arrangement with him and his son to wait till three in the
morning, then to conduct me to the port, and thence to
Nicaragua. At length the commandant's servant returned and conducted me to a house with a little shop
in front, where I was received by an old lady with a
buenos noces that almost surprised me into an idea that
I was welcome. I entered through the shop, and passed into a parlour which contained a hammock, an interlaced bedstead, and a very neat cartaret with a gauze
moscheto-netting, and pink bows at the corners. I was
agreeably disappointed with my posada, and while conversing with the old lady, was dozing over a cup of
chocolate, when I heard a lively voice at the door, and
a young lady entered, with two or three young men in
attendance, who came up to the table in front of me,
and throwing back a black mantilla, bade me buenos
noces, put out her hand, said that she had heard in
church that I was at her house, and was so glad of it;
no strangers ever came there; the place was complete-

ly out of the world, very dull, &c., &c. I was so surprised that I must have looked very stupid. She was
not regularly handsome, but her mouth and eyes were
beautiful; and her manner was so different from the
cold, awkward, and bashful air of her countrywomen,
so much like the frank and fascinating welcome which
a young lady at home might extend to a friend after a
long absence, that if the table had not been between
us I could have taken her in my arms and kissed her.
I pulled up my check collar, and forgot all my troubles
and perplexities. Though living in that little remote
town, like young ladies in large cities, she had a fancy
for strangers, which at the time I regarded as a delightful trait of character in a woman. Her every-day
beaux had no chance. At first they were very civil to
me, but they became short and crusty, and, very much
to my satisfaction, took themselves off. It was so long
since I had felt the least interest in a woman, that I
gave myself a benefit. The simplest stories of other
countries and other people were to her romance, and
her eye kindled as she listened; soon the transition
came from facts to feelings, and then that highest earth-
ly pleasure, of being lifted above every-day thoughts
by the enthusiasm of a high-minded girl.

We sat up till twelve o'clock. The mother, who at
first had wearied me, I found exceedingly agreeable;
indeed, I had seldom known a more interesting old
lady; for she pressed me to remain two or three days
and rest; said the place was dull, but that her daughter
would try to make it agreeable; and her daughter said
nothing, but looked unutterable things.

All pleasure is fleeting. Twelve o'clock came, an
unprecedented hour for that country. My ordinary
prudence in looking out for a sleeping-place had not

deserted me. Two little boys had taken possession of
the leather bed; the old lady had retired; the beautiful
little cartaret remained unoccupied, and the young lady
withdrew, telling me that this was to be my bed.   I
do not know why, but I felt uneasy.   I opened the mos-
cheto-net.   In that country beds are not used, and an
oxhide or mat, often not so clean as it might be, is the
substitute.   This was a mat, very fine, and clean as if
perfectly new.   At the head was a lovely pillow with
a pink muslin covering, and over it a thin white pillow-
case with a bewitching ruffle.   Whose cheek had rested
on that pillow?   I pulled off my coat, walked up and
down the room, and waked up one of the boys.   It
was as I supposed.   I lay down, but could not sleep,
and determined not to continue my journey the next
day.

At three o'clock the guide knocked at the door.   The
mules were already saddled, and Nicolas was putting
on the luggage.   I had often clung to my pillow, but
never as I did to that pink one with its ruffled border.
I told Nicolas that the guide must go home and wait
another day.   The guide refused.   It was the young
man; his father had already gone, and had ordered
him to follow.   Very soon I heard a light footstep, and
a soft voice expostulating with the guide.   Indignant at
his obstinacy, I ordered him away; but very soon I
reflected that I could not procure another, and might
lose the great object I had in view in making this long
journey.   I called him back, and attempted to bribe him;
but his only answer was, that his father had started at
the rising of the moon, and ordered him to follow.   At
length it was arranged that he should go and overtake
his father and bring him back; but perhaps his father
would not come.   I was pertinacious until I carried the

point, and then I was more indifferent. After all, why should I wait? Nicolas said we could get our clothes washed in Nicaragua. I walked out of doors, and resolved that it was folly to lose the chance of examining a canal route for the belle of Guanacaste. I hurried through my preparations, and bade her, I may say, an affectionate farewell. There is not the least chance that I shall ever see her again. Living in a secluded town, unknown beyond the borders of its own unknown state, between the Andes and Pacific Ocean, probably she is already the happy wife of some worthy townsman, and has forgotten the stranger who owes to her some of the happiest moments he passed in Central America.

It was now broad daylight. It was very rare that I had left a place with so much regret; but I turned my sorrow into anger, and wreaked it upon Nicolas and the guide. The wind was very high, and, sweeping over the great plain, raised such clouds of dust as made riding both disagreeable and difficult. This ought to have had some effect in restoring my equanimity, but it did not. All day we had on our right the grand range of Cordilleras, and crowning it at this point the great volcanoes of Rincon and Orosi. From thence a vast plain, over which the wind swept furiously, extended to the sea. At one o'clock we came in sight of the hacienda of Santa Teresa, standing on a great elevation, and still a long way before us. The hacienda was the property of Don Augustin Gutierres of San José, and, with two others, was under the charge of his son Don Manuel. A letter from his father had advised him of my coming, and he received me as an old acquaintance. The situation of the house was finer than that of any I had seen. It was high, and commanded a view of an immense plain, studded with trees in groups and in forest. The ocean was not visible, but we could see the opposite coast of the Gulf of Nicoya, and the point of the port of Colubre, the finest on the Pacific, only three and a half leagues distant. The hacienda contained a thousand mares and four hundred horses, more than a hundred of which were in sight from the door. It was grand enough to give the owner ideas of empire. Toward evening I counted from the door of the house seventeen deer, and Don Manuel told me that he had a contract for furnishing two thousand skins. In the season a good hunter gets twenty-five a day. Even the workmen will not eat them, and they are only shot for the hide and horns. He had forty workmen, and an ox was killed every day. Near the house was an artificial lake, more than a mile in circumference, built as a drinking-place for cattle. And yet the proprietors of these haciendas are not rich; the ground is worth absolutely nothing. The whole value is in the stock; and allowing ten dollars a head for the horses and mares would probably give the full value of this apparently magnificent estate.

Here, too, I could have passed a week with great satisfaction, but the next morning I resumed my journey. Though early in the dry season, the ground was parched and the streams were dried up. We carried a large calabash with water, and stopping under the shade of a tree, turned our mules out on the plain and breakfasted. I was riding in advance, with my poncha flying in the wind, when I saw a drove of cattle stop and look wildly at me, and then rush furiously toward me. I attempted to run, but, remembering the bullfights at Guatimala, I tore off my poncha, and had just time to get behind a high rock as the whole herd darted by at their full speed. We continued our route, from time to time catching glimpses of the Pacific, till we reached a clear, open place, completely protected from the wind, and called the Boca of the Mountain of Nicaragua. A large caravan had already encamped, and among the muleteers Nicolas found acquaintances from San José. Their cargoes consisted of potatoes, sweet bread, and dolces for Nicaragua.

Toward evening I climbed to the top of one of the hills, and had a magnificent sunset view. On the top the wind blew so fiercely that I was obliged to shelter myself under the lee. Behind me was the great range of Cordilleras, along which we had ridden all day, with their volcanoes ; on the left the headlands of the bays of Tortugas and Salina, and in front the great body of the Pacific Ocean ; and what was quite as agreeable a spectacle to a traveller, my mules were up to their knees in grass. I returned to the encampment, and found that my guide had made me a casita, or small house to sleep in. It was formed by cutting two sticks about four feet high, and as thick as a man's arm, and driving them into the ground, with a crotch in the top. Another stick was laid in the crotches, and against this other sticks were laid slanting, with leaves and branches wound in between them, so as to protect me from the dew, and tolerably well from the wind.

I never had a servant in Central America who was not a brute with mules. I was obliged to look out myself for their food, and also to examine that their backs were not hurt by the saddles. My macho I always saddled myself. Nicolas had saddled the cargo-mule so badly the day before, that when he took off the apparecho (a huge saddle covering half the beast) the shoulder was raw, and in the morning even pointing at it made her

shrink as if touched with a hot iron. I was unwilling
to put the apparecho upon her back, and tried to hire a
mule from one of the muleteers, but could not, and,
putting the cargo upon the other mule, made Nicolas
walk, and the cargo-mule go loose. I left the apparecho in the boca of the mountain : a great piece of
profligacy, as Nicolas and the guide considered it.

We wound for a short distance among the hills that
enclosed us, ascended a slight range, and came down
directly upon the shore of the sea. I always had a
high feeling when I touched the shore of the Pacific,
and never more so than at this desolate place. The
waves rolled grandly, and broke with a solemn roar.
The mules were startled, and my macho shrank from
the heaving water. I spurred him into it, and at a moment when I was putting in my pocket some shells
which Nicolas had picked up, he ran away. He had
attempted it several times before in the woods; and
now, having a fair chance, I gave him the full sweep
of the coast. We continued nearly an hour on the
shore, when we crossed a high, rough headland, and
again came down upon the sea. Four times we mounted headlands and again descended to the shore, and the
heat became almost intolerable. The fifth ascent was
steep, but we came upon a table covered with a thick
forest, through which we proceeded until we came to a
small clearing with two huts. We stopped at the first,
which was occupied by a black man and his wife. He
had plenty of corn; there was a fine pasture-ground
near, so hemmed in by the woods that there was no
danger of the mules escaping, and I hired the man and
woman to sleep out of doors, and give me the hovel to
myself.

CHAPTER XIX.

The Flores.—The San Juan.—Nature's Solitude.—Primitive Cookery.—Harbour of San Juan.—Route of the Great Canal to connect the Atlantic and Pacific Oceans.—Nicaragua.—Survey for the Canal.—Lake of Nicaragua.—Plan of the Canal.—Lockage.—Estimate of Cost.—Former Efforts to construct the Canal.—Its Advantages.—Central American Hospitality.—Tierra Caliente.—Horrors of Civil War.

I ROSE about an hour before daylight, and was in my saddle by break of day. We watered our mules at the River Flores, the boundary-line of the states of Costa Rica and Nicaragua. In an hour we reached Skamaika, the name given to a single hut occupied by a negro, sick and alone. He was lying on a bedstead made of sticks, the very picture of wretchedness and desolation, worn to a skeleton by fever and ague. Soon after we came to another hut, where two women were sick with fever. Nothing could be more wretched than these huts along the Pacific. They asked me for remedios, and I gave them some quinine, but with little hope of their ever benefiting by it. Probably both the negro and they are now in their graves.

At twelve o'clock we reached the River St. John, the mouth of which was the terminating point of the great canal. The road to Nicaragua crossed the stream, and ours followed it to the sea, the port being situated at its mouth. Our whole road had been desolate enough, but this far surpassed anything I had seen; and as I looked at the little path that led to Nicaragua, I felt as if we were leaving a great highway. The valley of the river is about a hundred yards broad, and in the season of rain the whole is covered with water; but at this time the stream was small, and a great part of its bed dry. The stones were bleached by the sun, and there was no track or impression which gave the slightest indication of a path. Very soon this stony bed became contracted and lost ; the stream ran through a different soil, and high grass, shrubs, and bushes grew luxuriantly up to its bank. We searched for the track on both sides of the river, and it was evident that since the last wet season no person had passed. Leaving the river, the bushes were higher than our heads, and so thick that at every two or three paces I became entangled and held fast ; at length I dismounted, and my guide cleared a way for me on foot with his machete. Soon we reached the stream again, crossed it, and entered the same dense mass on the opposite side. In this way we continued nearly two hours, with the river for our line. We crossed it more than twenty times, and when it was shallow rode in its bed. Farther down the valley was open, stony, and barren, and the sun beat upon it with prodigious force ; flocks of sopilotes or turkey-buzzards, hardly disturbed by our approach, moved away on a slow walk, or, with a lazy flap of the wings, rose to a low branch of the nearest tree. In one place a swarm of the ugly birds were feasting on the carcass of an alligator. Wild turkeys were more numerous than we had seen them before, and so tame that I shot one with a pistol. Deer looked at us without alarm, and on each side of the valley large black apes walked on the tops of the trees, or sat quietly in the branches, looking at us. Crossing the river for the last time, which became broader and deeper until it emptied into the Pacific, we entered the woods on the right, and reached the first station of Mr. Bailey ; but it was covered with young trees and bushes ; the woods were thicker than before, and the path entirely undistinguishable. I had read reports, papers, and pamphlets on the subject of the great canal, and expected at least to find a road to the port; but the desert of Arabia is not more desolate, and the track of the Children of Israel to the Red Sea a turnpike compared with it.

My beautiful gray, degraded into a cargo-mule, chafed under her burden; and here obstructed, and jerked first one way and then the other, the girths of the saddle became loose, the load turned on her side, and she rushed blindly forward, kicking, and threw herself among the bushes. Her back was badly hurt, and she was desperately frightened; but we were obliged to reload her, and, fortunately, we were near the end of our day's journey.

On the border of the woods we reached a stream, the last at which fresh water was procurable, and filling our calabash, entered a plain covered with high grass. In front was another piece of woodland, and on the left the River San Juan, now a large stream, emptying into the Pacific. In a few minutes we reached a small clearing, so near the shore that the waves seemed breaking at our feet. We tied our mules under the shade of a large tree on the edge of the clearing. The site of Mr. Bailey's rancho was on an eminence near, but hardly a vestige remained; and though it commanded a fine view of the port and the sea, it was so hot under the afternoon sun that I fixed our encampment under the large tree. We hung our saddles, saddlecloths, and arms upon its branches, and while Nicolas and José gathered wood and made a fire, I found, what was always the most important and satisfactory part of the day's journey, excellent pasture for the mules.

The next thing was to take care of ourselves. We had no trouble in deciding what to have for dinner.

We had made provision, as we supposed, for three days ; but, as usual, it always happened that, however abundant, it did not last more than one. At this time all was eaten up by ourselves or by vermin ; and, but for the wild turkey, we should have been obliged to dine upon chocolate. It was a matter of deeply-interesting consideration how the turkey should be cooked. Boiling it was the best way ; but we had nothing to boil it in except a small coffee-pot. We attempted to make a gridiron of our stirrups, and broil it ; but those of Nicolas were wooden, and mine alone were not large enough. Roasting was a long and tedious process ; but our guide had often been in such straits ; and fixing in the ground two sticks with crotches, he laid another across, split open the turkey, and securing it by sticks crosswise, hung it like a spread eagle before a blazing fire. When one side was burned, he turned the other. In an hour it was cooked, and in less than ten minutes eaten up. A cup of chocolate, heavy enough to keep it from rising if it had been eaten with its wings on, followed, and I had dined.

Rested and refreshed, I walked down to the shore. Our encampment was about in the centre of the harbour, which was the finest I saw on the Pacific. It is not large, but beautifully protected, being almost in the form of the letter U. The arms are high and parallel, running nearly north and south, and terminating in high perpendicular bluffs. As I afterward learned from Mr. Bailey, the water is deep, and under either bluff, according to the wind, vessels of the largest class can ride with perfect safety. Supposing this to be correct, there is but one objection to this harbour, which I derive from Captain D'Yriarte, with whom I made the voyage from Zonzonate to Caldera. He has been nine years navigating the coast of the Pacific, from Peru to the Gulf of California, and has made valuable notes, which he intends publishing in France; and he told me that during the summer months, from November to May, the strong north winds which sweep over the Lake of Nicaragua pass with such violence through the Gulf of Papajayo, that, during the prevalence of these winds, it is almost impossible for a vessel to enter the port of San Juan. Whether this is true to the extent that Captain D'Yriarte supposes, and if true, how far steam tugs would answer to bring vessels in against such a wind, is for others to determine. But at the moment there seemed more palpable difficulties.

I walked along the shore down to the estuary of the river, which was here broad and deep. This was the proposed termination of the great canal to connect the Atlantic and Pacific Oceans. I had read and examined all that had been published on this subject in England or this country; had conferred with individuals; and I had been sanguine, almost enthusiastic, in regard to this gigantic enterprise; but on the spot the scales fell from my eyes. The harbour was perfectly desolate; for years not a vessel had entered it; primeval trees grew around it; for miles there was not a habitation. I walked the shore alone. Since Mr. Bailey left not a person had visited it; and probably the only thing that keeps it alive even in memory is the theorizing of scientific men, or the occasional visit of some Nicaragua fisherman, who, too lazy to work, seeks his food in the sea. It seemed preposterous to consider it the focus of a great commercial enterprise; to imagine that a city was to rise up out of the forest, the desolate harbour to be filled with ships, and become a great portal for the thoroughfare of nations. But the scene was magnificent. The sun was setting, and the high western headland threw a deep shade over the water. It was perhaps the last time in my life that I should see the Pacific; and in spite of fever and ague tendencies, I bathed once more in the great ocean.

It was after dark when I returned to my encampment. My attendants had not been idle; blazing logs of wood, piled three or four feet high, lighted up the darkness of the forest. We heard the barking of wolves, the scream of the mountain-cat, and other wild beasts of the forest. I wrapped myself in my poncha and lay down to sleep. Nicolas threw more wood upon the burning pile; and, as he stretched himself on the ground, hoped we would not be obliged to pass another night in this desolate place.

In the morning I had more trouble. My gray mule running loose, and drinking at every stream, with her girths tight, had raised a swelling eight or ten inches. I attempted to put the cargo on my macho, with the intention of walking myself; but it was utterly impossible to manage him, and I was obliged to transfer it to the raw back of the cargo-mule.

At seven o'clock we started, recrossed the stream at which we had procured water, and returned to the first station of Mr. Bailey. It was on the River San Juan, a mile and a half from the sea. The river here had sufficient depth of water for large vessels, and from this point Mr. Bailey commenced his survey to the Lake of Nicaragua. I sent Nicolas with the mules by the direct road, and set out with my guide to follow, as far as practicable, his line of survey. I did not know, until I found myself in this wilderness, how fortunate I had been in securing this guide. He had been Mr. Bailey's pioneer in the whole of his exploration. He was a dark

Mestitzo, and gained his living by hunting bee-trees, and cutting them down for the wild honey, which made him familiar with all the water-courses and secret depths of almost impenetrable forests. He had been selected by Mr. Bailey out of all Nicaragua; and for the benefit of any traveller who may feel an interest in this subject, I mention his name, which is José Dionisio de Lerda, and he lives at Nicaragua.

It was two years since Mr. Bailey had taken his observations, and already, in that rank soil, the clearings were overgrown with trees twelve or fifteen feet high. My guide cleared a path for me with his machete; and working our way across the plain, we entered a valley which ran in a great ravine called Quebrada Grande, between the mountain ranges of Zebadea and El Platina. By a vigorous use of the machete I was enabled to follow the line of Mr. Bailey up the ravine to the station of Panama, so called from a large Panama-tree near which Mr. Bailey built his rancho. Up to this place manifestly there could be no difficulty in cutting a canal; beyond, the line of survey follows the small stream of El Cacao for another league, when it crosses the mountain; but there was such a rank growth of young trees that it was impossible to continue without sending men forward to clear the way. We therefore left the line of the canal, and crossing the valley to the right, reached the foot of the mountain over which the road to Nicaragua passes. A path had been opened for carrying Mr. Bailey supplies to that station, but it was difficult to find it. We took a long draught at a beautiful stream called Loco de Agua, and my guide pulled off his shirt and commenced with his machete. It was astonishing how he found anything to guide him, but he knew a tree as the face of a man. The side of the mountain was very steep, and besides large trees, was full of brambles, thorn-bushes, and ticks. I was obliged to dismount and lead my macho ; the dark skin of my guide glistened with perspiration, and it was almost a climb till we reached the top.

Coming out into the road, the change was beautiful. It was about ten feet wide, straight, and shaded by the noblest trees in the Nicaragua forests. In an hour we reached the boca of the mountain, where Nicolas was waiting with the mules under the shade of a large tree, which threw its branches fifty feet from its trunk, and seemed reared by a beneficent hand for the shelter of a weary traveller. Soon we reached another station of Mr. Bailey. Looking back, I saw the two great mountain ranges, standing like giant portals, and could but think what a magnificent spectacle it would be to see a ship, with all its spars and rigging, cross the plain, pass through the great door, and move on to the Pacific. Beyond, the whole plain was on fire ; the long grass, scorched by the summer's sun, crackled, flashed, and burned like powder. The road was a sheet of flame, and when the fire had passed the earth was black and hot. We rode some distance on the smoking ground along the line of flame, and finding a favourable place, spurred the mules through ; but part of the luggage took fire, my face and hands were scorched, and my whole body heated.

Off from the road, on the edge of the woods, and near the River Las Lahas, was another station of Mr. Bailey. From that place the line runs direct over a plain till it strikes the same river near the Lake of Nicaragua. I attempted to follow the lines again, but was prevented by the growth of underwood.

It was late in the afternoon, and I hurried on to

reach the Camino Real. Beautiful as the whole country had been, I found nothing equal to this two hours
before entering Nicaragua. The fields were covered
with high grass, studded with noble trees, and bordered at a distance by a dark forest, while in front, high
and towering, of a conical form, rose the beautiful volcano of the island. Herds of cattle gave it a home-like
appearance.

Toward dark we again entered the woods, and for
an hour saw nothing, but at length heard the distant
sound of the vesper bell, and very soon were greeted by
the barking of dogs in the suburbs of Nicaragua. Fires
were burning in the streets, which served as kitchens
for the miserable inhabitants, and at which they were
cooking their suppers. We passed round a miserable
plaza, and stopped at the house of the Licenciado Pine-
da. A large door was wide open; the licenciado was
swinging in one hammock, his wife and a mulatto
woman in another. I dismounted and entered his
house, and told him that I had a letter to him from Don
Manuel de Aguila. He asked me what I wished, and
when I told him a night's lodging, said that he could
accommodate me, but had no room for the mules. I
told him that I would go to the cura, and he said that
the cura could do no better than he. In a word, his
reception of me was very cool. I was indignant, and
went to the door, but without it was dark as Erebus.
I had made a long and tiresome journey through a desolate country, and that day had been one of extreme
labour. The first words of kindness came from the
lady of the licenciado. I was so tired that I was almost
ready to fall; I had left San José with the fever and
ague, had been twelve days in the saddle, and the last
two nights I had slept in the open fields. I owe it to

both, however, to say, that, the ice once broken, they
did all they could for my comfort; and, in fact, treated
me with distinguished attention. A traveller never
forgets the kindness shown him in a strange land, and
I never felt so sensible of it as in Central America; in
other countries, with money, a man can command comforts; there, whatever his means may be, he is entirely
dependant upon individual hospitality.

The whole of the next morning I devoted to making
inquiries on the subject of the canal route. More is
known of it in the United States than at Nicaragua. I
did not find one man who had been to the port of San
Juan, or even who knew Mr. Bailey's terminating point
on the Lake of Nicaragua. I was obliged to send for
my old guide, and after a noonday dinner started for
the lake. The town consisted of a large collection of
straggling houses, without a single object of interest.
Though the richest state in the confederacy in natural
gifts, the population is the most miserable.

Passing through the suburbs, very soon we entered
the woods and rode under a beautiful shade. We met
no one. Before reaching the lake we heard the waves
breaking upon the shore like the waves of the sea, and
when we emerged from the woods the view before us
was grand. On one side no land was visible; a strong
north wind was sweeping over the lake, and its surface
was violently agitated; the waves rolled and broke
upon the shore with solemn majesty, and opposite, in
the centre of the lake, were the islands of Isola and
Madeira, with giant volcanoes rising, as if to scale the
heavens. The great Volcano of Omotepeque reminded
me of Mount Etna, rising, like the pride of Sicily, from
the water's edge, a smooth unbroken cone, to the height
of nearly six thousand feet.

We rode for an hour along the shore, and so near the water that we were wetted by the spray. The bank was all wooded; and in one place, on a little clearing by the side of a stream, was a hut occupied by a mulatto, the view from which princes might envy. Farther on we passed some women washing, and at a distance of a league and a half reached the River Las Lahas, according to Mr. Bailey's survey the terminating point on the lake. A flock of wild-fowl were sitting on the water, and long-legged birds, with wings outstretched, were walking on the shore.

I had now examined, as well as circumstances would permit, the canal route from the Pacific to the Lake of Nicaragua. A direction had been given to my investigations by getting on the track of Mr. Bailey's survey; but I should be able to communicate nothing if it were not for Mr. Bailey himself, whom I afterward met at Grenada. This gentleman is a half-pay officer in the British navy. Two years before he was employed by the government of Central America to make a survey of this canal route, and he had completed all except the survey of an unimportant part of the River San Juan when the revolution broke out. The states declared their independence of the general government, and disclaimed all liability for its debts. Mr. Bailey had given his time and labour, and when I saw him had sent his son to make a last appeal to the shadow of the Federal Government; but before he reached the capital this government was utterly annihilated, and Mr. Bailey remains with no reward for his arduous services but the satisfaction of having been a pioneer in a noble work. On my arrival at Grenada he laid before me all his maps and drawings, with liberty to make what use of them I pleased. I passed an entire day in taking notes and memoranda, and receiving explanations, and the result of the whole is as follows :

The measurements began on the side of the Pacific Ocean, and were carried over to the Lake of Nicaragua. The chain was twenty-five varas in length, each vara being thirty-two and a half inches English, and I give the levels as taken from Mr. Bailey's survey.

At a distance of

Chains.		Elevation in Eng. feet.
17.50		8.93
34.37		12.04
52.38		7.99
67.50		16.82
80.95		26.90
103.06		38.12
120.07		52.62
134.94	La Desperansedera de la Quebrada la Palma. Boring 3½ feet, loose sand ; 66 feet, clay, not very firm	66.12
149.61		76.12
164.71		94.66
185.34		132.95
201.50	Panama, water on the surface. Boring 11 feet, gravel ; 24 feet 5 inches, slate-stone	201.50
221.87		223.00
226.14		214.235
235.48		241.35
253.63	First limestone *rock*	284.20
264.28		356.770
273.18		389.700
280.26		425.95
287.01		461.525
288.97		519.391
292.99	Top of the Palma, and summit-level. Boring 5 feet, yellow clay ; 59 feet, stone, soft and loose. No water	615.673
299.05		570.157
300.53	Second limestone rock	506.300
314.11		460.891
317.05		442.858
319.27		443.899

Chains.		Elevation in Eng. feet.
332.25	....	410.524
336.92	To this point national lands	393.216
340.28	Third limestone rock. Boring 31½ feet, water ;	
	49 feet, limestone, soft and loose	350.776
358.50	....	311.152
361.40	....	318.235
370.55	....	291.419
373.85	....	295.160
382.86	....	283.352
401.04	....	269.236
409.30	....	258.378
413.51	....	261.486
423.75	Water on the surface. Boring 3 feet, sand ; 12	
	feet, earth	247.780
437.55	....	237.570
448.90	....	250.370
464.78	....	228.237
477.76	....	214.695
489.29	....	200.530
	Between this and next, boring 5 feet, earth ; 10	
	feet, white clay ; 11 feet, water ; 38 feet,	
	soft stone.	
506.22	....	184.511
510.53	....	186.869
519.47	....	180.244
533.04	....	170.161
543.25	....	159.311
545.98	....	160.411
553.85	....	158.736
	In the next six stations the elevations do not differ	
	one foot.	
604.82	....	153.461
612.62	....	160.077
622.54	Water on the surface. Boring 12 feet, sand and	
	hard stone. This station is in a hole of the	
	Quebrada, very deep.......................	149.553
627.27	....	150.052
630.32	....	149.336
634.20	....	157.102
638.86	....	147.044
643.31	....	154.785
685.55	....	143.343
661.35	....	155.076

Chains.		Elevation in Eng. feet.
664.47	....	140.243
671.22	....	151.185
675.86	....	139.352
685.93	....	150.927
692.55	....	146.977
696.91	....	148.569
712.85	....	144.436
716.17	....	149.152
723.29	....	142.994
728.29	....	148.552
739.95	....	139.702
749.10	....	164.360
756.40	....	142.560
760.80	....	144.830
766.80	....	141.177
770.61	Water at 8 feet. Boring 12 feet, black earth ; 22 feet, white clay ; 4 feet, stone	142.718
774.73	....	140.560
779.49	....	142.743
805.50	....	138.485
808.31	Water on the surface. Boring 5 feet, sand ; 15 feet, stone	124.310
812.01	....	139.152
828.77	....	133.802
832.24	....	134.377
837.43	....	130.994
841.76	....	129.486
846.45	....	129.994
	In six stations there is a difference of but from one to two feet.	
880.12	Water on the surface. Boring 9 feet, loose sand ; 18 feet, soft stone	126.569
887.23	....	107.553
891.96	....	123.903
901.22	....	118.112
910.80	....	120.628
	In four stations there is a difference of but one foot.	
933.74	Boring 8 feet, black earth ; 10 feet, white mud ; 18 feet, soft stone.........................	
957.62	....	117.178
971.48	....	108.802
976.30	....	135.168

Chains.	Elevation in Eng. feet.
986.06	107.643
992.93	119.176
1001.03	108.576
1006.65	118.592
1014.28	108.692
1033.51	124.808
1036.44	126.663
1043.06	141.416
1047.39	157.583
1062.87	118.042
1068.43	131.942
1077.69	120.584
1083.96	125.784
1100.19	135.709
1113.35	152.176
1128.97	127.201
1133.79	163.276
1140.94	129.776
1145.18	151.401
1156.44	129.335
1176.61	140.835
1190.87	129.396
1193.77	132.801
1203.21	128.093
1210.14	140.985
1223.50	128.243

The result of the whole is as follows : The length from the Pacific to the Lake of Nicaragua is 28,365⅔ yards, or 15⅔ miles.

	Feet. in. dec
The sum of the ascents is	1047 5.45
The sum of the descents is	919 2.4
The difference is the height of the lake above the Pacific Ocean at low water	128 3.05

We now come to the communication with the Atlantic by means of the Lake of Nicaragua and the River San Juan. The lake is ninety-five miles long, in its broadest part about thirty, and averages, according to Mr. Bailey's soundings, fifteen fathoms of water. The length of the river, by measurement, with all its windings, from the mouth of the lake to the sea, is seventy-nine miles. There are no cataracts or falls ; all the obstructions are from rapids, and it is at all times navigable, both up and down, for piraguas drawing from three to four feet of water.

From the lake to the river of Los Savalos, about eighteen miles, the depth is from two to four fathoms. Here commence the rapids of Toros, which extend one mile, with water from one and a half to two fathoms. The river is then clear for four miles, with an average depth of from two to four fathoms. Then come the rapids of the Old Castle, but little more than half a mile in extent, with water from two to four fathoms. The river is clear again for about two miles, with water from two and a half to five fathoms, where begin the rapids of Mico and Las Balas, connected and running into each other, and both together not more than a mile, with water from one to three fathoms. Then the river is clear one mile and a half to the rapids of Machuca, which extend a mile, and are the worst of all, the water being more broken, from running over a broken rocky bottom. The river then runs clear, and without any obstruction for ten miles, with water from two to seven fathoms, to the River San Carlos, and then eleven miles, with some islands interspersed, with water from one to six fathoms, to the River Serapequea, the measurements of one fathom being about the points or bends, where there is an accumulation of sand and mud. It then continues seven miles clear, with water from two to five fathoms, to the Rio Colorado. The River Colorado runs *out of* the San Juan in another direction into the Atlantic. The loss to the latter, according to measure-

ment taken in the month of May, 1839, was twenty-
eight thousand one hundred and seventy-eight cubic
yards of water per minute, and in the month of July of
the same year, during the rising of the waters, it was
eighty-five thousand eight hundred and forty yards per
minute, which immense body might be saved to the
San Juan by damming up the mouth of the River Colorado. From this point there are thirteen miles, with
soundings of from three to eight fathoms. The bottom
is of sand and mud, and there are many small islands
and aggregations of sand without trees, very easily
cleared away. The last thirteen miles might be reduced to ten by restoring the river to its old channel,
which has been filled up by collections, at points, of
drifted matter. An old master of a piragua told Mr.
B. that within his memory trees grew half a mile
back. The soundings were all taken with the plotting-
scale when the river was low, and the port of San Juan,
though small, Mr. Bailey considers unexceptionable.

The foregoing memoranda were placed in the hands
of my friend Mr. Horatio Allen (now engaged as engineer on our Croton Aqueduct), who has kindly prepared from them the plan opposite.

I ought perhaps to remark, for the benefit of those
who are not familiar with such plans, that in order to
bring the profile of the country within a small compass,
the vertical lines, which represent elevations and de-
pressions, are on a scale many times greater than the
base lines or horizontal distances. Of the former, the
scale is one thousand feet, and of the latter it is twenty miles to the inch. This, of course, gives a distorted
view of the country; but, to preserve the relative proportions, it would be necessary for the base line in the
plan to be one thousand times longer.

The whole length of the canal from the Lake of Nic-

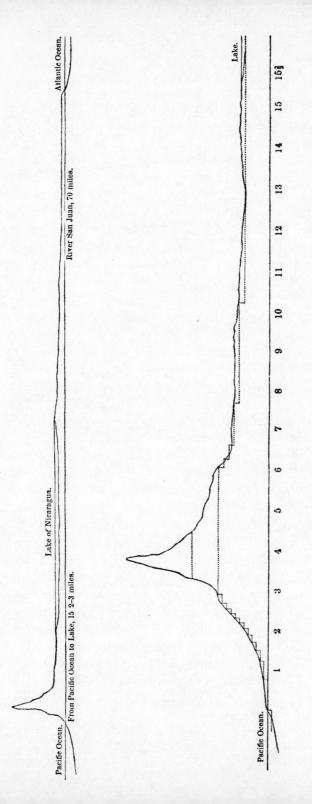

PROFILE OF LAND FOR PROPOSED CANAL.

Pacific Ocean.

Lake of Nicaragua.

Atlantic Ocean.

From Pacific Ocean to Lake, 15 2-3 miles.

River San Juan, 70 miles.

Lake.

Pacific Ocean.

1 2 3 4 5 6 7 8 9 10 11 12 13 14 15 15⅔

aragua to the Pacific is fifteen and two third miles. According to the plan, in the first eight miles from the lake but one lock is necessary. In the next mile sixty-four feet of lockage are required. In the next three miles there are about two of deep cutting and one of tunnel, and then a descent of two hundred feet in three miles by lockage, to the Pacific.

Thus far of the canal across the isthmus. The Lake of Nicaragua is navigable for ships of the largest class down to the mouth of the River San Juan. This river has an average fall of one and six sevenths feet per mile to the Atlantic. If the bed of the river cannot be cleared out, a communication can be made either by lock and dam, or by a canal along the bank of the river. The latter would be more expensive, but, on account of the heavy floods of the rainy season, it is preferable.

I am authorized to state that the physical obstructions of the country present no impediment to the accomplishment of this work. A canal large enough for the passage of boats of the usual size could be made at a trifling expense. A tunnel of the length required is not considered a great work in the United States. According to the plan of the Chesapeake and Ohio Canal, a tunnel is contemplated upward of four miles in length. The sole difficulty is the same which would exist in any route in any other region of country, viz., the great dimensions of the excavation required for a ship canal.

The data here given are, of course, insufficient for great accuracy; but I present a rough estimate of the cost of this work, furnished me with the plan. It is predicated upon the usual contract prices in the United States, and I think I am safe in saying that the cheapness of labour in Nicaragua will equalize any advantages and facilities that exist here.

The estimate is,

From the lake to the east end of the tunnel, from	$8,000,000 to	10,000,000
Descent to the Pacific	2,000,000 to	3,000,000
From the lake to the Atlantic, by canal along the bank of the river	10,000,000 to	12,000,000
	$20,000,000 to	25,000,000

which is but about the sum contemplated as the cost of our enlarged Erie Canal.

The idea of a communication between the Atlantic and Pacific is not new. Columbus wore out the last days of his checkered life in searching for a natural passage, and the vastness and sublimity of the enterprise suited the daring imagination of the early Spaniards.

From the formation of the continent and the falling off in height of the range of the Andes, it has ever since engaged the attention of reflecting men. Even during the deathlike sleep of Spanish dominion a survey was made under the direction of the captain-general; but the documents remained buried in the archives of Guatimala until the emancipation of the colonies, when they were procured and published by Mr. Thomson, who visited that country under a commission from the British government.*

In 1825 an envoy extraordinary from the new republic of Central America called to it the special attention of our government, requesting our co-operation in preference to that of any other nation, and proposed, by

---

* Thomson's Guatimala. By this survey the work appears much more easy than by Mr. Bailey's, but it purports to have been taken by the water level. Mr. Bailey knew of its existence, and had been the means of procuring it for Mr. Thomson.

means of a treaty, " effectually to secure its advantages to the two nations."

A chargé d'affaires was appointed by our government, who was specially instructed to assure the government of Central America of the deep interest taken by that of the United States in the execution of an undertaking " so highly calculated to diffuse an extensive influence on the affairs of mankind," and to investigate with the greatest care the facilities offered by the route, and to remit the information to the United States.

Unfortunately, being far removed from the capital, none of our diplomatic agents ever visited the spot; but in 1826, as appears by documents accompanying the report of a committee of the House of Representatives on a memorial "praying the aid of the government of the United States in procuring the construction of a ship channel or navigable canal across the isthmus between North and South America," a contract was made by the government of Central America with the agent of a New-York company, under the name, style, and designation of the " Central American and United States' Atlantic and Pacific Canal Company." The names of Dewitt Clinton and others of the most distinguished men of that day appear as associates, but the scheme fell through.

In 1830 the government of Central America made another contract with a society of the Netherlands, under the special patronage of the King of Holland, who embarked in it a large amount of his private fortune; but, owing to the difficulties between Holland and Belgium, and the separation of the two countries, this also fell through.

On the third of March, 1835, a resolution passed the Senate of the United States, " that the president be requested to consider the expediency of opening negotiations with the governments of other nations, and particularly with the governments of Central America and Grenada, for the purpose of effectually protecting, by suitable treaty stipulations with them, such individuals or companies as may undertake to open a communication between the Atlantic and Pacific Oceans, by the construction of a ship canal across the isthmus which connects North and South America, and of securing forever, by such stipulations, the free and equal right of navigating such canal to all nations, on the payment of such reasonable tolls as may be established, to compensate the capitalists who may engage in such undertaking and complete the work."

Under this resolution a special agent was appointed by General Jackson, who was instructed to proceed without delay by the most direct route to Port San Juan, ascend the River San Juan to the Lake of Nicaragua, and thence by the contemplated route of communication, by canal or railroad, to the Pacific Ocean. After having completed an examination of the route of the canal, he was directed to repair to Guatimala, the capital of that republic, and, with the aid of Mr. De Witt, the chargé d'affaires of the United States, procure all such public documents connected with the subject as might be had, and especially copies of all such laws as may have been passed to incorporate companies to carry into effect the undertaking of any convention or conventions that may have been entered into with a foreign power upon the subject, and of any plans, surveys, or estimates in relation to it. From Guatimala he was directed to proceed to Panama, and make observations and inquiries relative to the proposed connexion of the two oceans at that point. Unfortunately, from the difficulty of procuring a conveyance to the River San Juan, the agent went to Panama first, from adverse circumstances never reached Nicaragua, and died on his return to this country, before he reached Washington ; but, from his imperfect report, it appears to be the result of his observations that a ship canal was not practicable across the Isthmus of Panama. It is therefore valuable as turning attention, which was before divided between the two routes, exclusively to that by the Lake of Nicaragua. In regard to this route much has been written, many speculations and even estimates of the cost of constructing the canal have been made, but the actual knowledge on the subject has been very limited. In fact, the foregoing notes from Mr. Bailey's survey are the most reliable data that have ever been published. I can but hope that the same liberal spirit which prompted the sending out of an agent may induce our government to procure from Mr. Bailey and give to the world the whole of his maps and drawings.

As yet the subject of this communication has not taken any strong hold upon the public mind. It will be discussed, frowned upon, sneered at, and condemned as visionary and impracticable. Many in established business will oppose it as deranging the course of their trade. Capitalists will not risk their money in an unsettled and revolutionary country. The pioneers will be denounced and ridiculed as Clinton was when he staked his political fortunes upon the " big ditch" that was to connect the Hudson with Lake Erie ; but, if the peace of Europe be not disturbed, I am persuaded that the time is not far distant when the attention of the whole civilized and mercantile world will be directed toward it ; and steamboats will give the first impulse. In less than a year, English mailboats will be steaming to Cuba, Jamaica, and the principal ports of Spanish America, touching once a month at San Juan and Panama. To men of leisure and fortune, jaded with rambling over the ruins of the Old World, a new country will be opened. After a journey on the Nile, a day in Petra, and a bath in the Euphrates, English and American travellers will be bitten by moschetoes on the Lake of Nicaragua, and drink Champagne and Burton ale on the desolate shores of San Juan on the Pacific. The random remarks of the traveller for amusement, and the observations of careful and scientific men, will be brought together, a mass of knowledge will be accumulated and made public, and in my opinion the two oceans will be united.

In regard to the advantages of this work I shall not go into any details; I will remark, however, that on one point there exists a great and very general error. In the documents submitted to Congress before referred to, it is stated that "the trade of the United States and of Europe with China, Japan, and the Indian Archipelago would be facilitated and increased by reason of shortening the distance above four thousand miles;" and in that usually correct work, the Modern Traveller, it is stated that from Europe "the distance to India and China would be shortened more than 10,000 miles!" but by measurement on the globe the distance from Europe to India and China will not be shortened at all. This is so contrary to the general impression that I have some hesitation in making the assertion, but it is a point on which the reader may satisfy himself by referring to the globe. The trade of Europe with India and Canton, then, will not necessarily pass through this channel from any saving of distance; but, from conversations with masters of vessels and other practical men, I am induced to believe that, by reason of more favourable latitudes for winds and currents, it will be considered preferable to the passage by the Cape of Good Hope. At all events, all the trade of Europe with the western coast of the Pacific and the Polynesian Islands, and all her whale-fishing; and *all* the trade of the United States with the Pacific, without the exception of a single vessel, would pass through it; the amount of saving on which, in time, interest of money, navigating expenses and insurance, by avoiding the stormy passage around Cape Horn, I have no data for calculating.

On broad grounds, this work has been well characterized as " the mightiest event in favour of the peaceful intercourse of nations which the physical circumstances of the globe present to the enterprise of man." It will compose the distracted country of Central America; turn the sword, which is now drenching it with blood, into a pruning-hook; remove the prejudices of the inhabitants by bringing them into close connexion with people of every nation; furnish them with a motive and a reward for industry, and inspire them with a taste for making money, which, after all, opprobrious as it is sometimes considered, does more to civilize and keep the world at peace than any other influence whatever. A great city will grow up in the heart of the country, with streams issuing from it, fertilizing as they roll into the interior; her magnificent mountains, and valleys now weeping in desolation and waste, will smile and be glad. The commerce of the world will be changed, the barren region of Terra del Fuego be forgotten, Patagonia become a land of fable, and Cape Horn live only in the recollection of sailors and insurers. Steamboats will go smoking along the rich coasts of Chili, Peru, Equador, Grenada, Guatimala, California, our own Oregon Territory, and the Russian possessions on the borders of Behring's Straits. New markets will be opened for products of agriculture and manufactures, and the intercourse and communion of numerous and immense bodies of the human race will assimilate and improve the character of nations. The whole world is interested in this work. I would not speak of it with sectional or even national feeling; but if Europe is indifferent, it would be glory surpassing the conquest of kingdoms to make this greatest enterprise ever attempted by human force entirely our own work ; nay, more, to make it, as it was once attempted, entirely the work of our city ; for it is to furnish a new field for the action of that tremendous power which, first brought into being under our own eyes, is now changing the face of the whole moral, social, and political world. Is it too much to hope that, in honour of services poorly paid but never to be forgotten, a steamboat, bearing the glorious name of Fulton, may start from the spot where he made his first experiment, and open the great " highway of nations" to the Pacific Ocean?

Thursday, February 27. At three o'clock in the morning we left the yard of the licenciado. The inhabitants of the town were still sleeping. At daylight we passed a village, where, before the door of one of the houses, a traveller was making preparation to set out on a journey. We accosted him, and he said that he would overtake us on the road. At eight o'clock we reached a house, where we stopped to breakfast. The hospitality of Central America is in the country and in the villages ; here I never knew it to fail. The traveller may stop where he pleases, and have house, fire, and water free, paying only for the articles which he consumes. We had milk in abundance, and the charge was six cents. Before we resumed our journey the traveller whom we had passed at the last village arrived, and, after he had taken chocolate, we all started together. He was a merchant, on his way to Leon, accoutred in the style of the country, with pistols, sword, spatterdashes, and spurs; and as he was then suffering from fever and ague, wore a heavy woollen poncha, a striped cotton pocket-handkerchief around his head, and over it two straw hats, one inside of the other. A young man, mounted, and armed with a gun, was driving a cargo-mule, and three mozos with machetes followed on foot.

The whole of this region along the coast of the Pacific is called the Tierra Caliente. At half past two, after a desperately hot and dusty ride, without any water, we reached a hacienda, the name of which I have lost. It was built of poles and plastered with mud. The major-domo was a white man, in bad health, but very obliging, who lived by selling occasionally a fowl or a few eggs to a traveller, and corn and water for mules. There were no more of those beautiful streams which had given such a charm to my journey in Costa Rica. The earth was parched; water was a luxury sold for money. There was a well on the hacienda, and I paid two cents apiece for our mules to drink. There was a bedstead in the hut; at four o'clock I lay down for a few moments' rest, and did not wake till five the next morning. On a line with the head of my bed was a long log, squared and hollowed out, with a broad lid on the top, and secured by a lock and key, containing the corn and household valuables, and on the top of it were sleeping a woman, rather yellow, and a little girl. I took chocolate, and in a few minutes was in the saddle. Very soon we came in sight of the highlands of Buombacho, a high, dark range of mountains, behind which stood Grenada, which in half an hour we entered. Built by those hardy adventurers who conquered America, even yet it is a monument worthy of their fame. The houses are of stone, large and spacious, with balconies to the windows of turned wood, and projecting roofs, with pendent ornaments of wood curiously carved.

I rode to the house of Don Frederico Derbyshire, to whom I had a letter from friends in New-York. He had gone to the United States; but his clerk, a young Englishman, offered me the house, gave me a room, and in a few moments my travelling clothes were off and I was in the street. My first visit was to Mr. Bailey, who lived nearly opposite, with an English lady, whose husband had died two years before, and who, besides carrying on his business, received into her house the few Englishmen or foreigners whom chance brought to that place. My appearance at Grenada created surprise, and I was congratulated upon my liberation or escape from prison. News had reached there that I had been arrested (I do not know for what), and was in prison in San Salvador; and as all news had a party bias, it was told as another of the outrages of General Morazan. The house of this lady was a comfort to a battered traveller. I could have remained there a month; but, unfortunately, I heard news which did not allow me much time for rest. The black clouds which hung over the political horizon had burst, and civil war had broken out anew. The troops of Nicaragua, fourteen hundred strong, had marched into Honduras, and uniting with those of the latter state, had routed, with great slaughter, the troops of Morazan stationed at Taguzegalpa. The latter consisted of but four hundred and fifty men, under the command of General Cabanes, and the records of civil wars among Christian people nowhere present a bloodier page. No quarter was given or asked. After the battle, fourteen officers were shot in cold blood, and not a single prisoner lived as a monument of mercy. Cabanes, fighting desperately, escaped. Colonel Galindo, to whom I have before referred as having visited the ruins of Copan, known both in this country and in Europe for his investigation of the antiquities of that country, and to whom I had a letter of introduction from Mr. Forsyth, was murdered. After the battle, in attempting to escape, with two dragoons and a servant-boy, he passed through an Indian village, was recognised, and they were all murdered with machetes. A disgraceful quarrel ensued between Quejanos and Ferrera, the leaders of the Nicaragua and Honduras troops, for the paltry spoils; and the former got Ferrera into his power, and for twenty-four hours had him under sentence to be shot. Afterward the matter was accommodated, and the Nicaraguans returned to Leon in triumph, with three hundred and fifty muskets, several stands of colours, and as a proof of the way in which they had done their work, without a single prisoner.

At San Salvador there had been an ominous movement. General Morazan had resigned his office of chief of the state, retaining command of the army, and sent his wife and family to Chili. The crisis was at hand; the notes of war sounded fearfully, and it was all important for the prosecution of my ultimate designs and

for my personal safety to reach Guatimala while yet
the road was open.

I would have gone on immediately, but felt that I might
exert myself too far, and break down at an awkward
place.   In the afternoon, in company with Mr. Bailey
and Mr. Wood, I walked down to the lake. At the
foot of the street by which we entered, built out into the
lake, was an old fort, dismantled, and overgrown with
bushes and trees, a relic of the daring Spaniards who
first drove the Indians from the lake ; probably the very
fortress that Cordova built, and in its ruins beautifully
picturesque.   Under the walls, and within the shade of
the fort and trees growing near it, the Indian women
of Grenada were washing ; garments of every colour
were hanging on the bushes to dry and waving in the
wind ; women were wading out with their water-jars,
passing beyond the breakers to obtain it clear of sand ;
men were swimming, and servants were bringing horses
and mules to drink, all together presenting a beautifully
animated picture.   There were no boats on the water ;
but about half a dozen piraguas, the largest of which
was forty feet long, and drew three feet of water, were
lying on the shore.

END OF VOL. I.

A CATALOGUE OF SELECTED DOVER BOOKS
IN ALL FIELDS OF INTEREST

A CATALOGUE OF SELECTED DOVER BOOKS
IN ALL FIELDS OF INTEREST

THE NOTEBOOKS OF LEONARDO DA VINCI, edited by J.P. Richter. Extracts from manuscripts reveal great genius; on painting, sculpture, anatomy, sciences, geography, etc. Both Italian and English. 186 ms. pages reproduced, plus 500 additional drawings, including studies for Last Supper, Sforza monument, etc. 860pp. 7⅞ x 10¾. USO 22572-0, 22573-9 Pa., Two vol. set $15.90

ART NOUVEAU DESIGNS IN COLOR, Alphonse Mucha, Maurice Verneuil, Georges Auriol. Full-color reproduction of Combinaisons ornementales (c. 1900) by Art Nouveau masters. Floral, animal, geometric, interlacings, swashes — borders, frames, spots — all incredibly beautiful. 60 plates, hundreds of designs. 9⅜ x 8¹/₁₆. 22885-1 Pa. $4.00

GRAPHIC WORKS OF ODILON REDON. All great fantastic lithographs, etchings, engravings, drawings, 209 in all. Monsters, Huysmans, still life work, etc. Introduction by Alfred Werner. 209pp. 9⅛ x 12¼. 21996-8 Pa. $6.00

EXOTIC FLORAL PATTERNS IN COLOR, E.-A. Seguy. Incredibly beautiful full-color pochoir work by great French designer of 20's. Complete Bouquets et frondaisons, Suggestions pour étoffes. Richness must be seen to be believed. 40 plates containing 120 patterns. 80pp. 9⅜ x 12¼. 23041-4 Pa. $6.00

SELECTED ETCHINGS OF JAMES A. McN. WHISTLER, James A. McN. Whistler. 149 outstanding etchings by the great American artist, including selections from the Thames set and two Venice sets, the complete French set, and many individual prints. Introduction and explanatory note on each print by Maria Naylor. 157pp. 9⅜ x 12¼. 23194-1 Pa. $5.00

VISUAL ILLUSIONS: THEIR CAUSES, CHARACTERISTICS, AND APPLICATIONS, Matthew Luckiesh. Thorough description, discussion; shape and size, color, motion; natural illusion. Uses in art and industry. 100 illustrations. 252pp.
21530-X Pa. $3.00

TEN BOOKS ON ARCHITECTURE, Vitruvius. The most important book ever written on architecture. Early Roman aesthetics, technology, classical orders, site selection, all other aspects. Stands behind everything since. Morgan translation. 331pp.
20645-9 Pa. $3.75

THE CODEX NUTTALL, A PICTURE MANUSCRIPT FROM ANCIENT MEXICO, as first edited by Zelia Nuttall. Only inexpensive edition, in full color, of a pre-Columbian Mexican (Mixtec) book. 88 color plates show kings, gods, heroes, temples, sacrifices. New explanatory, historical introduction by Arthur G. Miller. 96pp. 11⅜ x 8½. 23168-2 Pa. $7.50

HOUDINI ON MAGIC, Harold Houdini. Edited by Walter Gibson, Morris N. Young. How he escaped; exposés of fake spiritualists; instructions for eye-catching tricks; other fascinating material by and about greatest magician. 155 illustrations. 280pp. 20384-0 Pa. $2.75

HANDBOOK OF THE NUTRITIONAL CONTENTS OF FOOD, U.S. Dept. of Agriculture. Largest, most detailed source of food nutrition information ever prepared. Two mammoth tables: one measuring nutrients in 100 grams of edible portion; the other, in edible portion of 1 pound as purchased. Originally titled Composition of Foods. 190pp. 9 x 12. 21342-0 Pa. $4.00

COMPLETE GUIDE TO HOME CANNING, PRESERVING AND FREEZING, U.S. Dept. of Agriculture. Seven basic manuals with full instructions for jams and jellies; pickles and relishes; canning fruits, vegetables, meat; freezing anything. Really good recipes, exact instructions for optimal results. Save a fortune in food. 156 illustrations. 214pp. 6⅛ x 9¼. 22911-4 Pa. $2.50

THE BREAD TRAY, Louis P. De Gouy. Nearly every bread the cook could buy or make: bread sticks of Italy, fruit breads of Greece, glazed rolls of Vienna, everything from corn pone to croissants. Over 500 recipes altogether. including buns, rolls, muffins, scones, and more. 463pp. 23000-7 Pa. $4.00

CREATIVE HAMBURGER COOKERY, Louis P. De Gouy. 182 unusual recipes for casseroles, meat loaves and hamburgers that turn inexpensive ground meat into memorable main dishes: Arizona chili burgers, burger tamale pie, burger stew, burger corn loaf, burger wine loaf, and more. 120pp. 23001-5 Pa. $1.75

LONG ISLAND SEAFOOD COOKBOOK, J. George Frederick and Jean Joyce. Probably the best American seafood cookbook. Hundreds of recipes. 40 gourmet sauces, 123 recipes using oysters alone! All varieties of fish and seafood amply represented. 324pp. 22677-8 Pa. $3.50

THE EPICUREAN: A COMPLETE TREATISE OF ANALYTICAL AND PRACTICAL STUDIES IN THE CULINARY ART, Charles Ranhofer. Great modern classic. 3,500 recipes from master chef of Delmonico's, turn-of-the-century America's best restaurant. Also explained, many techniques known only to professional chefs. 775 illustrations. 1183pp. 6⅝ x 10. 22680-8 Clothbd. $22.50

THE AMERICAN WINE COOK BOOK, Ted Hatch. Over 700 recipes: old favorites livened up with wine plus many more: Czech fish soup, quince soup, sauce Perigueux, shrimp shortcake, filets Stroganoff, cordon bleu goulash, jambonneau, wine fruit cake, more. 314pp. 22796-0 Pa. $2.50

DELICIOUS VEGETARIAN COOKING, Ivan Baker. Close to 500 delicious and varied recipes: soups, main course dishes (pea, bean, lentil, cheese, vegetable, pasta, and egg dishes), savories, stews, whole-wheat breads and cakes, more. 168pp. USO 22834-7 Pa. $2.00

150 MASTERPIECES OF DRAWING, edited by Anthony Toney. 150 plates, early 15th century to end of 18th century; Rembrandt, Michelangelo, Dürer, Fragonard, Watteau, Wouwerman, many others. 150pp. 8⅜ x 11¼. 21032-4 Pa. $4.00

THE GOLDEN AGE OF THE POSTER, Hayward and Blanche Cirker. 70 extraordinary posters in full colors, from Maîtres de l'Affiche, Mucha, Lautrec, Bradley, Cheret, Beardsley, many others. 9⅜ x 12¼. 22753-7 Pa. $5.95

SIMPLICISSIMUS, selection, translations and text by Stanley Appelbaum. 180 satirical drawings, 16 in full color, from the famous German weekly magazine in the years 1896 to 1926. 24 artists included: Grosz, Kley, Pascin, Kubin, Kollwitz, plus Heine, Thöny, Bruno Paul, others. 172pp. 8½ x 12¼. 23098-8 Pa. $5.00
23099-6 Clothbd. $10.00

THE EARLY WORK OF AUBREY BEARDSLEY, Aubrey Beardsley. 157 plates, 2 in color: Manon Lescaut, Madame Bovary, Morte d'Arthur, Salome, other. Introduction by H. Marillier. 175pp. 8½ x 11. 21816-3 Pa. $4.00

THE LATER WORK OF AUBREY BEARDSLEY, Aubrey Beardsley. Exotic masterpieces of full maturity: Venus and Tannhäuser, Lysistrata, Rape of the Lock, Volpone, Savoy material, etc. 174 plates, 2 in color. 176pp. 8½ x 11. 21817-1 Pa. $4.50

DRAWINGS OF WILLIAM BLAKE, William Blake. 92 plates from Book of Job, Divine Comedy, Paradise Lost, visionary heads, mythological figures, Laocoön, etc. Selection, introduction, commentary by Sir Geoffrey Keynes. 178pp. 8½ x 11. 22303-5 Pa. $4.00

LONDON: A PILGRIMAGE, Gustave Doré, Blanchard Jerrold. Squalor, riches, misery, beauty of mid-Victorian metropolis; 55 wonderful plates, 125 other illustrations, full social, cultural text by Jerrold. 191pp. of text. 8⅛ x 11. 22306-X Pa. $6.00

THE COMPLETE WOODCUTS OF ALBRECHT DÜRER, edited by Dr. W. Kurth. 346 in all: Old Testament, St. Jerome, Passion, Life of Virgin, Apocalypse, many others. Introduction by Campbell Dodgson. 285pp. 8½ x 12¼. 21097-9 Pa. $6.00

THE DISASTERS OF WAR, Francisco Goya. 83 etchings record horrors of Napoleonic wars in Spain and war in general. Reprint of 1st edition, plus 3 additional plates. Introduction by Philip Hofer. 97pp. 9⅜ x 8¼. 21872-4 Pa. $3.50

ENGRAVINGS OF HOGARTH, William Hogarth. 101 of Hogarth's greatest works: Rake's Progress, Harlot's Progress, Illustrations for Hudibras, Midnight Modern Conversation, Before and After, Beer Street and Gin Lane, many more. Full commentary. 256pp. 11 x 14. 22479-1 Pa. $7.95

PRIMITIVE ART, Franz Boas. Great anthropologist on ceramics, textiles, wood, stone, metal, etc.; patterns, technology, symbols, styles. All areas, but fullest on Northwest Coast Indians. 350 illustrations. 378pp. 20025-6 Pa. $3.75

EGYPTIAN MAGIC, E.A. Wallis Budge. Foremost Egyptologist, curator at British Museum, on charms, curses, amulets, doll magic, transformations, control of demons, deific appearances, feats of great magicians. Many texts cited. 19 illustrations. 234pp. USO 22681-6 Pa. $2.50

THE LEYDEN PAPYRUS: AN EGYPTIAN MAGICAL BOOK, edited by F. Ll. Griffith, Herbert Thompson. Egyptian sorcerer's manual contains scores of spells: sex magic of various sorts, occult information, evoking visions, removing evil magic, etc. Transliteration faces translation. 207pp. 22994-7 Pa. $2.50

THE MALLEUS MALEFICARUM OF KRAMER AND SPRENGER, translated, edited by Montague Summers. Full text of most important witchhunter's "Bible," used by both Catholics and Protestants. Theory of witches, manifestations, remedies, etc. Indispensable to serious student. 278pp. 6⅝ x 10. USO 22802-9 Pa. $3.95

LOST CONTINENTS, L. Sprague de Camp. Great science-fiction author, finest, fullest study: Atlantis, Lemuria, Mu, Hyperborea, etc. Lost Tribes, Irish in pre-Columbian America, root races; in history, literature, art, occultism. Necessary to everyone concerned with theme. 17 illustrations. 348pp. 22668-9 Pa. $3.50

THE COMPLETE BOOKS OF CHARLES FORT, Charles Fort. Book of the Damned, Lo!, Wild Talents, New Lands. Greatest compilation of data: celestial appearances, flying saucers, falls of frogs, strange disappearances, inexplicable data not recognized by science. Inexhaustible, painstakingly documented. Do not confuse with modern charlatanry. Introduction by Damon Knight. Total of 1126pp. 23094-5 Clothbd. $15.00

FADS AND FALLACIES IN THE NAME OF SCIENCE, Martin Gardner. Fair, witty appraisal of cranks and quacks of science: Atlantis, Lemuria, flat earth, Velikovsky, orgone energy, Bridey Murphy, medical fads, etc. 373pp. 20394-8 Pa. $3.50

HOAXES, Curtis D. MacDougall. Unbelievably rich account of great hoaxes: Locke's moon hoax, Shakespearean forgeries, Loch Ness monster, Disumbrationist school of art, dozens more; also psychology of hoaxing. 54 illustrations. 338pp. 20465-0 Pa. $3.50

THE GENTLE ART OF MAKING ENEMIES, James A.M. Whistler. Greatest wit of his day deflates Wilde, Ruskin, Swinburne; strikes back at inane critics, exhibitions. Highly readable classic of impressionist revolution by great painter. Introduction by Alfred Werner. 334pp. 21875-9 Pa. $4.00

THE BOOK OF TEA, Kakuzo Okakura. Minor classic of the Orient: entertaining, charming explanation, interpretation of traditional Japanese culture in terms of tea ceremony. Edited by E.F. Bleiler. Total of 94pp. 20070-1 Pa. $1.25

Prices subject to change without notice.
Available at your book dealer or write for free catalogue to Dept. GI, Dover Publications, Inc., 180 Varick St., N.Y., N.Y. 10014. Dover publishes more than 150 books each year on science, elementary and advanced mathematics, biology, music, art, literary history, social sciences and other areas.